Playfair

…AL

CW01636404

…aully

THE FRONT COVER—John Snow, now established as the finest fast bowler in the world

means

SLAZENGER

Slazenger

Superb quality equipment
and clothing for every sport.

THE NEW FACE OF CRICKET
by
GORDON ROSS

THIS, the summer of 1971, will be the last for cricket in its present structure. At a meeting of the Test and County Cricket Board at Lord's in March, the following proposals were accepted for the structure of cricket in 1972.

(1) Twenty three-day Championship matches, including on average, six home Saturday starts.

(2) A sponsored League Cup on the principle of the World Soccer Cup, early matches being played in four area Leagues. Each area is to comprise five Counties (three Minor Counties will make up the number). The first two in each League will qualify for the quarter-finals, which will then be played on a knock-out basis.

(3) The Gillette Cup as at present, but beginning later so that all rounds, except the first, are played after the completion of the League Cup.

(4) The John Player Sunday League as before.

The new League Cup is to be sponsored although no announcement has been made of this at present. All that is known is that the Gillette Company were offered the opportunity of converting the Gillette Cup into a League Cup and did not warm to the idea. They firmly believed that the Gillette Cup, which has been run on identical lines to the most successful competition in the world—the F.A. Cup, has thrived on its knock-out element, and since its success has been overwhelming, there was surely no point in tampering with it. Gillette's pioneer sponsorship of the one-day type of cricket in 1963 has clearly opened the way for others to follow, and although the purists will perhaps never wholly favour one-day cricket, the County Treasurers would probably be in the bankruptcy Court without it. Gillette's contribution to cricket, therefore, can be seen to be a sizeable one, and should always be looked at in its proper context.

The general cricket situation is much happier at the

beginning of this new season than it was a year ago, when the cancellation of the South African tour to England was the culmination of months of bitterness. Now, England has given cricket the shot in the arm it needed by winning back the Ashes. Ray Illingworth's side in Australia prevented Australia from winning a single Test Match, the first time that Australia had not won one Test in a Home series since 1888. This was a fine team effort in the face of many problems and some regrets, but overall, Illingworth revealed some stirring qualities, and he had in his team the world's leading batsman, the world's leading fast-bowler, and the world's leading wicket-keeper. Knott had a magnificent tour, culminating in his century in New Zealand in the second Test and missing by only four runs the distinction of scoring a hundred in each innings of a Test match, a feat not performed by an Englishman since Denis Compton did so against Australia at Adelaide in 1946–47. England should have no problems in overcoming the twin-tour teams this summer of Pakistan and India, but let it be remembered that India beat West Indies in a Test Match in March for the first time since the two countries began their rivalry. Dilip Sardesai's double-century in the First Test was the first ever made by an Indian against West Indies, so given good wickets, and the right conditions for their battery of spinners, the Indians, strengthened, one presumes, by Farokh Engineer, could be a very useful side indeed. Unhappily, neither touring party was chosen by the time the annual goes to press, so we are not able to include the pen-pictures of the visitors which normally, has been an integral part of the annual since its inception in 1948.

Kent's Late Run

The County Championship in 1970 was probably one of the most closely contested in its whole history. Kent, at one time bottom of the table, and making major contributions to the England side, surprised the field with a late run and deservedly took the title. Lancashire were emulating Leeds United in going for three titles. Whereas Leeds got none, Lancashire scooped two—and very nearly three. This is a side which will be watched with interest in 1971.

Two ways of getting a clean shave wherever you are.

The new Philishave Carshaver and the Philishave Compact both have all the famous Philips features such as rotary action and 90 microgroove floating heads, so you get the cleanest, closest shave possible. But in addition, they're both portable.

The Compact runs for six weeks off four penlight batteries. The Carshaver runs from the 12v. cigar lighter socket in the car.

So wherever you happen to be you can be sure of getting a perfect shave.

We want you to have the best.

Philishave
Carshaver £8·50.

Philishave
Compact £7·50.

PHILIPS

PHILIPS

It will be very difficult to get used to Brian Close in Somerset colours. The wrangle with Yorkshire has been lamentable (without taking sides either way) and to see this magnificent cricketer leave a side he has graced for so long is nothing less than a tragedy. It must be Somerset's gain, and with O'Keeffe, the Australian leg-spinner in the side, there will be great expectations on the cricket grounds of Somerset. A testing time will come early. When Somerset meet Lancashire in the First Round of the Gillette Cup at Taunton on May 15. Here is a quick repeat of last year's semi-final when the Taunton crowd was the biggest since Bradman's Australians were there in 1948. A Somerset success in the Gillette Cup would be heartily welcomed. They did once reach the Final, and were beaten by Kent, but more to the point, the winning of the Gillette Cup has so far been the prerogative of the South. They have won it three times with Sussex (twice) and Kent; The North—they have won it three times with Yorkshire (twice) and Lancashire, and the Midlands have won it twice—each time with Warwickshire as the victors. The West and Wales have so far not had a look in, although Worcester have twice been defeated Finalists.

Well Done, Selectors

Cyril Washbrook, great cricketer, great ambassador, now joins the England Test Panel of Selectors, a move warmly welcomed in every corner of the game. The decision by G. O. 'Gubby' Allen to withdraw his nomination for the Panel was indeed a commendable one. Had it gone forward, it would have been difficult, in view of his experience and position, for him to have been anything else but Chairman, and had Alec Bedser been demoted after picking a captain and a team to beat Australia, the cricket world (save for the few—no names, no packdrill!) would have been up in arms —and rightly so! This might be a moment to applaud the Selectors for the side they chose to tour Australia. They get very few pats on the back but plenty of carping criticism. I cannot believe that 'Plum' Warner or P. A. Perrin would have done much better!

Lively New Cricket Books

CRICKET: THE GREAT CAPTAINS

Edited by John Arlott

Great captains in cricketing history analysed by a team of authoritative writers

Illustrated £1·75

Old Trafford

John Marshall

The colourful story of this world-famous cricket ground.

Illustrated £2·00

Doug Walters

Looking for Runs

A fascinating account of the young Australian test star's rise to cricketing maturity.

To be Published in September. Illustrated £2·00

PELHAM BOOKS

52 Bedford Square, London, W.C.I.

THE REST OF THE WORLD WAS A GOOD SERIES

WHATEVER the pros and cons and the eternal discussions as to whether or not this should be regarded as an official Test series, there was some very good cricket played during it. There are points for both sides of the argument. The standard of the opposition was probably stronger than any one country could provide, but at the same time, England did select the side against which they were playing, and one also wonders whether the extra stimulant of playing for one's own country will produce that little bit extra from the players. Would the South African players, for instance, have found a little more had they been playing for South Africa? . . some think it would be very hard for Barlow to have found any more—he found quite enough as it was! Be all this as it may, it was a good series, although it was watched by an average of only 8,000 people a day; millions of televiewers, of course, can be added to the list, though not financially. The B.B.C. understandably did not find as much enthusiasm (or cash) for this series as they would have done for the world-beating South Africans, so cricket as a whole sustained a heavy financial blow.

The Guinness Trophy

The Rest of the World took the series by four Tests to one and thus won the *Guinness* Trophy (*Guinness* had been found as sponsors late in the day), but despite the fact that the series in terms of winning and losing was all over when the teams met for the last time at the Oval, this match still produced the best gate of the series, approximately 60,000 watching the five days. It was at the Oval that a new name emerged in Test cricket, that of Peter Lever of Lancashire, and his piece of bowling in the Rest of the World's first innings was his passport to Australia and to greater things. In the main it was the old guard with Illingworth fast making a name for himself as a batsman. He was second in the England batting averages with Boycott above him, and Fletcher, Luckhurst, D'Oliveira and Cowdrey just below him. Luckhurst, too, was now a certainty for Australia. The strength of the Rest of the World batting conjured up memories of Bradman's Australians in 1948. For a bowler to see such a talented player as Procter coming in at Number Eight must have been a forbidding sight. It was, of course, since Procter finished up with a batting average of 48.66. A good many Number One batsmen would envy such a record. Intikhab Alam, who, believe it or not, came in at Number Ten, had a batting average of 34.28. This was no real series for England bowlers—Illingworth's wickets cost him 41.90 apiece, Underwood's cost 40.42, Snow's 34.84 and d'Oliveira's 30.88. The games must have felt like the real thing to England's bowlers!

Unfamiliar First Four

The first Test created the impression that the gap between the two sides was unbridgable. With a strangely unfamiliar first four—Jones, Luckhurst, Denness and D'Oliveira, England, at one stage, were 44 for 7. Illingworth then scored 63 to avoid total ignomy, and England flickered to a total of 127. The Rest of the World replied with 546, Barlow scoring 119 and Sobers 183. England did eminently better in their second innings. One or two significant factors emerged. This was the beginning and it could be the end of Representative cricket for Alan Jones of Glamorgan; it was probably during this game that the Selectors began their thinking that Illingworth was the man to lead England in Australia. It was still somewhat surprising after this poor performance that England managed to swing the pendulum the full circle in the second match at Trent Bridge and won somewhat easily by 8 wickets. Luckhurst's performance (he scored a hundred in the second innings) brought him into serious consideration for Australia. But from this point onwards the Rest of the World took over and won the last three games. At Edgbaston by 5 wickets—a good match for D'Oliveira this—110 and 81. Shortly after 3 o'clock on the last day at Leeds, The Rest clinched the series. This was Barlow's Match—"The Wrecker"—4 wickets in 5 balls, and 7 for 64. Leeds had seen now't like this since Trueman, and so to the Oval and another win.

England v Rest of the World, 1970

FIRST TEST MATCH

PLAYED AT LORD'S, JUNE 17, 19, 20 and 22
REST OF THE WORLD WON BY AN INNINGS AND 80 RUNS

ENGLAND

A. Jones c Engineer b Procter	5	c Engineer b Procter.......	0
B. W. Luckhurst c Richards b Sobers.	1	c Engineer b Intikhab	67
M. H. Denness c Barlow b McKenzie	13	c Sobers b Intikhab	24
B. L. D'Oliveira c Engineer b Sobers	0	c Lloyd b Intikhab	78
P. J. Sharpe c Barlow b Sobers	4	b Sobers	2
†R. Illingworth c Engineer b Sobers...	63	c Barlow b Sobers...........	94
‡A. P. Knott c Kanhai b Sobers	2	lbw b Gibbs	39
J. A. Snow c Engineer b Sobers	2	b Intikhab	10
D. L. Underwood c Lloyd b. Barlow	19	c Kanhai b Intikhab	7
A. Ward c Sobers b McKenzie	11	st Engineer b Intikhab ...	0
K. Shuttleworth not out	1	not out	0
Extras (LB5, NB1)	6	(B4, LB8, NB6)	18
Total	127	....	339

REST OF THE WORLD

B. A. Richards c Sharpe b Ward	35
E.J.BarlowcUnderwoodbIllingworth	119
R. B. Kanhai c Knott b D'Oliviera .	21
R. G. Pollock b Underwood	55
C. H. Lloyd b Ward	20
†G. S. Sobers c Underwood b Snow .	183
‡F. M. Engineer b Ward	2
Intikhab Alam b Ward	61
M. J. Procter b Snow	26
G. D. McKenzie c Snow b Underwood	0
L. R. Gibbs not out	2
Extras (B10, LB5, NB7)	22
Total	546

BOWLING

R.O.W.	*O.*	*M.*	*R.*	*W.*		*O.*	*M.*	*R.*	*W.*
McKenzie	16.1	3	43	2	...	15	8	25	0
Procter	13	6	20	1	...	15	4	36	1
Sobers	20	11	21	6	...	31	14	43	2
Barlow	4	0	26	1	...	7	2	10	0
Intikhab	2	0	11	0	...	54	24	113	6
Gibbs	—	—	—	—	...	51	17	91	1
Lloyd	—	—	—	—	...	1	0	3	0
ENGLAND									
Snow	27	7	109	2	...				
Ward	33	4	121	4	...				
Shuttleworth	21	2	85	0	...				
D'Oliveira	18	5	45	1	...				
Underwood .	25.5	8	81	2	...				
Illingworth ...	30	8	83	1	...				

Fall of Wickets

	E. *1st*	*RoW* *1st*	*E.* *2nd*
1st	5	69	0
2nd	17	106	39
3rd	23	237	140
4th	23	237	148
5th	29	293	196
6th	31	298	313
7th	44	496	323
8th	94	537	334
9th	125	544	338
10th	127	546	339

SECOND TEST MATCH

PLAYED AT TRENT BRIDGE, JULY 2, 3, 4, 6 and 7
ENGLAND WON BY 8 WICKETS

REST OF THE WORLD

B. A. Richards c Knott b Greig	64	b Greig	30
E. J. Barlow c Cowdrey b D'Oliveira	11	b Greig	142
R. B. Kanhai c Fletcher b Greig	6	c Knott b D'Oliveira	6
R. G. Pollock b D'Oliveira	2	lbw b D'Oliveira	0
C. H. Lloyd not out	114	b Underwood	20
†G. S. Sobers b Greig	8	c Knott b Greig	18
‡F. M. Engineer c Knott b Greig	0	c & b Underwood	1
IntikhabAlam cCowdreyb D'Oliveira	12	c & b Brown	23
M. J. Procter b Brown	43	c Edrich b D'Oliveira	27
G. D. McKenzie c & b Brown	0	not out	6
L. R. Gibbs b D'Oliveira	1	b Snow	1
Extras (B4, LB9, NB2)	15	(B2, LB8, NB2)	12
Total	276		286

ENGLAND

J. H. Edrich c Engineer b Barlow	39	c Barlow b McKenzie	17
B. W. Luckhurst b Barlow	37	not out	113
M. C. Cowdrey c Richards b Barlow	1	lbw b Barlow	64
K. W. Fletcher c Engineer b Barlow	4	not out	69
B. L. D'Oliveira b Barlow	16		
†R. Illingworth b Sobers	97		
A. W. Greig c Gibbs b Sobers	14		
‡A. P. Knott c Kanhai b Intikhab	21		
D. J. Brown b Procter	3		
D. L. Underwood c Sobers b Intikhab	2		
J. A. Snow not out	27		
Extras (B1, LB7, NB10)	18	(LB14, W3, NB4)	21
Total	279	(2 wkts.)	284

BOWLING

ENGLAND	*O.*	*M.*	*R.*	*W.*	*O.*	*M.*	*R.*	*W.*
Snow	20	5	58	0	19.2	2	64	1
Brown	16	1	64	2	13	0	41	1
D'Oliveira	17.4	3	43	4	26	9	63	3
Greig	18	3	59	4	23	7	71	3
Underwood	9	4	25	0	26	13	35	2
Illingworth	4	2	12	0				
R.O.W.								
Procter	17	6	42	1	20	9	23	0
McKenzie	21	3	60	0	24	8	53	1
Sobers	20.5	3	49	2	18	7	24	0
Gibbs	6	3	8	0	31	10	40	0
Barlow	20	5	66	5	14	4	20	1
Intikhab	19	3	36	2	27	9	94	0
Kanhai					1	0	4	0
Pollock					0.2	0	5	0

Fall of Wickets

	RoW	*E*	*RoW*	*E*
	1st	*1st*	*2nd*	*2nd*
1st	31	78	68	44
2nd	46	82	87	164
3rd	55	86	87	—
4th	106	106	112	—
5th	126	109	141	—
6th	126	126	154	—
7th	172	179	220	—
8th	259	191	263	—
9th	267	195	281	—
10th	276	279	286	—

THIRD TEST MATCH

PLAYED AT EDGBASTON, JULY 16, 17, 18, 20 and 21
REST OF THE WORLD WON BY 5 WICKETS

ENGLAND

J. H. Edrich b P. Pollock	37	c Sobers b Intikhab	3
B. W. Luckhurst c Murray b Sobers	28	c Murray b Intikhab	35
M. C. Cowdrey lbw b Sobers	0	c Murray b P. Pollock	71
K. W. Fletcher c Murray b Sobers	0	run out	27
B. L. D'Oliveira c & b Lloyd	110	c Barlow b Sobers	81
†R. Illingworth c Murray b Procter	15	b Gibbs	43
A. W. Greig b Procter	55	c & b Sobers	22
‡A. P. Knott b Procter	21	not out	50
D. J. Brown b Procter	13	c Murray b Procter	32
D. L. Underwood c Sobers b Procter	1	b Sobers	0
J. A. Snow not out	3	b Sobers	21
Extras (LB7, NB4)	11	(B14, LB10)	24
Total	294		409

REST OF THE WORLD

B. A. Richards c Greig b Snow	47	b Underwood	32
E. J. Barlow b Snow	4	c Knott b Snow	0
R. B. Kanhai c Greig b Illingworth	71	c & b Underwood	37
R. G. Pollock b Snow	40		
C. H. Lloyd b Illingworth	101	b Illingworth	20
†G. S. Sobers b Illingworth	80	lbw b Illingworth	7
M. J. Procter b Snow	62	not out	25
‡D.L. Murray c Fletcher b Underwood	62		
Intikhab Alam c Knott b Illingworth	45	not out	15
P. M. Pollock not out	23		
L. R. Gibbs not out	3		
Extras (B10, LB13, NB2)	25	(B1, LB4)	5
Total (9 wkts. dec.)	563	(5 wkts.)	141

BOWLING

R.O.W.	*O.*	*M.*	*R.*	*W.*		*O.*	*M.*	*R.*	*W.*
Procter	24.1	7	46	5	...	22	10	26	1
Pollock, P.	15	1	62	1	...	18	5	48	1
Barlow	11	2	28	0	...	9	2	26	0
Sobers	20	11	38	3	...	51.5	20	89	4
Gibbs	19	5	41	0	...	42	16	80	1
Intikhab	19	4	45	0	...	63	29	116	2
Lloyd	7	1	23	1	...				
ENGLAND									
Snow	38	6	124	4	...	7	2	10	1
Brown	14	2	65	0	...	7	2	23	0
Greig	16	0	58	0	...				
D'Oliveira	24	8	58	0	...				
Underwood	44	17	90	1	...	15	2	52	2
Illingworth	49	13	131	4	...	15	4	51	2
Fletcher	2	0	12	0	...				

Fall of Wickets

	E *1st*	*RoW* *1st*	*E* *2nd*	*RoW* *2nd*
1st	56	7	20	3
2nd	56	80	58	72
3rd	66	157	132	79
4th	76	175	193	100
5th	134	330	271	107
6th	244	377	279	—
7th	258	450	317	—
8th	282	526	364	—
9th	290	538	364	—
10th	294		409	—

FOURTH TEST MATCH

PLAYED AT LEEDS, JULY 30, 31, AUGUST, 1, 3 and 4
REST OF THE WORLD WON BY 2 WICKETS

ENGLAND

G. Boycott c Murray b Barlow	15	c Pollock b Barlow	64
B. W. Luckhurst c Intikhab b Procter	35	c Gibbs b Barlow	92
M. C. Cowdrey c Murray b Barlow	1	b Barlow	0
K. W. R. Fletcher c Murray b Barlow	89	c Barlow b Lloyd	63
B. L. D'Oliveira c Richards b Procter	2	b Procter	21
†R. Illingworth c Murray b Barlow	58	b Intikhab	54
A. W. Greig b Procter	5	c Murray b Lloyd	0
‡A. P. Knott b Barlow	0	c Procter b Barlow	11
C. M. Old b Barlow	0	c Murray b Gibbs	37
D. Wilson c sub. b Barlow	0	not out	6
J. A. Snow not out	3	c Procter b Barlow	10
Extras (B4, LB7, NB3)	14	(B3, LB8, W1, NB6)	18
Total	222		376

REST OF THE WORLD

E. J. Barlow c Boycott b Greig	37	c Cowdrey b Snow	6
‡D. L. Murray c Snow b Wilson	95	lbw b Snow	10
Mushtaq Mohammad lbw b Greig	4	lbw b Illingworth	14
R. G. Pollock c Knott b Greig	3	b Snow	8
C. H. Lloyd b Old	35	c Luckhurst b Illingworth	20
†G. S. Sobers c Knott b Snow	114	c Cowdrey b Snow	59
M. J. Procter c Knott b Old	27	not out	22
Intikhab Alam c Knott b Greig	15	c D'Oliveira b Wilson	54
R. B. Kanhai c & b D'Oliveira	26	c Knott b Illingworth	4
L. R. Gibbs not out	0		
B. A. Richards		not out	21
Extras (LB13, W1, NB6)	20	(B4, LB4)	8
Total (9 wkts. dec.)	376	(8 wkts.)	226

BOWLING

R.O.W.	O.	M.	R.	W.	O.	M.	R.	W.
Procter	21	7	47	3	40	14	67	1
Sobers	20	11	24	0	34	9	65	0
Barlow	22.4	6	64	7	32	8	78	5
Gibbs	5	0	16	0	13	2	31	1
Intikhab	5	2	15	0	18.5	6	28	1
Mushtaq	12	4	27	0	14	4	44	0
Lloyd	10	2	15	0	17	7	45	2
ENGLAND								
Snow	28.1	7	80	1	27.5	5	82	4
Old	27	5	70	2	13	1	35	0
D'Oliveira	24	10	52	1	11	6	17	0
Greig	31	6	86	4	3	0	14	0
Wilson	20	5	48	1	18	9	29	1
Illingworth	8	2	20	0	21	8	41	3

Fall of Wickets

	E 1st	RoW 1st	E 2nd	RoW 2nd
1st	37	67	104	6
2nd	43	84	108	25
3rd	81	90	194	49
4th	91	152	227	58
5th	209	220	257	62
6th	218	280	267	177
7th	219	309	268	182
8th	219	376	300	183
9th	219	376	360	—
10th	222	—	376	—

FIFTH TEST MATCH

PLAYED AT THE OVAL, AUGUST 13, 14, 15, 17 and 18
REST OF THE WORLD WON BY 4 WICKETS

ENGLAND

B. W. Luckhurst b Procter	0	b Procter	0
G. Boycott c Sobers b Intikhab	24	c Barlow b Lloyd	157
M. C. Cowdrey c Murray b Sobers	73	b Intikhab	31
K. W. Fletcher c Murray b McKenzie	25	c Barlow b Sobers	63
D. L. Amiss b Mushtaq	24	c Murray b Lloyd	35
†R. Illingworth c Barlow b Intikhab	52	c Mushtaq b Lloyd	0
‡A. P. Knott not out	51	b Sobers	15
J. A. Snow c Barlow b McKenzie	20	c Mushtaq b Sobers	19
C. M. Old b McKenzie	0	b McKenzie	5
D. Wilson b McKenzie	0	b McKenzie	1
P. Lever b Barlow	13	not out	0
Extras (B2, LB7, NB3)	12	(B5, LB10, NB3)	18
Total	294		344

REST OF THE WORLD

B. A. Richards b Snow	14	b Wilson	14
E. J. Barlow c Amiss b Lever	28	b Snow	6
R. B. Kanhai c& b Wilson	13	c Fletcher b Snow	100
R. G. Pollock b Lever	114	b Illingworth	28
Mushtaq Mohammad b Lever	3	c Fletcher b Snow	8
†G. S. Sobers b Lever	79	not out	40
C. H. Lloyd c Knott b Lever	2	c Knott b Snow	68
M. J. Procter c Boycott b Lever	51	not out	9
‡D. L. Murray b Snow	5		
Intikhab Alam c Boycott b Lever	15		
G. D. McKenzie not out	4		
Extras (LB14, NB13)	27	(B2, LB8, W1, NB3)	14
Total	355	(6 wkts.)	287

BOWLING

R.O.W.	*O.*	*M.*	*R.*	*W.*	*O.*	*M.*	*R.*	*W.*
Procter	20	10	22	1	19	9	30	1
McKenzie	24	7	51	4	22.1	2	51	2
Barlow	16.2	2	36	1	16	2	42	0
Sobers	15	5	18	1	42	15	81	3
Intikhab	44	14	92	2	32	8	87	1
Mushtaq	28	10	63	1	1	0	1	0
Lloyd					18	3	34	3
ENGLAND								
Snow	32	8	73	2	23	6	81	4
Old	21	4	57	0	7	0	22	0
Wilson	18	5	58	1	24	8	70	1
Lever	32.5	9	83	7	10.1	2	34	0
Illingworth	15	3	57	0	23	5	66	1

Fall of Wickets

	E *1st*	*RoW* *1st*	*E* *2nd*	*RoW* *2nd*
1st	0	26	0	7
2nd	62	46	71	41
3rd	113	92	225	92
4th	150	96	289	215
5th	150	261	289	241
6th	236	267	319	265
7th	266	280	323	
8th	266	310	343	
9th	266	338	343	
10th	294	355	344	

AVERAGES

ENGLAND—BATTING AND FIELDING

	M.	I.	N.O.	Runs	H.S.	Avge.	100	50	Ct.	St.
G. Boycott	2	4	0	260	157	65.00	1	1	3	—
R. Illingworth	5	9	0	476	97	52.88	—	6	—	—
K. W. R. Fletcher	4	8	1	340	89	48.57	—	4	4	—
B. W. Luckhurst	5	10	1	408	113*	45.33	1	2	1	—
B. L D'Oliveira	4	7	0	308	110	44.00	1	2	2	—
M. C. Cowdrey	4	8	0	241	73	30.12	—	3	4	—
A. P. E. Knott	5	9	2	210	51*	30.00	—	2	14	—
J. H. Edrich	2	4	0	96	39	24.00	—	—	1	—
A. W. Greig	3	5	0	96	55	19.20	—	1	2	—
J. A. Snow	5	9	3	115	27*	19.16	—	—	2	—
D. J. Brown	2	3	0	48	32	16.00	—	—	2	—
C. M. Old	2	4	0	42	37	10.50	—	—	—	—
D. L. Underwood	3	5	0	29	19	5.80	—	—	4	—
D. Wilson	2	4	1	7	6*	2.33	—	—	1	—

Played in one match: D. L. Amiss 24, 35 (1c); M. H. Denness 13, 24; A. Jones 5, 0; P. Lever 13, 0*; P. J. Sharpe 4, 2 (1c); K. Shuttleworth 1*, 0*; A. Ward 11, 0.

BOWLING

	Overs	Mdns	Runs	Wkts.	Avge.	Best	5wI	10wM
P. Lever	43	11	117	7	16.71	7–83	1	—
A. W. Greig	91	16	288	11	26.18	4–59	—	—
B. L. D'Oliveira	120.4	41	278	9	30.88	4–43	—	—
J. A. Snow	222.2	48	681	19	34.84	4–81	—	—
D. L. Underwood	119.5	44	283	7	40.42	2–35	—	—
R. Illingworth	165	45	461	11	41.90	4–131	—	—

Also bowled: D. J. Brown 50–5–193–3; K. W. R. Fletcher 2–0–12–0; C. M. Old 68–10–184–2; K. Shuttleworth 21–2–85–0; A. Ward 33–4–121–4; D. Wilson 80–27–205–4.

REST OF THE WORLD—BATTING AND FIELDING

	M.	I.	N.O.	Runs	H.S.	Avge.	100	50	Ct.	St.
G. S. Sobers	5	9	1	588	183	73.50	2	3	7	—
C. H. Lloyd	5	9	1	400	114*	50.00	2	1	3	—
M. J. Procter	5	9	3	292	62	48.66	—	2	2	—
D. L. Murray	3	4	0	172	95	43.00	—	2	15	—
E. J. Barlow	5	9	0	353	142	39.22	2	—	10	—
B. A. Richards	5	8	1	257	64	36.71	—	1	3	—
Intikhab Alam	5	8	1	240	61	34.28	—	2	1	—
R. B. Kanhai	5	9	0	284	100	31.55	1	1	3	—
R. G. Pollock	5	8	0	250	114	31.25	1	1	1	—
Mushtaq Mohammad	2	4	0	29	14	7.25	—	—	2	—
G. D. McKenzie	3	4	2	10	6*	5.00	—	—	—	—
L. R. Gibbs	4	5	3	7	3*	3.50	—	—	2	—
F. M. Engineer	2	3	0	3	2	1.00	—	—	8	1

Played in one match: P. M. Pollock 23*

BOWLING

	Overs	Mdns	Runs	Wkts	Avge.	Best	5wI	10wM
E. J. Barlow	152	33	396	20	19.80	7–64	3	1
C. H. Lloyd	53	13	120	6	20.00	3–34	—	—
G. S. Sobers	272.4	106	452	21	21.52	6–21	1	—
M. J. Procter	211.1	82	359	15	23.93	5–46	1	—
G. D. McKenzie ...	122.2	31	283	9	31.44	4–51	—	—
Intikhab Alam	283.5	99	637	14	45.50	6–113	1	—

Also bowled: L. R. Gibbs 167–53–307–3; Mushtaq Mohammad 55–18–135–1; R. B. Kanhai 1–0–4–0; P. M. Pollock 33–6–110–2; R. G. Pollock 0.2–0–5–0.

ISN'T IT NICE TO KNOW . . .

Starting on this page, and continuing through the book at odd points, are questions that we hope will intigue our readers. Turn to page 151 to check on your answers.

1. What is the earliest known reference in history to the game of cricket?

2. Which County has played least matches in the Gillette Cup?

3. Which Minor County has beaten a First Class County in the Gillette Cup?

4. Which County Captain has the best record of success under his Captaincy?

5. Who was the first player to score 300 in a Test Match?

6. What is the best bowling performance for Leicestershire since the last war?

7. Which bowler has taken most wickets in a season?

8. What is the highest individual opening partnership in First-Class cricket?

ENGLAND 2 AUSTRALIA 0

FOR the first time since 1888, Australia failed to win a single Test in a Home series against England, and there were six Tests, too. England won two, so there can be little doubt as to which was the better side. England won by surmounting all manner of problems. The appointment of Illingworth as Captain had been questioned from the very start, principally by the Pro-Cowdrey element. The various injuries which bedevilled the side from start to finish (Alan Ward had to come home and was replaced by the inexperienced Bob Willis) must have made the team's Headquarters seem like a casualty clearing station. Press comment was distinctly unfavourable in the first few weeks of the tour when the side was written off in some quarters. But Illingworth never wavered in the belief that his players could win the series. It was just a pity that victory, which was won deservedly, leaves the memory of one or two incidents which have tarnished it a little—the Boycott affair, when he threw his bat away in disgust at having been given run-out, and the occasion in the last Test when Illingworth led his players off the field after beer cans were hurled on to the field of play. There was a very great deal of provocation here, but other captains have stood their ground on much more inflamed occasions than this, particularly in West Indies. Crowd behaviour is fast changing the world over, but it was still hard to believe that the England players were in physical danger, which was the reason given by England's captain for taking them off. It is very easy, on the other hand, to reach a decision in retrospect in the light of what has happened; it was a very different thing for Illingworth at the time in the heat of the moment, and it will be a real pity if this single incident is allowed to cloud judgment when assessing his merits as England's captain. Illingworth has many qualities of great merit. He was certainly able during a long and sustained tour to create a team spirit which saw the side through its moments of adversity. Without a team spirit the result of the tour could have been very different. The tour proved that England has the best opening batsman in the world in Boycott, with Edrich, and now Luckhurst not far behind him; it proved that we have the finest fast-bowler in the world in Snow, and certainly the best wicket-keeper in the world in Knott. English cricket, as a whole, can take great heart from the performance of our side in Australia. Australia, have been given a good deal of food for thought. After a hiding in South Africa they have now been decisively beaten at home, and changed their captain in a last desperate bid to level the series—without success. They have few players of world-class almost for the first time in Australian cricket history. Still, the outcome of this series was still in the balance until the very last day of the Final Test. Australia could have won this Test. Some thought at the start of the last day that Australia would win; as it happened they never looked like it. Ian Chappell, the new Captain, had put England in to bat on winning the toss. He had to show aggression, but it failed in the end.

Pre-Test Cricket

The series began at Brisbane. In a drawn game the critics suggested that England's performance was better than might have been expected judged by their pre-Test cricket. Admittedly, Australia scored 433, with a double century by Stackpole, and a century by Walters, but England, without a century-maker, replied with 464 and then put Australia out for 214, Shuttleworth bowling particularly well to pick up five wickets. It was runs again that dominated the Second Test at Perth—Perth's inaugural Test match, after many years of endeavour. England won the toss this time and with a splendid century by Luckhurst reached 397. Like Australia's first innings total in the first Test this was not enough; with Redpath and Greg Chappell hitting hundreds, Australia reached 440; a century by Edrich enabled England to declare at 287–6, and this was the second draw of the Series.

The Third Test at Melbourne joins those at Old Trafford in 1890, and 1938 in that not a ball was bowled. This one at Melbourne is different to the others because the match was called off after the third day and agreement was reached to play an additional match in Melbourne. For the purpose of the records, since the captains had tossed, the match will be recorded for posterity, so that the next Test at Sydney is officially 'The Fourth Test', but what it is called matters very little . . England won it, after Snow, in his most devastating mood, had taken 7 for 40 in Australia's second innings and bowled them out for 116. England won by the handsome margin of 299 runs. This was a game in which fortunes did not change. From the moment Boycott and Luckhurst put on 100 for the opening partnership England were in control. They led Australia by 96 runs on the first innings, Boycott then hit a magnificent 142 not out in the second, and Snow did the rest. Here was a great fillip for the England side.

Plethora of Runs

The fifth Test produced a plethora of runs. It was a draw from the word 'Go'. Australia 493 for 9 (Ian Chappell 111), England 392 (Luckhurst 109, D'Oliveira 117), Australia 169 for 4 declared, and England with no chance of getting the runs, used the occasion for batting practice and were 161 without loss at the close. The Sixth Test was drawn, but strong views were expressed about Illingworth's decision not to enforce the follow-on. He did not think that his tired bowlers were capable of bowling Australia out for a second time, and was afraid of England being shot out on a deteriorating wicket. He wanted to hold on to the one victory he had achieved. Now that we have won the last Test, Illingworth has been vindicated. England 470 (Edrich 130), Australia 235, England, batting again not having enforced the follow-on, scored 233 for 4 before declaring (Boycott 119 not out), and then Australia showed that the wicket was far from deteriorating by scoring 328 for 3 (Stackpole 136, Ian Chappell 104).

So it was all on the last one. That England won by 62 runs is now cricket history. This was a comparatively low scoring match without a century on either side and it was a victory contrived without the injured Boycott and in its last vital stages without Snow in the England attack. He had crippled his hand in a collision with the fence in trying to catch out Stackpole. A hard tough, competitive series was over. Illingworth was a hard captain . . but so were Jardine and Hutton . . without a hard captain the Ashes would probably still be in Australia.

Australia v. England, 1970-71

FIRST TEST MATCH

PLAYED AT BRISBANE, NOVEMBER 27, 28, 29, DECEMBER 1, 2

MATCH DRAWN

AUSTRALIA

†W. M. Lawry c Knott b Snow	4	c Snow b Fletcher	84
K. R. Stackpole c Knott b Snow	207	c Knott b Shuttleworth	8
I. M. Chappell run out	59	st Knott b Illingworth	10
K. D. Walters b Underwood	112	c Luckhurst b Snow	7
I.R.RedpathcIllingworthbUnderwood	22	c & b Underwood	28
A. P. Sheahan c Knott b Underwood	0	c Shuttleworth b Snow	36
‡R. W. Marsh b Snow	9	b Shuttleworth	14
T. J. Jenner c Cowdrey b Snow	0	c Boycott b Shuttleworth	2
G. D. McKenzie not out	3	b Shuttleworth	1
J. W. Gleeson c Cowdrey b Snow	0	b Shuttleworth	6
A. L. Thomson b Snow	0	not out	4
Extras (B7, LB4, NB6)	17	(B4, LB3, NB7)	14
Total	433		214

ENGLAND

G. Boycott c Marsh b Gleeson	37	c & b Jenner	16
B. W. Luckhurst run out	74	not out	20
‡A. P. Knott c Lawry b Walters	73		
J. H. Edrich c Chappell b Jenner	79		
M. C. Cowdrey c Chappell b Gleeson	28		
K.W.R.Fletcher c Marsh b McKenzie	34		
B.L.D'Oliveira c Sheahan b McKenzie	57		
†R. Illingworth c Marsh b Thomson	8		
J. A. Snow c Marsh b Walters	34		
D. L. Underwood not out	2		
K. Shuttleworth c Lawry b Walters	7		
Extras (B2, LB7, NB22)	31	(LB3)	[illegible]
Total	464	(1 wkt.)	3[illegible]

BOWLING

ENGLAND	*O.*	*M.*	*R.*	*W.*	*O.*	*M.*	*R.*	*W.*
Snow	32.3	6	114	6	20	3	48	2
Shuttleworth	27	6	81	0	17.5	2	47	5
D'Oliveira	16	2	63	0	7	5	7	0
Illingworth	11	1	47	0	18	11	19	1
Underwood	28	6	101	3	20	10	23	1
Cowdrey	1	0	10	0	2	0	8	0
Fletcher					9	1	48	1
AUSTRALIA								
McKenzie	28	5	90	2	3	0	6	0
Thomson	43	8	136	1	4	0	20	0
Gleeson	42	15	97	2				
Jenner	24	5	86	1	4.6	2	9	1
Stackpole	4	0	12	0	4	3	1	0
Walters	5.5	0	12	3				

Fall of Wickets

	A. *1st*	*E.* *1st*	*A.* *2nd*	*E.* *2nd*
1st	12	92	30	3[illegible]
2nd	163	136	47	
3rd	372	245	64	
4th	418	284	137	
5th	418	336	152	
6th	421	346	193	
7th	422	371	199	
8th	433	449	201	
9th	433	456	208	
10th	433	464	214	

SECOND TEST MATCH

PLAYED AT PERTH, DECEMBER 11, 12, 13, 15, 16
MATCH DRAWN

ENGLAND

G. Boycott c McKenzie b Gleeson	70	st Marsh b Gleeson	50
B. W. Luckhurst b McKenzie	131	c Stackpole b Walters	19
J. H. Edrich run out	47	not out	115
†A.P.E. Knott c Stackpole b Thomson	24	not out	30
K. W. R. Fletcher b Walters	22	lbw b Gleeson	0
M. C. Cowdrey c & b G. Chappell	40	c Marsh b Thomson	1
B. L. d'Oliveira c Stackpole b Thomson	8	b Gleeson	31
*R. Illingworth b McKenzie	34	c Marsh b Stackpole	29
J. A. Snow not out	4		
K. Shuttleworth b McKenzie	2		
P. Lever b McKenzie	2		
Extras (LB8, W1, NB4)	13	(B2, LB3, NB7)	12
Total	397	(6 wkts. dec.)	287

AUSTRALIA

*W. M. Lawry c Illingworth b Snow	0	not out	38
K. R. Stackpole c Lever b Snow	5	c sub (Hampshire) b Snow	0
I. M. Chappell c Knott b Snow	50	c sub (Hampshire) b Snow	17
K. D. Walters c Knott b Lever	7	b Lever	8
I. R. Redpath c & b Illingworth	171	not out	26
A. P. Sheahan run out	2		
G. S. Chappell c Luckhurst b Shuttleworth	108		
R. W. Marsh c d'Oliveira b Shuttleworth	44		
G. D. McKenzie c Lever b d'Oliveira	7		
J. W. Gleeson c Knott b Snow	15		
A. L. Thomson not out	12		
Extras (B5, LB4, NB10)	19	(B4, LB4, NB3)	11
Total	440	(3 wkts.)	100

BOWLING

AUSTRALIA	*O.*	*M.*	*R.*	*W.*	*O.*	*M.*	*R.*	*W.*
McKenzie	31.4	4	66	4	18	2	50	0
Thomson	24	4	118	2	25	3	71	1
G. Chappell	24	4	54	1	4	1	17	0
Gleeson	32	10	78	1	32	11	68	3
Walters	11	1	35	1	7	1	26	1
Stackpole	11	2	33	0	15	3	43	1
ENGLAND								
Snow	33.5	3	143	4	9	4	17	2
Shuttleworth	28	4	105	2	3	1	9	0
Lever	21	3	78	1	5	2	10	1
d'Oliveira	17	1	41	1	4	2	5	0
Illingworth	13	2	43	1	4	2	12	0
Boycott	1	0	7	0				
Fletcher	1	0	4	0	4	0	18	0
Cowdrey					3	0	18	0

Fall of Wickets

	E. 1st	*A. 1st*	*E. 2nd*	*A. 2nd*
1st	171	5	60	0
2nd	243	8	98	20
3rd	281	17	98	40
4th	291	105	101	
5th	310	107	152	
6th	327	326	209	
7th	389	393		
8th	389	408		
9th	393	426		
10th	397	440		

FOURTH TEST MATCH

PLAYED AT SYDNEY, JANUARY 9, 10, 12, 13, 14
ENGLAND WON BY 299 RUNS

ENGLAND

G. Boycott c Gleeson b Connolly	77	not out	142
B. W. Luckhurst lbw b Gleeson	38	c I. Chappell b McKenzie	5
J. H. Edrich c Gleeson b G. Chappell	55	run out	12
K.W.R. Fletcher c Walters b Mallett	23	c Stackpole b Mallett	8
B. L. d'Oliveira c Connolly b Mallett	0	c I. Chappell b G. Chappell	56
†R. Illingworth b Gleeson	25	st Marsh b Mallett	53
‡A. P. E. Knott st Marsh b Mallett	6	not out	21
J. A. Snow c Lawry b Gleeson	37		
P. Lever c Connolly b Mallett	36		
D. L. Underwood c G. Chappell b Gleeson	0		
R. G. D. Willis not out	15		
Extras (B5, LB2, W1, NB12)	20	(B9, LB4, NB9)	22
Total	332	(5 wkts. dec.)	319

AUSTRALIA

†W. M. Lawry c Edrich b Lever	9	not out	60
I. M. Chappell c Underwood b Snow	12	c d'Oliveira b Snow	0
I. R. Redpath c Fletcher b d'Oliveira	64	c Edrich b Snow	6
K. D. Walters c Luckhurst b Illingworth	55	c Knott b Lever	3
G. S. Chappell c & b Underwood	15	b Snow	2
K. R. Stackpole c Boycott b Underwood	33	c Lever b Snow	30
‡R.W.Marsh c d'Oliveira b Underwood	8	c Willis b Snow	0
A. A. Mallett b Underwood	4	c Knott b Willis	6
G. D. McKenzie not out	11	retired hurt	6
J. W. Gleeson c Fletcher b d'Oliveira	0	b Snow	0
A. N. Connolly b Lever	14	c Knott b Snow	0
Extras (NB11)	11	(B2, NB1)	3
Total	236		116

BOWLING

AUSTRALIA	*O.*	*M.*	*R.*	*W.*	*O.*	*M.*	*R.*	*W.*
McKenzie	15	3	74	0	15	0	65	1
Connolly	13	2	43	1	14	1	38	0
Gleeson	29	7	83	4	23	4	54	0
G. Chappell	11	4	30	1	15	5	24	1
Mallett	16.7	5	40	4	19	1	85	2
Walters	3	1	11	0	2	0	14	0
Stackpole	7	2	31	0	6	1	17	0
ENGLAND								
Snow	14	6	23	1	17.5	5	40	7
Willis	9	2	26	0	3	2	1	1
Lever	8.6	1	31	2	11	1	24	1
Underwood	22	7	66	4	8	2	17	0
Illingworth	14	3	59	1	9	5	9	0
d'Oliveira	9	2	20	2	7	3	16	0
Fletcher					1	0	6	0

Fall of Wickets

	E 1st	*A* 1st	*E* 2nd	*A* 2nd
1st	116	14	7	1
2nd	130	38	35	11
3rd	201	137	48	14
4th	205	160	181	21
5th	208	189	276	66
6th	219	199	—	66
7th	262	208	—	86
8th	291	208	—	116
9th	291	219	—	116
10th	332	236	—	—

FIFTH TEST MATCH

PLAYED AT MELBOURNE, JANUARY 21, 22, 23, 25, 26
MATCH DRAWN

AUSTRALIA

†W. M. Lawry c Snow b Willis	56	c sub(Shuttleworth)b Snow	42
K. R. Stackpole c Lever b d'Oliveira	30	c Knott b Willis	18
I. M. Chappell c Luckhurst b Snow	111	b Underwood	30
I. R. Redpath b Snow	72	c Knott b Snow	5
K. D. Walters b Underwood	55	not out	39
G. S. Chappell c Edrich b Willis	3	not out	20
‡R. W. Marsh not out	92		
K. J. O'Keeffe c Luckhurst b Illingworth	27		
J. W. Gleeson c Cowdrey b Willis	5		
J. R. F. Duncan c Edrich b Illingworth	3		
A. L. Thomson not out	0		
Extras (B10, LB17, NB12)	39	(B8, LB3, NB4)	15
Total (9 wkts. dec.)	493	(4 wkts. dec.)	169

ENGLAND

G. Boycott c Redpath b Thomson	12	not out	76
B. W. Luckhurst b Walters	109		
J. H. Edrich c Marsh b Thomson	9	not out	74
M. C. Cowdrey c and b Gleeson	13		
B. L. d'Oliveira c Marsh b Thomson	117		
†R. Illingworth c Redpath b Gleeson	41		
‡A. P. E. Knott lbw b Stackpole	19		
J. A. Snow b I. Chappell	1		
P. Lever run out	19		
D. L. Underwood c and b Gleeson	5		
R. G. D. Willis not out	5		
Extras (B17, LB14, NB11)	42	(B1, LB8, NB2)	11
Total	392	(0 wkt.)	161

BOWLING

ENGLAND	*O.*	*M.*	*R.*	*W.*	*O.*	*M.*	*R.*	*W.*
Snow	29	6	94	2	12	4	21	2
Lever	25	6	79	—	12	1	53	—
d'Oliveira	22	6	71	1				
Willis	20	5	73	3	10	1	42	1
Underwood	19	4	78	1	12	—	38	1
Illingworth	13	—	59	2				
AUSTRALIA								
Thomson	34	5	110	3	11	5	26	—
Duncan	14	4	30	—				
G. Chappell	8	—	21	—	5	—	19	—
O'Keeffe	31	11	71	—	19	3	45	—
Gleeson	25	7	60	3	3	1	18	—
Stackpole	17.5	4	41	1	13	2	28	—
Walters	5	2	7	1	7	1	14	—
I. Chappell	3	—	10	1				

Fall of Wickets

	A *1st*	*E* *1st*	*A* *2nd*	*E* *2nd*
1st	64	40	51	—
2nd	266	64	84	—
3rd	269	88	91	—
4th	310	228	132	—
5th	314	306	—	—
6th	374	340	—	—
7th	471	354	—	—
8th	477	362	—	—
9th	480	379	—	—
10th	—	392	—	—

SIXTH TEST MATCH

PLAYED AT ADELAIDE, JANUARY 29, 30, FEBRUARY 1, 2, 3
MATCH DRAWN

ENGLAND

G. Boycott run out	58	not out	119
J. H. Edrich c Stackpole b Lillee	130	b Thomson	40
K. W. R. Fletcher b Thomson	80	b Gleeson	5
‡A. P. E. Knott c Redpath b Lillee	7		
B.L.d'Oliveira c Marsh b G.Chappell	47	c Walters b Thomson	5
J.H.Hampshire c Lillee b G.Chappell	55	lbw b Thomson	3
†R. Illingworth b Lillee	24	not out	48
J. A. Snow b Lillee	38		
P. Lever b Thomson	5		
D. L. Underwood not out	1		
R. G. D. Willis c Walters b Lillee	4		
Extras (B1, LB5, W4, NB11)	21	(LB4, W1, NB8)	13
Total	470	(4 wkts. dec.)	233

AUSTRALIA

K. R. Stackpole b Underwood	87	b Snow	136
†W. M. Lawry c Knott b Snow	10	c Knott b Willis	21
I. M. Chappell c Knott b Lever	28	c Willis b Underwood	104
I. R. Redpath c Lever b Illingworth	9	not out	21
K. D. Walters c Knott b Lever	8	not out	36
G. S. Chappell c Edrich b Lever	0		
‡R. W. Marsh c Knott b Willis	28		
A. A. Mallett c Illingworth b Snow	28		
J. H. Gleeson c Boycott b Willis	16		
D. Lillee c Boycott b Lever	10		
A. Thomson not out	6		
Extras (LB2, NB3)	5	(B2, LB3, NB5)	10
Total	235	(3 wkts.)	328

BOWLING

AUSTRALIA	*O.*	*M.*	*R.*	*W.*	*O.*	*M.*	*R.*	*W.*
Thomson	29.7	6	94	2	19	2	79	3
Lillee	28.3	0	84	5	7	0	40	0
Walters	9	2	29	0	3	0	5	0
G. Chappell	18	1	54	2	5	0	27	0
Gleeson	19	1	78	0	16	1	69	1
Mallett	20	1	63	0	1	1	0	0
Stackpole	12	2	47	0				
ENGLAND								
Snow	21	4	73	2	17	3	60	1
Lever	17.1	2	49	4	17	4	49	0
Underwood	21	6	45	1	35	7	85	1
Willis	12	3	49	2	13	1	48	1
Illingworth	5	2	14	1	14	7	32	0
d'Oliveira					15	4	28	0
Fletcher					4	0	16	0

Fall of Wickets

	E *1st*	*A* *1st*	*E* *2nd*	*A* *2nd*
1st	107	61	103	65
2nd	276	117	128	267
3rd	289	131	143	271
4th	289	141	151	
5th	385	145		
6th	402	163		
7th	458	180		
8th	464	219		
9th	465	221		
10th	470	235		

SEVENTH TEST MATCH

PLAYED AT SYDNEY, FEBRUARY 12, 13, 14, 16 and 17
ENGLAND WON BY 62 RUNS

ENGLAND

J. H. Edrich c G. Chappell b Dell	30	c I. Chappell b O'Keeffe	57
B.W. Luckhurst c Redpath b Walters	0	c Lillee b O'Keeffe	59
K. W. R. Fletcher c Stackpole b O'Keeffe	33	c Stackpole b Eastwood	20
J. H. Hampshire c Marsh b Lillee	10	c I. Chappell b O'Keeffe	24
B. L. d'Oliveira b Dell	1	c I. Chappell b Lillee	47
†R. Illingworth b Jenner	42	lbw b Lillee	29
‡A. P. Knott c Stackpole b O'Keeffe	27	b Dell	15
J. A. Snow b Jenner	7	c Stackpole b Dell	20
P. Lever c Jenner b O'Keeffe	4	c Redpath b Jenner	17
D. L. Underwood not out	8	c Marsh b Dell	0
R. G. D. Willis b Jenner	11	not out	2
Extras (B4, LB4, W1, NB2)	11	(B3, LB3, NB6)	12
Total	184		302

AUSTRALIA

K. Eastwood c Knott b Lever	5	b Snow	0
K. R. Stackpole b Snow	6	b Illingworth	67
‡R. W. Marsh c Willis b Lever	4	b Underwood	16
†I. M. Chappell b Willis	25	c Knott b Lever	6
I. R. Redpath c & b Underwood	59	c Hampshire b Illingworth	14
K.D. Walters st Knott b Underwood	42	c d'Oliveira b Willis	1
G. S. Chappell b Willis	65	st Knott b Illingworth	30
K. O'Keeffe c Knott b Illingworth	3	c sub (Shuttleworth) b d'Oliveira	12
D. Lillee c Knott b Willis	6	c Hampshire b d'Oliveira	
T. J. Jenner b Lever	30	c Fletcher b Underwood	4
A. Dell not out	3	not out	3
Extras (LB5, W1, NB10)	16	(B2, NB5)	7
Total	264		160

BOWLING

AUSTRALIA	*O.*	*M.*	*R.*	*W.*	*O.*	*M.*	*R.*	*W.*
Lillee	13	5	32	1	14	0	43	2
Dell	16	8	32	2	26.7	3	65	3
Walters	4	0	10	1	5	0	18	0
G. Chappell	3	0	9	0				
Jenner	16	3	42	3	21	5	39	1
O'Keeffe	24	8	48	3	26	8	96	3
Eastwood					5	0	21	1
Stackpole					3	1	8	0
ENGLAND								
Snow	18	2	68	1	2	1	7	1
Lever	14.6	3	43	3	12	2	23	1
d'Oliveira	12	3	24	0	5	1	15	2
Willis	12	1	58	3	9	1	32	1
Underwood	16	3	39	2	13.6	5	28	2
Illingworth	11	3	16	1	20	7	39	3
Fletcher					1	0	9	0

Fall of Wickets

	E. 1st	*A. 1st*	*E. 2nd*	*A. 2nd*
1st	5	11	94	0
2nd	60	13	125	22
3rd	68	32	158	71
4th	69	66	165	82
5th	98	147	234	96
6th	145	162	251	131
7th	156	178	276	142
8th	165	235	298	154
9th	165	239	299	154
10th	184	264	302	160

TEST MATCH AVERAGES

Played 6: England Won 2, Drawn 4, Abandoned 1.

ENGLAND—BATTING AND FIELDING

	M.	I.	N.O.	Runs	H.S.	Aver.	100	50	Ct.	St.
G. Boycott	5	10	3	657	142*	93.85	2	5	4	—
J. H. Edrich	6	11	2	648	130	72.00	2	4	5	—
B. W. Luckhurst	5	9	1	455	131	56.87	2	2	5	—
R. Illingworth	6	10	1	333	53	37.00	—	1	4	—
B. L. D'Oliveira	6	10	0	369	117	36.90	1	2	4	—
A. P. E. Knott	6	9	2	222	73	31.71	—	1	21	3
K. W. R. Fletcher	5	9	0	225	80	25.00	—	1	3	—
J. A. Snow	6	7	1	141	38	23.50	—	—	2	—
J. H. Hampshire	2	4	0	92	55	23.00	—	1	2	—
M. C. Cowdrey	3	4	0	82	40	20.50	—	—	3	—
R. G. D. Willis	4	5	3	37	15*	18.50	—	—	3	—
P. Lever	5	6	0	83	36	13.83	—	—	5	—
D. L. Underwood	5	6	3	16	8*	5.33	—	—	4	—
K. Shuttleworth	2	2	0	9	7	4.50	—	—	1	—

ENGLAND—BOWLING

	Overs	Mdns.	Runs	Wkts	Aver.	Best	5wI	10wM
J. A. Snow	225.5	47	708	31	22.83	7–40	2	—
R. G. D. Willis	88	16	329	12	27.41	3–58	—	—
D. L. Underwood	194.6	50	520	16	32.50	4–66	—	—
P. Lever	143.5	25	439	13	33.76	4–49	—	—
K. Shuttleworth	75.5	13	242	7	34.57	5–47	1	—
R. Illingworth	132	43	349	10	34.90	3–39	—	—
B. L. D'Oliveira	114	28	290	6	48.33	2–15	—	—

Also bowled: G. Boycott 1–0–7–0; M. C. Cowdrey 6–0–36–0; K. W. R. Fletcher 20–1–101–1.

AUSTRALIA—BATTING AND FIELDING

	M.	I.	N.O.	Runs	H.S.	Aver.	100	50	Ct.	St.
K. R. Stackpole	6	12	0	627	207	52.25	2	2	9	—
I. R. Redpath	6	12	2	497	171	49.70	1	3	5	—
W. M. Lawry	5	10	2	324	84	40.50	—	3	3	—
I. M. Chappell	6	12	0	452	111	37.66	2	2	7	—
K. D. Walters	6	12	2	373	112	37.30	1	2	3	—
G. S. Chappell	5	8	1	243	108	34.71	1	1	3	—
R. W. Marsh	6	9	1	215	92*	26.87	—	1	11	3
A. L. Thomson	4	5	4	22	12*	22.00	—	—	—	—
G. D. McKenzie	3	5	3	28	11*	14.00	—	—	1	—
K. J. O'Keeffe	2	3	0	42	27	14.00	—	—	—	—
A. A. Mallett	2	3	0	38	28	12.66	—	—	—	—
A. P. Sheahan	2	3	0	38	36	12.66	—	—	1	—
T. J. Jenner	2	4	0	36	30	9.00	—	—	2	—
J. W. Gleeson	5	7	0	42	16	6.00	—	—	4	—
D. K. Lillee	2	3	0	16	10	5.33	—	—	2	—

Played in one Test: A. N. Connolly 14, 0 (2 ct.); A. R. Dell 3*, 3*; J. R. F. Duncan 3; K. H. Eastwood 5, 0.

AUSTRALIA—BOWLING

	Overs	Mdns.	Runs	Wkts.	Aver.	Best	5wI	10wM
A. R. Dell	42.7	11	97	5	19.40	3–65	—	—
D. K. Lillee	62.3	5	199	8	24.87	5–84	1	—
K. D. Walters	61.5	8	181	7	25.85	3–12	—	—
T. J. Jenner	65.6	15	176	6	29.33	3–42	—	—
A. A. Mallett	56.7	8	188	6	31.33	4–40	—	—
J. W. Gleeson	221	57	605	14	43.21	4–83	—	—
K. J. O'Keeffe	100	30	260	6	43.33	3–48	—	—
G. D. McKenzie	110.4	14	351	7	50.14	4–66	—	—
G. S. Chappell	93	15	255	5	51.00	2–54	—	—
A. L. Thomson	189.7	33	654	12	54.50	3–79	—	—

Also bowled: I. M. Chappell 3–0–10–1; A. N. Connolly 27–3–81–1; J. R. F. Duncan 14–4–30–0; K. H. Eastwood 5–0–21–1; K. R. Stackpole 92.5–20–261–2.

Note: This is the first time since 1887–88 that Australia has failed to win a match in a home series.

LIST OF COUNTY CHAMPIONS

1873	Nottinghamshire / Gloucestershire	1898	Yorkshire	1935	Yorkshire
		1899	Surrey	1936	Derbyshire
1874	Derbyshire	1900	Yorkshire	1937	Yorkshire
1875	Nottinghamshire / Lancashire / Sussex	1901	Yorkshire	1938	Yorkshire
		1902	Yorkshire	1939	Yorkshire
		1903	Middlesex	1946	Yorkshire
1876	Gloucestershire	1904	Lancashire	1947	Middlesex
1877	Gloucestershire	1905	Yorkshire	1948	Glamorgan
1878	Middlesex	1906	Kent	1949	Middlesex / Yorkshire
1879	Nottinghamshire / Lancashire	1907	Nottinghamshire		
		1908	Yorkshire	1950	Lancashire / Surrey
1880	Nottinghamshire / Gloucestershire	1909	Kent		
		1910	Kent	1951	Warwickshire
1881	Lancashire	1911	Warwickshire	1952	Surrey
1882	Lancashire / Nottinghamshire	1912	Yorkshire	1953	Surrey
		1913	Kent	1954	Surrey
1883	Nottinghamshire	1914	Surrey	1955	Surrey
1884	Nottinghamshire	1919	Yorkshire	1956	Surrey
1885	Nottinghamshire	1920	Middlesex	1957	Surrey
1886	Nottinghamshire	1921	Middlesex	1958	Surrey
1887	Surrey	1922	Yorkshire	1959	Yorkshire
1888	Surrey	1923	Yorkshire	1960	Yorkshire
1889	Nottinghamshire / Lancashire / Surrey	1924	Yorkshire	1961	Hampshire
		1925	Yorkshire	1962	Yorkshire
		1926	Lancashire	1963	Yorkshire
1890	Surrey	1927	Lancashire	1964	Worcestershire
1891	Surrey	1928	Lancashire	1965	Worcestershire
1892	Surrey	1929	Nottinghamshire	1966	Yorkshire
1893	Yorkshire	1930	Lancashire	1967	Yorkshire
1894	Surrey	1931	Yorkshire	1968	Yorkshire
1895	Surrey	1932	Yorkshire	1969	Glamorgan
1896	Yorkshire	1933	Yorkshire	1970	Kent
1897	Lancashire	1934	Lancashire		

NEW ZEALAND v ENGLAND 1971

England Preserve Their Record In New Zealand

IT was a tired and battle-worn party which ended its strenuous tour of Australia and landed in New Zealand to contest two more Test matches—eight in all. Luck, which has not exactly accompanied the side on its ventures from start to finish, did at least come down on England's side in the First Test, when Underwood found a wicket which was tailor-made for him. He produced all his skills in these conditions to take 6 for 12 and shoot New Zealand out for 65. He followed this up with 6 more wickets in the second innings to give him a match aggregate of 12 for 97. When Underwood took his third wicket in the second innings he reached a total of 1,000 wickets in first-class cricket. Underwood, who is not yet 26, is the first bowler for generations to perform this feat at such a tender age. Wilfred Rhodes and George Lohmann were younger when they did it. Underwood's consistency is seen in the fact that he has never taken 200 wickets in a season. It was D'Oliveira's batting contribution (he made exactly 100) which won this First Test, England getting home by eight wickets.

In the Second Test, it looked as though by scoring over 300 in their first innings England had placed themselves in a position where defeat was only a remote possibility—yet they had to fight out of a tight corner before it was all over, and the fight back was spearheaded by two cripples, Cowdrey and D'Oliveira, both of whom needed runners. This was a match to remember for Alan Knott (and by Peter Lever for his batting, too) who scored a century in the first innings and was only four runs short of a second century in the same match when he was out for 96 in the second innings. Had he been able to collect the other four runs he would have become the first Englishman to score a hundred in each innings of a Test match since Denis Compton achieved the feat at Adelaide in 1946–47.

FIRST TEST MATCH

PLAYED AT CHRISTCHURCH, FEBRUARY 25, 26, 27, MARCH 1
ENGLAND WON BY 8 WICKETS

NEW ZEALAND

†G. T. Dowling	c Edrich b Underwood	13	c Luckhurst b Lever	1
B. A. G. Murray	c Taylor b Shuttleworth	1	b Shuttleworth	1
B.F. Congdon	c Taylor b Shuttleworth	1	b Underwood	55
R. W. Morgan	c Luckhurst b Shuttleworth	6	b Underwood	0
M. J. F. Shrimpton	c Fletcher b Underwood	0	c Illingworth b Underwood	8
G. M. Turner	b Underwood	11	b Underwood	76
V. Pollard	b Wilson	18	lbw b Underwood	34
‡K. J. Wadsworth	c Fletcher b Underwood	0	c Fletcher b Wilson	1
R. S. Cunis	b Underwood	0	b Shuttleworth	35
H.J. Howarth	st Taylor b Underwood	0	c Illingworth b Underwood	25
R. O. Collinge	not out	3	not out	7
Extras	(B9, LB1, W1, NB1)	12	(B6, LB3, W1, NB1)	11
Total		65		254

ENGLAND

B. W. Luckhurst	c Wadsworth b Collinge	10	not out	29
J. H. Edrich	lbw b Cunis	12	c Wadsworth b Collinge	2
K. W. R. Fletcher	b Collinge	4	c Howarth b Collinge	2
J. H. Hampshire	c Turner b Howarth	40	not out	51
B. L. d'Oliveira	b Shrimpton	100		
†R. Illingworth	b Shrimpton	36		
‡R.W. Taylor	st Wadsworth b Howarth	4		
D. Wilson	c Murray b Howarth	5		
P. Lever	b Howarth	4		
K. Shuttleworth	b Shrimpton	5		
D. L. Underwood	not out	0		
Extras	(B1, LB9, NB1)	11	(B1, LB4)	5
Total		231	(2 wkts.)	89

ENGLAND	*O.*	*M.*	*R.*	*W.*		*O.*	*M.*	*R.*	*W.*
Lever	5	4	1	0	...	15	3	30	1
Shuttleworth	8	1	14	3	...	12	1	27	2
D'Oliveira	3	1	2	0	...				
Underwood	11.6	7	12	6	...	32.3	7	85	6
Illingworth	6	3	12	0	...	17	5	45	0
Wilson	4	2	12	1	...	21	6	56	1
N. ZEALAND									
Collinge	12	2	39	2	...	7	2	20	2
Cunis	13	2	44	1	...	8	0	17	0
Howarth	19	7	46	4	...	4	0	17	0
Pollard	9	3	45	0	...	3	0	9	0
Shrimpton	11.5	0	35	3	...	3	0	21	0
Congdon	3	0	11	0	...				

Fall of Wickets

	NZ 1st	*E 1st*	*NZ 2nd*	*E 2nd*
1st	4	20	1	3
2nd	7	26	6	11
3rd	19	31	83	
4th	28	95	83	
5th	33	188	99	
6th	54	213	151	
7th	54	220	152	
8th	62	224	209	
9th	62	231	239	
10th	65	231	256	

SECOND TEST MATCH

PLAYED AT AUCKLAND, MARCH 5, 6, 7, 8

MATCH DRAWN

ENGLAND

B. W. Luckhurst c Dowling b Cunis	14	c Wadsworth b Webb	15
J. H. Edrich c Morgan b Webb	1	c Burgess b Collinge	24
M. C. Cowdrey c Congdon b Cunis	54	b Collinge	45
J. H. Hampshire c Turner b Cunis	9	c Wadsworth b Cunis	0
B. L. d'Oliveira c Morgan b Congdon	58	b Collinge	5
†R. Illingworth c Wadsworth b Cunis	0	c Turner b Collinge	22
‡A. P. E. Knott b Collinge	101	b Cunis	96
P. Lever c Wadsworth b Cunis	64	lbw b Howarth	0
K. Shuttleworth c Wadsworth b Cunis	0	c Wadsworth b Morgan	11
R. G. D. Willis c Burgess b Collinge	7	lbw b Cunis	3
D. L. Underwood not out	1	not out	8
Extras (B2, NB6, LB4)	12	(B5, LB3)	8
Total	321		237

NEW ZEALAND

†G. T. Dowling c and b Underwood	53	not out	31
G. M. Turner c and b Underwood	65	not out	8
B. E. Congdon b Underwood	0		
R. W. Morgan c and b Underwood	8		
M. G. Burgess c Edrich b Willis	104		
M. J. F. Shrimpton lbw b Underwood	46		
‡K. J. Wadsworth c Hampshire b Willis	16		
R. S. Cunis not out	5		
H. J. Howarth not out	2		
R. O. Collinge } M. G. Webb } did not bat			
Extras (B7, LB3, NB4)	14	(LB1)	1
Total (7 wkts. dec.)	313	(0 wkts)	40

BOWLING

N. ZEALAND	*O.*	*M.*	*R.*	*W.*		*O.*	*M.*	*R.*	*W.*
Webb	18	0	94	1	...	11	0	50	1
Collinge	18.6	5	51	2	...	9	6	41	4
Cunis	24	4	76	6	...	21.7	5	52	3
Howarth	7	0	41	0	...	21	8	37	1
Congdon	2	0	18	1	...				
Shrimpton	3	0	29	0	...	6	0	33	0
Morgan					...	6	0	16	1
ENGLAND									
Shuttleworth	17	3	49	0	...	4	0	12	0
Willis	14	2	54	2	...	6	1	15	0
Lever	19	3	43	0	...	2	0	6	0
Underwood	38	12	108	5	...	2	2	0	0
Illingworth	18	4	45	0	...				
Luckhurst					...	2	0	6	0

Fall of Wickets

	E 1st	*NZ 1st*	*E 2nd*	*NZ 2nd*
1st	8	91	26	—
2nd	38	91	27	—
3rd	59	121	62	—
4th	111	142	67	—
5th	111	283	143	—
6th	145	302	152	—
7th	294	307	177	—
8th	297	—	199	—
9th	317	—	218	—
10th	321	—	237	—

TOUR AVERAGES

M.C.C. in AUSTRALIA and NEW ZEALAND

Played 16: Won 4, Drawn 11, Lost 1, Abandoned 1.

BATTING AND FIELDING

	M.	*I.*	*N.O.*	*Runs*	*H.S.*	*Aver.*	100	50	*Ct.*	*St.*
G. Boycott	12	22	6	1535	173	95.93	6	7	6	—
J. H. Edrich	14	25	5	1136	130	56.80	3	7	8	—
B. W. Luckhurst	11	20	3	954	135	56.11	4	3	11	—
B. L. D'Oliveira	13	20	3	870	162*	51.17	4	3	6	—
A. P. E. Knott	12	17	5	539	101	44.91	1	2	24	4
J. H. Hampshire......	10	17	3	463	156*	33.07	1	3	6	—
R. Illingworth	14	21	4	537	53	31.58	—	1	6	—
K. W. R. Fletcher ...	12	21	1	602	80	30.10	—	5	10	—
M. C. Cowdrey	11	18	1	511	101	30.05	1	3	3	—
J. A. Snow	10	10	1	150	38	16.66	—	—	2	—
R. W. Taylor	5	6	0	98	31	16.33	—	—	14	5
P. Lever.................	13	13	1	188	64	15.66	—	1	6	—
R. G. D. Willis.......	9	8	3	74	27	14.80	—	—	4	—
D. Wilson	6	3	0	35	19	11.66	—	—	3	—
K. Shuttleworth	9	10	2	88	24	11.00	—	—	3	—
A. Ward	2	3	1	15	8*	7.50	—	—	—	—
D. L. Underwood ...	13	14	7	41	13*	5.85	—	—	11	—

BOWLING

	Overs	*Mdns.*	*Runs*	*Wkts.*	*Aver.*	*Best*	*5wI*	*10wM*
D. L. Underwood ...	422	110	1123	43	26.11	6–12	3	1
J. A. Snow	306.5	57	1021	38	26.86	7–40	2	—
R. G. D. Willis.......	182	29	738	23	32.08	4–81	—	—
K. Shuttleworth	188.5	23	662	17	38.94	5–47	1	—
P. Lever	311.2	48	951	23	41.34	4–17	—	—
R. Illingworth	284	71	883	20	44.15	3–39	—	—
K. W. R. Fletcher ...	40.3	2	232	5	46.40	3–43	—	—
B. L. D'Oliveira	192	34	569	12	47.41	2–15	—	—
D. Wilson	120.7	19	406	8	50.75	3–32	—	—

Also bowled: G. Boycott 4.4–0–31–1; M. C. Cowdrey 24–0–127–3; J. H. Hampshire 9–0–53–0; B. W. Luckhurst 2–0–6–0; A. Ward 38.5–3–166–4.

WEST INDIES v INDIA

At the time of going to press with this annual this series was still unfinished. Full details will appear in next year's annual.

PAKISTAN HERE THIS SUMMER

As the touring party from Pakistan had not been chosen at the time of going to Press it has not been possible to include the biographies of the visitors which have always been an integral part of the Playfair Annual. This is particularly unfortunate with Pakistan, as the side is sure to contain quite a few players who have not been seen in action here before though Intikhab Alam, the captain, is known to all of us as a Surrey player.

The best guide of the likely composition of the side is the match between a Pakistan XI and the Rest of the World played at Karachi in December in aid of the Flood Disaster Fund. The Pakistan team was; Javed Burki, Sadiq Mohammed, Saeed Ahmed, Asif Iqbal, Mushtaq Mohammed, Shafqat Rana, Intikhab Alam, Wasim Bari, Salim Altaf, Sarfraz Nawaz, Pervez Sajjad. Pakistan won this match by 226 runs against a team which included Kanhai, Sobers, Lloyd, and Engineer.

PAKISTAN TOUR FIXTURES, 1971

		MAY		
Sat.	1	Worcestershire		Worcester
Wed.	5	Warwickshire		Edgbaston
Sat.	8	Northamptonshire		Northampton
Wed.	12	Hampshire		Portsmouth
Sat.	15	Cambridge U.		Cambridge
Wed.	19	Nottinghamshire		Trent Bridge
Sat.	22	M.C.C.		Lord's
Wed.	26	Kent		Gravesend
Sat.	29	Gloucestershire		Bristol
		JUNE		
Thurs.	3	**First Test Match**	**England v Pakistan**	**Edgbaston (five days)**
Wed.	9	Yorkshire		Bradford
Sat.	12	Oxford U.		Oxford
Thurs.	17	**Second Test Match**	**England v Pakistan**	**Lord's (five days)**
Wed.	23	Glamorgan		Swansea
Sat.	26	Lancashire		Old Trafford
Wed.	30	Scotland		Selkirk
		JULY		
Sat.	3	Derbyshire		Chesterfield
Thurs.	8	**Third Test Match**	**England v Pakistan**	**Headingley (five days)**
Wed.	14	Surrey		The Oval

ENGLAND v PAKISTAN

1954 TO 1968-69

SERIES BY SERIES

Season		*Touring Team Captain*	*P.*	*E. W.*	*P. W.*	*D.*
1954	In England	A. H. Kardar (P)	4	1	1	2
1961–62	In Pakistan	E. R. Dexter (E)	3	1	0	2
1962	In England	Javed Burki (P)	5	4	0	1
1967	In England	Hanif Mohammad (P)	3	2	0	1
1968–69	In Pakistan	M. C. Cowdrey (E)	3	0	0	3
		At Lord's	3	1	0	2
		At The Oval	3	2	1	0
		At Leeds	1	1	0	0
		At Manchester	1	0	0	1
		At Nottingham	3	2	0	1
		At Birmingham	1	1	0	0
		At Karachi	2	0	0	2
		At Lahore	2	1	0	1
		At Dacca	2	0	0	2
		In England	12	7	1	4
		In Pakistan	6	1	0	5
		Total	18	8	1	9

RECORD WICKET PARTNERSHIPS FOR ENGLAND:

1st	198	G. Pullar & R. W. Barber at Dacca	1961–62
2nd	248	M. C. Cowdrey & E. R. Dexter at The Oval	1962
3rd	201	K. F. Barrington & T. W. Graveney at Lord's	1967
4th	188	E. R. Dexter & P. H. Parfitt at Karachi	1961–62
5th	192	D. C. S. Compton & T. E. Bailey at Nottingham	1954
6th	153*	P. H. Parfitt & D. A. Allen at Birmingham	1962
7th	67	P. H. Parfitt & J. T. Murray at Leeds	1962
8th	99	P. H. Parfitt & D. A. Allen at Leeds	1962
9th	76	T. W. Graveney & F. S. Trueman at Lord's	1962
10th	51	D. A. Allen & J. B. Statham at Leeds	1962

RECORD WICKET PARTNERSHIPS FOR PAKISTAN

1st	122	Hanif Mohammad & Alim-ud-Din at Dacca	1961–62
2nd	137	Imtiaz Ahmed & Mushtaq Mohammad at The Oval	1962
3rd	156	Hanif Mohammad & Javed Burki at Dacca	1961–62
4th	153	Javed Burki & Mushtaq Mohammad at Lahore	1961–62
5th	197	Javed Burki & Nasim-ul-Ghani at Lord's	1962

6th	81	Imtiaz Ahmed & Mushtaq Mohammad at Karachi	1961–62
7th	51	Saeed Ahmed & Nasim-ul-Ghani at Nottingham	1962
8th	130	Hanif Mohammad & Asif Iqbal at Lord's	1967
9th	190	Asif Iqbal & Intikhab Alam at The Oval	1967
10th	52	Afaq Hussain & Haseeb Ahsan at Lahore	1961–62

HIGHEST INNINGS TOTALS:

England

558–6d	at Nottingham	1954
544–5d	at Birmingham	1962
507	at Karachi	1961–62
502–7	at Karachi	1968–69
480–5d	at The Oval	1962
440	at The Oval	1967

LOWEST INNINGS TOTALS:

England

130	at The Oval (1st inns.)	1954
143	at The Oval (2nd inns)	1954
274	at Dacca	1968–69

HIGHEST INNINGS TOTALS:

Pakistan

404–8	at Karachi	1961–62
393–7d	at Dacca	1961–62
387–9d	at Lahore	1961–62
355	at Lord's	1962
354	at Lord's	1967

LOWEST INNINGS TOTALS:

Pakistan

87	at Lord's	1954
90	at Manchester	1954
100	at Lord's	1962
114	at Nottingham	1967
131	at Leeds	1962

HIGHEST INDIVIDUAL INNINGS FOR ENGLAND

278	D. C. S. Compton	at Nottingham	1954
205	E. R. Dexter	at Karachi	1961–62
182	M. C. Cowdrey	at The Oval	1962
172	E. R. Dexter	at The Oval	1962
165	G. Pullar	at Dacca	1961–62
159	M. C. Cowdrey	at Birmingham	1962
153	T. W. Graveney	at Lord's	1962

A total of 21 centuries have been scored for England.

HIGHEST INDIVIDUAL INNINGS FOR PAKISTAN

187*	Hanif Mohammad	at Lord's	1967
146	Asif Iqbal	at The Oval	1967
140	Javed Burki	at Dacca	1961–62
138	Javed Burki	at Lahore	1961–62

A total of 10 centuries have been scored for Pakistan.

A CENTURY IN EACH INNINGS OF A MATCH

FOR ENGLAND

NIL

FOR PAKISTAN

111 & 104	Hanif Mohammad	at Dacca	1961–62

A CENTURY ON DEBUT IN ENGLAND v PAKISTAN TESTS

FOR ENGLAND

139	K. F. Barrington	at Lahore	1961–62
159	M. C. Cowdrey	at Birmingham	1962

FOR PAKISTAN

138	Javed Burki	at Lahore	1961–62

HIGHEST RUN AGGREGATE IN A TEST RUBBER FOR:

England in England	453	(Av. 90.60)	D. C. S. Compton	1954
England in Pakistan	303	(Av. 101.00)	E. R. Dexter	1961–62
Pakistan in England	401	(Av. 44.55)	Mushtaq Mohammad	1962
Pakistan in Pakistan	407	(Av. 67.83)	Hanif Mohammad	1961–62

BEST INNINGS BOWLING FIGURES FOR:

England in England	7–56	J. H. Wardle at The Oval	1954
England in Pakistan	5–30	D. A. Allen at Dacca	1961–62
Pakistan in England	6–46	Fazal Mahmood at The Oval	1954
Pakistan in Pakistan	5–112	Antao D'Souza at Karachi	1961–62

MOST WICKETS IN A MATCH FOR ENGLAND:

9–110	L. J. Coldwell at Lord's (on Test debut)	1962
9–116	F. S. Trueman at Lord's	1962
9–145	J. D. F. Larter at The Oval	1962

TEN WICKETS OR MORE IN A MATCH FOR PAKISTAN

12–99	Fazal Mahmood at The Oval	1954

HIGHEST WICKET AGGREGATE IN A TEST RUBBER FOR:

England in England	F. S. Trueman	22	(Av. 19.95)	1962
England in Pakistan	D. A. Allen	13	(Av. 25.69)	1961–62
Pakistan in England	Fazal Mahmood	20	(Av. 20.40)	1954
Pakistan in Pakistan	Antao D'Souza	9	(Av. 22.88)	1961–62
	Saeed Ahmed	9	(Av. 24.88)	1968–69

HIGHEST MATCH AGGREGATE: 1176–34 wkts. at Lahore 1961–62

LOWEST MATCH AGGREGATE: 509–28 wkts. at Nottingham 1967

Future Cricket Tours

TO ENGLAND		M.C.C. TOURS OVERSEAS	
1972	Australia	1971–72	India and Pakistan
1973	N. Zealand and W. Indies	1972–73	No tour
1974	India and Pakistan	1973–74	W. Indies
1975	South Africa	1974–75	Australia and N. Zealand
1976	W. Indies	1975–76	No tour
1977	Australia	1976–77	South Africa
		1977–78	India and Pakistan

OTHER TOURS

1971–72	New Zealand to West Indies (prov.)
1971–72	South Africa to Australia and New Zealand
1972–73	Australia to West Indies
1973–74	New Zealand to Australia (prov.)
	Australia to New Zealand (prov.)
1975–76	Australia to South Africa
1977–78	West Indies to Australia

INDIA, OUR SECOND 1971 TOURISTS

As this is a split-tour summer, the Indians follow Pakistan to England. Once again the tour party is not known at the time of going to press, but it may not be too difficult to guess this side as the Indians are at present on tour in West Indies and won the Second Test—their first victory over West Indies in the whole series of matches between the two countries. A double century by Sardesai—the first ever by an Indian against West Indies, has made him one player to look out for. The tour party was; A. L. Wadekar (Captain), S. Abid Ali, B. S. Bedi, S. A. Durrani, S. M. Gavaskar, D. Govindraj, M. L. Jaisimha, K. Jayantilal, B. A. Jeejeebhoy, P. Krishnamurthy, A. V. Mankad, E. A. S. Prasanna, D. N. Sardesai, E. D. Solkar, S. Venkataraghavan, G. R. Vishwanath, It is presumed that Farokh Engineer would join the party in England.

INDIA TOUR FIXTURES, 1971

		JUNE		
Wed.	23	Middlesex		Lord's
Sat.	26	Essex		Colchester
Wed.	30	D. H. Robins's XI		Eastbourne
		JULY		
Sat.	3	Kent		Canterbury
Wed.	7	Leicestershire		Leicester
Sat.	10	Warwickshire		Edgbaston
Wed.	14	Glamorgan		Cardiff
Sat.	17	Hampshire		Bournemouth
Thurs.	22	**First Test Match**	**England v India**	**Lord's (five days)**
Wed.	28	Minor Counties		Lakenham, Norfolk
Sat.	31	Surrey		The Oval
		AUGUST		
Thurs.	5	**Second Test Match**	**England v India**	**Old Trafford (five days)**
Wed.	11	Yorkshire		Headingley
Sat.	14	Nottinghamshire		Trent Bridge
Thurs.	19	**Third Test Match**	**England v India**	**The Oval (five days)**
Wed.	25	Sussex		Hove
Sat.	28	Somerset		Taunton
		SEPTEMBER		
Wed.	1	Worcestershire		Worcester
Sat.	4	T. N. Pearce's XI		Scarborough

ENGLAND v INDIA

1932 TO 1967

SERIES BY SERIES

Season		Touring Team Captain	P.	E. W.	I. W.	D.
1932	In England	C. K. Nayudu (I)	1	1	0	0
1933–34	In India	D. R. Jardine (E)	3	2	0	1
1936	In England	Maharaj of Vizianagram (I)	3	2	0	1
1946	In England	Nawab of Pataudi, Senior (I)	3	1	0	2
1951–52	In India	N. D. Howard (E)	5	1	1	3
1952	In England	V. S. Hazare (I)	4	3	0	1
1959	In England	D. K. Gaekwad (I)	5	5	0	0
1961–62	In India	E. R. Dexter (E)	5	0	2	3
1963–64	In India	M. J. K. Smith (E)	5	0	0	5
1967	In England	Nawab of Pataudi, Junior (I)	3	3	0	0
		At Lord's	6	6	0	0
		At The Oval	4	2	0	2
		At Leeds	3	3	0	0
		At Manchester	4	2	0	2
		At Nottingham	1	1	0	0
		At Birmingham	1	1	0	0
		At Bombay	4	1	0	3
		At Calcutta	4	0	1	3
		At Madras	4	1	2	1
		At New Delhi	3	0	0	3
		At Kanpur	3	1	0	2
		In England	19	15	0	4
		In India	18	3	3	12
		Total	37	18	3	16

RECORD WICKET PARTNERSHIPS FOR ENGLAND

1st	159	P. E. Richardson & G. Pullar at Bombay	1961–62
2nd	164	G. Pullar & K. F. Barrington at New Delhi	1961–62
3rd	169	R. Subba Row & M. J. K. Smith at The Oval	1959
4th	266	W. R. Hammond & T. S. Worthington at The Oval	1936
5th	182	J. Hardstaff & P. A. Gibb at Lord's	1946
6th	159	T. W. Graveney & T. G. Evans at Lord's	1952
7th	102	R. Illingworth & R. Swetman at The Oval	1959
8th	138	R. W. V. Robins & H. Verity at Manchester	1936

9th	81	R. W. Barber & G. A. R. Lock at Kanpur..........1961–62
10th	57	J. T. Murray & R. N. S. Hobbs at Birmingham 1967

RECORD WICKET PARTNERSHIPS FOR INDIA

1st	203	V. M. Merchant & Mushtaq Ali at Manchester.........1936
2nd	168	F. M. Engineer & A. L. Wadekar at Leeds 1967
3rd	211	V. M. Merchant & V. S. Hazare at New Delhi 1951–52
	211	V. M. Mankad & V. S. Hazare at Lord's 1952
4th	222	V. S. Hazare & V. L. Manjrekar at Leeds 1952
5th	190	Nawab of Pataudi, Jnr. & C. G. Borde at New Delhi 1963–64
6th	105	V. S. Hazare & D. G. Phadkar at Leeds 1952
7th	153	C. G. Borde & S. A. Durani at Bombay 1963–64
8th	101	R. G. Nadkarni & F. M. Engineer at Madras 1961–62
9th	54	G. S. Ramchand & S. G. Shinde at Lord's 1952
10th	51	R. G. Nadkarni & B. S. Chandrasekhar at Calcutta 1963–64

HIGHEST INNINGS TOTALS:
England

571–8d	at Manchester	1936
559–8d	at Kanpur	1963–64
550–4d	at Leeds	1967
537	at Lord's	1952
500–8d	at Bombay	1961–62
497–5d	at Kanpur	1961–62
490	at Manchester	1959
483–8d	at Leeds	1959
471–8d	at The Oval	1936

LOWEST INNINGS TOTALS:
England

134	at Lord's	1936
183	at Madras	1951–52
203	at New Delhi	1951–52
203	at Kanpur	1951–52
203	at Birmingham	1967

HIGHEST INNINGS TOTALS:
India

510	at Leeds	1967
485–9d	at Bombay	1951–52
467–8d	at Kanpur	1961–62
466	at New Delhi	1961–62
463–4	at New Delhi	1963–64
457–9d	at Madras	1951–52
457–7d	at Madras	1963–64

LOWEST INNINGS TOTALS:
India

58	at Manchester	1952
82	at Manchester	1952
92	at Birmingham	1967
93	at Lord's	1936
98	at The Oval	1952
110	at Lord's	1967
121	at Kanpur	1951–52

HIGHEST INDIVIDUAL INNINGS FOR ENGLAND

246*	G. Boycott	at Leeds	1967
217	W. R. Hammond	at The Oval	1936
205*	J. Hardstaff	at Lord's	1946
175	T. W. Graveney	at Bombay	1951–52
172	K. F. Barrington	at Kanpur	1961–62
167	W. R. Hammond	at Manchester	1936
160	M. C. Cowdrey	at Leeds	1959

A total of 28 centuries have been scored for England.

HIGHEST INDIVIDUAL INNINGS FOR INDIA

203*	Nawab of Pataudi, Junior	at New Delhi	1963–64
192	B. K. Kunderan	at Madras	1963–64
189*	V. L. Manjrekar	at New Delhi	1961–62
184	V. M. Mankad	at Lord's	1952

164*	......V. S. Hazare	......at New Delhi	1951–52
155	......V. S. Hazare	......at Bombay	1951–52
154	......V. M. Merchant	......at New Delhi	1951–52

A total of 27 centuries have been scored for India.

A CENTURY IN EACH INNINGS OF A MATCH

No instance for either side.

A CENTURY ON DEBUT IN ENGLAND v INDIA TESTS

FOR ENGLAND

246*	......G. Boycott	......at Leeds	1967
109	......B. L. D'Oliveira	......at Leeds	1967
175	......T. W. Graveney	......at Bombay	1951–52
100	......M. J. K. Smith	......at Manchester	1959
136	......B. H. Valentine (on Test debut)	at Bombay	1933–34
138*	......A. J. Watkins	......at New Delhi	1951–52

FOR INDIA

118	......L. Amarnath (on Test debut)	...at Bombay	1933–34
112	......A. A. Baig (on Test debut)	......at Manchester	1959
105	......Hanumant Singh (on Test Debut)	.......at New Delhi	1963–64

HIGHEST RUN AGGREGATE IN A TEST RUBBER FOR:

England in England.........	399 (Av. 79.80)	...L. Hutton	1952
England in India	594 (Av. 99.00)	...K. F. Barrington	.1961–62
India in England	333 (Av. 55.50)	...V. S. Hazare	1952
India in India	586 (Av. 83.71)	...V. L. Manjrekar	1961–62

BEST INNINGS BOWLING FIGURES FOR:

England in England.........	8–31	F. S. Trueman at Manchester	.1952
England in India	7–49	H. Verity at Madras	1933–34
India in England	6–35	Amar Singh at Lord's	1936
India in India	8–55	V. M. Mankad at Madras	.1951–52

TEN WICKETS OR MORE IN A MATCH FOR ENGLAND

11–93	......A. V. Bedser at Manchester	1946
11–145	......A. V. Bedser at Lord's	1946
11–153	......H. Verity at Madras	1933–34
10–78	......G. O. Allen at Lord's	1936

TEN WICKETS OR MORE IN A MATCH FOR INDIA

12–108	......V. M. Mankad at Madras	1951–52
10–177	......S. A. Durani at Madras	1961–62

HIGHEST WICKET AGGREGATE IN A TEST RUBBER FOR:

England in England......	F. S. Trueman......	29 (Av. 13.31)	1952
England in India	F. J. Titmus	27 (Av. 27.66)	1963–64
India in England	S. P. Gupte	17 (Av. 34.64)	1959
India in India	V. M. Mankad	34 (Av. 16.79)	1951–52

HIGHEST MATCH AGGREGATE: 1,350–28 wkts. at Leeds, 1967

LOWEST MATCH AGGREGATE: 482–31 wkts. at Lord's, 1936

LANCASHIRE WIN THE CUP

Sussex in the Final yet again

by Gordon Ross

THE Gillette Cup went North again to keep a nice geographical balance—The North have won it three times—Yorkshire, twice, and Lancashire; the South have won it three times, Sussex, twice, and Kent; the Midlands (Warwickshire) have won it twice, so it should be the Midlands turn in 1971! The West and Wales are the only barren areas in the eight years of the competition. Lancashire's victory was not really a surprise. They had shown their ability the previous season at one day cricket and repeated the performance in the Sunday League in 1970 to complete a double, and there were few moments during all four Gillette Cup Matches in which they played, that Lancashire looked in danger of defeat. By scoring 278 at Bristol they left Gloucestershire what looked a hopeless task, although Gloucestershire made an uncommonly good attempt at getting the runs. A comfortable five wicket victory over Hampshire was achieved in the next Round, but when Somerset were 100 for 1 in the Semi-Final at Taunton there were momentary doubts as to Lancashire's ability to win this one. In the end they did so comfortably by four wickets, and so to the Final and another match which Lancashire controlled virtually from start to finish. Their out-cricket, having lost the toss, kept Sussex on tenterhooks all the time, Lloyd in particular, whose very presence in the cover regions seemed to have almost a mesmerising affect on the Sussex batsmen; no less than three of them were run-out—Suttle, Griffith and Snow, all very experienced cricketers. Not that Lloyd stood out head and shoulders above the rest in the field; Pilling's work in the deep and especially his throwing was of the highest order; in fact the whole Lancashire side looked aggressive in the field; it was they who intended to call the tune in giving their bowlers exhilarating support. The Sussex innings soldiered on in fits and starts without ever giving the impression that it was likely to dominate. Sussex followers, at 149 for 5, might have cherished the hope of a total beyond Lancashire's compass, but only the most devout of them could have expected Lancashire to fail in reaching a total of 185. At 37 for 2, well, was it just possible? . . not really, with Pilling, Clive Lloyd, Sullivan, Engineer and Bond to come. As it happened, Bond was never needed. Pilling had taken things under his wing, and although the non-partisans plus the Lancastrians were bitterly sorry to see Lloyd go, Engineer is a Test-class batsman, made for a situation like this one. So Sussex, appearing in their fourth final in eight years, were disappointed for the second time. It is still a proud record to have accomplished, to have taken part in four finals although Surrey will certainly have mixed feelings about it. When the last ball was about to be bowled at the Oval in the Semi-Final, Surrey had pretty good reason to think that they would be at Lord's for the second time, but history has it that a piece of mis-fielding off this ball allowed Sussex to snatch a near impossible situation from the fire.

THE GILLETTE CUP, 1971

FIRST ROUND

Ties to be played on May 15th

Essex v. Bedfordshire (at Chelmsford).
Kent v. Northamptonshire (at Canterbury).
Northumberland v. Lincolnshire (at Jesmond).
Somerset v. Lancashire (at Taunton).
Staffordshire v. Glamorgan (Longton, Stoke).
Surrey v. Hertfordshire (at The Oval).

SECOND ROUND

Ties to be played on June 12th

Surrey or Hertfordshire v. Middlesex.
Warwickshire v. Northumberland or Lincolnshire (at Edgbaston).
Hampshire v. Nottinghamshire (at Portsmouth).
Leicestershire v. Derbyshire (at Leicester).
Essex or Bedfordshire v. Staffordshire or Glamorgan.
Worcestershire v. Somerset or Lancashire (at Worcester).
Kent or Northamptonshire v. Yorkshire.
Sussex v. Gloucestershire (at Hove).

GILLETTE CUP COMPETITION
1970 RESULTS

FIRST ROUND

Cornwall v Glamorgan at Truro, April 26th and 27th
Glamorgan 171–7 in 60 overs (Walker 51*).
Cornwall 99 (Walker 5–21).
Result: Glamorgan won by 72 runs.
Man of the Match: P. M. Walker.
Adjudicator: H. Gimblett.

Middlesex v Norfolk at Lord's, April 28th
Middlesex 264–5 in 60 overs (Russell 80, Murray 63).
Norfolk 117 (Edrich, W. J. 36).
Result: Middlesex won by 147 runs.
Man of the Match: J. T. Murray.
Adjudicator: Gordon Ross.

Oxfordshire v Worcestershire at Cowley, April 25th and 27th
Oxfordshire 99 (Holder 3–14).
Worcestershire 101–3 (D'Oliveira 32*).
Result: Worcestershire won by 7 wickets.
Man of the Match: B. L. D'Oliveira.
Adjudicator: C. J. Barnett.

Warwickshire v Nottinghamshire at Edgbaston, April 28th
Warwickshire 215–9 in 60 overs (Smith, M. J. K. 50, Jameson 44).
Nottinghamshire 216–5 (Sobers 70*, Smedley 51).
Result: Nottinghamshire won by 5 wickets.
Man of the Match: G. S. Sobers.
Adjudicator: D. Kenyon.

Yorkshire v Surrey at Harrogate, April 26th and 27th
Surrey 134–8 in 60 overs (Close 3–27).
Yorkshire 76 (Jackman 7–33, Willis 3–25).
Result: Surrey won by 58 runs.
Man of the Match: R. D. Jackman.
Adjudicator: C. Washbrook.

Buckinghamshire v Bedfordshire at High Wycombe, May 9th
Bedfordshire 102 (Wynn 35, Pickett 4–20, Lever 3–19).
Buckinghamshire 105–2 (Turner 56, Leach 39*).
Result: Buckinghamshire won by 8 wickets.
Man of the Match: C. A. Pickett.
Adjudicator: W. J. Edrich.

SECOND ROUND

Buckinghamshire v Hampshire at Chesham, May 30th

Hampshire 278–3 in 60 overs (Reed 143*, Richards 69).
Buckinghamshire 136 (Hooker 65).
Result: Hampshire won by 142 runs.
Man of the Match: B. L. Reed.
Adjudicator: W. J. Edrich.

Essex v Sussex at Chelmsford, May 30th

Essex 174–9 in 60 overs (Edmeades 40).
Sussex 175–6 (Buss, M. A. 72).
Result: Sussex won by 4 wickets.
Man of the Match: M. A. Buss.
Adjudicator: A. V. Bedser.

Glamorgan v Surrey at Swansea, May 30th

Glamorgan 149 (Jones, A. 52, Storey 3–13, Jackman 3–25).
Surrey 151–3 (Edrich 66*, Younis Ahmed 63).
Result: Surrey won by 7 wickets.
Man of the Match: S. J. Storey.
Adjudicator: H. Gimblett.

Gloucestershire v Lancashire at Bristol, May 30th

Lancashire 278–8 in 60 overs (Lloyd, D. 62, Lloyd, C. H. 53, Brown 4–56).
Gloucestershire 251 (Nicholls 75, Simmons 3–39).
Result: Lancashire won by 27 runs.
Man of the Match: R. B. Nicholls.
Adjudicator: D. Kenyon.

Kent v Worcestershire at Canterbury, May 30th

Kent 297–3 in 60 overs (Luckhurst 96, Cowdrey 83*).
Worcestershire 228 (Cass 43, Brown 3–31, Underwood 3–33).
Result: Kent won by 69 runs.
Man of the Match: B. W. Luckhurst.
Adjudicator: J. D. Robertson.

Leicestershire v Nottinghamshire at Leicester, May 30th

Nottinghamshire 216–5 in 60 overs (Bolus 75*, Sobers 51).
Leicestershire 173 (Illingworth 59, Taylor 4–32).
Result: Nottinghamshire won by 43 runs.
Man of the Match: J. B. Bolus.
Adjudicator: C. Washbrook.

Middlesex v Derbyshire at Lord's, May 30th

Derbyshire 161–9 in 60 overs (Harvey 34, Titmus 5–26).
Middlesex 162–8 (Russell 54, Featherstone 50, Rumsey 3–15).
Result: Middlesex won by 2 wickets.
Man of the Match: F. J. Titmus.
Adjudicator: F. R. Brown.

Northamptonshire v Somerset at Northampton, May 30th
Somerset 248–6 in 60 overs (Virgin 103, Robinson 40, Crump 3–43).
Northamptonshire 198 (Steele 58, Jones 5–56).
Result: Somerset won by 50 runs.
Man of the Match: R. Virgin.
Adjudicator: R. T. Simpson.

THIRD ROUND

Kent v Sussex at Canterbury, July 8th
Sussex 199 (Greenidge 56, Greig 54, Woolmer 3–26).
Kent 152 (Luckhurst 48, Greig 5–42).
Result: Sussex won by 47 runs.
Man of the Match: A. W. Greig.
Adjudicator: F. R. Brown.

Lancashire v Hampshire at Old Trafford, July 8th
Hampshire 142 (Marshall 43, Livingstone 41, Lever 5–30).
Lancashire 143–5 (Wood 63*).
Result: Lancashire won by 5 wickets.
Man of the Match: P. Lever.
Adjudicator: D. Kenyon.

Nottinghamshire v Somerset at Trent Bridge, July 8th and 9th
Nottinghamshire 232–5 in 60 overs (Harris 101, Sobers 96*).
Somerset 233–5 (Robinson 57, Virgin 52, Halfyard 3–47).
Result: Somerset won by 5 wickets.
Man of the Match: G. I. Burgess.
Adjudicator: W. J. Edrich.

Surrey v Middlesex at The Oval, July 8th
Surrey 280–5 in 60 overs (Edrich 91, Younis Ahmed 87, Edwards 51, Price 3–63).
Middlesex 272–9 in 60 overs (Parfitt 52, Featherstone 47, Willis 6–49).
Result: Surrey won by 8 runs.
Man of the Match: R. G. D. Willis.
Adjudicator: C. Washbrook.

SEMI-FINALS

Somerset v Lancashire at Taunton, July 22nd
Somerset 207 (Virgin 65, Wood 3–35, Lloyd 3–39).
Lancashire 210–6 (Sullivan 50, Lloyd, C. H. 43).
Result: Lancashire won by 4 wickets.
Man of the Match: B. Wood.
Adjudicator: C. J. Barnett.

Surrey v Sussex at The Oval, July 22nd
Surrey 196 (Edwards 50, Snow 4–35, Greig 3–45).
Sussex 196–8 in 60 overs (Graves 45, Pataudi 42).
Result: Sussex won by having 2 wickets in hand when the series were level after 60 overs.
Man of the Match: J. A. Snow.
Adjudicator: D. Kenyon.

GILLETTE CUP FINAL

Played at Lord's, September 5th
Sussex v Lancashire
Lancashire won by 6 wickets

SUSSEX

M. A. Buss	b Simmons	42
G. A. Greenidge	b Shuttleworth	2
R. J. Langridge	c D. Lloyd b C. H. Lloyd	9
‡J. M. Parks	b Hughes	34
A. W. Greig	b Hughes	15
P. J. Graves	b Hughes	16
K. G. Suttle	run out	23
†M. G. Griffith	run out	10
A. Buss	not out	13
J. A. Snow	run out	0
J. S. Spencer	not out	5
Extras (B4, LB6, NB5)		15
Total (9 wkts.)		184

LANCASHIRE

B. Wood	c Snow b M. A. Buss	22
D. Lloyd	b Spencer	12
H. R. Pilling	not out	70
C. H. Lloyd	c Greenidge b M. Buss	29
J. Sullivan	c Parks b Greig	15
‡F. M. Engineer	not out	31
Extras (LB5, NB1)		6
Total (4 wkts.) 55.1 overs		185

Did not bat: †J. D. Bond, D. P. Hughes, J. Simmons, K. Shuttleworth, P. Lever.

BOWLING

LANCASHIRE	*O.*	*M.*	*R.*	*W.*
Shuttleworth	12	0	31	1
Lever	12	3	31	0
C. H. Lloyd	12	1	46	1
Simmons	12	1	30	1
Hughes	12	2	31	3
SUSSEX				
Snow	12	2	31	0
A. Buss	10.1	1	31	0
Spencer	11	1	40	1
M. A. Buss	12	2	34	2
Greig	10	0	43	1

Fall of Wickets

	Suss.	*Lancs.*
1st	7	33
2nd	34	37
3rd	68	86
4th	113	113
5th	114	
6th	149	
7th	161	
8th	164	
9th	173	

Man of the Match: H. R. Pilling.
Adjudicator: A. V. Bedser.
Umpires: C. S. Elliott and A. E. Fagg.

GILLETTE CUP COMPETITION

PRINCIPAL RECORDS

Highest Innings Total: 327–7 off 60 overs, Glos v Berkshire (Reading) 1966.

Highest Innings Total by a Minor County: 219–9 off 59.4 overs, Cheshire v Norfolk (Macclesfield) 1968.

Highest Innings Total by side batting second: 272–9 off 60 overs, Middlesex v Surrey (Oval) 1970.

Highest Innings Total by side batting first and losing: 250–8 off 60 overs, Middlesex v Surrey (The Oval) 1965.

Lowest Innings Total: 49 off 35.2 overs, Sussex v Derbyshire (Chesterfield) 1969.

Lowest Innings Total by side batting first and winning: 98 off 56.2 overs, Worcs v Durham (Chester-le-Street) 1968.

Highest Individual Innings: 146 G. Boycott, Yorks v Surrey (Lord's) 1965.

Highest Individual Innings by a Minor County player: 105 T. A. Bell, Herts v Berkshire (Hitchin) 1966.

Record Partnerships:

1st wkt.	227	R. E. Marshall & B. L. Reed, Hants v Bedfordshire (Goldington)	1968
2nd wkt.	192	G. Boycott & D.B. Close, Yorks v Surrey (Lord's)	1965
3rd wkt.	145	R. G. Headley & T. W. Graveney, Worcs v Surrey (Worcester)	1963
4th wkt.	169	M. J. Harris & G. S. Sobers, Notts v Somerset (Nottingham)	1970
5th wkt.	134	J. M. Parks & G. C. Cooper, Sussex v Durham (Hove)	1964
6th wkt.	91	P. D. Briggs & G. Hardstaff, Cheshire v Norfolk (Macclesfield)	1968
7th wkt.	86*	T. W. Graveney & G. R. Cass, Worcs v Derbyshire (Derby)	1969
8th wkt.	55	B. S. V. Timms & A. T. Castell, Hants v Sussex (Hove)	1967
9th wkt.	75	B. A. Langford & D. G. Doughty, Somerset v Glamorgan (Cardiff)	1963
10th wkt.	45	A. T. Castell & D. W. White, Hants v Lancs (Manchester)	1970

"Hat-tricks": J. D. F. Larter, Northants v Sussex (Northampton) 1963
D. A. D. Sydenham, Surrey v Cheshire (Hoylake) .1964
R. N. S. Hobbs, Essex v Middlesex (Lord's) 1968

Seven wickets in an Innings: 7–15 A. L. Dixon, Kent v Surrey (The Oval) 1967

P. J. Sainsbury (Hants—7–30 in 1965 and R. D. Jackman (Surrey)—7–33 in 1970 have also achieved this feat.

Most "Man of the Match" awards: 4 R. W. Barber (Warwickshire), D.M. Green (Lancs and Glos), C. Milburn (Northants).

Cumberland and Shropshire are the only minor counties who have not appeared in the competition.

A total of 38 out of 163 matches have taken more than one day to complete.Three matches have taken place outside the assigned period of three days.

27 centuries have been scored in the competition.

LANCASHIRE'S SUNDAY LEAGUE AGAIN

LANCASHIRE, for the second time, were worthy winners of the John Player League, though many will regard their winning of the Gillette Cup as having the greater merit. The Sunday League still has too many artificialities about it—enforced shortened run for the fast bowlers and ludicrous situations when bad weather interferes with play, are but two of them. Many games have drawn enormous crowds (Old Trafford on August 30th was quite memorable) but too many commentators and writers are letting themselves be carried away on the question of crowds. It might be interesting for them to know that the average attendance last summer for John Player League matches was between two and three thousand—substantially better, of course, than the County Championship, which was a mere five hundred, but not necessarily a figure to be shouted from the housetops. Since some of the crowds were very big, some must have been very small in order to produce the average that they did. This is not intended to detract from Lancashire's performance. They proved themselves a first-class all-round cricket team, very nearly pulling off all three competitions, all different in concept, all needing specialist talents. Only once in the Sunday League did Lancashire allow the opposition to reach 200. Shuttleworth headed the League bowling average with 24 wickets at 11 runs each, and in an age where spinners are rarely used in one-day cricket, Simmons (off-spin) and Hughes (Left-arm) finished third and fourth respectively. Only twice were Lancashire bowled out. Harry Pilling set a new Sunday League record by scoring 625 runs, and was the only player to top a thousand runs in the two seasons of the competition. Clive Lloyd, with 521 runs, 15 sixes, and a Ford 'Capri' for scoring a seventy-ball century against Somerset, provided the power onslaught. Engineer, Sullivan, Snellgrove and David Lloyd all averaged over twenty and scored their runs so quickly that Lancashire were able to maintain the fastest run-rate of the League—5.13 runs per over.

FINAL TABLE, 1970

	P.	W.	L.	N.R.	Pts.
1. Lancashire (1)	16	13	2	1	53
2. Kent (4)	16	12	4	0	48
3. Derbyshire (15)	16	11	5	0	44
4. Essex (3)	16	8	5	3	35
5. Warwickshire (9)	16	8	6	2	34
6. Worcestershire (12)	16	8	7	1	33
7. Leicestershire (11)	16	7	7	2	30
8. Gloucestershire (6)	16	7	7	2	30
9. Surrey (5)	16	7	7	2	30
10. Nottinghamshire (13)	16	7	9	0	28
11. Middlesex (7)	16	6	8	2	26
12. Hampshire (2)	16	6	10	0	24
13. Northamptonshire (14)	16	6	10	0	24
14. Yorkshire (7)	16	5	9	2	22
15. Somerset (15)	16	5	9	2	22
16. Glamorgan (9)	16	5	9	2	22
17. Sussex (17)	16	3	10	3	15

Figures in brackets 1969 positions.

Where teams finished with equal points the positions have been decided by their runs-per over rate throughout the season.

Highest Innings Total: 288–6 off 40 overs Sussex v Middx (Hove) 1969.

Highest Innings Total by side batting second: 254–7 off 39 overs Leics v Sussex (Leicester) 1969.

Highest Innings Total by side batting first and losing: 253–7 off 40 overs Sussex v Leics (Leicester) 1969.

Lowest completed Innings Total: 56 off 27.1 overs, Middlesex v Worcs (Kidderminster) 1969.

Highest Individual Innings: 155* B. A. Richards, Hants v Yorks (Hull) 1970.

Record Partnerships: 16 centuries have been scored in the League.

1st wkt. 182 M. H. Denness & B. W. Luckhurst, Kent v Somerset (Weston-super-Mare) 1970.
2nd wkt. 170* R. T. Virgin & G. S. Chappell, Somerset v Surrey (Brislington) 1969.
3rd wkt. 182 H. Pilling & C. H. Lloyd, Lancs v Som (Manchester) 1970.
4th wkt. 175* M. J. K. Smith & D. L. Amiss, Warwickshire v Yorks (Birmingham) 1970.
5th wkt. 97 R. Illingworth & G. F. Cross, Leics v Glamorgan (Coalville) 1970.
6th wkt. 90 B. F. Davison & R. Illingworth, Leics v Surrey (Oval) 1970.
7th wkt. 92 B. E. A. Edmeades & S. Turner, Essex v Notts (Chelmsford) 1969.
8th wkt. 88 B. A. Davis & M. A. Nash, Glam v Kent (Swansea) 1970.
9th wkt. 48* R. N. S. Hobbs & J. K. Lever, Essex v Yorks (Colchester) 1970.
10th wkt. 37* J. A. Snow & D. L. Bates, Sussex v Hants (Hove) 1969.

Four wickets in four balls: A. Ward, Derbyshire v Sussex (Derby) 1970.

Hat-tricks (excluding above): R. Palmer, Somerset v Glos (Bristol) 1970.

Seven wickets in an innings: 7–15 R. A. Hutton, Yorks v Worcs (Leeds) 1969.

WHAT A CHAMPIONSHIP!

KENT—Champions in their Centenary Year for the first time since 1913! What a fantastic struggle lies behind that cold statement. Kent won despite losing their leading players at various stages in the season, Cowdrey, Denness, Luckhurst, Knott and Underwood all answering England's call. In addition, Graham, one of their most effective bowlers in the past four seasons, suffered trouble with his feet and missed half Kent's matches. On the first day of July, Kent occupied bottom place in the table. Unbelievably, by the start of September they had moved into second place with two matches to play and four teams were then still in the fight. Glamorgan (who had yet to play Lancashire), Kent, Lancashire and Surrey, who were down in seventh place, but their final matches were against Kent and Lancashire so technically they had a chance. Kent took over at the top of the table with 229 points with one match to play, followed by Glamorgan with their final tally of 220, and then Lancashire with 211 and one game to go. Lancashire, 18 points behind, had to sit in the wings while Kent took on Surrey at the Oval. All Kent needed to make sure of the title was a reasonable return from bonus points. For one moment it looked as if the weather might defeat them when play was not possible until the middle of the afternoon, but Cowdrey, on the basis that bowling points were probably easier to get than batting points, put Surrey in and the move worked.

Cowdrey's Proud Achievement

Fittingly, it was Colin Cowdrey himself who scored a century, and who made sure of the necessary bonus points and Kent were Champions. To lead Kent to a Championship success will be one of Cowdrey's proudest achievements. He has been a great man for Kent cricket to which he has devoted himself utterly. Fortune did not favour him and allow him a similar triumph with England in Australia. This was a season in which some magnificent cricket was played in the County Championship, followed keenly by enthusiasts from the stop press columns of their evening papers, but not, alas from the boundary's edge.

THE COUNTIES AND THEIR PLAYERS

Compiled by Michael Fordham

NOTE: All career records and Test Match appearances included in this section are complete to 30th September, 1970

B	Born	OB	Off-break
RHB	Right-hand bat	LB	Leg-break
LHB	Left-hand bat	LBG	Leg-break and googly
RF	Right-arm fast	SLA	Slow left-arm orthodox
RFM	Right-arm fast medium	SLC	Slow left-arm "chinaman"
RM	Right-arm medium	WK	Wicket-keeper
LF	Left-arm fast	*	Not out or unfinished stand
LFM	Left-arm fast medium	HS	Highest score
LM	Left-arm medium	BB	Best bowling figures

The county of the cricketer's birth-place is given in the less obvious cases,

"Debut" denotes "first-class debut" and "Cap" means "1st XI county cap".

"Wisden 1969" indicates that a player was selected as one of Wisden's Five Cricketers of the Year for his achievements in 1969.

Owing to the increasing number of privately arranged overseas tours of short duration, only those which may be regarded as major tours have been included.

The matches between England and the Rest of the World have been treated as official Test Matches for player's Test appearances, etc.

DERBYSHIRE

Formation of present club: 1870.
Colours: Chocolate, amber and pale blue.
Badge: Rose and crown.
County Champions (2): 1874 and 1936.
Gillette Cup Finalists: 1969.
John Player League: Third in 1970.

Secretary.—Major D. J. Carr, County Cricket Ground, Nottingham Road, Derby, DE2 6DA.
Captain.—I. R. Buxton.

Anthony John ("Tony") BORRINGTON (Spondon Park G.S.).—B Derby 8/12/1948. RHB. Played for M.C.C. Schools at Lord's in 1967. Played in one John Player League match in 1970. Has yet to appear in first-class cricket. Is student at Loughborough College.

Ian Ray BUXTON (Wirksworth G.S.).—B Cromford (Derbyshire) 17/4/1938. RHB, RM. Soccer for Derby County, Luton Town and Notts County. Debut 1959, Cap 1962. Appointed vice-captain in 1969 and county captain in 1970. 1,000 runs (5)—1,219 runs (av 28.34) in 1964 best. "Hat-trick" v Oxford U (Derby) 1969. HS: 118* v Lancs (Derby) 1964. BB. 7–33 v Oxford U (Derby) 1969. Career record: 9,566 runs (av 23.73), 5 centuries, 396 wkts (av 25.31).

Thomas John Peter EYRE (New Mills G.S.).—B Brough (Derbyshire) 17/10/1939. LHB, RFM. Debut 1959. Cap 1967. Reported to M.C.C. in 1965 by umpire N. Oldfield through not being completely satisfied with his bowling action. HS: 102 v Leics (Chesterfield) 1969. BB: 8–65 v Somerset (Chesterfield) 1969. Career record: 3,314 runs (av 16.16), 1 century, 327 wkts (av 27.72).

Peter John Keith GIBBS (Hanley H. S. and Oxford).—B Buglawton (Cheshire) 17/8/1944. RHB, OB. Played for Staffordshire from 1961 to 1965. Debut for Oxford U. 1964. Blue 1964, 1965 and 1966. Debut for county 1966. Cap 1968. 1,000 runs (3)—1,441 runs (av 41.17) in 1970 best. HS: 138 v Somerset (Chesterfield) 1969. Career record: 6,459 runs (av 28.83), 8 centuries, 4 wkts (av 80.25).

Ian William HALL (The Brunt's G.S., Mansfield).—B Sutton Scarsdale (Derbyshire) 27/12/1939. RHB. Debut 1959. Cap 1961. Testimonial in 1971. 1,000 runs (4)—1,262 runs (av 26.29) in 1965 best. Scored two centuries in match (101 and 101) v Kent (Folkestone) 1965. HS: 136 v Northants (Derby) 1963. Soccer (IR) for Derby County and Mansfield Town. Career record: 9,552 runs (av 24.55), 7 centuries.

John Frank HARVEY (Cambridge Central Technical School).—B Cambridge 27/9/1939. RHB, OB. Debut 1961 for M.C.C. v Scotland whilst on M.C.C. staff at Lord's. Debut for Derbyshire 1963 joining staff by special registration. Cap 1968. 1,000 runs (2)—1,136 runs (av 31.55) in 1968 best. HS: 168 v Northants (Ilkeston) 1969. Career record: 5,948 runs (av 23.69), 4 centuries, 1 wkt (av 21.00).

Michael HENDRICK.—B Darley Dale (Derbyshire) 22/10/1948. RHB, RFM. Debut 1969. HS: 9* v Glamorgan (Cardiff) 1969. BB: 4–77 v Sussex (Buxton) 1970. Career record: 15 runs, (av 7.50), 12 wkts (av 34.91).

Michael Harry PAGE (Francis Askew H.S., Hull).—B Blackpool 17/6/1941. RHB, OB. Debut and cap 1964 scoring 990 runs (av 27.50) in debut season. 1,000 runs (3)—1,344 runs (av 40.72) in 1970 best. HS: 162 v Leics (Leicester) 1969. Career record: 6,790 runs (av 27.26), 6 centuries, 6 wkts (av 75.50).

Frederick Edward ("Fred") RUMSEY (Cooper's Company School, London).—B Stepney 4/12/1935. RHB, LFM. Debut for Worcestershire 1960. Released after end of 1961 season, but re-appeared in 1962 in two matches. Debut for Somerset and Cap 1963. Left staff after 1968 season having obtained post with Derbyshire as Public Relations Officer. Specially registered for county for 1960. Played mostly in Gillette Cup and John Player League. Tests: 5 in 1964 and 1965. 100 wkts (3)—119 wkts (av 16.18) in 1965 best. HS: 45 Somerset v Sussex (Weston-super-Mare) 1967. BB: 8–26 Somerset v Hants (Bath) 1965. Career record: 1,015 runs (av 8.45), 580 wkts (av 20.29).

Philip Edgar RUSSELL (Ilkeston G.S.).—B Ilkeston 9/5/1944. RHB, RM/OB. Debut 1965. HS: 72 v Glamorgan (Swansea) 1970. BB: 6–61 v Glamorgan (Swansea) 1970. Career record: 705 runs (av 15.66), 97 wkts (av 28.08).

David Henry Kilner SMITH (Bingley G.S.).—B Shipley (Yorks) 29/6/1940. LHB, occasional WK. Debut 1965. Cap 1968. 1,000 runs (3)—1,397 runs (av 28.51) in 1968 best. HS: 136 v Lancs (Derby) 1970. Career record: 4,915 runs (av 26.71), 4 centuries, 1 wkt (av 23.00).

Edwin SMITH.—B Grassmoor (Chesterfield), 2/1/1934. RHB, OB. Debut 1951 taking 8–21 in his second match v Worcs (Chesterfield). Cap 1954. Testimonial (£2,810) in 1966. Took 105 wkts (av 17.65) in 1955. HS: 90 v Notts (Ilkeston) 1962. BB: 9–46 (14–112 match) v Scotland (Edinburgh) 1955. Career record: 6,926 runs (av 13.26), 1,186 wkts (av 25.64).

Frederick William ("Fred") SWARBROOK.—B Derby 17/12/1950. LHB, SLA. Debut 1967 aged 16 years 6 months, youngest player ever to appear for county. HS: 90 v Essex (Leyton) 1970. BB: 6–48 v Warwickshire (Coventry) 1970. Soccer for Derby County Juniors. Career record: 528 runs (av 17.03), 80 wkts (av 28.33).

Robert William ("Bob") TAYLOR.—B Stoke-on-Trent 17/7/1941. RHB, WK. Played for Bignall End (N. Staffs and S. Cheshire League) when only 15 and for Staffordshire from 1958 to 1960. Debut 1960 for Minor Counties v South Africans (Stoke-on-Trent). Debut for Derbyshire in 1961, when he deputised for the injured Dawkes. Cap 1962. Tour: Australia and New Zealand 1970–71. Dismissed 80 batsmen (77 ct 3 st) in 1962. 83 batsmen (81 ct 2 st) in 1963 and 86 batsmen (79 ct 7 st) in 1965. Dismissed 10 batsmen in match, all caught v Hants (Chesterfield) 1963 and 7 in innings, all caught, v Glamorgan (Derby) 1966. HS: 65 v Warwickshire (Birmingham) 1969. Career record: 4,467 runs (av 14.89), 689 dismissals (630 ct 59 st).

Alan WARD.—B Dronfield (Derbyshire) 10/8/1947. RHB, RF. Debut 1966. Cap 1969. Elected Best Young Cricketer of the Year in 1969 by the Cricket Writers Club. Tests: 4 in 1969 and 1970. Tour: Australia 1970–71 returning home early owing to injury. Took 4 wickets in 4 balls in John Player League match v Sussex (Derby) 1970. HS: 44 v Notts (Ilkeston) 1969. BB: 6–30 v Sussex (Buxton) 1970. Career record: 356 runs (av 9.88), 177 wkts (av 19.13).

David WILDE.—B Glossop 3/7/1950. LHB, LFM. Played in one John Player League match in 1970. Has yet to appear in first-class cricket.

Christopher Peter ("Chris") WILKINS.—B Kingwilliamstown (South Africa) 31/7/1944. RHB, RM. Occasional WK. Debut for Border in Currie Cup 1962–63 and has played continuously for province since. Debut for county and cap 1970. Scored 1,638 runs (av 39.95) in 1970. Scored century in 73 minutes for Rest of World v T. N. Pearce's XI (Scarborough) 1970. HS: 133 Border v Natal B (East London) 1968–69. HS in England: 102* v Worcs (Chesterfield) and 102 Rest of World v T. N. Pearce's XI (Scarborough) 1970. BB: 4–21 v Leics (Derby) 1970. Career record: 3,474 runs (av 35.81), 5 centuries, 15 wkts (av 39.26).

COUNTY AVERAGES

County Championship: Played 24, Won 7, Drawn 10, Lost 7
All First-Class Matches: Played 25, Won 7, Drawn 11, Lost 7

BATTING AND FIELDING

Cap		*M.*	*I.*	*N.O.*	*Runs*	*H.S.*	*Avge.*	100	50	*Ct.*	*St.*
1968	P. J. K. Gibbs	21	38	3	1441	112*	41.17	2	11	19	—
1964	M. H. Page	20	35	2	1344	113	40.72	1	9	19	—
1970	C. P. Wilkins	25	44	5	1510	102*	38.71	2	9	17	—
1968	J. F. Harvey	16	26	4	726	80	33.00	—	6	3	—
1968	D. H. K. Smith	25	46	3	1241	136	28.86	1	3	20	—
1961	I. W. Hall	19	32	6	701	107	26.96	1	1	20	—
1962	I. R. Buxton	25	42	7	863	72	24.65	—	5	10	—
1962	R. W. Taylor	25	34	5	543	56	18.72	—	2	50	10
1954	E. Smith	24	28	10	303	28	16.83	—	—	10	—
—	F. W. Swarbrook	24	30	8	367	90	16.68	—	1	16	—
—	P. E. Russell	18	20	4	234	72	14.62	—	1	10	—
1967	T. J. P. Eyre	11	11	2	87	31	9.66	—	—	6	—
1969	A. Ward	16	19	4	115	26	7.66	—	—	9	—
—	M. Hendrick	5	5	3	6	3*	3.00	—	—	2	—

Played in one match: F. E. Rumsey 2*.

BOWLING

	Type	*Overs*	*Mdns*	*Runs*	*Wkts*	*Avge.*	*Best*	*5wI.*	*10wM*
I. R. Buxton	RM	422.2	142	1018	46	22.13	6/34	2	—
A. Ward	RF	416.1	90	1247	55	22.67	6/30	2	1
P. E. Russell	RM/OB	547.4	179	1325	50	26.50	6/61	2	—
F. W. Swarbrook	SLA	613.4	184	1694	57	29.71	6/48	3	—
E. Smith	OB	794.1	246	2227	73	30.50	7/84	1	—
M. Hendrick	RFM	97	14	343	9	38.11	4/77	—	—
C. P. Wilkins	RM	152	27	484	12	40.33	4/21	—	—
T. J. P. Eyre	RFM	236.2	65	749	15	49.93	4/57	—	—

Also bowled: P. J. K. Gibbs 3-1-14-0; F. E. Rumsey 30.5-5-97-2; R. W. Taylor 1-0-4-0; D. H. K. Smith 4.2-3-3-1; M. H. Page 23-9-53-2.

County Records

Highest Innings Totals:	For ...645 v Hampshire (Derby)	1898
	Agst...662 by Yorkshire (Chesterfield)	1898

DERBYSHIRE

Lowest Innings Totals:	For	... 16 v Nottinghamshire (Nottingham) 1879
	Agst	... 23 by Hampshire (Burton-on-Trent) 1958
Highest Individual Inngs.:	For	...274 G. Davidson v Lancashire (Manchester)1896
	Agst	...343* P. A. Perrin for Essex (Chesterfield) ...1904
Best bowling figs. in an Inngs.:	For	...10–40 W. Bestwick v Glamorgan (Cardiff)1921
	Agst	...10–47 T. F. Smailes for Yorkshire (Sheffield)1939
Best bowling figs in a match	For	...16–84 C. Gladwin v Worcs. (Stourbridge)...1952
	Agst	...16–101 G. Giffen for Australians (Derby)...1886

Most runs in a season	2165	(av. 48.11) D. B. Carr 1959
runs in a career...........	20516	(av. 31.41) D. Smith......1927–1952
100s in a season...........	6	by L. F. Townsend 1933
100s in a career...........	30	by D. Smith 1927–1952
wickets in a season	168	(av. 19.55) T. B. Mitchell 1935
wickets in a career	1670	(av. 17.11) H. L. Jackson 1947–1963

RECORD WICKET STANDS

1st	322	H. Storer & J. Bowden v Essex (Leyton).....................	1929
2nd	349	C. S. Elliott & J. D. Eggar v Nottinghamshire (Nottingham)	1947
3rd	246	J. Kelly & D. B. Carr v Leicestershire (Chesterfield)......	1957
4th	328	P. Vaulkhard & D. Smith v Nottinghamshire (Nottingham)	1946
5th	191	A. G. Slater & A. Morton v Hampshire (Basingstoke)...	1914
6th	212	G. M. Lee & T. S. Worthington v Essex (Chesterfield)...	1932
7th	241*	G. H. Pope & A. E. G. Rhodes v Hampshire (Portsmouth)	1948
8th	182	A. H. M. Jackson & W. Carter v Leicestershire (Leicester)	1922
9th	283	A. R. Warren & J. Chapman v Warwickshire (Blackwell)	1910
10th	93	J. Humphries & J. Horsley v Lancashire (Derby).........	1914

Home Matches in Championship

Glos (Chesterfield)—D 236 (Gibbs 104, Smith 6–86) and 148–5d. (Gibbs 69). G 115 (Buxton 4–16, Ward 4–42) and 171 (Pullar 73). *D (10 points) won by 98 runs. (D 7 bonus points. G 5 bonus points.)*

Warwicks (Derby)—D 280 (Gibbs 62, Taylor 56) and 164–4 (Smith, D. H. K. 55). W 468–7d. (Kanhai 165, Smith, M. J. K. 61, Ibadulla 53, Russell 4–109). *Match drawn. (D 5 bonus points, W 7 bonus points.)*

Sussex (Buxton)—S 75 (Ward 6–30) and 299 (Buss, M. 76, Langridge 50, Hendrick 4–77, Ward 4–83). D 253 (Denman 4–45, Greig 4–64) and 124–2 (Gibbs 53). *D (10 points) won by 8 wickets. (D 9 bonus points, S 5 bonus points.)*

Hants (Chesterfield)—D 180 (Wilkins 59, Castell 4–46) and 281–8 (Harvey 80, Taylor 50). H 302–6d. (Richards 153). *Match drawn. (D 3 bonus points, H 10 bonus points.)*

Glam (Derby)—D 269–5d (Gibbs 77, Wilkins 75*) and 106–6 (Cordle 4–35). G 85 (Buxton 6–34) and 288 (Lewis 128). *D* (10 *points*) *won by* 4 *wickets.* (*D* 9 *bonus points, G* 2 *bonus points.*)

Yorks (Chesterfield)—D 307–7d (Wilkins 95, Gibbs 65, Page 58, Smith, D. H. K. 56, Nicholson 5–82) and 201–4d (Page 72, Wilkins 54). Y 246–6d (Boycott 99) and 266–6 (Hampshire 120*). *Y* (10 *points*) *won by* 4 *wickets.* (*D* 5 *bonus points, Y* 1 *bonus point.*)

Lancs (Derby)—L 270–9d (Bond 89, Sullivan 72) and 204 (Bond 58). D 468–5d (Smith, D. H. K. 136, Page 113, Wilkins 96, Gibbs 72) and 10–0. *D* (10 *points*) *won by* 10 *wickets.* (*D* 8 *bonus points, L* 1 *bonus point*).

Northants (Chesterfield)–D 228 (Wilkins 68, Swinburne 4–91) and 286–4d (Wilkins 101, Harvey 57*, Gibbs 51). N 293 (Breakwell 97, Crump 75, Swarbrook 5–65) and 115–3. *Match drawn.* (*D* 5 *bonus points, N* 3 *bonus points.*)

Surrey (Burton-on-Trent)—D 276 (Harvey 50, Arnold 4–68) and 209–5d (Harvey 52*). S 253–9d (Younis 66, Russell 4–68) and 100–4 (Younis 52*) *Match Drawn.* (*D* 6 *bonus points, S* 8 *bonus points.*)

Worcs (Chesterfield)—D 268 (Harvey 80, Buxton 57, Carter 4–64) and 349–3d (Wilkins 102*, Gibbs 83, Page 80). W 305–3d (Turner 142*, Graveney 64*) and 100–4. *Match drawn.* (*D* 3 *bonus points, W* 7 *bonus points.*)

Leics (Derby)—L 175 (Tolchard R. 55, Wilkins 4–21). D 94–1. *Match drawn.* (*D* 5 *bonus points, L* 1 *bonus point.*)

Notts (Ilkeston)—N 326 (Smedley 84, Harris 50, Smith, E. 4–76) and 143–1d (Bolus 64*, Harris 64). D 178 (Wilkins 61, Sobers 4–32) and 163 (White 5–28). *N* (10 *points*) *won by* 128 *runs.* (*D* 3 *bonus points, N* 7 *bonus points.*)

ESSEX

Formation of present club: 1876
Colours: Blue, gold and red.
Badge: Three scimitars with word 'Essex' underneath.
Best final position in Championship: Third in 1897.
Gillette Cup Third round (2): 1966 and 1969.
John Player League: Third in 1969.

Secretary.—Major C. A. Brown, M.B.E.,
The County Ground, New Writtle Street, Chelmsford, CM2 0RW.
Captain.—B. Taylor.

ESSEX

David Laurence ACFIELD (Brentwood & Cambridge).—B Chelmsford 24/7/1947. RHB, OB. Debut 1966. Blue 1967, 1968. Cap 1970. HS: 42 Cambridge U v Leics (Leicester) 1967. BB: 6–28 Cambridge U v Sussex (Cambridge) 1967. Has also obtained Blue for Fencing (sabre). Has appeared in internationals in this sport and represented Great Britain in Olympic Games at Mexico City. Career record: 632 runs (av 8.10), 254 wkts (av 28.29).

Gordon BARKER.—B Leeds 6/7/1931. RHB, RM. Fine field. Scored 107* v Canadians (Clacton) on debut in 1954. Cap 1955. Benefit (£2,400) in 1965. Testimonial in 1971. 1,000 runs (15)—1,741 runs (av 36.27) in 1960 best. HS: 181* v Kent (Colchester) 1961 (completing century before lunch on first day). Soccer for Southend United. Career record: 22,122 runs (av 29.49), 30 centuries, 4 wkts (av 45.25).

Keith David BOYCE.—B St. Peter, Barbados 11/10/1943. RHB, RFM. Very good outfield. Debut for Barbados v Cavaliers in one match in 1964–65. Joined county in 1965 and made debut in two matches v Cambridge U and West Indians in 1966. Cap 1967 when he scored 910 runs (av 20.22) and took 81 wkts (av 27.24). Scored 908 runs (av 20.63) and took 88 wkts (av 23.54) in 1968. Played for Barbados in 1968–69 Shell Shield competition. Won single-wicket tournament at Lord's in 1969. Returned to Barbados in 1970–71 to play against India. HS: 147* v Hants (Ilford) 1969. BB: 9–61 (13–108 match) v Cambridge U (Brentwood) 1966, in debut match for county. Career record: 3,735 runs (av 20.29), 3 centuries, 363 wkts (av 25.24).

Michael John Herbert BOYERS (Sir George Monoux G.S., Walthamstow).—B Plaistow 16/4/1948. RHB, RFM. Played in Schools' matches at Lord's 1966 and 1967. Debut 1969. One match v Middlesex (Westcliff). Did not play in 1970. Has played rugger for Loughborough College where he is a student. Career record: 2 runs (av 1.00).

Victor Charles George BROOKS (East Ham G.S.).—B East Ham 29/6/48. LHB. Played in two John Player League matches in 1969. Debut 1970. One match v Jamaica XI. HS: 15 v Jamaica XI (Leyton) 1970. Career record: 15 runs (av 15.00).

Raymond Eric ("Ray") EAST.—B Manningtree (Essex) 20/6/1947. RHB, SLA. Debut 1965. Cap 1967. HS: 58 v New Zealanders (Westcliff) 1969. BB: 8–63 (15–115 match) v Warwickshire (Leyton) 1968. Career record: 1,300 runs (av 11.92), 303 wkts (av 24.36).

Brian Ernest Arthur EDMEADES.—B Matlock (Derbyshire) 17/9/1941. RHB, RM. Debut 1961. Cap 1965. 1,000 runs (3)—1,620 runs (av 35.21) in 1970 best. Took 106 wkts (av 18.59) in 1966. HS: 148 v Somerset (Taunton) 1969. BB: 7–37 v Glamorgan (Leyton) 1966. Career record: 7,390 runs (av 24.30), 10 centuries, 319 wkts (av 25.17).

Keith William Robert FLETCHER.—B Worcester 20/5/1944. RHB, LB. Debut 1962. Cap 1963. Tests: 10 between 1968 and 1970. Tours:

Pakistan 1966–67, Ceylon and Pakistan 1968–69, Australia and New Zealand 1970–71. 1,000 runs (8)—1,890 runs (av 41.08) in 1968 best. HS: 228* v Sussex (Hastings) 1968. BB: 4–50 M.C.C. under-25 v North Zone (Peshawar) 1966–67. Career record: 13,893 runs (av 34.05), 19 centuries, 11 wkts (av 55.27).

Bruce C. FRANCIS.—Born Sydney 18/2/1948. RHB. Debut for New South Wales 1968–69. Played for county 2nd XI and for Accrington in Lancashire League in 1970. Has joined county for 1971 on 3 year contract. HS: 126 New South Wales v Queensland (Sydney) 1969–70. Is a graduate of Sydney University. Career record: 841 runs (av 28.03), 2 centuries.

Robin Nicholas Stuart HOBBS (Raine's Foundation School, Stepney).—B Chippenham (Wilts) 8/5/1942. RHB, LBG. Outstanding cover fielder. Debut 1961. Cap 1964. Tests: 6 between 1967 and 1968–69. Tours: South Africa 1964–65, Pakistan 1966–67, West Indies 1967–68, Ceylon and Pakistan 1968–69. 100 wkts (2)—102 wkts (av 21.40) in 1970 best. HS: 100 v Glamorgan (Ilford) 1968. BB: 8–63 (13–164 match) v Glamorgan (Swansea) 1966. "Hat-trick" v Middlesex (Lord's) 1968 in Gillette Cup. Career record: 3,087 runs (av 11.43), 1 century, 765 wkts (av 25.19).

Anthony Mervyn ("Tony") JORDEN (Monmouth School and Cambridge).—B Radlett (Herts) 28/1/1947. RHB, RFM. Debut 1966. Blue 1968, 1969 and 1970 (captain in 1969 and 1970). HS: 67* Cambridge U v Derbyshire (Cambridge) 1968. BB: 5–95 Cambridge U v Sussex (Hove) 1969. Plays rugby (full-back) for Blackheath, and played for England v France 1969–70. Rugby Blues 1968 and 1969. Career record: 1,112 runs (av 11.23), 176 wkts (av 30.38).

John Kenneth LEVER.—B Ilford 24/2/1949. RHB, LFM. Outfield, Debut 1967. Cap 1970. HS: 91 v Glamorgan (Cardiff) 1970. BB: 6–72 v Cambridge U (Cambridge) 1969. Career record: 526 runs (av 10.11), 170 wkts (av 28.47).

Keith Rupert PONT.—B Wanstead 16/1/1953. Brother of Kelvin Pont who was formerly on M.C.C. staff at Lord's. RHB, RM. Debut 1970. One match v Jamaica XI. HS: 5 v Jamaica XI (Leyton) 1970. Plays hockey for Brentwood. Career record: 5 runs (av 5.00).

Edward Robert ("Eddie") PRESLAND.—B Highbeach, Loughton (Essex) 27/3/1943. RHB RM/OB. Debut 1962. Not re-engaged after 1965 season but has played occasionally since. HS: 51 v Northants (Northampton) 1967. Soccer for West Ham United and Crystal Palace. Career record: 625 runs (av 16.89) 13 wkts (av 58.53).

Graham John SAVILLE (Sir George Monoux G.S. Walthamstow).—B Leytonstone 5/2/1944. RHB, LBG. Fine slip fielder. Debut 1963. Left staff after 1966 season. Played for Norfolk from 1967 to 1969 and for Minor Counties in 1968 and 1969. Rejoined staff and cap 1970. Scored 1,133 runs (av 29.81) in 1970. HS: 116 Minor Counties v West Indians (Stoke-on-Trent) 1969. Career record: 2,554 runs (av 23.86), 2 centuries.

Brian TAYLOR.—B West Ham 19/6/1932. LHB, WK. Debut 1949 gained regular place as batsman in 1954. Cap 1956. Elected Best Young Cricketer of the Year in 1956 by the Cricket Writers' Club. Testimonial (£2,500) in 1966. Appointed county captain in 1967. Has played in 267 consecutive Championship matches since May 1961, and has missed only one other first-class match during this period. Tour: South Africa 1956–57. 1,000 runs (8)—1,837 runs (av 30.61) in 1959 best. Dismissed 91 batsmen (81 ct 10 st) in 1962. HS: 135 v Middlesex (Lord's) 1959. Soccer (left-back) for Brentford and Bexley United (Southern League). Was player-manager of latter club. Career record: 17,575 runs (av 22.07), 9 centuries, 1,149 dismissals (966 ct 183 st), 1 wkt (av 29.00).

Stuart TURNER.—B Chester 18/7/1943. RHB, RM. Debut 1965. Cap 1970. HS: 121 v Somerset (Taunton) 1970. BB: 4–10 v Somerset (Chelmsford) 1969. Career record: 1,141 runs (av 15.01), 2 centuries, 131 wkts (av 24.41).

Kenneth William WALLACE.—B Romford 27/8/1936. RHB, RM. Played for county 2nd XI for some years. Debut 1967. HS: 55 v Hants (Ilford) 1967. Career record: 148 runs (av 12.33).

Brian WARD.—B Chelmsford 28/2/1944. RHB, RM. Plays in contact lenses. On M.C.C. groundstaff 1961–66. Played for Derbyshire 2nd XI 1965–66. Debut 1967. Cap 1970. Scored 948 runs (av 21.06) in 1968. HS: 164* v Notts (Nottingham) 1970. Career record: 3,074 runs (av 22.43), 3 centuries, 3 wkts (av 2.33).

N.B. The following players whose particulars appeared in the 1970 Annual have been omitted: B. L. Irvine (to remain in South Africa) and H. R. Sherman. In addition S. C. Dinsdale a left-hand batsman who played one match for Rhodesia in 1969–70 and R. Richards a wicket-keeper who made his debut against the Jamaica XI at Leyton have not been included as they are unlikely to play again for the county. Sadiq Mohammad who made his debut for the county against the Jamaica XI is also not included, as he has joined Gloucestershire and his particulars will be found under that county.

The career records of Dinsdale, Richards and Sadiq Mohammad will be found elsewhere in this Annual.

GILLETTE CUP WINNERS

1963 Sussex	1967 Kent
1964 Sussex	1968 Warwickshire
1965 Yorkshire	1969 Yorkshire
1966 Warwickshire	1970 Lancashire

COUNTY AVERAGES

County Championship: Played 24, Won 4, Drawn 14, Lost 6
All First-Class Matches: Played 27, Won 5, Drawn 16, Lost 6

BATTING AND FIELDING

Cap		*M.*	*I.*	*N.O.*	*Runs*	*H.S.*	*Avge.*	100	50	*Ct.*	*St.*
1963	K. W. R. Fletcher ...	18	30	4	1218	169*	46.84	4	5	17	—
1965	B. E. A. Edmeades .	26	49	3	1620	120*	35.21	4	10	7	—
1970	J. K. Lever	16	17	11	189	91	31.50	—	1	2	—
1956	B. Taylor	27	46	7	1176	113*	30.15	2	5	51	19
1970	G. J. Saville	25	45	7	1133	103	29.81	1	7	24	—
1955	G. Barker	25	45	6	1111	124	28.48	2	6	5	—
1970	B. Ward	18	32	1	774	164*	24.96	1	2	6	—
1964	R. N. S. Hobbs	25	39	11	568	83*	20.28	—	1	25	—
—	E. R. Presland	10	17	2	300	45	20.00	—	—	11	—
1967	R. E. East	25	31	8	424	50*	18.43	—	1	19	—
1967	K. D. Boyce	27	46	1	728	70	16.17	—	4	23	—
1970	S. Turner	25	40	6	545	121	16.02	1	—	26	—
—	S. C. Dinsdale	5	7	0	97	29	13.85	—	—	4	—
1970	D. L. Acfield..........	19	20	10	137	34	13.70	—	—	6	—

Played in one match: V. C. G. Brooks 15; A. M. Jorden 8; K. R. Pont 5; Sadiq Mohammad 20; K. W. Wallace 4; R. Richards did not bat.

BOWLING

	Type	*Overs*	*Mdns*	*Runs*	*Wkts*	*Avge.*	*Best*	5*wI.*	10*wM*
R. N. S. Hobbs	LBG	668.5	169	1907	90	21.18	7/59	4	—
S. Turner	RM	720.1	184	1646	70	23.51	4/53	—	—
D. L. Acfield....	OB	532.1	150	1263	51	24.76	5/39	2	—
K. D. Boyce	RFM	759.4	112	2303	87	26.47	5/39	5	—
R. E. East	SLA	677	229	1458	53	27.50	6/22	1	—
B.E.A.Edmeades	RM	70	18	143	5	28.60	2/21	—	—
J. K. Lever	LFM	356	65	1078	31	34.77	4/32	—	—

Also bowled: K. W. R. Fletcher 16.5-1-79-2; A. M. Jorden 15-1-39-2; K. R Pont 4-1-9-0; E. R. Presland 16-0-78-1.

County Records

Highest Innings Totals:	For ...692 v Somerset (Taunton)...................	1895
	Agst...803–4d by Kent (Brentwood).................	1934
Lowest Inngs Totals:	For ... 30 v Yorkshire (Leyton).....................	1901
	Agst... 31 by Derbyshire (Derby) and by Yorkshire (Huddersfield)......................	1914 & 1935
Highest Individual Inngs:	For ...343* P. A. Perrin v Derbyshire (Chesterfield)	1904
	Agst...332 W. H. Ashdown for Kent (Brentwood)	1934
Best Bowling figs in an Inngs:	For ...10–32 H. Pickett v Leicestershire (Leyton)...	1895
	Agst...10–40 G. Dennett for Gloucestershire (Bristol)	1906
Best bowling figs in a match	For ...17–119 W. Mead v Hampshire (Southampton)	1895
	Agst...17–56 C. W. L. Parker for Gloucestershire (Gloucester)	1925

Most runs in a season......	2308	(av 56.29) J. O'Connor................1934
runs in a career	29162	(av 36.18) P. A. Perrin......1896–1928
100s in a season......	9	by J. O'Connor and D. J. Insole 1934 & 1955
100s in a career	71	by J. O'Connor 1921–1939
wickets in a season...	172	(av 27.13) T. P. B. Smith............1947
wickets in a career...	1611	(av 26.26) T. P. B. Smith......1929–1951

RECORD WICKET STANDS

1st 270	A. V. Avery & T. C. Dodds v Surrey (The Oval)	1946
2nd 294	A. V. Avery & P. A. Gibb v Northampton (Northampton)	1952
3rd 343	P. A. Gibb & R. Horsfall v Kent (Blackheath)	1951
4th 298	A. V. Avery & R. Horsfall v Worcestershire (Clacton)	1948
5th 287	C. T. Ashton & J. O'Connor v Surrey (Brentwood)	1934
6th 206	J. W. H. T. Douglas & J. O'Connor v Gloucestershire (Cheltenham)	1923
	B. R. Knight & R. A. G. Luckin v Middlesex (Brentwood)	1962
7th 261	J. W. H. T. Douglas & J. Freeman v Lancashire (Leyton)	1914
8th 263	D. R. Wilcox & R. M. Taylor v Warwickshire (Southend)	1946
9th 251	J. W. H. T. Douglas & S. N. Hare v Derbyshire (Leyton)	1921
10th 218	F. H. Vigar & T. P. B. Smith v Derbyshire (Chesterfield)	1947

Home Matches in Championship

Northants (Chelmsford)—E 314–8d (Hobbs 83*, Saville 69, Sarfraz 4–108) and 194 (Mushtaq 4–56, Crump 4–63). N 268–9d (Willey 50, Turner 4–53) and 152 (Acfield 4–34). *E (10 points) won by* 88 *runs.* (*E* 7 *bonus points, N* 6 *bonus points.*)

Leics (Chelmsford)—L 268 (Inman 76, Dudleston 58, Hobbs 4–60) and 158 (Boyce 5–39, Hobbs 4–74). E 239 (Edmeades 79, Barker 61, McKenzie 4–62) and 191–1 (Edmeades 120*). *E* (10 *points*) *won by* 9 *wickets.* (*E* 6 *bonus points, L* 8 *bonus points.*)

Glam (Ilford)—E 208 (Fletcher 88, Nash 5–76) and 196 (Edmeades 54, Nash 4–58). G 258 (Lewis 72, Boyce 4–67) and 150–5 (Davis, B. A. 52*). *G* (10 *points*) *won by* 5 *wickets.* (*G* 9 *bonus points, E* 5 *bonus points*).

Lancs (Ilford)—E 270 (Fletcher 103, Simmons 4–26, Shuttleworth 4–52) and 203–7d (Taylor 55). L 202 (Lever 4–43) and 102–9 (Lever 4–32). *Match drawn.* (*E* 9 *bonus points, L* 6 *bonus points.*)

Kent (Harlow)—K 330–7d (Denness 167*, Ealham 88). E 179 (Taylor 63, Saville 61, Shepherd 5–41) and 127 (Graham 6–67, Dye 4–51). *K* (10 *points*) *won by an innings and* 24 *runs.* (*E* 3 *bonus points, K* 8 *bonus points.*)

Middx (Westcliff)—E 388–7d (Fletcher 90, Barker 89, Saville 74). M 116 (Hobbs 6–31) and 37–2. *Match drawn.* (*E* 6 *bonus points, M* 1 *bonus point.*)

Yorks (Colchester)—Y450–4d (Boycott 260*, Hampshire 80, Sharpe 58). E 226 (Edmeades 78, Hutton 4–60) and 123 (Cope 7–36). *Y* (10 *points*) *won by an innings and* 101 *runs.* (*E* 4 *bonus points, Y* 8 *bonus points.*)

Surrey (Colchester)—S 210 (Hobbs 4–28) and 284–5d (Stewart 96*, Younis 66). E 273 (East 50*, Pocock 5–88) and 128–7. *Match drawn.* (*E* 6 *bonus points, S* 6 *bonus points.*)

Som (Leyton)—S 298 (Virgin 95, Robinson 67, Hobbs 4–41). E 137 (Cartwright 7–56) and 104 (Cartwright 5–38). *S* (10 *points*) *won by an innings and* 57 *runs.* (*E* 2 *bonus points, S* 6 *bonus points.*)

Derbys (Leyton)—E 341 (Boyce 70, Edmeades 67, Russell 4–71) and 192–7d (Edmeades 69). D 288 (Wilkins 93, Swarbrook 90, Buxton 56, Boyce 5–76) and 179 (Wilkins 90, Hobbs 7–59). *E* (10 *points*) *won by* 66 *runs.* (*E* 8 *bonus points, D* 8 *bonus points.*)

Worcs (Chelmsford)—W 290 (Headley 84, Hobbs 4–68) and 207–9d (Graveney 62, Hobbs 5–79). E 311 (Taylor 86, Ward 50) and 116–5. *Match drawn.* (*E* 8 *bonus points, W* 7 *bonus points.*)

Glos (Chelmsford)—G 308 (Shepherd 77) and 237 (Acfield 5–39). E 325–8d (Fletcher 169*, Procter 4–57) and 215–6 (Edmeades 106, Mortimore 4–69). *Match drawn.* (*E* 10 *bonus points, G* 9 *bonus points.*)

GLAMORGAN

Formation of present club: 1888.
Colours: Blue and gold.
Badge: Gold daffodil.
County Champions (2): 1948 and 1969.
Gillette Cup Third round (2): 1964 and 1969.

Secretary.—W. Wooller, 6 High Street, Cardiff, CF1 1YU.
Captain.—A. R. Lewis.

Anthony Elton ("Tony") CORDLE:—B St. Michael, Barbados 21/9/1940. RHB, RFM. Debut 1963. Cap 1967. HS: 56* v Sussex (Cardiff) 1969 and 56 v Yorks (Sheffield) 1968. BB: 9–49 (13–110 match) v Leics (Colwyn Bay) 1969. Career record: 2,556 runs (av 15.12), 295 wkts (av 23.16).

GLAMORGAN

Francis John DAVIS (Blundell's and Oxford).—B Cardiff 26/3/1939. RHB, SLA. Debut 1959 in one match v Indian touring team. Debut for Oxford U and Blue 1963. Re-appeared for Glamorgan in two matches in 1963 and again in one match in 1965. On staff for 1966 season, but left at end of season and appeared in one match in 1967. Re-appeared in two John Player League matches in 1970. HS: 63 Oxford U v Northants (Oxford) 1963. BB: 5–67 Oxford U v Cambridge U (Lord's) 1963. Career record: 552 runs (av 16.23), 52 wkts (av 32.57).

Roger Clive DAVIS (Blundell's).—B Cardiff 15/1/1946. Brother of F. J. Davis. RHB, OB. Debut 1964. Cap 1969. HS: 116 v Derbyshire (Derby) 1969. BB: 6–82 v Glos (Cheltenham) 1970. Career record: 3,231 runs (av 18.56), 1 century, 113 wkts (av 25.87).

Geoffrey Phillip ELLIS.—B Llandudno (Caernarvonshire) 24/5/1950. RHB. Debut 1970. HS: 55 v Glos (Swansea) 1970. Career record: 318 runs (av 26.50).

Leonard Winston HILL.—B Caerleon (Monmouthshire) 14/4/1942. RHB. Cover field. Debut 1964. Did not play in 1968 or 1969, but re-appeared in 1970. HS: 80 v Oxford U. (Oxford) 1970. Soccer (right-half) for Newport County. Career record: 967 runs (av 20.57).

John Anthony HOPKINS.—B Maesteg 16/6/1953. Younger brother of J. D. Hopkins formerly on staff and now with Middlesex. RHB, WK. Debut 1970. One match v Leics (Leicester). HS: 4 v Leics (Leicester) 1970. Career record: 6 runs (av 3.00).

Alan JONES.—B Swansea 4/11/1938. LHB, OB. Joined staff 1955. Debut 1957. Cap 1962. Played for Western Australia in 1963–64. Tests: 1 v Rest of World 1970. 1,000 runs (10)—1,865 runs (av 34.53) in 1966 and 1,862 runs (av 38.00) in 1968 best. Scored two centuries in match (187* and 105*) v Somerset (Glastonbury) 1963. Shared in 2nd wkt partnership record for county, 238 with A. R. Lewis v Sussex (Hastings) 1962. HS: 187* v Somerset (Glastonbury) 1963. Career record: 18,253 runs (av 31.79), 26 centuries, 2 wkts (av 104.00).

Eifion Wyn JONES.—B Velindre (Glamorgan) 25/6/1942. Brother of A. Jones. RHB, WK. Debut 1961. Cap 1967 Dismissed 94 batsmen (85 ct 9 st) in 1970. Dismissed 7 batsmen (6 ct 1 st) in innings v Cambridge U (Cambridge) 1970. HS: 146* v Sussex (Hove) 1968. Career record: 2,886 runs (av 18.50), 2 centuries, 342 dismissals (314 ct, 28 st).

MAJID JAHANGIR KHAN (Aitchison College, Lahore and Cambridge) —B Jullundur (India) 28/9/1946. Son of Dr Jahangir Khan, pre-war Indian Test cricketer and Cambridge Blue. RHB, RM. Debut 1961–62 for Lahore B v Khairpur at age of 15 scoring 111* and taking 6–67 and has since played continuously for various Lahore sides. Debut for county and cap 1968. "Wisden 1969". Blue 1970. University captain 1971. Tests: 7 for Pakistan in 1964–65 and 1967. Tours: England 1963 with Pakistan Eaglets and 1967. 1,000 runs (3)—1,862 runs (av 46.55) in 1970 best. Scored 973 runs (av 42.30) on 1967 tour. Scored 147* in 89 minutes before lunch with 13 6's and 10 4's and hitting 30 runs off one over from R. C. Davis on third morning of match against county at Swansea. Scored 147 before lunch v West Indians (Swansea) and 114* before lunch Worcs (Cardiff) in 1969. "Hat-trick" v Oxford U (Oxford) 1969. HS: 241 Lahore Greens v Bahawalpur (Lahore) 1965–66. HS in England: 200 Cambridge U v Oxford U (Lord's) 1970. BB: 6–67 in debut match. BB in England: 4–18 Pakistan Eaglets v Northants (Peterborough) 1963. Career record: 9,313 runs (av 42.14), 25 centuries, 120 wkts (av 25.50).

Graham Charles KINGSTON (St. Julian's High School, Newport).—B. Newport (Mon.) 1/11/1950. RHB, RM. Debut 1967. HS: 22 v Sussex (Hove) 1970. Plays both rugger and soccer and is son of C. Kingston, international soccer referee. Career record: 124 runs (av 13.77), 3 wkts (av 42.00).

Anthony Robert ("Tony") LEWIS (Neath C.G.S. and Cambridge).—B Swansea 6/7/1938. RHB, LB. Debut 1955. Cap 1960. Blue 1960, 1961 and 1962 (capt. 1962). Appointed assistant secretary 1962. Resigned post in 1963. Appointed county captain in 1967. Captain of M.C.C. team to Asia 1969–70. 1,000 runs (10)—2,198 runs (av 41.47) in 1966 best. His 2,052 runs for Glamorgan in 1966 was only 19 runs short of county record. Shared in 2nd wkt partnership record for County, 238 with A. Jones v Sussex (Hastings) 1962. HS: 223 v Kent (Gravesend) 1966. BB: 3–18 v Somerset (Neath) 1967. Career record: 17,225 runs (av 32.56), 26 centuries, 6 wkts (av 70.83).

Michael John LLEWELLYN.—B Clydach 27/11/1953. LHB, OB. Debut 1970. One match v Oxford U. HS: 15 v Oxford U (Oxford) 1970. BB: 4–35 v Oxford U (Oxford) 1970. Career record: 15 runs (av 7.50), 6 wkts (av 21.50).

Kevin James LYONS (Lady Mary's Boys High School, Cardiff).—B. Cardiff 18/12/1946. RHB, RM. Cover-point. Debut 1967. HS: 58* v Oxford U (Oxford) 1970. Soccer player. Career record: 658 runs (av 15.66).

Malcolm Andrew NASH (Wells Cathedral School).—B Abergavenny (Monmouthshire) 9/5/1945. LHB, LM. Debut 1966. Cap 1969. HS: 69 v Leics (Leicester) 1967. BB: 7–15 v Somerset (Swansea) 1968. Plays hockey and has captained Welsh Under-23 XI. Career record: 1,754 runs (av 16.86), 241 wkts (av 22.72).

Alan REES.—B Port Talbot (Glamorgan) 17/2/1938. RHB, RM. Fine field. Played cricket for Welsh schools. Debut 1955 (one match). Reappeared in 1959. Cap 1963. Left staff after 1968 season, but still available if required and appeared in one John Player League match in both 1969 and 1970 and also in Gillette Cup match v Surrey in 1970. 1,000 runs (4)—1,206 runs (av 30.15) in 1964 best. Scored the first two centuries of his career in successive innings in 1964. Was dismissed handled the ball v Middlesex (Lord's) 1965. HS: 111* v Lancs (Cardiff) 1964. Won three Rugby caps for Wales in 1961–62, v England, Scotland and France before turning professional for Leeds in Rugby League. Retired from Rugby football in 1965. Career record: 7,681 runs (av 24.07), 2 centuries, 6 wkts, (av 66.33).

Graham Edward Arthur REYNOLDS (Newport H.S.).—B Newport (Mon). 23/9/1939. LHB, RM. Outfield. Debut 1970. One match v Jamaica XI. Played in three John Player League matches in 1969 taking 5–37 v Notts (Nottingham) and five League matches in 1970. HS: 9* v Jamaica XI (Swansea) 1970. Has played soccer for Newport County. Career record: 9 runs, 2 wkts (av 12.00).

Donald John ("Don") SHEPHERD (Gowerton County G.S.).—B Port-eynon (Glamorgan) 12/8/1927. RHB, RM/OB. Debut 1950. Cap 1952. Benefit (£3,200) in 1960. Testimonial (£5,000) in 1968. "Wisden 1969". 100 wkts (12)—177 wkts (av 15.36) in 1956 best. "Hat-trick" v Northants (Swansea) 1964. Has taken more wickets for Glamorgan than any other bowler and in 1969 became first Glamorgan bowler to take 2,000 wkts in first-class cricket. HS: 73 v Derby (Cardiff) 1961. BB: 9–47 v Northants (Cardiff) 1954 and 9–48 v Yorks (Swansea) 1965. Career record: 5,410 runs (av 9.71), 2,127 wkts (av 21.01).

Peter Michael WALKER (Highlands North School, Johannesburg).—B Bristol 17/2/1936. Tall (6ft. 4in.) RHB, LM/SLA. Joined staff in 1954. Debut 1956. Cap 1958. Left staff after 1962 season, but rejoined in 1963, missing first half of season. Benefit (£4,500) in 1966. Played for Transvaal in 1956–57 and 1957–58 and Western Province in 1962–63. Tests (3): v South Africa 1960. 1 000 runs (10)—1,564 runs (av 34.00) in 1959 best. Took 101 wkts (av 24.04) in 1961 and with 1,347 runs (av 24.94) as well as 73 catches achieved double. Also had good all-round season in 1959 with 1,564 runs, 80 wkts (av 27.82) and 65 catches. Held 69 catches in 1960. Held 8 catches in match v Derbyshire (Swansea) 1970. Has held more catches for Glamorgan than any other player. HS: 152* v Middlesex (Lord's) 1962. BB: 7–58 v Middlesex (Lord's) 1962. Career record: 16,160 runs (av 26.14), 11 centuries, 766 wkts (av 27.87).

David Lawrence WILLIAMS (Neath C.G.S.).—B Tonna, Neath 20/11/1946. LHB, RFM. Joined staff and made debut 1969 after playing for 2nd XI in 1967 and 1968. HS: 37* v Essex (Chelmsford) 1969. BB: 7–60 v Lancs (Blackpool) 1970. Rugger player. Career record: 151 runs (av 5.39), 122 wkts (24.16).

N.B. The following players whose particulars appeared in the 1970 Annual are omitted: B. A. Davis (returned to Trinidad), I. J. Jones (retired through injury), D. W. Lewis, R. J. Thomas and O. S. Wheatley. In addition H. Jenkins a left hand batsman who played one match v Oxford U has not been included as he is unlikely to play again.

The career records of Davis and Jenkins will be found elsewhere in this Annual.

Know where you're going — with
MICHELIN MAPS AND GUIDES

COUNTY AVERAGES

County Championship: Played 24, Won 9, Drawn 9, Lost 6
All First-Class Matches: Played 28, Won 10, Drawn 10, Lost 8

BATTING AND FIELDING

Cap		*M.*	*I.*	*N.O.*	*Runs*	*H.S.*	*Avge.*	100	50	*Ct.*	*St.*
1962	A. Jones	19	36	2	1389	161*	40.85	5	5	11	—
1960	A. R. Lewis	25	47	5	1596	128	38.00	2	10	22	—
1968	M. J. Khan	10	19	1	646	157	35.88	2	3	16	—
1969	B. A. Davis	27	52	3	1532	91	31.26	—	14	29	—
—	G. P. Ellis	9	15	3	318	55	26.50	—	2	1	—
—	L. W. Hill	7	12	2	244	80	24.40	—	1	8	—
1958	P. M. Walker	27	49	6	1049	114	24.39	1	6	39	—
1969	R. C. Davis	27	47	6	823	69	20.07	—	4	36	—
—	K. J. Lyons	15	28	4	452	58*	18.83	—	1	5	—
1969	M. A. Nash	26	42	7	606	61	17.31	—	2	13	—
1967	E. W. Jones	28	49	12	626	56*	16.91	—	2	85	9
1967	A. E. Cordle	26	41	7	564	48	16.58	—	—	8	—
—	G. C. Kingston	5	8	1	84	22	12.00	—	—	1	—
1952	D. J. Shepherd	27	30	12	180	36*	10.00	—	—	9	—
—	D. L. Williams	26	22	10	35	5*	2.91	—	—	4	—

Played in one match: J. A. Hopkins 2, 4; H. Jenkins 65, 16* (1 ct); M. J. Llewellyn 0, 15 (2 ct); G. E. A. Reynolds 9*.

BOWLING

	Type	*Overs*	*Mdns*	*Runs*	*Wkts*	*Avge*	*Best*	*5wI.*	*10wM*
D. J. Shepherd	RM/OB	1123.3	420	2031	106	19.16	7/48	6	2
M. J. Khan	RM	80	25	173	9	19.22	3/17	—	—
M. J. Llewellyn	OB	43.2	13	129	6	21.50	4/35	—	—
M. A. Nash	LM	705.2	202	1761	79	22.29	6/42	5	—
R. C. Davis	OB	520.5	145	1373	54	25.42	6/82	1	—
D. L. Williams	RFM	619.1	164	1604	61	26.29	7/60	4	—
P. M. Walker	LM/SLA	686	224	1599	60	26.65	6/33	3	—
A. E. Cordle	RFM	451.3	114	1179	37	31.86	4/35	—	—

Also bowled: B. A. Davis 24-6-85-1; A. Jones 9-1-44-1; G. C. Kingston 33-6-126-3; K. J. Lyons 26-0-93-0; G. E. A. Reynolds 17-11-24-2.

County Records

Highest Innings Totals:	For ...587–8d v Derbyshire (Cardiff)	1951
	Agst...653–6d by Gloucestershire (Bristol)	1928
Lowest Innings Totals:	For ... 22 v Lancashire (Liverpool)	1924
	Agst... 33 by Leicestershire (Ebbw Vale)	1965
Highest Individual Inngs.:	For ...287* E.Davies v Gloucestershire (Newport)	1939
	Agst...302* W. R. Hammond for Glos. (Bristol)	1934
	302 W. R. Hammond for Glos. (Newport)	1939

Best Bowling figs in an inngs	For	...10–51 J. Mercer v Worcs (Worcester)......1936
	Agst	...10–18 G. Geary for Leics (Pontypridd) ...1929
Best Bowling figs in a match	For	...17–212 J. C. Clay v Worcs (Swansea) 1937
	Agst	...16–96 G. Geary for Leics (Pontypridd) ...1929
Most runs in a season	2071	(av. 49.30) W. G. A. Parkhouse...1959
runs in a career	26104	(av. 27.82) E. Davies.........1924–1954
100s in a season	7	by W. G. A. Parkhouse 1950
100s in a career	32	by W. G. A. Parkhouse 1948–1964
wickets in a season...	176	(av. 17.34) J. C. Clay 1937
wickets in a career ...	2085	(av. 20.66) D. J. Shepherd...1950–1970

RECORD WICKET STANDS

1st	274	E. Davies & A. H. Dyson v Leicestershire (Leicester)......1937
2nd	238	A. Jones & A. R. Lewis v Sussex (Hastings)..................1962
3rd	313	E. Davies & W. E. Jones v Essex (Brentwood)...............1948
4th	263	G. Lavis & C. Smart v Worcestershire (Cardiff)............1934
5th	264	M. Robinson & S. W. Montgomery v Hampshire (Bournemouth) 1949
6th	230	W. E. Jones & B. L. Muncer v Worcestershire (Worcester) 1953
7th	195*	W. Wooller & W. E. Jones v Lancashire (Liverpool)......1947
8th	202	D. Davies & J. J. Hills v Sussex (Eastbourne)...............1928
9th	203*	J. J. Hills & J. C. Clay v Worcestershire (Swansea).........1929
10th	131*	C. Smart & W. D. Hughes v South Africans (Cardiff)......1935

Home Matches in Championship

Kent (Swansea)—G 170 (Davis B.A. 55, Graham 4–46, Underwood 4–65) and 193–8d (Davis B.A. 83*). K 103 (Shepherd 6–43) and 214 (Walker 5–86). *G (10 points) won by* 46 *runs (G* 5 *bonus points, K* 3 *bonus points.)*

Hants (Cardiff)—H 350–5d (Marshall 87, Richards 61, Turner 60) and 138–7d (Shepherd 4–49). G 298–7d (Jones, A. 161*) and 157–7. *Match drawn.* (*G* 3 *bonus points, H* 6 *bonus points.*)

Som (Swansea)—S 264 (Walker 4–78) and 213–9d (Langford 50*, Walker 4–58, Shepherd 4–65). G 290–8d (Jones, A. 56, Walker 51, Davis, B.A. 51) and 188–7 (Davis, B.A. 62). *G (10 points) won by* 3 *wickets.* (*G* 5 *bonus points, S* 3 *bonus points.*)

Worcs (Neath)—W 114 (Shepherd 4–34) and 204 (Hemsley 52). G 84 (Holder 6–21) and 139 (Gifford 6–56). *W (10 points) won by* 95 *runs.* (*G* 5 *bonus points, W* 5 *bonus points.*)

Surrey (Cardiff)—S 259–9d (Roope 111, Storey 57) and 72–3. G 252–6d (Walker 63*, Lewis 58). *Match drawn.* (*G* 5 *bonus points, S* 4 *bonus points.*)

Notts (Cardiff)—N 321–7d (Smedley 149, Frost 50, Davis, R. C. 4–60) and 64–2. G 154 (White 6–58) and 228 (Davis, B. A. 61, Lewis 52, White 4–92). *N (10 points) won by* 8 *wickets.* (*G* 2 *bonus points, N* 6 *bonus points.*)

Glos (Swansea)—Glam 286 (Jones, A. 100, Ellis 55) and 176 (Lewis 57). G 142 (Nash 5–60) and 196 (Davis, R. C. 4–55). *Glam* (10 *points*) *won by* 124 *runs.* (*Glam* 8 *bonus points, G* 2 *bonus points.*)

Essex (Cardiff)—G 304–8d (Jones, A. 105, Lewis, A. 78) and 148–9d (Hobbs 5–88, East 4–41). E 285 (Lever 91, Boyce 61) and 77–9 (Walker 6–33). *Match drawn.* (*G* 7 *bonus points, E* 3 *bonus points.*)

Sussex (Swansea)—S 195–9d ana 5–0d. G 47–4d and 154–1 (Davis, B. A. 66*, Khan 55*). *G* (10 *points*) *won by* 9 *wickets* (*G* 3 *bonus points, S* 3 *bonus points.*)

Northants (Cardiff)—N 247 and 193–7d (Mushtaq 70, Lightfoot 63). G 200 (Swinburne 5–81) and 165–6 (Lewis, A. R. 88). *Match drawn.* (*G* 5 *bonus points, N* 6 *bonus points.*)

Derbys (Swansea)—G 261 (Davis, B. A. 91, Walker 57, Russell 6–61) and 136–6. D 87 (Shepherd 6–33) and 309 (Russell 72, Page 71, Shepherd 6–106). *G* (10 *points*) *won by* 4 *wickets.* (*G* 8 *bonus points, D* 4 *bonus points.*)

Lancs (Cardiff)—L 303–5d (Pilling 89, Lloyd, C. H. 58, Wood 51) and 77–5. G 138 and 301–5d (Walker 114, Lewis, A. R. 78). *Match drawn.* (*G* 2 *bonus points, L* 11 *bonus points.*)

GLOUCESTERSHIRE

Formation of present club: 1871.
Colours: Blue, gold, brown, sky-blue, green and red.
Badge: Coat of Arms of the City and County of Bristol.
County Champions (2): 1876 and 1877.
Joint Champions (2): 1873 and 1880.
Gillette Cup Semi-Finalists: 1968.

Secretary.—G. W. Parker, O.B.E., County Ground, Nevil Road, Bristol, BS7 9EJ.
Captain.—A. S. Brown.

David Arthur ALLEN (Cotham G.S.).—B Bristol 29/10/1935. RHB, OB. Debut 1953. Cap 1959. Elected Best Young Cricketer of the Year in 1960 by the Cricket Writer's Club. Tests: 39 between 1959–60 and 1966. Tours: West Indies 1959–60, New Zealand 1960–61, India and Pakistan 1961–62, Australia 1962–63, South Africa 1964–65, Australia and New Zealand 1965–66. 1,000 runs (2)—1,165 runs (av 24.78) in 1964 best. Took 124 wkts (av 19.43) to achieve double 1961. HS: 121* v Notts (Nottingham) 1961. BB: 8–34 v Sussex (Lydney) 1969. Career record: 9,016 runs (av 18.90), 1 century, 1,173 wkts (av 23.47).

Michael ("Mike") BISSEX.—B Bath 28/9/1944. RHB, SLA. Debut 1961. Cap 1970. Tour: Pakistan 1966–67. Scored 1,316 runs (av 37.60) in 1970. HS: 104* v Oxford U (Bristol) 1964, and 104 v Kent (Cheltenham) 1970. BB: 7–70 v Surrey (Oval) 1967. Career record: 5,603 runs (av 20.90), 2 centuries, 180 wkts (av 28.10).

Anthony Stephen ("Tony") BROWN (Fairfield G.S., Bristol).—B Bristol 24/6/1936. RHB, RM. Debut 1953. Cap 1957. Appointed county captain in 1969. Benefit 1969. Scored 1,149 runs (av 20.15) in 1964. 100 wkts (2)—110 wkts (av 23.08) in 1959 and 110 wkts (av 26.40) in 1962. Held 7 catches in innings v Notts (Nottingham) 1966 to equal world record held by M. J. Stewart (Surrey). HS: 109* v Glamorgan (Bristol) 1965. BB: 8–80 v Essex (Leyton) 1963. Career record: 9,407 runs (av 17.71), 2 centuries, 962 wkts (av 25.98).

Jack DAVEY (Tavistock G.S.).—B Tavistock (Devon) 4/9/1944. LHB, LFM. Played for Devonshire in 1964 and 1965. Debut 1966. HS: 17 v Lancs (Cheltenham) and 17 v Leics (Cheltenham) 1967. BB: 6–95 v Notts (Gloucester) 1967. Career record: 149 runs (av 5.51), 133 wkts (av 30.28).

David Michael GREEN (Manchester G.S. and Oxford).—B Llanengan (Caernarvon) 10/11/1939. RHB, RM. Debut for Oxford U and Lancs 1959 scoring 1,049 runs (av 24.97) in his first season. Blue 1959, 1960 and 1961. Cap 1962. Joined Lancs staff in 1964 and appointed vice-captain in 1965. Not re-engaged after 1967 season and joined Glos by special registration in 1968. Cap 1968. "Wisden 1968". Left staff after 1970 season, but may play in John Player League matches in 1971. 1,000 runs (7)—2,137 runs (av 40.32) in 1968 best. Only player ever to have scored 2,000 runs in a season (2,037 runs in 1965) without a century. Has won "Man of the Match" award in Gillette Cup Competition on four occasions, equalling record. HS: 233 v Sussex (Hove) 1968 sharing in 1st wkt partnership record for county in County Championship, 315 with C. A. Milton. BB: 5–61 Oxford U v Sussex (Hove) 1959. Career record: 13,325 runs (av 29.03), 14 centuries, 115 wkts (av 38.34).

Roger David Verdon KNIGHT (Dulwich and Cambridge).—B Streatham 6/9/1946. LHB, RM. Debut for Cambridge U 1967. Blue 1967, 1968, 1969 and 1970. Debut for Surrey 1968. Has joined county by special registration for 1971. Scored 1,007 runs (av 28.77) in 1969. HS: 164* Cambridge U v Essex (Cambridge) 1970. BB: 6–65 Cambridge U v Essex (Cambridge) 1970. Plays rugger. Career record: 3,126 runs (av 26.94), 2 centuries, 74 wkts (av 36.35).

Barrie John MEYER.—B Bournemouth 21/8/1932. RHB, WK. Debut 1957. Cap 1958. Benefit 1971. Soccer (IL) for Bristol Rovers, Plymouth Argyle, Newport County and Bristol City. HS: 63 v Indians (Cheltenham) 1959, v Oxford U (Bristol) 1962 and v Sussex (Bristol) 1964. Career record: 5,164 runs (av 14.10), 781 dismissals (669 ct, 112 st).

Clement Arthur MILTON (Cotham G.S.).—B Bristol 10/3/1928. RHB, RM. Debut 1948. Cap 1949. "Wisden 1958". Benefit (£3,235) in 1961.

Appointed county captain for 1968, relinquished appointment after end of season. Soccer (OR) for Arsenal and Bristol City, capped for England v Austria at Wembley 1951–52 after only 12 League games. Became one of the few double internationals when he made Test Debut v New Zealand (Leeds) 1958, scoring 104* in his first innings. Tests: 6 between 1958 and 1959. Tour: Australia 1958–59, returning home early through injury. 1,000 runs (16)—2,089 runs (av 46.42) in 1967 best. Scored two centuries in match v Sussex (Eastbourne) 1961 (150 and 100*) and v Kent (Bristol) 1962 (110* and 102*). Shared in 1st wkt partnership record for county in County Championship, 315 with D. M. Green v Sussex (Hove) 1968. Held 44 catches in 1954 and won trophy for most catches by a fielder. Held 63 catches in 1956 and won trophy for second time. Held 8 catches in match v Sussex (Hove) 1952. HS: 170 v Sussex (Cheltenham) 1965. BB: 5–64 v Glamorgan (Gloucester) 1950. Career record: 30,269 runs (av 34.16), 55 centuries, 79 wkts (av 45.94).

John Brian MORTIMORE.—B Bristol 14/5/1933. RHB, OB. Debut 1950. Cap 1954. County captain from 1965 to 1967. Benefit (£3,600) in 1965. Tests: 9 between 1958–59 and 1964. Tours: Australia and New Zealand 1958–59 (flown out as reinforcement in November), India 1963–64. 1,000 runs (5)—1,425 runs (av 26.88) in 1963 best. 100 wkts (3)—113 wkts (av 18.28) in 1959 best. Doubles (3): 1959, 1963 and 1964. Took 4 wkts in 5 balls v Lancs (Cheltenham) 1962. HS: 149 v Notts (Nottingham) 1963. BB: 8–59 (13–104 match) v Oxford U (Oxford) 1959. Career record: 14,513 runs (av 18.58), 4 centuries, 1,550 wkts (av 22.50).

Ronald Bernard ("Ron") NICHOLLS.—B Sharpness (Glos) 4/12/1933. RHB, OB. Occasional WK. Good field at cover. Goalkeeper with Bristol Rovers, Cardiff City, Fulham and Bristol City. Debut 1951. Cap 1957. Benefit (£3,750) in 1966. 1,000 runs (14)—2,059 runs (av 36.76) in 1962 best. Scored century before lunch in Gillette Cup match v Berks (Reading) 1966. Has twice won "Man of the Match" award in Gillette Cup Competition. HS: 217 v Oxford U (Oxford) 1962, sharing in 1st wkt partnership record for county, 395 with D. M. Young. Career record: 20,380 runs (av 26.29), 17 centuries, 7 wkts (av 74.42).

Michael John ("Mike") PROCTER (Hilton College, Natal).—B Durban 15/9/1946. RHB, RF. Vice-captain of South African Schools team to England 1963. Debut for county 1965 in one match v South Africans. Returned home to make debut for Natal in 1965–66 Currie Cup Competition. Joined staff in 1968. Cap 1968. "Wisden 1969". Transferred to Western Province for 1969–70 Currie Cup Competition and Rhodesia in 1970–71. Tests (12): 7 for South Africa v Australia 1966–67 and 1969–70 and 5 for Rest of World v England 1970. Scored 1,167 runs (av 29.92) in 1968. Took 108 wkts (av 15.02) in 1969. Scored 6 centuries in 6 consecutive innings for Rhodesia 1970–71. HS: 254 Rhodesia v Western Province (Salisbury) 1970–71. HS in England: 134 v Middlesex (Bristol) 1968. BB: 7–25 Natal v Rhodesia (Salisbury) 1966–67. BB in England: 7–65 v Worcs (Worcester) 1969. Plays rugger, hockey, tennis, golf and squash rackets. Career record: 4,402 runs (av 28.03), 7 centuries, 414 wkts (av 18.05).

SADIQ MOHAMMAD.—B Junagadh (India) 3/5/1945. LHB, LBG. Youngest of family of five cricket-playing brothers which include Hanif and Mushtaq Mohammad. Debut in Pakistan 1959–60 at age of 14 years 9 months and played subsequently for various Karachi sides and Pakistan International Airways. Played for Northants 2nd XI in 1967 and 1968, for Nelson in Lancs League in 1968 and subsequently for Poloc, Glasgow in Scottish Western Union. Played for D. H. Robins XI v Oxford U 1969 and for Essex v Jamaica XI in 1970. Has joined county as special overseas registration. Tests: 3 for Pakistan v New Zealand 1969–70. HS: 167 Karachi Blues v Rawalpindi Greens (Karachi) 1969–70. BB: 5–29 Pakistan International Airways v Dacca (Dacca) 1964–65. Career record: 1,869 runs (av 36.64), 3 centuries, 41 wkts (av 27.26).

David Robert SHEPHERD.—B Bideford (Devon) 27/12/1940. RHB, RM. Played for Devonshire from 1959 to 1964. Played for Minor Counties v Australians, 1964. Debut 1965 scoring 108 in first match v Oxford U Cap 1969. 1,000 runs (2)—1,079 runs (av 26.97) in 1970 best. HS: 153 v Middlesex (Bristol) 1968. Has played rugger for Bideford. Career record: 4,641 runs (av 23.55), 8 centuries, 1 wkt (av 5.00).

David Robert SMITH.—B Bristol 5/10/1934. RHB, RM. Debut 1956. Cap 1957. Benefit (£3,800) in 1968. Soccer (OL) for Bristol City and Millwall. Tests (5): 5 v India 1961–62. Tours: New Zealand 1960–61, India and Pakistan 1961–62. 100 wkts (5)—143 wkts (av 20.30) in 1960 best. HS: 74 v M.C.C. (Lord's) 1961. BB: 7–20 v Sussex (Stroud) 1962. Career record: 4,970 runs (av 12.30), 1,250 wkts (av 23.72).

John Patrick SULLIVAN (Withywood Comprehensive, Bristol).—B Bristol 11/3/1948. RHB. Occasional WK. Debut 1968. HS: 53 v Notts (Nottingham) 1970. Plays soccer. Career record: 225 runs (av 17.30).

Stuart Alker WESTLEY (Lancaster Royal G.S. and Oxford).—B Preston 21/3/1947. RHB, WK. Debut for Oxford U 1968. Blue 1968 and 1969. Debut for county 1969 (four matches) following injury to B. J. Meyer after having played for Lancs 2nd XI. Did not play in 1970. HS: 93* Oxford U v Warwickshire (Oxford) 1969. Has played rugger for University and Fylde R.U.F.C. Career record: 454 runs (av 15.13), 63 dismissals (56 ct. 7 st.)

N.B. The following players whose particulars appeared in the 1970 Annual have been omitted: D. G. Bevan (left staff), H. Heard, H. Jarman, R. W. Phillips (not re-engaged) and G. Pullar (retired). The career records of Bevan, Phillips and Pullar will be found elsewhere in this Annual.

ISN'T IT NICE TO KNOW . . . *Check answers page* 151

9. Who has scored the slowest 50 in Test Cricket?
10. Which touring team scored the highest number of runs in one day against an English County?

COUNTY AVERAGES

County Championship: Played 24, Won 3, Drawn 13, Lost 8
All First-Class Matches: No others played

BATTING AND FIELDING

Cap		M.	I.	N.O.	Runs	H.S.	Avge.	100	50	Ct.	St.
1970	M. Bissex	24	44	9	1316	104	37.60	1	9	19	—
1968	M. J. Procter	15	24	4	642	115	32.10	1	3	14	—
1957	R. B. Nicholls	24	46	2	1341	100	30.47	1	7	7	—
1957	A. S. Brown	24	39	10	878	104*	30.27	1	2	19	—
1968	D. M. Green	24	46	0	1355	146	29.45	2	8	11	—
1949	C. A. Milton	14	26	5	600	149*	28.57	1	2	12	—
1969	D. R. Shepherd	23	42	2	1079	111	26.97	1	6	6	—
—	G. Pullar	6	10	1	227	73	25.22	—	1	2	—
—	R. W. Phillips	9	15	0	281	82	18.73	—	1	8	—
—	J. P. Sullivan	5	9	0	168	53	18.66	—	1	2	—
1959	D. A. Allen	20	26	7	337	41	17.73	—	—	12	—
1957	D. R. Smith	23	28	3	400	61*	16.00	—	1	27	—
1954	J. B. Mortimore	18	26	5	318	46	15.14	—	—	10	—
1958	B. J. Meyer	24	27	13	163	34	11.64	—	—	43	8
—	D. G. Bevan	3	5	0	53	17	10.60	—	—	1	—
—	J. Davey	8	10	7	25	11	8.33	—	—	4	—

BOWLING

	Type	Overs	Mdns	Runs	Wkts	Avge	Best	5wI.	10wM
M. J. Procter	RF	435.5	99	1039	50	20.78	6/38	1	—
J. B. Mortimore	OB	577.1	116	1561	54	28.90	5/43	2	—
D. A. Allen	OB	501.4	129	1460	48	30.41	4/53	—	—
D. R. Smith	RM	622.1	115	2020	61	33.11	6/86	1	—
J. Davey	LFM	208.2	35	736	22	33.45	4/37	—	—
A. S. Brown	RM	469.3	92	1308	38	34.42	6/48	1	—
M. Bissex	SLA	393	88	1242	35	35.48	5/34	2	—

Also bowled: D. M. Green 31-9-82-0; R. B. Nicholls 5-2-16-0; G. Pullar 1-1-0-0.

County Records

Highest Innings Totals:	For	653–6d v Glamorgan (Bristol) 1928
	Agst	774–7d by Australians (Bristol) 1948
Lowest Innings Totals:	For	17 v Australians (Cheltenham) 1896
	Agst	12 by Northamptonshire (Gloucester) 1907
Highest Individual Inngs.:	For	318* W. G. Grace v Yorkshire (Cheltenham) 1876
	Agst	296 A. O. Jones for Notts (Nottingham) 1903
Best Bowling figs. in an Inngs.	For	10–40 G. Dennett v Essex (Bristol) 1906
	Agst	10–66 A. A. Mailey for Aust (Cheltenham) 1921 and K. Smales for Notts (Stroud) 1956
Best Bowling figs. in a match	For	17–56 C. W. L. Parker v Essex (Gloucester) 1925
	Agst	15–87 A. J. Conway for Worcestershire (Moreton-in-the-Marsh) 1914
Most runs in a season		2860 (av 69.75) W. R. Hammond 1933
runs in a career		33664 (av 57. 05) W. R. Hammond 1920–1951

100s in a season	13 by W. R. Hammond	1938
100s in a career............	113 by W. R. Hammond	1920–1951
wickets in a season	222 (av 16.80 & 16.37) T. W. Goddard	.........1937 & 1947
wickets in a career	3171 (av 19.43) C. W. L. Parker	...1903–1935

RECORD WICKET STANDS

1st 395	D. M. Young & R. B. Nicholls v Oxford Univ. (Oxford)	...1962
2nd 256	C. T. M. Pugh & T. W. Graveney v Derbyshire (Chesterfield)	...1960
3rd 336	W. R. Hammond & B. H. Lyon v Leicestershire (Leicester)	...1933
4th 321	W. R. Hammond & W. L. Neale v Leicestershire (Gloucester)	...1937
5th 261	W. G. Grace & W. O. Moberley v Yorkshire (Cheltenham)	1876
6th 320	G. L. Jessop & J. H. Board v Sussex (Hove)	...1902
7th 248	W. G. Grace & E. L. Thomas v Sussex (Hove)	...1896
8th 239	W. R. Hammond & A. E. Wilson v Lancashire (Bristol)	...1938
9th 193	W. G. Grace & S. A. Kitcat v Sussex (Bristol)	...1896
10th 131	W. R. Gouldsworthy & J. G. Bessant v Somerset (Bristol)	1923

Home Matches in Championship

Sussex (Bristol)—S 240 (Buss, M. A. 63, Greig 55, Parks 52, Brown 4–61) and 230–7d (Greig 62). G 177 (Shepherd 69, Snow 4–45, Buss, A. 4–57) and 297–6 (Green 69, Procter 67*). *G* (10 *points*) *won by* 4 *wickets.* (*G* 5 *bonus points, S* 8 *bonus points.*)

Som (Bristol)—G 245 (Shepherd 111, Cartwright 6–58) and 220–5d (Shepherd 87*, Green 50, Burgess 4–73). S 170 (Brown 6–48) and 157. *G* (10 *points*) *won by* 138 *runs.* (*G* 8 *bonus points, S* 3 *bonus points.*)

Middx (Bristol)—M 379–6d (Russell 102, Murray 92, Featherstone 83) and 160–4d (Parfitt 63*). G 296–5d (Green 130, Nicholls 100) and 140 (Titmus 5–29). *M* (10 *points*) *won by* 103 *runs.* (*G* 6 *bonus points, M* 4 *bonus points.*)

Northants (Bristol)—N 277–6d (Mushtaq 77, Prideaux 75) and 119–5d G 132 (Sarfraz 5–43) and 55–2. *Match drawn.* (*G* 3 *bonus points, N* 10 *bonus points.*)

Worcs (Bristol)—W 313–2d (Turner 154*, Ormrod 118) and 210–4d (Ormrod 83, Turner 56). G 213 (Gifford 4–44) and 263–7 (Nicholls 69, Bissex 66, Holder 5–73). *Match drawn.* (*G* 2 *bonus points, W* 8 *bonus points.*)

Surrey (Gloucester)—G 314–9d (Brown 79*, Bissex 75) and 157–6d (Jackman 4–37). S 230 (Stewart 79, Edrich 50) and 195–7 (Storey 55, Mortimore 4–77). *Match drawn.* (*G* 4 *bonus points, S* 5 *bonus points.*)

Warwicks (Gloucester)—W 319–8d (Amiss 110, Smith, M. J. K. 94). G 142 (Bissex 83, Lewington 4–39) and 358 (Milton 149*, Hemmings 4–88). *Match drawn.* (*G* 1 *bonus point, W* 6 *bonus points.*)

Hants (Cheltenham)—G 190 (Procter 61, Bissex 50, Jesty 4–37) and 229 (Smith, D. R. 61*, Bissex 54, Wheatley 4–75). H 173 (Mortimore 5–58) and 249–6 (Richards 94). *H* (10 *points*) *won by* 4 *wickets.* (*G* 6 *bonus points, H* 5 *bonus points*).

Glam (Cheltenham)—G 324 (Nicholls 85, Davis, R. C. 6–82) and 152 (Shepherd 5–46, Walker 5–66). Glam 356–9d (Khan 157, Lewis 87, Davis, B. A. 63) and 124–5 (Allen 4–53). *Glam* (10 *points*) *won by* 5 *wickets.* (*G* 7 *bonus points, Glam* 10 *bonus points.*)

Kent (Cheltenham)—G 289 (Bissex 104, Underwood 6–68) and 190 (Nicholls 63, Underwood 5–82), K 140 (Mortimore 5–43) and 340–9 (Asif Iqbal 109, Denness 97, Allen 4–92). *K* (10 *points*) *won by* 1 *wicket.* (*G* 8 *bonus points, K* 3 *bonus points.*)

Yorks (Bristol)—G 226–7d (Milton 62, Shepherd 52) and 96–3d. Y 132–3d (Padgett 53*) and 62–3 (Boycott 52*). *Match drawn.* (*G* 4 *bonus points, Y* 3 *bonus points.*)

Leics (Bristol)—L 108–6d (Mortimore 4–36) and 185–4d (Haywood 65). G 82–3d and 121–7. *Match drawn.* (*G* 3 *bonus points, L* 1 *bonus point.*)

HAMPSHIRE

Formation of present club: 1863.
Colours: Blue, gold and white.
Badge: Tudor rose and crown.
County Champions: 1961.
Gillette Cup Semi-Finalists: 1966.
John Player League Runners-up: 1969.

Secretary.—E. D. R. Eagar, County Cricket Ground, Northlands Road, Southampton, SO9 2TY.
Captain.—R. M. C. Gilliat.

Alan Terry CASTELL.—B Oxford 6/8/1943. RHB, RM changing from LBG in 1966, although still bowls occasionally in the latter style. Debut 1961. HS: 76 v Surrey (Southampton) 1962, sharing in 9th wkt partnership record for county, 230 with D. A. Livingstone. BB: 6–22 v Somerset (Bath) 1969. Career record: 1,443 runs (av 16.58), 202 wkts (av 30.99).

Robert Michael Henry ("Bob") COTTAM.—B Cleethorpes (Lincolnshire) 16/10/1944. RHB, RFM. Debut 1963. Cap 1965. Elected Best Young Cricketer of the Year in 1968 by the Cricket Writers Club. Tests: 2 v Pakistan 1968–69. Tour: Ceylon and Pakistan 1968–69. 100 wkts (3)—130 wkts (av 17.56) in 1968 best. HS: 35 v Somerset (Portsmouth) 1969. BB: 9–25 v Lancs (Manchester) 1965 (the best bowling figures ever in an innings for the county). Career record: 575 runs (av 5.98), 642 wkts (av 20.90).

Richard Michael Charles GILLIAT (Charterhouse and Oxford).—B Ware (Herts), 20/5/1944. LHB, LB. Fine field in any position. Debut for Oxford U 1964. Blue 1964, 1965, 1966 and 1967 (Capt. 1966). Debut for county 1966. Appointed assistant secretary in 1967, county vice-captain in 1969 and captain for 1971. Cap 1969. Played in only two matches in 1970 owing to injury. Scored 1,386 runs (av 39.60) in 1969. HS: 223* v Warwickshire (Southampton) 1969. Blues for soccer 1964, 1965 and 1966 (Capt. in 1966). Career record: 4,905 runs (av 28.18), 9 centuries, 1 wkt (av 32.00).

Cuthbert Gordon GREENIDGE.—B St. Peter, Barbados 1/5/1951. RHB, RM. Debut 1970. HS: 73 v Leics (Southampton) 1970. Career record: 351 runs (av 35.10).

John Wakefield HOLDER.—B St. George, Barbados 19/3/1945. RHB, RFM. Joined staff 1966. Debut 1968, taking 5–96 in first innings of debut match v Somerset (Portsmouth). HS: 28* v Glamorgan (Portsmouth) 1970. BB: 5-36 v Warwickshire (Birmingham) 1970. Career record: 211 runs (av 12.41), 80 wkts (av 24.00).

Trevor Edward JESTY.—B Gosport 2/6/1948. RHB, RM. Good field in any position. Debut 1966. Took 3 wkts in 4 balls v Somerset (Portsmouth) 1969. HS: 73* v Sussex (Bournemouth) 1970. BB: 4–25 v Somerset (Portsmouth) 1969. Career record: 1,246 runs (av 23.07), 65 wkts (av 36.92).

Richard Victor LEWIS (Peter Symond's School, Winchester).—B Winchester 6/8/1947. RHB. Useful field. Debut 1967. HS: 114 v Oxford U (Oxford) 1968. Plays soccer. Career record: 1,176 runs (av 17.04), 1 century.

Daintes Abbia ("Danny") LIVINGSTONE (Antigua G.S. and Bathurst Heights Collegiate S., Toronto).—B St. John's (Antigua), 21/9/1933. LHB, RM. Safe slip field. Debut 1959. Cap 1961. 1,000 runs (6)—1,817 runs (av 37.08) in 1962 best. Scored two centuries in match (117 and 105*) v Kent (Canterbury) 1964. HS: 200 v Surrey (Southampton) 1962 sharing in 9th wkt partnership record for county, 230 with A. T. Castell. Shared in 4th wkt partnership record for county, 263 with R. E. Marshall v Middlesex (Lord's) 1970. Career record: 12,150 runs (av 27.99), 16 centuries, 1 wkt (av 92.00).

Roy Edwin MARSHALL.—B St. Thomas, Barbados 25/4/1930. RHB, RM/OB. Debut for Barbados 1945–46 (aged 15¾ years). Tours: England

1950, scoring 1,117 runs (av 39.89), Australia and New Zealand 1951–52, with West Indians and India with Commonwealth team 1953–54. Tests (4): 2 v Australia and 2 v New Zealand, 1951–52. League cricket for Lowerhouse (Central Lancs League) 1951 and 1952. Debut for Hants 1953. Qualified and cap 1955. "Wisden" 1958. Benefit (£5,865) in 1961. Testimonial in 1971. County captain from 1966 to 1970. 1,000 runs (16)—2,607 runs (av 43.45) in 1961 best. Shared in 1st wkt partnership record for county, 249 with J. R. Gray v Middlesex (Portsmouth) 1960 and in 4th wkt record, 263 with D. A. Livingstone v Middlesex (Lord's) 1970. Has won "Man of the Match" award in Gillette Cup Competition on three occasions. Scored century before lunch in Gillette Cup match v Lincolnshire (Basingstoke) 1967 and also v Bedfordshire (Goldington) 1968, sharing in partnership of 227 for 1 st wkt with B. L. Reed—record for any wkt in Gillette Cup. HS: 228* v Pakistan (Bournemouth) 1962. BB: 6–36 v Surrey (Portsmouth) 1956. Career record: 33,143 runs (av 35.67), 63 centuries, 176 wkts (av 28.93).

Richard Johnston McILWAINE (Portsmouth G.S.).—B Southsea 16/3/1950. RHB, RM. Played for Public Schools v English Schools C.A. at Lord's 1967. Joined county staff 1969. Debut 1969. HS: 17 v Northants (Bournemouth) 1969. Career record: 29 runs (av 14.50), 4 wkts (av 68.25).

Barry Lindsay REED (Winchester).—B Southsea 17/9/1937. RHB. Debut 1958 in one match v Cambridge U. Did not play again until 1965. Cap 1967. 1,000 runs (3)—1,136 runs (av 24.17) in 1967 best. Shared in partnership of 227 for 1st wkt with R. E. Marshall v Bedfordshire (Goldington) 1968—record for any wkt in Gillette Cup Competition. Has twice won "Man of the Match" award in the Competition. HS: 138 v Oxford U (Oxford) 1970. Career record: 4,962 runs (av 24.32), 2 centuries.

Barry Anderson RICHARDS (Durban H.S.).—B Durban 21/7/1945. RHB, OB. Captain of South African Schools team to England 1963. Debut for Natal 1964–65. Appeared for Glos in one match in 1965 v South Africans, but decided not to qualify and returned home. Joined Hants on 3 year contract in 1968 and scored 2,395 runs (av 47.90) in first full season, including over 2,000 runs in County Championship. "Wisden" 1968. Played for South Australia 1970–71. Tests: 9, 4 for South Africa v Australia 1969–70 and 5 for Rest of World v England 1970. Scored two centuries in match (130 and 104*) v Northants (Northampton) 1968. Holds record for highest score in John Player League 155* v Yorks (Hull) 1970. 1,000 runs (3)—2,395 runs (av 47.90) in 1968 best. Also scored 1,172 runs (av 73.25) in South Africa 1969–70—record aggregate by a South African. HS: 356 South Australia v Western Australia (Perth) 1970–71 scoring 325* on first day of match. HS in England: 206 v Notts (Portsmouth) 1968. BB: 7–63 v Rest of World (Bournemouth) 1968. Career record: 9,307 runs (av 53.48), 25 centuries, 34 wkts (av 34.20).

Peter James SAINSBURY.—B Southampton 13/6/1934. RHB, SLA and brilliant field anywhere. Debut 1954. Cap 1955. Benefit (£6,035) in 1965. Tour: Pakistan 1955–56. 1,000 runs (6)—1,533 runs (av 30.05) in

1961 best. Took 102 wkts (av 18.50) in 1955. Held 56 catches in 1957. Won "Man of the Match" award twice in successive matches in Gillette Cup Competition in 1965. HS: 163 v Oxford U (Oxford) 1962. BB: 7–25 v Essex (Southampton) 1955. Career record: 15,882 runs (av 26.03), 5 centuries, 951 wkts (av 25.66).

Derek SHACKLETON ("Shack").—B Todmorden (Yorks) 12/8/1924. RHB, RM. Debut 1948. Cap 1949. Benefit (£5,000) in 1958. Testimonial (£5,000) in 1967. "Wisden" 1958. Retired after 1968 season to take coaching job at Canford School, and now plays only in John Player League matches. Tests: 7 between 1950 and 1963. Tours: India with Commonwealth 1950–51 and M.C.C. 1951–52. 100 wkts (20)—172 wkts (av 20.15) in 1962 best. His 100 wkts in 20 consecutive seasons is a record. Only Wilfred Rhodes, a slow bowler, has taken 100 wkts in more seasons (23). Has taken more wkts than any other bowler now playing first-class cricket, is the third Hants bowler to take over 2,000 wkts and the second to take over 2,500 wkts. Has taken more wkts (2,669) for county than any other bowler exceeding A. S. Kennedy's figure of 2,549 wkts in 1967. HS: 87* v Essex (Bournemouth) 1949. BB: 9–30 v Warwicks (Portsmouth) 1960 and 8–4 (14–29 match) v Somerset (Weston-super-Mare) 1955. Has also taken 9 wkts in an innings on three other occasions. Career record: 9,561 runs (av 14.59), 2,857 wkts (av 18.65).

George Robert ("Bob") STEPHENSON (Derby School).—B Derby 19/11/1942. RHB, WK. Debut for Derbyshire 1967 following injury to R. W. Taylor. Joined Hants by special registration in 1969 following resignation of B. S. V. Timms. Cap 1969. Dismissed 80 batsmen (73 ct 7 st) in 1970. HS: 82 v Sussex (Bournemouth) 1970. Soccer for Derby County, Shrewsbury Town and Rochdale. Career record: 1,049 runs (av 15.89), 158 dismissals (146 ct, 12 st).

David Roy TURNER.—B Chippenham (Wilts) 5/2/1949. LHB, RM. Fine field in any position. Played for Wiltshire in 1965. Debut 1966. Cap 1970. Scored 1,165 runs (av 32.36) in 1970. HS: 181* v Surrey (Oval) 1969. Career record: 2,433 runs (av 24.33), 2 centuries, 1 wkt (av 5.00).

Keith James WHEATLEY (Lord Wandsworth College, Long Sutton, Hants).—B Guildford 20/1/1946. RHB, OB. Good field. Debut 1965. HS: 79* v Kent (Maidstone) 1969. BB: 4–1 v Glamorgan (Southampton) 1968. Career record: 1,781 runs (av 18.55), 69 wkts (av 28.31).

David William ("Butch") WHITE.—B Warwick 14/2/1935. LHB, RFM. Played for Warwicks 2nd XI in 1955. Debut 1957. Cap 1960. Benefit (£4,547) in 1969. Missed second half of last season owing to cartilage injury. Tests (2): v Pakistan 1961–62. Tour: India and Pakistan 1961–62. 100 wkts (4)—124 wkts (av 19.10) in 1960 best. "Hat-tricks" (2): v Sussex (Portsmouth) 1961 and v Sussex (Hove) 1962. Took 4 wkts in 5 balls for M.C.C. v Services (Calcutta) 1961–62. HS: 58* v Essex (Portsmouth) 1963. BB: 9–44 v Leics (Portsmouth) 1966. Career record: 3,002 runs (av 10.87), 1,124 wkts (av 23.27).

Lawrence Roosevelt ("Larry") WORRELL (Combermere H.S., Barbados).—B St. Thomas, Barbados 28/8/1943. RHB, OB. Second cousin of Sir Frank Worrell. Served in Army from 1964 to 1970. Debut 1969. One match v New Zealanders. Also played for Dorset in Minor Counties Championship. Did not play in 1970. Will be qualified for start of 1971 season.

N.B. The following player whose particulars appeared in the 1970 Annual is omitted: W. D. Buck.

COUNTY AVERAGES

County Championship: Played 24, Won 4, Drawn 14, Lost 6
All First-Class Matches: Played 25, Won 4, Drawn 15, Lost 6

BATTING AND FIELDING

Cap		*M.*	*I.*	*N.O.*	*Runs*	*H.S.*	*Avge.*	100	50	*Ct.*	*St.*
1968	B. A. Richards	15	25	1	1410	153	58.75	3	11	12	—
1960	D. W. White	14	12	9	150	57	50.00	—	1	3	—
1955	R. E. Marshall	25	41	2	1590	189*	40.76	2	10	10	—
1967	B. L. Reed	12	21	0	816	138	38.85	1	5	7	—
—	C. G. Greenidge	7	11	1	351	73	35.10	—	4	6	—
1970	D. R. Turner	23	39	3	1165	116	32.36	1	7	12	—
1961	D. A. Livingstone	23	37	4	1020	103	30.90	1	6	15	2
—	K. J. Wheatley	14	26	5	538	73	25.61	—	2	8	—
—	T. E. Jesty	22	32	9	572	73*	24.86	—	3	12	—
1955	P. J. Sainsbury	23	36	7	688	70	23.72	—	2	20	—
—	A. T. Castell	21	24	5	370	73	19.47	—	1	20	—
1969	G. R. Stephenson	24	32	8	422	82	17.58	—	2	73	7
—	R. V. Lewis	11	22	1	311	74	14.80	—	1	10	—
—	J. W. Holder	15	14	4	144	28*	14.40	—	—	4	—
1965	R. M. H. Cottam	22	21	11	79	16	7.90	—	—	12	—

Played in two matches: R. M. C. Gilliat 0*, 3 (1 ct); R. J. McIlwaine 10 (1 ct).

BOWLING

	Type	*Overs*	*Mdns*	*Runs*	*Wkts*	*Avge*	*Best*	*5wI.*	*10wM*
K. J. Wheatley	OB	106.5	31	253	15	16.86	4/38	—	—
J. W. Holder	RFM	471	99	1280	55	23.27	5/36	1	—
D. W. White	RFM	439.4	113	1074	45	23.86	7/61	2	—
R. M. H. Cottam	RFM	763.1	173	1988	77	25.81	7/106	3	—
P. J. Sainsbury	SLA	803.5	310	1885	71	26.54	5/40	2	—
A. T. Castell	RM/LBG	570.4	109	1714	43	39.86	4/24	—	—
T. E. Jesty	RM	496	101	1403	32	43.84	4/37	—	—

Also bowled: C. G. Greenidge 1-1-0-0; R. J. McIlwaine 25-3-98-2; R. E. Marshall 16-10-7-1; B. A. Richards 39-8-138-3; D. R. Turner 1-0-4-1.

County Records

Highest Innings Totals:	For ...672–7d v Somerset (Taunton)	1899
	Agst...742 by Surrey (The Oval)	1909
Lowest Innings Totals:	For ... 15 v Warwickshire (Birmingham)	1922
	Agst... 23 by Yorkshire (Middlesbrough)	1965
Highest Individual Innings	For ...316 R. H. Moore v Warwickshire (Bournemouth)	1937
	Agst...302* P. Holmes for Yorkshire (Portsmouth)	1920
Best bowling figs in an Inngs.:	For ...9–25 R. M. H. Cottam v Lancs (Manchester)	1965
	Agst...9–21 L. B. Richmond for Notts (Nottingham)	1921
Best bowling figs. in a match	For ...16–88 J. A. Newman v Somerset (Weston-super-Mare)	1927
	Agst...17–119 W. Mead for Essex (Southampton)	1895
Most runs in a season	2854 (av 79.27) C. P. Mead	1928
runs in a career	48892 (av 48.84) C. P. Mead	1905–1936
100s in a season	12 by C. P. Mead	1928
100s in a career	138 by C. P. Mead	1905–1936
wickets in a season	190 (av 15.61) A. S. Kennedy	1922
wickets in a career	2669 (av 18.22) D. Shackleton	1948–1969

RECORD WICKET STANDS

1st 249	R. E. Marshall & J. R. Gray v Middlesex (Portsmouth)	1960
2nd 321	G. Brown & E. I. M. Barrett v Gloucestershire (Southampton)	1920
3rd 344	C. P. Mead & G. Brown v Yorkshire (Portsmouth)	1927
4th 263	R. E. Marshall & D. A. Livingstone v Middlesex (Lord's)	1970
5th 235	G. Hill & D. F. Walker v Sussex (Portsmouth)	1937
6th 411	R. M. Poore & E. G. Wynyard v Somerset (Taunton)	1899
7th 325	G. Brown & C. H. Abercrombie v Essex (Leyton)	1913
8th 178	C. P. Mead & C. P. Brutton v Worcestershire (Bournemouth)	1925
9th 230	D. A. Livingstone & A. T. Castell v Surrey (Southampton)	1962
10th 192	A. Bowell & W. H. Livsey v Worcestershire (Bournemouth)	1921

Home Matches in Championship

Surrey (Bournemouth)—S 257 (Long 69*, Storey 58, Cottam 4–63) and 210–7d (Younis 66*, White 4–52). H 176 (Richards 76, Intikhab 5–29) and 281 (Marshall 121, Castell 73, Jackman 4–74). *S* (10 *points*) *won by* 10 *runs*. (*H* 5 *bonus points, S* 7 *bonus points.*)

Kent (Portsmouth)—K 310 (Shepherd 105, Denness 64, Sainsbury 5–58) and 176–6d. H 277–8d (Turner 84, Marshall 77, Graham 4–95) and 74–0 (Richards 60*). *Match drawn.* (*H* 6 *bonus points, K* 4 *bonus points.*)

Lancs (Southampton)—H 325–9d (Livingstone 91, Turner 80) and 184–5d L 251 (White 5–57) and 232–9 (Hayes 99, Sainsbury 4–92). *Match drawn.* (*H* 6 *bonus points, L* 5 *bonus points.*)

Worcs (Southampton)—W 200 (Graveney 59, Sainsbury 5–40) and 325–6d (Turner 137). H 303–5d (Richards 94, Reed 89, Livingstone 70) and 116–2 (Richards 66). *Match drawn.* (*H* 10 *bonus points, W* 3 *bonus points.*)

Notts (Portsmouth)—N 333–5d (Smedley 100, Sobers 78, Harris 68) and 167–3d (Bolus 90*). H 200 (Jesty 70*) and 98–9 (Sobers 5–39). *Match drawn.* (*H* 4 *bonus points, N* 11 *bonus points.*)

Middx (Basingstoke)—M 243 (Smith 60, Featherstone 52) and 189–7d (Radley 85, Russell 52). H 207 (Wheatley 60, Titmus 4–49) and 228–6 (Reed 74, Marshall 67, Connolly 4–80). *H* (10 *points) won by* 4 *wickets.* (*H* 7 *bonus points, M* 8 *bonus points.*)

Essex (Bournemouth)—H 280 (Wheatley 73, Marshall 54) and 189–5d (Marshall 54, Acfield 5–83). E 201 and 155–6 (Edmeades 56*, Barker 54). *Match drawn.* (*H* 7 *bonus points, E* 4 *bonus points.*)

Sussex (Bournemouth)—H 150 (Buss, M. A. 7–58) and 337–7 (Stephenson 82, Lewis 74, Jesty 73*, Sainsbury 55, Greig 4–85). S 258–9d (Parks 79). *Match drawn.* (*H* 4 *bonus points, S* 9 *bonus points.*)

Glam (Portsmouth)—H 412–8d (Marshall 83, Turner 69, Greenidge 65, Livingstone 63) and 194–8d (Marshall 70). G 361–9d (Khan 116, Davis, B. A. 67, Nash 57, Sainsbury 4–87) and 141–3 (Khan 60, Davis, B. A. 52). *Match drawn.* (*H* 9 *bonus points, G* 7 *bonus points.*)

Glos (Portsmouth)—G 191–5 (Bissex 73*). *Match abandoned.* (*H* 2 *bonus points, G* 1 *bonus point.*)

Leics (Southampton)—L 175 (Davison 74, Cottam 4–44) and 355 (Marner 86, Davison 76, Booth 62, Sainsbury 4–85). H 394–9d (Richards 124, Greenidge 73, Livingstone 70). *Match drawn.* (*H* 10 *bonus points, L* 3 *bonus points.*)

Som (Bournemouth)—H 311 (Turner 99, Richards 75, Marshall 65, Cartwright 4–45, Robinson 4–84) and 135–2d (Richards 81). S 211 (Clarkson 71, Robinson 50, Wheatley 4–38) and 239–4 (Virgin 108. Clarkson 63). *S* (10 *points) won by* 6 *wickets.* (*H* 11 *bonus points, S* 7 *bonus points.*)

Join the world-wide

PLAYFAIR CLUB

There is no subscription. All you do is purchase the handsome green and gold tie £1 (including postage) from:

The Playfair Club, 161, Queen Victoria St., London E.C.4

KENT

Formation of present club: 1859, reorganised 1870.
Colours: Red and white.
Badge: White horse.
County Champions (5): 1906, 1909, 1910, 1913 and 1970.
Gillette Cup Winners: 1967.
John Player League Runners-up: 1970.

Secretary.—L. E. G. Ames, St. Lawrence Ground, Canterbury.
Captain.—M. C. Cowdrey.

ASIF IQBAL RAZVI (Osmania University, Hydrerabad, India).—B Hyderabad 6/6/1943. Nephew of Ghulam Ahmed, former Indian off-break bowler and Test Cricketer. RHB, RM. Good fielder. Debut 1959–60 for Hyderabad in Ranji Trophy. Migrated to Pakistan in 1961 and has since appeared for various Karachi teams and Pakistan International Airways. Captained Pakistan under-25 v England under-25 in 1966–67. Debut for county and cap 1968. "Wisden" 1967. Tests: 17 for Pakistan between 1964–65 and 1969–70. 1,000 runs (2)—1,379 runs (av 39.40) in 1970 best. Scored 146 v England (Oval) 1967 sharing in 9th wkt partnership of 190 with Intikhab Alam after Pakistan were 65–8—record 9th wkt stand in Test cricket. Tours: Pakistan to Australia and New Zealand 1964–65, England 1967, Pakistan Eaglets to England 1963, Pakistan "A" to Ceylon 1964, Pakistan International Airways to East Africa 1964. HS: 159 v Northants (Northampton) 1969. BB: 6–45 Pakistan Eaglets v Cambridge U (Cambridge) 1963. Career record: 7,990 runs (av 33.71), 10 centuries, 198 wkts (av 29.60).

Alan **BROWN** (High Oakham G.S.).—B Rainworth (Notts) 17/10/1935 RHB, RFM. Soccer (CH) for Gravesend and Northfleet. Debut 1957. Cap 1961. Joint benefit in 1971 with D. M. Sayer. Tests (2): 1 v India and 1 v Pakistan 1961–62. Tour: India and Pakistan 1961–62. Took 116 wkts (av 19.04) in 1965. Took 4 wkts in 5 balls v Notts (Folkestone) 1959. HS: 81 v Glamorgan (Folkestone) 1968. BB: 8–47 v Warwickshire (Nuneaton) 1963. Career record: 2,189 runs (av 9.72), 743 wkts (av 24.64).

Michael Colin **COWDREY** (Tonbridge and Oxford).—B Bangalore (India) 24/12/1932. RHB, LBG. Was 5 years in XI at Tonbridge. Debut 1950. Cap 1951 (youngest Kent player to have received this award). Oxford Blue 1952, 1953 and 1954 (captain 1954). Elected Best Young Cricketer of the Year in 1953 by the Cricket Writers' Club. "Wisden 1955." Appointed Kent captain in 1957. Tests: 108 between 1954–55 and 1970, captaining England in 27 Tests between 1959–60 and 1968–69. Has played more Tests and Test Innings and held more catches than any other player. Shared in 4th wkt partnership of 411 with P. B. H. May v W.I. (Birmingham) 1957—record 4th wkt stand in Test cricket and record stand for any wkt for England. Shared in 9th wkt partnership of 163* with A.C. Smith v N.Z. (Wellington) 1962–63, record 9th wkt stand for England in Test cricket. Tours: Australia and New Zealand 1954–55, 1958–59, 1962–63, 1965–66, 1970–71 (vice-captain on last four tours), South Africa 1956–57, West Indies 1959–60 (vice captain), 1967–68 (captain), India 1963–64 (withdrew from tour after selection as captain owing to injury but subsequently flown out as replacement and took over vice-captaincy from M. J. Stewart), Ceylon and Pakistan (captain) 1968–69. 1,000 runs (18)—2,093 runs (av 63.42) in 1965 best. Has also scored 1,000 runs on following tours (6): 1954–55, 1956–57, 1958–59, 1959–60, 1962–63 and 1965–66. Has scored two 100's in match on three occasions: 110 and 103 M.C.C. v New South Wales (Sydney) 1954–55, 115* and 103* v Essex (Gillingham) 1955 and 149 and 121 v Australians (Canterbury) 1961. Scored 30,000th run of his career in Australia 1965–66 and is fourth Kent batsman to have achieved this target. Has won "Man of the Match" award in Gillette Cup Competition on three occasions. HS: 307 M.C.C. v South Australia (Adelaide) 1962–63. HS in England: 250 v Essex (Blackheath) 1959. BB: 4–22 v Surrey (Blackheath) 1951. Blues for Rackets and Tennis. Career record: 37,060 runs (av 43.70), 94 centuries, 54 wkts (av 53.57).

Michael Henry ("Mike") DENNESS (Ayr Academy).—B Bellshill (Lanarkshire) 1/12/1940. RHB, RM/OB. Debut for Scotland 1959. Debut for Kent 1962. Cap 1964. County vice-captain. Tests: 2 in 1969 and 1970. 1,000 runs (8)—1,606 runs (av 31.49) in 1966 best. HS: 174 v Derbyshire (Folkestone) 1965. Career record: 12,232 runs (av 30.58), 12 centuries, 1 wkt (av 36.00).

John Cooper James DYE.—B Gillingham 24/7/1942. RHB, LFM. Plays in contact lenses. Debut 1962. Cap 1966. HS: 27* v Sussex (Tunbridge Wells) 1970. BB: 6–37 v Leics (Hinckley) 1964. Career record: 314 runs (av 5.41), 337 wkts (av 24.78).

Alan George Ernest EALHAM:—B Ashford (Kent) 30/8/1944. RHB, OB. Outfield. Debut 1966. Cap 1970. Held 5 catches in innings v Glos (Folkestone) 1966, all in outfield off D. L. Underwood. HS: 103* v Oxford U (Oxford) 1969. Career record: 2,387 runs (av 24.11), 1 century, 1 wkt (av 21.00).

Richard ELMS.—B Sutton (Surrey) 5/4/1949. RHB, LFM. Debut 1970 (one match v Hants, Maidstone). Career record: 4 wkts (av 22.00).

John Norman GRAHAM (Queen Elizabeth G.S., Hexham).—B Hexham (Northumberland) 8/5/1943. Very tall (6ft 7½ ins). RHB, RM. Debut 1964. Cap 1967. Took 104 wkts (av 13.90) in 1967. HS: 23 v Cambridge U (Cambridge) 1968. BB: 8–20 v Essex (Brentwood) 1969. Career record: 243 runs (av 4. 11), 341 wkts (av 19.14).

Graham William JOHNSON (Shooters Hill G.S. and London School of Economics).—B Beckenham 8/11/1946. RHB, OB. Debut 1965. Cap 1970. Scored 927 runs (av 23.76) in 1970. HS: 116 v Sussex (Tunbridge Wells) 1970. BB: 6–35 (12–151 match) v Surrey (Blackheath) 1970. Career record: 1,709 runs (av 20.84), 3 centuries, 44 wkts (av 30.47).

Bernard JULIEN.—B Trinidad 13/3/1950. RHB, LM/SLA/SLC. Debut for North of Trinidad v South of Trinidad (Pointé-á-Pierre) 1967–68. Has played subsequently for Trinidad in Shell Shield Competition. Debut for county 1970 (one match v Cambridge U). Will be qualified in 1971. "Hat-trick" for North of Trinidad v South of Trinidad (Port of

Spain) 1968–69. HS: 54 in same match. BB: 7–63 in same match. Career record: 209 runs (av 19.00), 31 wkts (av 23.93).

Alan Phillip Eric KNOTT.—B Belvedere 9/4/1946. RHB, WK. Can bowl OB. Debut 1964. Cap 1965. Elected Best Young Cricketer of the Year in 1965 by Cricket Writers' Club. "Wisden 1969". Played for Tasmania 1969–70 whilst coaching there. Tests: 23 between 1967 and 1970. Tours: Pakistan 1966–67, West Indies 1967–68, Ceylon and Pakistan 1968–69, Australia and New Zealand 1970–71. Scored 1,033 runs (av 25.82) in 1968. HS: 102 v Notts (Newark) 1969. Dismissed 84 batsmen (74 ct 10 st) in 1965, 81 batsmen (73 ct 8 st) in 1966 and 98 batsmen (90 ct 8 st) in 1967. Dismissed 7 batsmen (7 ct) on debut in Test Cricket v Pakistan (Nottingham) 1967. Career record: 5,580 runs (av 24.15), 2 centuries, 551 dismissals (476 ct 75 st), 1 wkt (av 43.00).

David Alan LAYCOCK.—B Woolwich 2/9/1947. RHB. Debut 1969. HS: 58 v Leics (Canterbury) 1969, in debut innings. Career record: 151 runs (av 21.57).

Stuart Edward LEARY (Sea Point High School for Boys, Cape Town). B Cape Town 30/4/1933. RHB, LB. Good close field. Debut 1951. Cap 1957. Benefit (£9,100) in 1967. 1,000 runs (9)—1,440 runs (av 38.91) in 1961 best. Held six consecutive catches in innings v Cambridge U (Cambridge) 1958. HS: 158 v Northants (Kettering) 1963. BB: 5–22 v Glamorgan (Swansea) 1961. Soccer (CF) for Charlton Athletic and Queen's Park Rangers. Career record: 16,087 runs (av 31.23), 18 centuries, 145 wkts (av 33.80).

Brian William LUCKHURST.—B Sittingbourne 5/2/1939. RHB, SLA. Joined staff 1954. Debut 1958. Cap 1963. Tests: 5 v Rest of the World 1970. Tour: Australia and New Zealand 1970–71. 1,000 runs (9)—1,914 runs (av 47.85) in 1969 best. Scored two centuries in match (113 and 100*) v Rest of World (Canterbury) 1968. HS: 203* v Cambridge U (Cambridge) 1970. BB: 4–32 v Somerset (Gravesend) 1962. Career record: 13,736 runs (av 36.82), 27 centuries, 44 wkts (av 51.54).

David NICHOLLS (Gravesend G.S.).—B Dereham (Norfolk) 8/12/1943. LHB, reserve WK. Debut 1960. Cap 1969. HS: 211 v Derbyshire (Folkestone) 1963. Career record: 3,062 runs (av 18.67), 1 century, 123 dismissals (118 ct 5 st), 1 wkt (av 4.00).

John Neil SHEPHERD (Alleyn's School, Barbados).—B St. Andrew, Barbados 9/11/1943. RHB, RM. Leg slip. Debut 1964–65 in one match for Barbados v Cavaliers. Debut for county 1966. Cap 1967. Played for Barbados Colts v M.C.C. 1967–68 and for Barbados in 1968–69 and 1970–71 Shell Shield Competition. Tests: 3 West Indies v England 1969. Tour: West Indies to England 1969. Scored 1,157 runs (av 29.66) and took 96 wkts (av 18.72) in 1968. HS: 170 v Northants (Folkestone) 1968. BB: 8–40 West Indies v Glos (Bristol) 1969. Career record: 3,365 runs (av 24.74), 4 centuries, 281 wkts (av 23.65).

Derek Leslie UNDERWOOD (Beckenham and Penge G.S.).—B Bromley 8/6/1945. RHB, LM. Debut 1963, taking 100 wkts and being the youngest player ever to do so in debut season. Cap 1964 (second youngest Kent player to have received this award). Elected Best Young Cricketer of the Year in 1966 by the Cricket Writers' Club. "Wisden" 1968. Tests: 19 between 1966 and 1970. Tours: Pakistan 1966–67, Ceylon and Pakistan 1968–69, Australia and New Zealand 1970–71. 100 wkts (6)—157 wkts (av 13.80) in 1966 best. HS: 80 v Lancs (Manchester) 1969. BB: 9–28 v Sussex (Hastings) 1964 and 9–37 v Essex (Westcliff) 1966. Career record: 1,655 runs (av 8.44), 965 wkts (av 17.90).

Robert Andrew WOOLMER (Skinners' School, Tunbridge Wells).—B Kanpur (India) 14/5/1948. RHB, RM. Debut 1968. Cap 1970. HS: 58 v Essex (Tunbridge Wells) 1970. BB: 7–47 v Sussex (Canterbury) 1969. Career record: 588 runs (av 16.33), 53 wkts (av 24.52).

N.B. The following player whose particulars appeared in the 1970 Annual is omitted: A. L. Dixon (retired). His career record will be found elsewhere in this Annual.

COUNTY AVERAGES

County Championship: Played 24, Won 9, Lost 5, Drawn 10
All First-Class Matches: Played 25, Won 10, Lost 5, Drawn 10

BATTING AND FIELDING

Cap		*M.*	*I.*	*N.O.*	*Runs*	*H.S.*	*Avge.*	100	50	*Ct.*	*St.*
1963	B. W. Luckhurst	17	26	3	1205	203*	52.39	3	6	25	—
1951	M. C. Cowdrey	17	27	6	1013	126	48.23	3	5	15	—
1964	M. H. Denness	23	39	2	1494	167*	40.37	2	10	33	—
1968	Asif Iqbal	24	40	5	1379	109	39.40	3	7	23	—
1970	A. G. E. Ealham	15	19	5	544	88	38.85	—	4	7	—
1957	S. E. Leary	19	30	5	669	88	26.76	—	3	19	—
1960	A. L. Dixon	9	13	5	211	44	26.37	—	—	1	—
1970	G. W. Johnson	25	40	1	927	116	23.76	3	3	24	—
1967	J. N. Shepherd	25	36	4	734	105	22.93	1	2	23	—
1965	A. P. E. Knott	17	20	5	309	47	20.60	—	—	48	2
1970	R. A. Woolmer	15	20	5	270	58	18.00	—	1	10	—
1969	D. Nicholls	8	12	0	154	41	12.83	—	—	20	—
1961	A. Brown...............	13	16	5	129	52	11.72	—	1	3	—
1964	D. L. Underwood ...	18	18	6	118	32	9.83	—	—	6	—
1966	J. C. J. Dye	15	12	5	52	27*	7.42	—	—	2	—
1967	J. N. Graham	12	13	4	36	11*	4.00	—	—	5	—

Played in one match: R. Elms did not bat; B. Julien 5 (1 ct); D. A. Laycock 8 (1 ct).

ISN'T IT NICE TO KNOW . . . *Check answer page* 151

11. What performance is S. C. Griffith, the M.C.C. secretary most remembered by?

BOWLING

	Type	Overs	Mdns	Runs	Wkts	Avge.	Best	5wI.	10wM
D. L. Underwood	LM	731.3	263	1760	82	21.46	7/103	7	2
R.A. Woolmer	RM	286	84	777	32	24.28	6/53	3	—
G. W. Johnson	OB	225.1	47	671	26	25.80	6/35	2	1
J. N. Graham	RM	384.1	86	1036	40	25.90	6/67	2	—
J. N. Shepherd	RM	894.5	231	2320	86	26.97	6/33	6	—
J. C. J. Dye ...	LFM	417.4	104	1064	38	28.00	5/69	1	—
A. Brown......	RFM	369	84	1065	34	31.32	5/35	1	—
Asif Iqbal	RM	137	29	363	10	36.30	3/46	—	—
A. L. Dixon .	RM/OB	130.4	32	371	6	61.83	3/24	—	—

Also bowled: M. C. Cowdrey 11-0-47-1; A. G. E. Ealham 1-0-4-0; R. Elms 27-9-88-4; B. Julien 24-10-58-2; S. E. Leary 15-0-67-0; B. W. Luckhurst 4-0-23-0.

County Records

Highest Innings Totals:	For ...803–4d v Essex (Brentwood)..................1934
	Agst...676 by Australians (Canterbury)...............1921
Lowest Innings Totals:	For ... 18 v Sussex (Gravesend)........................1867
	Agst... 16 by Warwickshire (Tonbridge).............1913
Highest Individual Inngs.	For ...332 W. H. Ashdown v Essex (Brentwood) 1934
	Agst...344 W. G. Grace for M.C.C. (Canterbury)...1876
Best Bowling figs in an Inngs.	For 10–30 C. Blythe v Northamptonshire (Northampton) 1907
	Agst...10–48 C. H. G. Bland for Sussex (Tonbridge) 1899
Best Bowling figs in a match	For ...17–48 C. Blythe v Northamptonshire (Northampton) 1907
	Agst...17–106 T. W. Goddard for Gloucestershire (Bristol) 1939

Most runs in a season......... 2894 (av 59.06) F. E. Woolley.........1928
runs in a career ....48483 (av 42.05) F. E. Woolley...1906–1938
100s in a season......... 10 by F. E. Woolley.........1928 & 1934
100s in a career .... 112 by F. E. Woolley............1906–1938
wickets in a season ... 262 (av 14.74) A. P. Freeman.........1933
wickets in a career...... 3359 (av 14.45) A. P. Freeman 1914–1936

RECORD WICKET STANDS

1st 283	A. E. Fagg & P.R. Sunnucks v Essex (Colchester).........1938
2nd 352	W. H. Ashdown & F. E. Woolley v Essex (Brentwood)...1934
3rd 321	A. Hearne & J. R. Mason v Nottinghamshire (Nottingham) 1899
4th 297	H. T. W. Hardinge & A. P. F. Chapman v Hampshire (Southampton) 1926
5th 277	F. E. Woolley & L. E. G. Ames v New Zealanders (Canterbury) 1931
6th 284	A. P. F. Chapman & G. B. Legge v Lancashire (Maidstone) 1927
7th 248	A. P. Day & E. Humphreys v Somerset (Taunton).........1908
8th 157	A. L. Hilder & C. Wright v Essex (Gravesend)...............1924
9th 161	B. R. Edrich & F. Ridgway v Sussex (Tunbridge Wells)...1949
10th 235	F. E. Woolley & A. Fielder v Worcestershire (Stourbridge) 1909

Home Matches in Championship

Lancs (Dartford)— L 360 (Lloyd, C. H. 163, Pilling 66, Sullivan 51) and 93–3d. K 218–7d (Luckhurst 72, Denness 61) and 163–1. *Match drawn.* (*K* 6 *bonus points, L* 11 *bonus points.*)

Warwicks (Gravesend)—W 204 (Kanhai 107, Underwood 7–103) and 246 (Amiss 91, Underwood 7–110). K 227 (Leary 65) and 130 (McVicker 5–16). *W* (10 *points*) *won by* 93 *runs.* (*K* 7 *bonus points, W* 6 *bonus points.*)

Northants (Dover)—N 340 (Mushtaq 67, Willey 80, Watts 60, Dye 5–69, Brown 4–77). K 176 (Leary 50, Breakwell 4–55) and 110 (Breakwell 8–39). *N* (10 *points*) *won by an innings and* 54 *runs.* (*K* 4 *bonus points, N* 8 *bonus points.*)

Sussex (Tunbridge Wells)—S 300–9d (Greenidge 121) and 288–3 (Graves 117*, Greig 113*). K 498–9d (Cowdrey 126, Johnson 116, Shepherd 52, Buss, A. 4–96). *Match drawn.* (*K* 7 *bonus points, S* 3 *bonus points.*)

Essex (Tunbridge Wells)—K 250 (Cowdrey 65, Asif 51) and 274–5d (Cowdrey 106, Shepherd 60, Woolmer 58). E 322–7d (Edmeades 80, Saville 75, Taylor 66) and 206–5 (Fletcher 75, Edmeades 66). *E* (10 *points*) *won by* 5 *wickets.* (*K* 4 *bonus points, E* 8 *bonus points.*)

Derbys (Maidstone)—D 270–9d (Page 74) and 27–1. K 307–7d (Asif 93, Cowdrey 76, Denness 63). *Match drawn.* (*K* 8 *bonus points, D* 4 *bonus points.*)

Hants (Maidstone)—K 354–8d (Johnson 106, Leary 88, Asif Iqbal 78, Cottam 4–114) and 159–4d (Denness 84, Johnson 51). H 226 (Reed 63, Jesty 58) and 238 (Turner 116). *K* (10 *points*) *won by* 49 *runs.* (*K* 10 *bonus points, H* 5 *bonus points.*)

Worcs (Canterbury)—W 309–8d (Graveney 114, Ormrod 81) and 147–3d (Turner 56). K 172 (Asif 73) and 218–6 (Ealham 69*, Gifford 5–96). *Match drawn.* (*K* 1 *bonus point, W* 6 *bonus points.*)

Middx (Canterbury)—K 207 (Johnson 63, Titmus 7–81) and 243–4d (Asif 88, Cowdrey 84*). M 95 (Shepherd 6–33) and 319–7 (Murray 97, Parfitt 83, Underwood 5–86). *Match drawn.* (*K* 7 *bonus points, M* 4 *bonus points.*)

Surrey (Blackheath)—K 325–3d (Asif 106*, Denness 81, Luckhurst 67) and 148–4d (Cowdrey 56*). S 211 (Johnson 6–35) and 250 (Johnson 6–116) *K* (10 *points*) *won by* 12 *runs.* (*K* 11 *bonus points, S* 2 *bonus points.*)

Notts (Folkestone)—N 376–4d (Sobers 123*, Smedley 92, Hassan 55, Harris 53) and 215–6d (Bolus 73). K 310–7d (Luckhurst 156*, Ealham 57) and 283–7 (Denness 90, Luckhurst 58, Asif 56). *K* (10 *points*) *won by* 3 *wickets.* (*K* 6 *bonus points, N* 7 *bonus points.*)

Leics (Folkestone)—L 152 (Marner 54, Shepherd 5–64) and 229 (Davison 63, Underwood 6–58). K 421–7d (Johnson 108, Denness 66, Asif 63). *K* (10 *points*) *won by an innings and* 40 *runs.* (*K* 13 *bonus points, L* 2 *bonus points.*)

LANCASHIRE

Formation of present club: 1864.
Colours: Red, green and blue.
Badge: Red rose.
County Champions (8): 1881, 1897, 1904, 1926, 1927, 1928, 1930 and 1934.
Joint Champions (5): 1875, 1879, 1882, 1889 and 1950.
Gillette Cup Winners: 1970.
John Player League Champions (2): 1969 and 1970.

Secretary.—J. B. Wood, Old Trafford, Manchester, M16 0PX
Captain.—J. D. Bond.

David BAILEY (Malvern College).—B West Hartlepool 9/9/1944. Brother of H. J. Bailey, captain of Durham. RHB, OB. Excellent cover-point. Played for Durham from 1961 to 1967. Debut 1968. Did not play in 1970. HS: 136 v Kent (Manchester) 1969. Plays soccer. Career record: 845 runs (av 24.14), 1 century.

John David ("Jackie") BOND (Bolton School).—B Kearsley (Lancs) 6/5/1932. RHB. Debut 1955. Cap 1961. Appointed County Captain in 1968. Benefit (£7,230) in 1970. 1,000 runs (2)—2,125 runs (av 36.01) in 1962 best. HS: 157 v Hants (Manchester) 1962. Career record: 11,018 runs (av 27.00), 13 centuries.

James ("Jimmy") CUMBES.—B East Didsbury (Lancs) 4/5/1944. RHB, RFM. Outfield. Debut 1963. Not re-engaged at end of 1967 season and made debut for Surrey in 1968. Not re-engaged after 1970 season and has re-joined county for 1971. HS: 25* Surrey v West Indians (Oval) 1969. BB: 6–35 Surrey v Oxford U (Oxford) 1968. Soccer (goalkeeper) for Tranmere Rovers and West Bromwich Albion. Career record: 76 runs (av 8.44), 103 wkts (av 21.72).

Farokh Maneksha ENGINEER (Don Boscoe H.S., Bombay and Bombay University)—B Bombay 25/2/1938. RHB,WK., LB. Debut for Combined Universities v West Indies 1958–59. Debut for Bombay in Ranji Trophy 1959–60 and played continuously for state and for West Zone in Duleep Trophy to 1967–68. Debut for county and cap 1968. Returned home after 1969 season to play against New Zealand and Australia. Tests: 32, 30 for India between 1961–62 and 1969–70 and 2 for Rest of World in 1970. Tours: Indian Starlets to Pakistan 1959–60, India to West Indies 1961–62. England 1967, Australia and New Zealand 1967–68. Scored 94* before lunch on recall to Indian team against West Indies (Madras) 1966–67. Scored century before lunch for West Zone v Central Zone in Duleep Trophy (Bombay) 1964–65. Scored 1,050 runs (av 47.72) in 1964–65 and 952 runs (av 32.82) in 1969. Dismissed 91 batsmen (86 ct 5 st) in 1970. HS: 162 Bombay v Bengal (Calcutta) 1962–63. HS in England: 103* v Glamorgan (Swansea) 1969. Career record: 7,886 runs (av 28.88), 6 centuries, 465 dismissals (373 ct 92 st), 1 wkt (av 117.00).

Keith GOODWIN.—B Oldham 21/6/1938. RHB, WK. Debut 1960. Cap 1965, gaining regular place in team following departure of G. Clayton. Became 2nd XI captain following signing of F. M. Engineer, but reappears occasionally through absence of Engineer. Held 6 catches in John Player League match v Worcs (Worcester) 1969, the record for this League. HS: 23 v Glamorgan (Swansea) 1965. Career record: 575 runs (av 5.86), 231 dismissals (211 ct 20 st).

Frank Charles HAYES (De La Salle College, Salford and Sheffield University).—B Preston 6/12/1946. RHB, RM, Slip field. Debut 1970 scoring 94 and 99 in first two matches after scoring 203* for 2nd XI v Warwickshire 2nd XI (Birmingham). HS: 99 v Hants (Southampton) 1970. Amateur soccer player. Career record: 780 runs (av 39.00).

David Paul HUGHES (Newton-le-Willows G.S.).—B Newton-le-Willows (Lancs) 13/5/1947. RHB, SLA. Good close field. Debut 1967. Cap 1970. HS: 55 v Kent (Manchester) 1970. BB: 7–24 v Oxford U (Oxford) 1970. Career record: 1,009 runs (av 14.01), 163 wkts (av 27.59).

Andrew KENNEDY.—B Blackburn 4/11/1949. LHB. Debut 1970 (one match v Jamaica XI). HS: 25 v Jamaica XI (Manchester) 1970. Career record: 26 runs (av 26.00).

Peter LEVER (Todmorden G.S.).—B Todmorden (Yorks) 17/9/1940. RHB, RFM. Debut 1960. Cap 1965. Tests: 1 v Rest of the World 1970. Tour: Australia and New Zealand 1970–71. "Hat-trick" v Notts (Manchester) 1969. Has won "Man of the Match" award twice in Gillette Cup Competition. HS: 83 v Essex (Colchester) 1966. BB: 7–83 England v Rest of the World (Oval) 1970 on Test debut. Career record: 2,577 runs (av 15.33), 458 wkts (av 26.00).

Clive Hubert LLOYD (Chatham H.S., Georgetown).—B Georgetown (Guyana) 31/8/1944. Cousin of L. R. Gibbs. LHB, RM. Brilliant field. Plays in glasses. Debut 1963–64 for British Guiana (now Guyana). Played for Haslingden in Lancashire League in 1967 and also for Rest of World XI in 1967 and 1968. Debut for county v Australians 1968. Cap 1969. Tests: 23, 18 for West Indies between 1966–67 and 1969 and 5 for Rest of World, 1970. Scored 118 on debut v England (Port of Spain) 1967–68, 129 on debut v Australia (Brisbane) 1968–69 and 82 and 78* on debut v India (Bombay) 1966–67 Tours: India and Ceylon 1966–67, Australia and New Zealand 1968–69, England 1969. 1,000 runs (2)—1,603 runs (av 47.14) in 1970 best. Also scored 1,000 runs in Australia and New Zealand 1968–69. HS: 205* W. Indians v South Island (Dunedin) 1968–69. HS in England 201* West Indians v Glamorgan (Swansea) 1969. BB: 4–48 v Leics (Manchester) 1970. Career record: 6,543 runs (av 47.75), 16 centuries, 61 wkts (av 35.09).

David LLOYD.—B Accrington 18/3/1947. LHB, SLA. Leg-slip. Debut 1965. Cap 1968. 1,000 runs (2)—1,238 runs (av 31.74) in 1969 best. HS: 148* v Cambridge U (Cambridge) 1968. BB: 7–38 v Glos (Lydney) 1966. Career record: 4,378 runs (av 26.05), 5 centuries, 86 wkts (av 27.63).

Harry PILLING.—B Ashton-under-Lyne (Lancs) 23/2/1943. RHB, OB. Debut 1962. Cap 1965. 1,000 runs (5)—1,606 runs (av 36.50) in 1967 best. Scored two centuries in match (119* and 104*) v Warwickshire (Manchester) 1970. HS: 133* v Hants (Portsmouth) 1963. Career record: 7,886 runs (av 29.98), 13 centuries.

Kenneth ("Ken") **SHUTTLEWORTH.**—B St. Helen's 13/11/1944. RHB, RFM. Outfield. Debut 1964. Cap 1968. Tests: 1 v Rest of World 1970. Tour: Australia and New Zealand 1970–71. HS: 71 v Glos (Cheltenham) 1967. BB: 7–41 v Essex (Leyton) 1968. Career record: 1,394 runs (av 16.02), 312 wkts (av 21.88).

Jack SIMMONS.—B Clayton-le-Moors (Lancs) 28/3/1941. RHB, OB. Debut for 2nd XI 1959. Played for Blackpool in Northern League as professional. Debut 1968. HS: 112 v Sussex (Hove) 1970. BB: 5–45 v Kent (Manchester) 1970. Plays soccer in Lancs Combination. Career record: 631 runs (av 17.05), 1 century, 75 wkts (av 33.06).

Kenneth Leslie ("Ken") SNELLGROVE.—B Shepton Mallet (Somerset) 12/11/1941. RHB. Debut 1965. HS: 138 v Middlesex (Manchester) 1970. Former soccer player in Cheshire League. Career record: 1,523 runs (av 21.45), 2 centuries.

John SULLIVAN.—B Ashton-under-Lyne (Lancs) 5/2/1945. RHB, RM. Outfield with very good throw. Debut 1963. Cap 1969. Former amateur boxer. HS: 80* (retiring hurt) v Derbyshire (Buxton) 1967. BB: 4–44 v Surrey (Oval) 1970. Career record: 3,049 runs (av 19.54), 41 wkts (av 26.68).

Barry WOOD.—B Ossett (Yorks) 26/12/1942. RHB, RM. Brother of R. Wood who played occasionally for Yorkshire some years ago. Debut for Yorks 1964. Did not play in 1965 and joined Lancs by special registration, making debut for county in 1966. Cap 1968. 1,000 runs (2)—1,457 runs (av 39.37) in 1970 best. HS: 144 v Yorks (Manchester) 1970. BB: 7–52 v Middlesex (Manchester) 1968. Career record: 3,987 runs (av 27.30), 7 centuries, 74 wkts (av 25.74).

N.B. The following players whose particulars appeared in the 1970 Annual have been omitted: G. Atkinson (left staff) and J. S. Savage. In addition P. A. Gooch (LHB, RFM) and M. W. Staziker (RHB, RM) who made their debuts in 1970 have not been re-engaged.

The career records of Gooch and Staziker will be found elsewhere in this Annual.

For holiday addresses at home

buy **HOLIDAY HAUNTS IN GT. BRITAIN**

From your newsagent 20p

COUNTY AVERAGES

County Championship: Played 24, Won 6, Drawn 16, Lost 2
All First-Class Matches: Played 26, Won 7, Drawn 17, Lost 2

BATTING AND FIELDING

Cap		*M.*	*I.*	*N.O.*	*Runs*	*H.S.*	*Avge.*	100	50	*Ct.*	*St.*
1969	C. H. Lloyd	18	28	2	1203	163	46.26	3	6	9	—
1968	B. Wood	26	44	7	1457	144	39.37	5	5	15	—
1965	H. Pilling	25	41	7	1315	120*	38.67	4	5	8	—
—	F. C. Hayes............	16	22	3	719	99	37.84	—	5	18	—
—	K. L. Snellgrove	8	14	1	474	138	36.46	1	1	3	—
1961	J. D. Bond	25	33	9	780	89	32.50	—	5	25	—
1968	D. Lloyd	22	39	4	1039	124	29.68	3	4	19	—
1968	F. M. Engineer	22	33	4	797	89	27.48	—	5	78	4
1969	J. Sullivan..............	21	32	3	669	72	23.06	—	3	17	—
1965	P. Lever	21	12	7	112	26*	22.40	—	—	12	—
—	J. Simmons	25	28	8	423	112	21.15	1	2	9	—
1970	D. P. Hughes	26	28	9	343	55	18.05	—	1	16	—
1968	K. Shuttleworth	20	14	7	114	20	16.28	—	—	5	—
1965	K. Goodwin	4	6	2	16	6	4.00	—	—	14	2
—	P. A. Gooch	4	3	1	0	0*	0.00	—	—	3	—

Played in two matches: M. W. Staziker 1*, 0*.
Played in one match: A. Kennedy 25, 1*.

BOWLING

	Type	*Overs*	*Mdns*	*Runs*	*Wkts*	*Avge.*	*Best*	*5wI.*	*10wM*
B. Wood	RM	287	80	601	31	19.38	5/54	1	—
J. Sullivan	RM	183.2	51	470	22	21.36	4/44	—	—
K. Shuttleworth	RFM	596.5	145	1599	74	21.60	6/60	5	1
P. Lever	RFM	647.2	163	1657	76	21.80	6/37	2	1
D. P. Hughes ...	SLA	803.3	248	2377	82	28.98	7/24	4	1
C. H. Lloyd	RM	270	72	698	22	31.72	4/48	—	—
J. Simmons	OB	559.2	153	1478	40	36.95	5/45	1	—
P. A. Gooch	RFM	83.1	18	252	6	42.00	4/52	—	—
D. Lloyd	SLA	93	27	316	7	45.14	2/14	—	—

Also bowled: F. M. Engineer 4-1-10-0; F. C. Hayes 7-3-10-0; H. Pilling 0.2-0-4-0; M. W. Staziker 57-11-269-1;

County Records

Highest Innings Totals:	For ...801 v Somerset (Taunton)	1895
	Agst...634 by Surrey (The Oval).........................	1895
Lowest Innings Totals:	For ... 25 v Derbyshire (Manchester)...............	1871
	Agst... 22 by Glamorgan (Liverpool)	1924
Highest Individual Inngs.:	For ...424 A. C. MacLaren v Somerset (Taunton)	1895
	Agst...315*T. Hayward for Surrey (The Oval)......	1898
Best bowling figs in an Inngs.:	For ...10–55 J. Briggs v Worcestershire (Manchester)	1900
	Agst...10—40 G. O. Allen for Middlesex (Lord's)	1929

LANCASHIRE

Best bowling For ...17–91 H. Dean v Yorkshire (Liverpool)......1913
figs in a match: Agst...16–65 G. Giffen for Australians (Manchester) 1886

Most runs in a season ...... 2633 (av 56.02) J. T. Tyldesley............1901
runs in a career ......32267 (av 41.68) J. T. Tyldesley ...1895–1923
100s in a season ...... 11 by C. Hallows 1928
100s in a career ...... 91 by E. Tyldesley..................1909–1936
wickets in a season... 198 (av 18.55) E. A. McDonald.........1925
wickets in a career ... 1816 (av 15.12) J. B. Statham......1950–1968

RECORD WICKET STANDS

1st	368	A. C. MacLaren & R. H. Spooner v Gloucestershire (Liverpool)	1903
2nd	371	F. Watson & E. Tyldesley v Surrey (Manchester)	1928
3rd	306	E. Paynter & N. Oldfield v Hampshire (Southampton)	1938
4th	324	A. C. MacLaren & J. T. Tyldesley v Nottinghamshire (Nottingham)	1904
5th	235*	N. Oldfield & A. E. Nutter v Nottinghamshire (Manchester)	1939
6th	278	J. Iddon & H. R.W. Butterworth v Sussex (Manchester)	1932
7th	245	A. H. Hornby & J. Sharp v Leicestershire (Manchester)	1912
8th	150	A. Ward & C. R. Hartley v Leicestershire (Leicester)	1900
9th	142	L. O. S. Poidevin & A. Kermode v Sussex (Eastbourne)	1907
10th	173	J. Briggs & R. Pilling v Surrey (Liverpool)	1885

Home Matches in Championship

Leics (Old Trafford)—Leics 102 (Lever 4–23, Lloyd, C. 4–48) and 185 (Inman 87, Shuttleworth 6–76). Lancs 123 (Cross 4–28, McKenzie 4–35) and 167–4 (Wood 72*). *Lancs* (10 *points*) *won by* 6 *wickets*. (*Lancs* 5 *bonus points*, *Leics* 5 *bonus points*.)

Northants (Liverpool)—N 156 (Shuttleworth 5–54) and 257 (Prideaux 60, Mushtaq 53). L 368–8d (Lloyd, D. 108, Lloyd, C. H. 89, Sullivan 57) and 49–1. *L* (10 *points*) *won by* 9 *wickets*. (*L* 12 *bonus points*, *N* 3 *bonus points*.)

Kent (Old Trafford)—L 300–9d (Hughes 55, Lloyd, D. 50, Graham 5–105, Shepherd 4–85) and 165–6d. K 232 (Johnson 92, Gooch 4–52) and 203–9 (Denness 92, Luckhurst 58, Simmons 5–45). *Match drawn*. (*L* 5 *bonus points*, *K* 5 *bonus points*.)

Glos (Old Trafford)—L 400–7d (Pilling 109, Lloyd, C. H. 102, Bond 54*) and 225–5d (Pilling 69, Engineer 71). G 370–9d (Procter 115, Green 71) and 152–4. *Match drawn*. (*L* 10 *bonus points*, *G* 9 *bonus points*.)

Warwicks (Old Trafford)—L 310–5d (Pilling 119*, Lloyd, C. H. 58, Bond 53*, Ibadulla 4–34) and 218–4d (Pilling 104*, Lloyd, C. H. 73). W 251–5d (Jameson 158*) and 23–1. *Match drawn*. (*L* 5 *bonus points*, *W* 6 *bonus points*.)

Middx (Old Trafford)—M 344–9d (Smith 117, Radley 58, Featherstone 51, Wood 5–54) and 243–8d (Parfitt 67, Russell 63, Hughes 4–64). L 348–8d (Snellgrove 138, Hayes 94) and 242–5 (Pilling 120*). *L* (10 *points*) *won by 5 wickets.* (*L* 8 *bonus points, M* 8 *bonus points.*)

Notts (Old Trafford)—N 135–9d and 103–0d (Bolus 52*, Harris 50*). L 50–2d. *Match drawn.* (*L* 4 *bonus points, N* 1 *bonus point.*)

Som (Southport)—S 283 (Kitchen 99, Denning 50, Lever 4–49) and 156 (Kitchen 58, Shuttleworth 5–44). L 278 (Hayes 72, Wood 64, Jones 4–88) and 154–9 (Jones 5–47). *Match drawn.* (*L* 7 *bonus points, S* 8 *bonus points.*)

Glam (Blackpool)—G 188 (Walker 53*, Hughes 5–89) and 127–8 (Wood 4–29, Lever 4–39). L 176 (Wood 68, Williams 7–60). *Match drawn.* (*L* 4 *bonus points, G* 5 *bonus points.*)

Derbys (Old Trafford)—D 264 (Buxton 72, Gibbs 53, Lever 6–57). L 7–0. *Match abandoned.* (*L* 2 *bonus points, D* 2 *bonus points.*)

Sussex (Blackpool)—S 193 (Graves 51, Hughes 4–63) and 100 (Hughes 4–43). L 418 (Wood 138, Lloyd, D. 124, Snellgrove 60, Buss, A. 6–117). *L* (10 *points*) *won by an innings and* 125 *runs.* (*L* 11 *bonus points, S* 2 *bonus points.*)

Yorks (Old Trafford)—L 430–7d (Wood 144, Hayes 82*, Pilling 66, Lloyd, C. H. 64) and 61–1d. Y 282–3d (Boycott 98, Hutton 81) and 45–1. *Match drawn.* (*L* 5 *bonus points, Y* 3 *bonus points.*)

LEICESTERSHIRE

Formation of present club: 1879.
Colours: Scarlet and dark green.
Badge: Running fox (gold) on green background.
Best final position in Championship: Third (2), 1953 and 1967.
Gillette Cup Third Round (2): 1968 and 1969.

Secretary.—F. M. Turner, County Ground, Grace Road, Leicester, LE2 8AD.
Captain.—R. Illingworth.

Roy James BARRATT.—B Leicester 3/5/1942. LHB, SLA. Debut 1961. Left staff after 1962 season. Re-appeared in 1964 and 1965 and again from 1968 to 1970. HS: 39 v Yorks (Leicester) 1961. BB: 7–35 v Glos (Leicester) 1969. Career record: 604 runs (av 8.38), 141 wkts (av 28.41).

LEICESTERSHIRE

Jack BIRKENSHAW (Rothwell G.S.).—B Rothwell (Yorks) 13/11/1940. LHB, OB. Played for Yorks 1958 to 1960. Specially registered and made debut for Leics in 1961. Cap 1965. Scored 951 runs (av 30.67) in 1969. 100 wkts (2)—111 wkts (av 21.41) in 1967 best. "Hat-tricks" (2)—v Worcs. (Worcester) 1967 and v Cambridge U (Cambridge) 1968. Shared in 7th wkt. partnership record for county, 206 with B. Dudleston v Kent (Canterbury) 1969. HS: 131 v Surrey (Guildford) 1969. BB: 7–28 v Cambridge U (Cambridge) 1968. Career record: 7,199 runs (av 22.28), 3 centuries, 535 wkts (av 27.52).

Brian Joseph BOOTH.—B Blackburn 3/12/1935. RHB, LBG. Joined Lancashire staff 1950. Debut for Lancashire 1956. Cap 1961. Joined Leicestershire by special registration. Debut and cap 1964. 1,000 runs (8)—1,752 runs (av 31.85) in 1961 best. Scored two centuries in match (109 and 104) v Middlesex (Lord's) 1965. HS: 183* Lancs v Oxford U (Manchester) 1961. BB: 7–143 Lancs v Worcs (Southport) 1959. Career record: 13,787 runs (av 27.90) 16 centuries, 140 wkts (av 31.97).

Graham Frederick CROSS.—B Leicester 15/11/1943. RHB, RM. Close field. Debut 1961. Plays soccer for Leicester City (half-back) and made 11 appearances for England in Under-23 International matches in 1962–63, 1963–64 and 1965–66 seasons. HS: 78 v Hants (Portsmouth) 1964. BB: 4–28 v Lancs (Manchester) 1970. Career record: 1,596 runs (av 17.53), 73 wkts (av 29.50).

Brian Fettes DAVISON (Gifford Technical H.S., Rhodesia).—B Bulawayo, Rhodesia 21/12/1946. RHB, RM. Debut for Rhodesia 1967–68 in Currie Cup competition. Debut for county 1970 after having played for International Cavaliers. HS: 76 v Hants (Southampton) 1970. BB: 5–52 Rhodesia v Griqualand West (Bulawayo) 1967–68. BB in England: 4–99 v Northants (Leicester) 1970. Has played hockey for Rhodesia. Career record: 602 runs (av 22.29), 34 wkts (av 28.41).

Barry DUDLESTON.—B Bebington (Cheshire) 16/7/1945. RHB, SLA. Short leg field. Debut 1966. Cap 1969. 1,000 runs (2)—1,374 runs (av 31.22) in 1970 best. HS: 171* v Kent (Canterbury) 1969, sharing in 7th wkt. partnership record for county, 206 with J. Birkenshaw. Career record: 3,309 runs (av 26.90), 7 centuries 5 wkts (av 53.80).

Paul Raymond HAYWOOD (Wyggeston G.S., Leicester).—B Leicester 30/3/1947. RHB. Cover point. Debut 1969. HS: 65 v Glos (Bristol) 1970. Has played hockey for county and Midlands under-23. Career record: 512 runs (av 19.69).

Raymond ("Ray") ILLINGWORTH.—B Pudsey 8/6/1932. RHB, OB who can bowl seamers. Debut for Yorks 1951. Cap 1955. "Wisden 1959." Benefit (£6,604) in 1965. Left Yorks after 1968 season and joined Leics by special registration in 1969 being appointed county captain. Cap 1969. Tests: 41 between 1958 and 1970 captaining England in 11 Test matches in 1969 and 1970. Tours: West Indies 1959–60, Australia and New Zealand 1962–63, 1970–71 (captain). 1,000 runs (8)—1,726 runs (av 46.64) in 1959 best. 100 wkts (10)—131 wkts (av 14.36) in 1968 best. Doubles (6): 1957, 1959–62 and 1964. Had match double of 100 runs and 10 wkts Yorks v Kent (Dover) 1964 (135 and 14–101). HS: 162 Yorks v Indians (Sheffield) 1959. BB: 9–42 Yorks v Worcs (Worcester) 1957. Career record: 18,511 runs (av 28.13) 19 centuries 1,674 wkts (av 19.26).

Clive INMAN (St. Peter's College, Colombo).—B Colombo (Ceylon) 29/1/1936. LHB, OB. Played for Ceylon 1956–57 to 1958–59. Debut for county 1961 in one match v Australians. Played for Ceylon v M.C.C. 1961–62. Qualified for county championship in 1963 and scored over 1,000 runs in first full season. Cap 1963. Benefit in 1970. Tour: Pakistan with Ceylon team 1966–67. 1,000 runs (7)—1,735 runs (av 36.91) in 1968 best. Scored 51 in 8 mins v Notts (Nottingham) 1965 including 32 in one over off N. Hill, record for fastest 50 in first-class cricket and equalling record at that time for highest number of runs off 6-ball over. HS: 178 v Essex (Leicester) 1965. Career record: 11,708 runs (av 33.74), 17 centuries, 1 wkt (av 76.00).

Raymond ("Ray") JULIAN.—B Cosby (Leics) 23/8/1936. RHB, WK. Debut 1953 (aged 16). Cap 1961. Played as regular WK between 1959 and 1965, but lost place to R. W. Tolchard in 1966. Has remained on staff and was appointed 2nd XI captain in 1967. Re-appeared in one match in 1968 and another in 1970. HS: 51 v Worcs (Worcester) 1962. Career record: 2,581 runs (av 9.73) 418 dismissals (379 ct 39 st).

Graham Douglas McKENZIE (John Curtis H.S., Fremantle).—B Cottesloe, Perth, Western Australia 24/6/1941. RHB, RFM. Debut for Western Australia 1959–60. Debut for county and cap 1969. Tests: 60, 57 for Australia between 1961 and 1969–70 and 3 for Rest of World, 1970. Tours: Australia to England 1961, 1964 and 1968, India and Pakistan 1964–65, West Indies 1964–65, South Africa 1966–67, India and South Africa 1969–70. Took 200th wkt in Test Cricket against West Indies in 1968–69 and is youngest ever bowler to achieve targets of 100, 150 and 200 wkts inTests. His 100 wkts was achieved in record timeof 3 years 165 days. HS: 76 Australia v South Africa (Sydney) 1963–64. HS in England: 50 Australians v Notts (Nottingham) 1964 and 50 Australians v Kent (Canterbury) 1968. BB: 8–71 Australia v West Indies (Melbourne) 1968–69. BB in England: 7–67 v Glamorgan (Leicester) 1970. Career record: 4,092 runs (av 15.44), 819 wkts (av 28.36).

Peter Thomas MARNER (Greenhill G.S., Oldham).—B Oldham 31/3/1936. RHB, RM. Debut for Lancs 1952 (aged 16). Cap 1958. Not re-engaged after 1964 season and joined Leics by special registration. Debut and Cap 1965. Appointed vice-captain in 1969. Left staff after 1970 season and will play as professional for Todmorden in Lancashire League, but will be available for one-day matches. 1,000 runs (12)—1,685 runs (av 38.29) in 1958 best. Has won "Man of the Match" award in Gillette Cup Competition on three occasions, twice in successive matches in 1969. HS: 142* Lancs v Leics (Manchester) 1963. BB: 7–29 v Glamorgan (Coalville) 1966. Career record: 17,513 runs (av 28.33), 18 centuries, 360 wkts (av 31.62).

Michael Eric John Charles ("Mick") NORMAN (Northampton G.S.).—B Northampton 19/1/1933. RHB, RM. Debut for Northants 1952. Cap 1960. Left staff after 1965 season. Debut and cap for Leics 1966. Left staff after 1969 season to become a teacher and will only be available in school holidays in future. 1,000 runs (8)—1,964 runs (av 33.86) in 1960 best. HS: 221* v Cambridge U (Cambridge) 1967. Career record: 16,276 runs (av 29.86), 23 centuries, 2 wkts (av 82.00).

John Devereaux Dubricious PEMBER.—B Creaton (Northants) 8/6/1940. RHB, RM. Played for 2nd XI in 1967. Debut 1968. HS: 53 v Northants (Leicester) 1970. BB: 5–45 v Somerset (Taunton) 1968. Career record: 251 runs (av 16.73), 40 wkts (av 31.50).

Charles Terry SPENCER.—B Leicester 18/8/1931. RHB, RFM. Debut and Cap 1952. Test trial 1953. Benefit (£3,500) in 1964. Took 123 wkts (av 19.56) in 1961. Retired after 1969 season, but re-appeared in 5 John Player League matches in 1970. HS: 90 v Essex (Leicester) 1964, sharing in 8th wkt partnership record for county, 164 with M. R. Hallam. BB: 9–63 v Yorks (Huddersfield) 1954. Career record: 5,712 runs (av 10.92), 1,319 wkts (av 26.68).

John Frederick STEELE.—B Stafford 23/7/1946. Younger brother of D. S. Steele of Northants. RHB, SLA. Debut 1970. Was 12th man for England v Rest of World (Lord's) a month after making debut. HS: 22 v Worcs (Worcester) 1970. BB: 5–43 v Warwickshire (Nuneaton) 1970. Career record: 167 runs (av 10.43), 29 wkts (av 32.00).

Peter Michael STRINGER.—B Leeds 23/2/1943. LHB, RFM. Debut for Yorks 1967. Left county after 1969 season and made debut for Leics by special registration in 1970. HS: 17 v Glamorgan (Leicester) 1970. BB: 5–43 v Yorks (Sheffield) 1970. Career record: 210 runs (av 8.07), 75 wkts (av 26.45).

Jeffrey Graham TOLCHARD (Malvern College).—B Torquay 17/3/1944. Brother of R. W. Tolchard. RHB. Good cover point. Played for Devon in 1963 and from 1966 to 1969. Debut 1970. HS: 43 v Yorks (Leicester) in debut match. Student at Loughborough College. Has played soccer for Torquay United. Career record: 189 runs (av 17.18).

Roger William TOLCHARD (Malvern College).—B Torquay 15/6/1946. RHB, WK. Played for Devon in 1963 and 1964. Also played for Hants 2nd XI and Public Schools v Combined Services (Lord's) in 1964. Debut 1965. Cap 1966. Appointed vice-captain for 1970. HS: 126* v Cambridge U (Cambridge) 1970. Has had soccer trial for Leicester City. Career record: 3,457 runs (av 23.04), 2 centuries, 322 dismissals (285 ct 37 st)

N.B. The following player whose particulars appeared in the 1970 Annual has been omitted: B. R. Knight (left staff and now resides in Australia).

COUNTY AVERAGES

County Championship: Played 24, Won 5, Drawn 13, Lost 6
All First-Class Matches: Played 25, Won 6, Drawn 13, Lost 6

BATTING AND FIELDING

Cap		*M.*	*I.*	*N.O.*	*Runs*	*H.S.*	*Avge.*	100	50	*Ct.*	*St.*
1965	P. T. Marner	23	41	2	1409	115	36.12	2	10	28	—
1963	C. Inman	24	44	5	1280	105	32.82	3	7	9	—
1966	R. W. Tolchard	24	39	7	963	126*	30.09	2	4	52	8
1969	B. Dudleston	24	46	4	1259	112	29.97	3	5	24	—
1966	M. E. J. C. Norman	9	16	1	429	88	28.60	—	2	2	—
1964	B. J. Booth	20	35	4	820	84	26.45	—	5	6	—
—	B. F. Davison	7	11	0	285	76	25.90	—	3	4	—
1969	R. Illingworth	17	28	4	556	102*	23.16	1	—	5	—
—	J. D. D. Pember	10	11	6	104	53	20.80	—	1	5	—
—	P. R. Haywood	13	26	1	503	65	20.12	—	3	4	—
1965	J. Birkenshaw	25	39	6	570	64*	17.27	—	2	16	—
—	J. G. Tolchard	9	14	3	189	43	17.18	—	—	2	—
—	G. F. Cross	8	15	2	188	53	14.46	—	1	3	—
1969	G. D. McKenzie	19	25	1	281	37	11.70	—	—	11	—
—	R. J. Barratt	3	6	2	42	14*	10.50	—	—	6	—
—	J. F. Steele	19	22	6	167	22	10.43	—	—	22	—
—	P. M. Stringer	19	26	9	109	17	6.41	—	—	5	—

Played in one match: M. R. Hallam 11 (1 ct); R. Julian 0, 19 (1 ct)

BOWLING

	Type	*Overs*	*Mdns*	*Runs*	*Wkts*	*Avge.*	*Best*	*5wI.*	*10wM*
G. D. McKenzie	RFM	614.2	155	1577	82	19.23	7/67	4	1
R. Illingworth	OB	339.1	97	751	31	24.22	5/35	1	—
G. F. Cross	RM	93.1	19	293	11	26.63	4/28	—	—
J. Birkenshaw	OB	721.1	191	1769	63	28.07	6/72	5	1
P. M. Stringer	RFM	482.4	133	1288	43	29.95	5/43	1	—
J. F. Steele	SLA	399.4	146	928	29	32.00	5/43	1	—
P. T. Marner	RM	269.4	47	790	24	32.91	5/70	1	—
J. D. D. Pember	RM	171.4	40	473	12	39.41	2/18	—	—
B. F. Davison	RM	105	22	285	7	40.71	4/99	—	—

Also bowled: R. J. Barratt 51-16-119-3; B. J. Booth 34-6-115-3; B. Dudleston 12.4-0-76-2; P. R. Haywood 2-1-5-0; C. Inman 3-0-14-0; M. E. J. C. Norman 9-0-44-0; J. G. Tolchard 1-0-5-0.

County Records

Highest Innings Totals:	For ...701–4d v Worcestershire (Worcester)	1906
	Agst...739–7d by Nottinghamshire (Nottingham)	1903
Lowest Innings Totals:	For ... 25 v Kent (Leicester)	1912
	Agst... 35 by Northants (Northampton)	1907
Highest individual Inngs.:	For ...252* S. Coe v Northants (Leicester)	1914
	Agst...341 G. H. Hirst for Yorkshire (Leicester)	1905
Best bowling figs in an Inngs.:	For ...10–18 G. Geary v Glamorgan (Pontypridd)	1929
	Agst...10–32 H. Pickett for Essex (Leyton)	1895
Best bowling figs in a match:	For ...16–96 G. Geary v Glamorgan (Pontypridd)	1929
	Agst...16–102 C. Blythe for Kent (Leicester)	1909

LEICESTERSHIRE

Most runs in a season .... 2446 (av 52.04) L. G. Berry 1937
runs in a career............30143 (av 30.32) L. G. Berry......1924–1951
100s in a season .... 7 by L. G. Berry and W. Watson.........1937 and 1959
100s in a career............ 45 by L. G. Berry................1924–1951
wickets in a season ...... 170 (av 18.96) J. E. Walsh 1948
wickets in a career ...... 2130 (av 23.19) W. E. Astill......1906–1939

RECORD WICKET STANDS

1st 380 C. J. B. Wood & H. Whitehead v Worcestershire (Worcester) 1906
2nd 287 W. Watson & A. Wharton v Lancashire (Leicester).........1961
3rd 316* W. Watson & A. Wharton v Somerset (Taunton)............1961
4th 270 C. S. Dempster & G. S. Watson v Yorkshire (Hull).........1937
5th 226* R. MacDonald & F. Geeson v Derbyshire (Glossop).... 1901
6th 262 A. T. Sharpe & G. H. S. Fowke v Derbyshire (Chesterfield) 1911
7th 206 B. Dudleston & J. Birkenshaw v Kent (Canterbury).........1969
8th 164 M. R. Hallam & C. T. Spencer v Essex (Leicester) 1964
9th 160 W. W. Odell & R. T. Crawford v Worcestershire (Leicester) 1902
10th 157 W. E. Astill & W. H. Marlow v Gloucestershire (Cheltenham) 1933

Home Matches in Championship

Surrey (Leicester)—L 235 (Marner 115, Cross 53, Buss, A. 5–71, Snow 4–49) and 168 (Buss, M. 6–63). S 234–6d (Parks 63) and 95–6. *Match drawn.* (*L 5 bonus points, S 7 bonus points.*)

Kent (Leicester)—K 342–6d (Luckhurst 135, Asif 102*). L 153 and 185 (Marner 67, Shepherd 6–89, Underwood 4–30). *K* (10 *points*) *won by an innings and* 4 *runs.* (*L* 1 *bonus point, K* 8 *bonus points.*)

Warwicks (Leicester)—W 162 (McKenzie 4–67) and 210. L 149 (Blenkiron 4–24) and 121 (Gibbs 5–22). *W* (10 *points*) *won by* 102 *runs.* (*L* 5 *bonus points, W* 5 *bonus points.*)

Derbys (Leicester)—D 237 (Harvey 55) and 112 (Illingworth 5–35). L 291 (Dudleston 104, Tolchard, R. 92, Smith 4/121) and 60–2. *L* (10 *points*) *won by* 8 *wickets.* (*L* 8 *bonus points, D* 6 *bonus points.*)

Essex (Leicester)—L 175 (Boyce 5–77) and 262 (Inman 80, Haywood 62, Hobbs 4–52). E 182 (Boyce 52, McKenzie 4–58) and 174–9 (Fletcher 63, McKenzie 4–50). *Match drawn.* (*L* 6 *bonus points, E* 6 *bonus points.*)

Surrey (Leicester)—S 305–7d (Roope 100*, Long 92) and 184–2d (Younis 77, Edwards 52). L 206 (Inman 55, Arnold 5–54) and 177–6. *Match drawn.* (*L* 4 *bonus points, S* 7 *bonus points.*)

Glam (Leicester)—G 164 (Davis, R. C. 54, McKenzie 5–60) and 186 (Walker 50*, McKenzie 7–67). L 274 (Illingworth 102*, Inman 57, Nash 6–90) and 77–1 (Marner 63*). *L* (10 *points*) *won by* 9 *wickets.* (*L* 6 *bonus points, G* 4 *bonus points.*)

Yorks (Leicester)—Y 242 (Hampshire 107) and 208 (Padgett 55, Birkenshaw 5–59). L 321–9d (Booth 74, Dudleston 71, Haywood 60) and 112 (Old 4–17). *Y* (10 *points*) *won by* 17 *runs.* (*Y* 5 *bonus points, L* 9 *bonus points.*)

Hants (Leicester)—L 198 (Tolchard, R. 51, Cottam 4–44, Holder 4–49). H 237–4 (Richards 150). *Match abandoned.* (*L* 3 *bonus points, H* 8 *bonus points.*)

Notts (Leicester)—N 114 (White 53, McKenzie 6–53) and 299 (Bolus 72, Birkenshaw 5–85). L 411 (Norman 88, Tolchard, R. 83*, Inman 76, Marner 53, Forbes 4–68) and 4–0. *L* (10 *points*) *won by* 10 *wickets.* (*L* 9 *bonus points, N* 2 *bonus points.*)

Northants (Leicester)—L 309 (Tolchard, R. 104*, Pember 53, Sarfraz 4–84) and 208–6 (Dudleston 105*). N 432–9d (Ackerman 208, Lightfoot 82, Davison 4–99, Marner 4–120). *Match drawn.* (*L* 4 *bonus points, N* 8 *bonus points.*)

Middx (Leicester)—M 157 (McKenzie 6–49) and 244–4d (Radley 71*, Russell 52). L 200–7d (Titmus 4–45) and 204–5 (Marner 79, Dudleston 60). *L* (10 *points*) *won by* 5 *wickets.* (*L* 7 *bonus points, M* 3 *bonus points.*)

MIDDLESEX

Formation of present club: 1863.
Colours: Blue.
Badge: Three Seaxes.
County Champions (5): 1878, 1903, 1920, 1921 and 1947.
Joint Champions: 1949.
Gillette Cup Semi-Finalists (2): 1965 and 1968.

Secretary.—A. W. Flower, Lord's Cricket Ground, St. John's Wood Road, London, NW8 8QN.
Captain.—J. M. Brearley.

James Stephen ("Jim") ALLDIS.—B Paddington 27/12/1949. LHB, SLA. Debut 1970 (two matches) after being on M.C.C. groundstaff. HS: 4* v Hants (Basingstoke) 1970. Career record: 7 runs (av 2.33), 1 wkt (av 37.00).

Graham Derek **BARLOW** (Ealing G.S.).—B Folkestone 26/3/1950. LHB. Cover field. Played in M.C.C. Schools matches at Lord's 1968. Debut 1969. HS: 38 v Glamorgan (Lord's) 1970. Career record: 194 runs (av 19.40).

Christopher James Robert ("Sam") **BLACK** (Michaelhouse School, Natal and Stowe School).—B Johannesburg 15/12/1947. RHB, RM. Played in M.C.C. Schools matches at Lord's in 1966. Debut 1970 (two matches). HS: 9 v Northants (Northampton) 1970. Plays hockey for Hampstead. Career record: 15 runs (av 7.50).

John Michael **BREARLEY** (City of London School & Cambridge).—B Harrow 28/4/1942. RHB. Occasional WK. Debut 1961 scoring 1,222 runs (av 35.94) in first season. Blue 1961, 1962, 1963 and 1964 (capt. in 1963 and 1964). Cap 1964. Elected Best Young Cricketer of the Year in 1964 by the Cricket Writers' Club. Did not play in 1966 or 1967, but re-appeared in latter half of each season between 1968 and 1970. Appointed county captain for 1971. Holds record for most runs scored for Cambridge U (4,068 runs, av 39.49). Tours: South Africa 1964–65, Pakistan 1966–67 (captain). 1,000 runs (3)—2,178 runs (av 44.44) in 1964 best. HS: 312* M.C.C. under-25 v North Zone (Peshawar) 1966–67. HS in England: 169 Cambridge U v Combined Services (Uxbridge) 1964. Career record: 8,937 runs (av 33.98), 13 centuries, 186 dismissals (174 ct 12 st), 1 wkt (av 91.00).

Norman George ("Smokey") **FEATHERSTONE** (King Edward VII High School, Johannesburg).—B Que Que, Rhodesia 20/8/1949. RHB, OB. Member of South African Schools Team to England 1967. Debut for Transvaal B 1967–68 in Currie Cup Competition. Debut for county 1968 Qualified for championship matches in 1969. Returned home to play for Transvaal in 1969–70 Currie Cup competition. Scored 1,096 runs (av 28.10) in 1970. HS: 94 v Surrey (Lord's) 1970. Career record: 2,054 runs (av 26.33), 7 wkts (av 52.14).

Jeffris David ("Dai") **HOPKINS**.—B Bridgend (Glamorgan) 23/8/1950. RHB, WK. Joined staff in 1969 as reserve WK after being on Glamorgan and M.C.C. staffs. Debut in one match v Lancs (Lord's) 1969, and played in one match in 1970 v Cambridge U. HS: 4 v Cambridge U (Cambridge) 1970. Career record: 4 runs (av 1.33), 9 dismissals (9 ct).

Keith Vaughan **JONES**.—B Park Royal (Middlesex) 28/3/1942. RHB, RM. Debut 1967. Joined staff 1969. HS: 56* v Northants (Northampton) 1970. BB: 6–78 v Somerset (Lord's) 1969. Career record: 717 runs (av 18.86), 70 wkts (av 28.22).

Harry Chand **LATCHMAN** (Christopher Wren Comprehensive, Shepherd's Bush).—B Kingston (Jamaica) 26/7/1943. RHB, LBG. Slip field. Debut 1965. Cap 1968. HS: 43 v Cambridge U (Cambridge) 1970. BB: 7–91 v Pakistanis (Lord's) 1967. Career record: 913 runs (av 9.92), 274 wkts (av 26.08).

John Thomas MURRAY.—B Kensington 1/4/1935. RHB, WK. Can bowl RM. Debut 1952. Cap 1956. Benefit (£8,010) in 1966. "Wisden" 1966. Tests: 21 between 1961 and 1967. Tours: New Zealand 1960–61, India and Pakistan 1961–62, Australia and New Zealand 1962–63 and 1965–66, Pakistan with Commonwealth team 1963–64, South Africa 1964–65, Ceylon and Pakistan 1968–69. 1,000 runs (6)—1,160 runs (av 28.29) in 1965 best. Achieved wicket-keeper's "double" in 1957 with 1,025 runs and 104 dismissals (82 ct 22 st); only L. E. G. Ames had previously recorded this feat. Dismissed 102 batsmen (95 ct 7 st) in 1960. Dismissed 6 batsmen (6 ct) in innings v India (Lord's) 1967, to equal record for a wicketkeeper in a Test Match. Dismissed 9 batsmen (8 ct 1 st) in match v Hants (Lord's) 1965. Has twice won "Man of the Match" award in Gillette Cup Competition. HS: 142 M.C.C. v N.E. Transvaal (Pretoria) 1964–65. HS in England: 133* v Oxford U (Oxford) 1963. Career record: 15,207 runs (av 23.50), 14 centuries, 1,274 dismissals (1,063 ct 211 st), 6 wkts (av 37.66).

Peter Howard PARFITT (King Edward VII School, King's Lynn and Fakenham G.S.).—B Billingford (Norfolk) 8/12/1936. LHB, OB. Played for Norfolk from 1953 to 1955. Joined staff 1956 on special registration. Debut 1956. Cap 1960. Elected Best Young Cricketer of the Year in 1961 by the Cricket Writers' Club. "Wisden" 1962. County captain from 1968 to 1970. Benefit (£10,000+) in 1970. Soccer as amateur for Norwich City. Tests: 34 between 1961–62 and 1969. Tours: India and Pakistan 1961–62, Australia and New Zealand 1962–63 and 1965–66, India 1963–64 (flown out as replacement), South Africa 1964–65. 1,000 runs (12)—2,121 runs (av 45.12) in 1962 best. Also scored 1,000 runs (1,043 runs, av 41.72) in India and Pakistan 1961–62. Has scored two centuries in a match twice—105 and 101* v Notts (Nottingham) 1961 and 122 and 114 v Pakistan (Lord's) 1962. Scored three centuries in successive innings (all against Pakistan) in 1962, as part of a sequence of seven consecutive fifties. Shared in 6th wkt partnership of 240 with B. R. Knight v N.Z. (Auckland) 1962–63, record 6th wkt stand for England in Test Cricket. HS: 200* v Notts (Nottingham) 1964. BB: 6–45 v Oxford U (Oxford) 1969. Career record: 23,756 runs (av 35.93), 51 centuries, 248 wkts (av 30.71).

Hugh PEARMAN (King Alfred School, Golders Green and Cambridge).—B Birmingham 1/6/1945. Younger brother of R. Pearman who played for county some years ago. RHB, SLA. Short-leg field. Debut for Cambridge U and county 1969. Blue 1969. HS: 43* v Warwickshire (Lord's) 1970. BB: 4–56 Cambridge U v Oxford U (Lord's) 1969. Plays soccer. Career record: 233 runs (av 15.53), 16 wkts (av 35.43).

John Sidney Ernest PRICE (St. Marylebone G.S.).—B Harrow 22/7/1937. LHB, RF. Debut 1961. Cap 1963. Tests: 10 between 1963–64 and 1964–65. Tours: India 1963–64, South Africa 1964–65. Took 94 wkts (av 18.74) in 1966. HS: 53* D. H. Robins XI v West Indians (Eastbourne) 1969. BB: 8–48 v Derbyshire (Lord's) 1966. Career record: 710 runs (av 7.17), 621 wkts (av 23.69).

Clive Thornton RADLEY (King Edward VI G.S., Norwich).—B Hertford 13/5/1944. RHB, LB. Debut 1964. Cap 1967. 1,000 runs (4)—1,414 runs (av 38.21) in 1969 best. HS: 139 v Sussex (Hove) 1967. Shared in 6th wkt partnership record for county, 227 with F. J. Titmus v South Africans (Lord's) 1965. Career record: 6,237 runs (av 31.02), 8 centuries, 2 wkts (av 9.00).

William Eric RUSSELL.—B Dumbarton 3/7/1936. RHB, RM. Debut 1956. Cap 1959. Benefit (£8,005) in 1969. Tests: 10 between 1961–62 and 1967. Tours: New Zealand 1960–61, India and Pakistan 1961–62, Australia and New Zealand 1965–66. 1,000 runs (12)—2,342 runs (av 45.92) in 1964 best. Shared in 1st wkt partnership record for county, 312 with M. J. Harris v Pakistanis (Lord's) 1967. HS: 193 v Hants (Bournemouth) 1964. BB: 3–20 M.C.C. v President's XI (Wellington) 1965–66. Career record: 23,033 runs (av 34.84), 37 centuries, 22 wkts (av 44.40).

Timothy SELWOOD (William Ellis School, Highgate).—B Prestatyn (Flintshire) 1/9/1944. RHB, RM. Debut 1966. Played only in one John Player League match in 1970. Trained as a teacher at St. Luke's College, Exeter. HS: 35 v Somerset (Lord's) 1969. Career record: 105 runs (av 13.12).

Michael John SMITH (Enfield G.S.).—B Enfield 4/1/1942. RHB, SLA. Debut 1959. Cap 1967. 1,000 runs (3)—1,705 runs (av 39.65) in 1970 best. HS: 181 v Lancs (Manchester) 1967. BB: 4–13 v Glos (Lord's) 1961. Career record: 7,768 runs (av 29.53), 14 centuries, 53 wkts (av 32.86).

Frederick John ("Fred") TITMUS (The William Ellis School, Highgate).—B St. Pancras 24/11/1932. RHB, OB. Debut 1949 (aged 16). Cap 1953. "Wisden" 1962. Benefit (£6,833) in 1963. Appointed county captain in 1965, but resigned post during 1968 season. Won single-wicket tournament at Lord's in 1966. Tests: 49 between 1955 and 1967–68. Tours: Pakistan 1955–56, Australia and New Zealand 1962–63, India 1963–64, South Africa 1964–65, Australia 1965–66, West Indies 1967–68 (vice-captain), returning home early through loss of four toes in accident. 1,000 runs (8)—1,703 runs (av 37.02) in 1961 best. 100 wkts (15)—191 wkts (av 16.31) in 1955 best. Doubles (8): 1955 to 1957, 1959 to 1962, 1967. Missed double by 62 runs in 1963 and by 76 runs in 1968. Shared in 6th wkt partnership record for county, 227 with C. T. Radley v South Africans (Lord's) 1965. Has won "Man of the Match" award in Gillette Cup Competition on three occasions. "Hat-trick" v Somerset (Weston-super-Mare) 1966. Took 4 wkts in 6 balls for England v New Zealand (Leeds) 1965. HS: 137* M.C.C. v South Australia (Adelaide) 1962–63. HS in England: 120* v Sussex (Hove) 1961. BB: 9–52 v Cambridge U (Cambridge) 1962 and 9–57 v Lancs (Lord's) 1964. Soccer (IL) for Watford and Hendon. Career record: 19,215 runs (av 24.07), 5 centuries, 2,292 wkts (av 21.88).

N.B. The following players whose particulars appeared in the 1970 Annual are omitted: **A. N. Connolly** (retired), **T. M. Cordaroy, R. S. Herman** (not re-engaged) and **C. J. Payne.**
The career records of Connolly, Herman and Payne will be found elsewhere in this Annual.

COUNTY AVERAGES

County Championship: Played 24, Won 5, Drawn 14, Lost 5
All First-Class Matches: Played 26, Won 7, Drawn 14, Lost 5

BATTING AND FIELDING

Cap		*M.*	*I.*	*N.O.*	*Runs*	*H.S.*	*Avge.*	100	50	*Ct.*	*St.*
1959	W. E. Russell	22	37	2	1580	128*	45.14	3	9	18	—
1960	P. H. Parfitt	23	40	6	1400	133	41.17	3	10	31	—
1967	M. J. Smith	25	45	2	1705	151	39.65	6	6	13	—
1967	C. T. Radley	26	44	4	1329	116	33.22	1	9	19	—
1964	J. M. Brearley	10	17	1	471	85	29.43	—	4	4	—
1956	J. T. Murray	25	41	4	1043	97	28.18	—	6	29	13
—	N. G. Featherstone	26	43	4	1096	94	28.10	—	9	26	—
—	H. Pearman	3	3	1	51	43*	25.50	—	—	3	—
—	K. V. Jones	22	32	14	417	56*	23.16	—	2	14	—
1953	F. J. Titmus	25	36	12	459	38	19.12	—	—	14	—
—	G. D. Barlow	4	7	0	129	38	18.42	—	—	—	—
1968	H. C. Latchman	13	13	2	137	43	12.45	—	—	7	—
1969	R. S. Herman	9	7	2	57	24*	11.40	—	—	—	—
—	C. J. Payne	3	5	0	37	22	7.40	—	—	—	—
1969	A. N. Connolly	20	21	3	123	26	6.83	—	—	5	—
1963	J. S. E. Price	25	19	13	27	7	4.50	—	—	12	—

Played in two matches: J. S. Alldis 1, 0, 2, 4*; C. J. R. Black 9, 6.
Played in one match: J. D. Hopkins 4 (5 ct).

BOWLING

	Type	*Overs*	*Mdns*	*Runs*	*Wkts*	*Avge.*	*Best*	5w*I.*	10w*M*
J. S. E. Price	RF	659.4	138	1875	79	23.73	8/56	3	1
F. J. Titmus	OB	1021.3	303	2512	100	25.12	7/81	6	1
A N Connolly	RFM	598.2	145	1610	52	30.96	5/32	1	—
K. V. Jones	RM	462.5	108	1329	42	31.64	5/64	2	—
P. H. Parfitt	OB	239.3	49	858	27	31.77	3/38	—	—
H. C. Latchman	LBG	324	67	1139	30	37.96	5/46	1	—
R. S. Herman	RFM	187	34	556	14	39.71	4/57	—	—

Also bowled: J. S. Alldis 15-5-37-1; C. J. R. Black 20-5-62-0; N. G. Featherstone 31-6-121-0; J. T. Murray 6.3-0-29-1; H. Pearman 25-5-85-0; M. J. Smith 1-0-4-0.

County Records

Highest Innings Totals:	For ...642–3d v Hampshire (Southampton)	1923
	Agst...665 by West Indians (Lord's)	1939
Lowest Innings Totals:	For ... 20 v M.C.C. (Lord's)	1864
	Agst... 31 by Gloucestershire (Bristol)	1924
Highest Individual Inngs.:	For ...331* J. D. Robertson v Worcs. (Worcester)	1949
	Agst...316* J. B. Hobbs for Surrey (Lord's)	1926
Best bowling figs in an Inngs.:	For ...10–40 G. O. Allen v Lancs (Lord's)	1929
	Agst... 9–38 R. C. Robertson-Glasgow for Somerset (Lord's)	1924

Best bowling figs in a match:	For ...16–114	G. Burton v Yorks (Sheffield)......1888 J. T. Hearne v Lancs (Manchester) 1898
	Agst...16–109	C. W. L. Parker for Glos. (Cheltenham)..............................1930
Most runs in a season.........	2650	(av 85.48) W. J. Edrich............1947
runs in a career............	40302	(av 49.81) E. Hendren......1907–1937
100s in a season	13	by D. C. S. Compton...............1947
100s in a career............	119	by E. Hendren...............1907–1937
wickets in a season	158	(av 14.63) F. J. Titmus............1955
wickets in a career	2133	(av 17.94) J. T. Hearne ...1888–1923

RECORD WICKET STANDS

1st 310	W. E. Russell & M. J. Harris v Pakistanis (Lord's)	1967
2nd 380	F. A. Tarrant & J. W. Hearne v Lancashire (Lord's)......	1914
3rd 424*	W. J. Edrich & D. C. S. Compton v Somerset (Lord's)......	1948
4th 325	J. W. Hearne & E. Hendren v Hampshire (Lord's).........	1919
5th 338	R. S. Lucas & T. C. O'Brien v Sussex (Hove)...............	1895
6th 227	C. T. Radley & F. J. Titmus v South Africans (Lord's) ...	1965
7th 271*	E. Hendren & F. T. Mann v Nottinghamshire (Nottingham)..	1925
8th 182*	M. H. C. Doll & H. R. Murrell v Nottinghamshire (Lord's)	1913
9th 160*	E. Hendren & T. J. Durston v Essex (Leyton)...............	1927
10th 230	R. W. Nicholls & W. Roche v Kent (Lord's)..................	1899

Home Matches in Championship

Hants (Lord's)—M 265–6d (Smith 72) and 279–6d (Russell 118, Parfitt 62). H 343–5d (Marshall 189*, Livingstone 103) and 173–8 (Marshall 74, Titmus 5–47). *Match drawn.* (*M* 5 *bonus points, H* 10 *bonus points.*)

Glam (Lord's)—G 282–7d (Jones, A. 88, Davis, B. A. 85) and 174–6d (Jones, A. 71*). M 215 (Nash 6–42) and 203–8 (Radley 90*). *Match drawn. M* 3 *bonus points, G* 6 *bonus points*).

Worcs (Lord's)—W 126 (Titmus 4–49) and 94–1. M 81–4d. *Match drawn.* (*M* 5 *bonus points, W* 2 *bonus points.*)

Sussex (Lord's)—M 369–5d (Smith, M. J. 151, Radley 85, Murray 66). S 191 (Latchman 4–80) and 353 (Parks 67, Griffith 63, Herman 4–57). *Match drawn.* (*M* 10 *bonus points, S* 3 *bonus points.*)

Derbys (Lord's)—M 229 (Radley 116, Parfitt 52, Russell 5–42) and 293–8d (Radley 73, Featherstone 71, Jones 50*). D 366 (Hall 107, Titmus 4–105) and 16–2. *Match drawn.* (*M* 6 *bonus points, D* 8 *bonus points.*)

Kent (Lord's)—M 157 (Russell 57, Woolmer 5–24) and 212 (Parfitt 73*, Woolmer 4–41, Shepherd 4–67). K 110 (Price 8–56) and 123 (Price 6–33). *M* (10 *points*) *won by* 136 *runs.* (*M* 5 *bonus points, K* 5 *bonus points.*)

Lancs (Lord's)—M 126 (Lever 6–37) and 240 (Radley 83, Featherstone 61, Lever 4–59). L 343–9d (Wood 99, Simmons 52*) and 26–0. *L (10 points) won by* 10 *wickets. (M* 2 *bonus points, L* 7 *bonus points.)*

Northants (Lord's)—N 332–5d (Mushtaq 151*, Willey 68*) and 93–3. M 289–9d (Brearley 82, Featherstone 68, Willey 5–14). *Match drawn. (M* 6 *bonus points, N* 7 *bonus points.)*

Yorks (Lord's)—Y 235 (Hampshire 67, Titmus 5–62) and 182–5d (Sharpe 53). M 171 (Russell 80, Hutton 4–39) and 250–7 (Smith M. J. 118, Hutton 6–83). *M* (10 *points) won by* 3 *wickets. (M* 4 *bonus points, Y* 6 *bonus points.)*

Warwicks (Lord's)—W 321–9d (Smith, M. J. 95, Jameson 59, Hemmings 54, Price 5–76) and 176–5d) Amiss 82*). M 248 (Radley 56, Brown 5–58) and 139–6. *Match drawn. (M* 3 *bonus points, W* 6 *bonus points.)*

Essex (Lord's)—M 251–7d (Parfitt 103*, Turner 4–78). E 275–5 (Edmeades 115, Barker 53*). *Match drawn. (M* 6 *bonus points, E* 8 *bonus points.)*

Surrey (Lord's)—M 291–6d (Featherstone 94, Brearley 73) and 194 (Brearley 85, Parfitt 60). S 300–5d (Edrich 133, Stewart 50) and 186–3 (Stewart 55). *S* (10 *points) won by* 7 *wickets. (M* 3 *bonus points, S* 8 *bonus points.)*

Are you a regular reader of Playfair Cricket Monthly? A year's subscription costs only £2.10 and you'll be sure of all-the-year-round cricket reading

NORTHAMPTONSHIRE

Formation of present club: 1820, reorganised 1878.
Colours: Maroon.
Badge: Tudor rose.
County Championship Runners Up (3):
1912, 1957 and 1965.
Gillette Cup Semi-Finalists: 1963.

Secretary.—K. C. Turner, County Ground, Wantage Rd., Northampton, NN1 4TJ.
Captain.—P. J. Watts.

Hylton Michael ACKERMAN (Dale College, Kingwilliamstown, South Africa).—B Springs (South Africa) 28/4/1947. LHB, RM. Played for South Africa Schools XI 1962–64, touring England in 1963. Debut for Border in one match in 1963–64 Currie Cup Competition age 16. Transferred to N.E. Transvaal for 1966–67 season and to Natal for 1968–

69 season. Debut for county v Indians 1967 and in championship in 1968. Cap 1969. 1,000 runs (2)—1,565 runs (av 33.29) in 1970 best. HS: 208 v Leics (Leicester) 1970. Career record: 5,648 runs (av 32.64), 10 centuries, 14 wkts (av 44.50).

Raymond Reginald BAILEY.—B Bedford 16/5/1944. RHB, RFM. Played for Bedfordshire in 1963. Debut 1964 taking 5 wkts in innings three times in first four matches. Bowled unchanged in match with B.S. Crump v Glamorgan (Cardiff) 1967. Did not play in 1968, played in only one match in 1969, and did not play in 1970. HS: 18* v Warwickshire (Birmingham) 1965. BB: 5–25 v Hants (Northampton) 1964. Soccer for Bedford Town and Gillingham (CH). Career record: 147 runs (av 9.18), 72 wkts (av 24.50).

Dennis BREAKWELL (Ounsdale Comprehensive School, Wombourne, Wolverhampton).—B Brierley Hill (Staffs) 2/7/1948. LHB, SLA. Debut 1969 after being on staff for some years. HS: 97 v Derbyshire (Chesterfield) 1970. BB: 8–39 v Kent (Dover) 1970. Career record: 580 runs (av 15.67), 105 wkts (av 25.51).

Brian Stanley CRUMP.—B Stoke-on-Trent 25/4/1938. RHB, RM. Joined county staff 1959. Debut 1960, scoring 1,000 runs (av 34.48) in his first season. Cap 1962. 1,000 runs (2)—1,396 runs (av 29.08) in 1961 best. 100 wkts (2)—112 wkts (av 18.88) in 1965 best. Bowled unchanged in match with R. R. Bailey v Glamorgan (Cardiff) 1967. HS: 120 v Glos (Peterborough) 1961. BB: 7–29 v Glamorgan (Cardiff) 1967. Career record: 7,266 runs (av 22.84), 2 centuries, 787 wkts (av 23.98).

Alan HODGSON.—B Moorside Consett, Co. Durham. 24/10/1951. LHB, RFM. Debut 1970. One match v Cambridge U (Northampton) 1970. Career record: 2 wkts (av 6.00).

Robert Leslie JOHNS (St. Albans School, Keele and Oxford Universities).—B Southampton, Hants 30/6/1946. RHB, OB. Debut for Oxford U and blue 1970. Has joined County for 1971. HS: 61* Oxford U v Cambridge U (Lord's) 1970. BB: 4–76 Oxford U v Notts (Oxford) 1970. Career record: 273 runs (av 21.00), 13 wkts (av 51.61).

Lawrence Alan ("Laurie") JOHNSON.—B West Horsley (Surrey) 12/8/1936. RHB, WK. On Surrey staff 1952 to 1957. Joined Northants and made debut 1958. Cap 1960. Gained regular place in side in 1967 following retirement of K. V. Andrew. HS: 50 v Worcs (Dudley) 1967. Dismissed 10 batsmen (10 ct) in match v Sussex (Worthing) 1963 and (8 ct 2 st) v Warwickshire (Birmingham) 1965. Career record: 1,366 runs (av 10.11), 293 dismissals (234 ct 59 st).

Michael Keith KETTLE (Hillside School, Bulawayo, Rhodesia).—B Stamford (Lincolnshire) 18/3/1944. RHB, LM. Close field. Debut 1963. Left staff after 1970 to return to Rhodesia, but may play occasionally in future. HS: 88 v Essex (Northampton) 1963. BB: 6–67 v Sussex (Northampton) 1968. Career record: 1,117 runs (av 13.14), 179 wkts (av 26.81).

Peter LEE.—B Arthingworth (Northants) 27/8/1945. RHB, RFM. Debut 1967. HS: 26 v Glos (Northampton) 1969. BB: 6–86 v Lancs (Northampton) 1969. Career record: 145 runs (av 11.15), 45 wkts (av 36.00).

MUSHTAQ MOHAMMAD.—B Junagadh (India) 22/11/1943. RHB, LBG. Fourth of family of five cricket-playing brothers which includes Hanif Mohammad. Debut 1956–57 at age of 13 years 41 days for Karachi Whites v Hyderabad (Hyderabad) scoring 87 and taking 5–28. Made Test debut v West Indies 1958–59 at age of 15 years 124 days and youngest player ever to do so. Scored two Test centuries before the age of 19, the only player ever to have scored a Test century under this age. "Wisden" 1962. Joined Northants in 1964. Won single-wicket tournament at Lord's in 1965. Qualified for county championship in 1966. Returned to Pakistan in 1966–67 and played against M.C.C. Under-25 team. Cap 1967. Tests: 24, 22 for Pakistan between 1958–59 and 1969–70, and 2 for Rest of World in 1970. Tours: Pakistan to India 1960–61, England 1962 and also in 1963 with Pakistan Eaglets. 1,000 runs (6)—1,831 runs (av 59.06) in 1969 best. Scored 1,112 runs (av 61.77) in 1961–62. Scored two centuries in match (128* and 123) for D. H. Robins XI v West Indians (Eastbourne) 1969. HS: 303* Karachi Blues v Karachi University (Karachi) 1967–68. HS in England: 176 Pakistan v Cambridge U (Cambridge) 1962. BB: 7–18 Karachi Whites v Khairpur (Karachi) 1963–64. BB in England: 7–67 v Kent (Wellingborough) 1968. Career record: 16,170 runs (av 42.32), 37 centuries, 477 wkts (av 22.55).

Wayne M. OSMAN.—B Hertfordshire 19/8/1950. LHB. Debut 1970 (one match). HS: 9 v Cambridge U (Northampton) 1970. Career record: 9 runs (av 9.00).

Roger Malcolm PRIDEAUX (Tonbridge and Cambridge).—B Chelsea 31/7/1939. RHB, RM. Debut for Cambridge U 1958. Blue 1958, 1959 and 1960. Played for Kent 1960 and 1961. Appointed Asst.-Sec to Northants 1961 and subsequently joined playing staff. Cap 1962. County captain from 1967 to 1970, relinquishing appointment through being unable to play regularly in 1971. Tests: 3 in 1968 and 1968–69. Tours: Canada in August 1959, New Zealand 1960–61, Ceylon and Pakistan 1968–69. 1,000 runs (11)—1,993 runs (av 41.52) in 1968 best. Scored two centuries in match (102 and 106) for Cambridge U v Somerset (Taunton) 1960 and (106 and 100) v Notts (Nottingham) 1966 as part of three consecutive centuries for Northants. Scored century in 52 mins (118 in 60 mins) for South v North (Blackpool) 1961—fastest for 24 years. Shared in 1st wkt partnership record for county in county championship, 293 with C. Milburn v Essex (Clacton) 1966. HS: 202* v Oxford U (Oxford) 1963. Career record: 20, 593 runs (av 33.98), 34 centuries.

SARFRAZ NAWAZ (Government College, Lahore).—B Lahore, Pakistan 1/12/1948. RHB, RFM. Debut 1967–68 for West Pakistan Governor's **XI** v Punjab University at Lahore and subsequently played for Lahore Greens in Ayub Trophy. Played against M.C.C. in 1968–69. Debut for county 1969. Tests: 1 Pakistan v England 1968–69. HS: 44* v Notts

(Nottingham) 1970. BB: 5–43 v Glos (Bristol) 1970. Career record: 298 runs (av 18.62), 82 wkts (av 30.87).

George SHARP.—B West Hartlepool 12/3/1950. RHB, WK. Can also bowl LM. Debut 1968. HS: 55* v Warwickshire (Birmingham) 1970. England Boys Table Tennis player. Career record: 165 runs (av 41.25), 17 dismissals (14 ct 3 st).

David Stanley STEELE.—B Stoke-on-Trent 29/9/1941. Cousin of B. S. Crump and brother of J. F. Steele of Leics. RHB, SLA. Short-leg field. Played for Staffordshire from 1958 to 1962. Debut for Northants 1963. Cap 1965. 1,000 runs (3)—1,193 runs (av 27.74) in 1965 best. HS: 118* v Leics (Leicester) 1966. BB: 8–29 v Lancs (Northampton) 1966. Career record: 6,532 runs (av 26.02), 4 centuries, 151 wkts (av 23.26).

William James ("Jim") STEWART.—B Carmarthen 31/10/1934. RHB, OB. Debut for Warwickshire 1955. Cap 1957. Had big toe of left foot amputated during 1962–63 winter. Benefit (£8,346) in 1967. Specially registered for Northants in 1970, but has only played for 2nd XI so far. Tour: New Zealand 1960–61. 1,000 runs (6)—2,318 runs (av 43.73) in 1962 best. Hit 17 sixes (10 in first innings) in scoring 155 and 125 Warwickshire v Lancs (Blackpool) 1959. Hit four centuries in five inns. (155, 4, 156, 155 and 125) in 1959. HS: 182* Warwickshire v Leics (Hinckley) 1962. Played centre-three-quarter for Coventry RFC and had Welsh trial. Career record: 14,773 runs (av 34.11), 25 centuries, 2 wkts (av 7.50).

John Warwick SWINBURNE (Leeds University).—B Wath-on-Dearne, Yorkshire 4/12/1939. RHB, OB. Played for Devon from 1964 to 1969 and was also professional for Middleton in Central Lancashire League in 1968 and 1969. Debut 1970. HS: 13 v Derbyshire (Chesterfield) 1970. BB: 5–81 v Glamorgan (Cardiff) 1970. Is a schoolteacher. Career record: 36 runs (av 3.60), 34 wkts (av 31.05).

Patrick James WATTS (Stratton School, Biggleswade).—B Henlow (Beds) 16/6/1940. Brother of P. D. Watts who also played for county. LHB, RM. Debut 1959, scoring 1,118 runs (av 28.66) in his first season. Cap 1962. Left staff after 1966 season, but re-joined staff in 1970. Appointed county captain for 1971. 1,000 runs (5)—1,798 runs (av 43.85) in 1962 best. HS: 145 v Hants (Bournemouth) 1962. BB: 6–18 v Somerset (Taunton) 1965. Career record: 9,492 runs (av 26.96), 7 centuries, 313 wkts (av 24.82).

Peter WILLEY.—B Sedgefield (Co. Durham) 6/12/1949. RHB, RM. Debut 1966 aged 16 years 5 months scoring 78 in second innings of first match v Cambridge U (Cambridge). Scored 923 runs (av 28.84) in 1970. HS: 99* v Somerset (Taunton) 1970. BB: 5–14 v Middlesex (Lord's) 1970. Career record: 2,171 runs (av 20.67), 85 wkts (av 28.96).

Roy WILLS.—B Northampton 5/12/1944. RHB. Slip field. Amateur soccer player. Debut 1963. Did not play in 1970. HS: 151* v Cambridge U (Cambridge) 1966. Career record: 824 runs (av 17.16), 1 century.

N.B. The following players whose particulars appeared in the 1970 Annual have been omitted: J. D. F. Larter, A. Lightfoot (retired), C. Milburn (retired through eye injury) and B. L. Reynolds (retired). In addition, G. W. Bradfield a right hand batsman made his debut in one match against Cambridge University in 1970, but he has been omitted as he is unlikely to play again.

The Career records of Bradfield, Lightfoot and Reynolds will be found elsewhere in this Annual.

COUNTY AVERAGES

County Championship: Played 24, Won 4, Drawn 14, Lost 6
All First-Class Matches: Played 25, Won 5, Drawn 14, Lost 6

BATTING AND FIELDING

Cap		*M.*	*I.*	*N.O.*	*Runs*	*H.S.*	*Avge.*	100	50	*Ct.*	*St.*
1962	R. M. Prideaux	23	43	5	1641	176*	43.18	4	7	10	—
—	G. Sharp	7	9	5	165	55*	41.25	—	1	11	3
1967	Mushtaq Mohammad	20	37	2	1397	151*	39.91	1	9	12	—
1962	B. S. Crump	22	29	13	612	75	38.25	—	3	6	—
1961	A. Lightfoot	13	24	2	837	96	38.04	—	5	9	—
1969	H. M. Ackerman	25	46	1	1506	208	33.46	3	6	31	—
—	P. Willey	25	40	9	917	99*	29.58	—	7	15	—
1962	P. J. Watts	24	41	6	966	103	27.60	1	4	22	—
1965	D. S. Steele	22	39	3	913	90*	25.36	—	6	26	—
1956	B. L. Reynolds	10	19	3	358	83	22.37	—	1	5	—
—	Sarfraz Nawaz	21	19	9	208	44*	20.80	—	—	13	—
—	D. Breakwell	25	32	7	478	97	19.12	—	2	10	—
1960	L. A. Johnson	18	21	6	159	41	10.60	—	—	29	7
—	J. W. Swinburne	10	11	1	36	13	3.60	—	—	4	—
—	P. Lee	5	2	0	4	4	2.00	—	—	2	—

Played in two matches: M. K. Kettle 1, 4, 7* (1 ct).
Played in one match: G. W. Bradfield 50; A. Hodgson did not bat; W. M. Osman 9 (2 ct).

BOWLING

	Type	*Overs*	*Mdns*	*Runs*	*Wkts*	*Avge.*	*Best*	*5wI.*	*10wM*
D. S. Steele	SLA	60.4	26	139	8	17.37	3/17	—	—
D. Breakwell	SLA	646.4	210	1619	68	23.80	8/39	2	1
P. Willey	RM	401.3	105	957	37	25.86	5/14	2	—
Mushtaq Mohammad	LBG	460.5	84	1517	57	26.61	4/56	—	—
Sarfraz Nawaz	RFM	634.5	145	1747	59	29.61	5/43	1	—
J. W. Swinburne	OB	345.5	81	1056	34	31.05	5/81	2	—
B. S. Crump	RM	589.1	154	1562	47	33.23	5/48	1	—
P. J. Watts	RM	257	72	679	18	37.72	3/2	—	—
P. Lee	RFM	93	11	299	7	42.71	2/21	—	—

Also bowled: H. M. Ackerman 2.2-0-8-0; A. Hodgson 12-5-12-2; L. A. Johnson 12-0-60-1; M. K. Kettle 31-8-93-4; R. M. Prideaux 3-1-3-0; B. L. Reynolds 11-0-47-0.

County Records

Highest Innings Totals:	For ...557–6d v Sussex (Hove)	1914
	Agst...670–9d by Sussex (Hove)	1921
Lowest Innings Totals:	For ... 12 v Gloucestershire (Gloucester)	1907
	Agst... 43 by Leicestershire (Peterborough)	1968
Highest individual Inngs.:	For ...300 R. Subba Row v Surrey (The Oval)	1958
	Agst...333 K. S. Duleepsinhji for Sussex (Hove)	1930
Best bowling figs in an Inngs:	For ...10–127 V. W. C. Jupp v Kent (Tunbridge Wells)	1932
	Agst...10–30 C. Blythe for Kent (Northampton)	1907
Best bowling figs in a match:	For ...15–31 G. E. Tribe v Yorkshire (Northampton)	1958
	Agst...17–48 C. Blythe for Kent (Northampton)	1907
Most runs in a season	2198 (av 51.11) D. Brookes	1952
runs in a career	28980 (av 36.13) D. Brookes	1934–1959
100s in a season	8 by R. Haywood	1921
100s in a career	67 by D. Brookes	1934–1959
wickets in a season	175 (av 18.70) G. E. Tribe	1955
wickets in a career	1097 (av 21.31) E. W. Clark	1922–1947

RECORD WICKET STANDS

1st 361	N. Oldfield & V. H. Broderick v Scotland (Peterborough)	1953
2nd 307*	T. L. Livingston & D. Barrick v Sussex (Northampton)	1953
3rd 320	T. L. Livingston & F. Jakeman v South Africans (Northampton)	1951
4th 232	G. J. Thompson & S. G. Smith v Hampshire (Portsmouth)	1910
5th 347	D. Brookes & D. Barrick v Essex (Northampton)	1952
6th 376	R. Subba Row & A. Lightfoot v Surrey (The Oval)	1958
7th 229	W. W. Timms & F. A. Walden v Warwickshire (Northampton)	1926
8th 155	F. R. Brown & A. E. Nutter v Glamorgan (Northampton)	1952
9th 156	R. Subba Row & S. Starkie v Lancashire (Northampton)	1955
10th 148	R. Bellamy & V. Murdin v Glamorgan (Northampton)	1925

Home Matches in Championship

Hants (Northampton)—H 245 (Richards 73, Reed 63) and 182 (Breakwell 4–31). N 249 (Crump 53*, Cottam 5–87, White 4–71) and 179–7 (Mushtaq 55). *N (10 points) won by 3 wickets. (N 8 bonus points, H 7 bonus points.)*

Middx (Northampton)—M 327–9d (Smith, M. J. 114) and 178–6d (Jones 56). N 261 (Prideaux 125, Jones 5–64) and 174–7. *Match drawn. (N 4 bonus points, M 6 bonus points.)*

Som (Northampton)—S 298–9d (Robinson 140, Hill 64, Breakwell 5–84) and 159–4d. N 169 (Cartwright 4–27) and 214–5 (Steele 65*). *Match drawn. (N 2 bonus points, S 8 bonus points.)*

Notts (Northampton)—N 303–9d (Prideaux 142*, Sobers 4–46) and 267–4d (Ackerman 91, Reynolds 83, Mushtaq 58). Notts 306–6d (Bolus 98, Sobers 80, Hassan 67, Crump 4–65) and 230–6 (Smedley 78, Sobers 56*, Harris 52). *Match drawn.* (*N 5 bonus points, Notts 5 bonus points.*)

Sussex (Kettering)—S 244 (Parks 62, Griffith 62) and 85 (Crump 5–48). N 288–9d (Steele 90*, Willey 66, Prideaux 60, Buss A. 4–44) and 44–1. *N* (10 *points) won by* 9 *wickets.* (*N* 6 *bonus points, S* 4 *bonus points.*)

Warwicks (Northampton)—W 343–5d (Ibadulla 81*) and 202–8d (Smith, M. J. K. 92, Mushtaq 4–70). N 314–6d. (Prideaux 176*, Mushtaq 68) and 229 (Steele 58, Blenkiron 4–38). *W* (10 *points) won by* 2 *runs.* (*N* 7 *bonus points, W* 5 *bonus points.*)

Essex (Northampton)—E 323–4d (Taylor 113*, Barker 105) and 209–8d (Boyce 69). N 267 (Lightfoot 96, Boyce 4–80) and 126–5. *Match drawn.* (*N* 4 *bonus points, E* 8 *bonus points.*)

Derbys (Northampton)—D 266 (Page 85, Gibbs 84) and 225 (Page 97). N 226 (Mushtaq 77, Willey 52) and 207 (Swarbrook 5–42). *D* (10 *points) won by* 58 *runs.* (*N* 4 *bonus points, D* 5 *bonus points.*)

Yorks (Northampton)—Y 411 (Close 128, Sharpe 67, Cope 66, Sarfraz 4–67, Swinburne 4–136). N 243 (Prideaux 56, Ackerman 52, Bore 5–51) and 250–4 (Lightfoot 88*, Prideaux 83). *Match drawn.* (*N* 6 *bonus points, Y* 10 *bonus points.*)

Worcs (Wellingborough)—N 234 (Mushtaq 73, Steele 53, Gifford 5–42) and 146 (Ackerman 82, Gifford 4–30) W 157 (Swinburne 4–71) and 229–3 (Turner 110*). *W* (10 *points) won by* 7 *wickets.* (*N* 5 *bonus points, W* 2 *bonus points.*)

Leics (Northampton)—L 214 (Booth 74, Swinburne 5–84, Breakwell 4–54) and 264–6d (Inman 105). N 187 (Ackerman 97, Birkenshaw 6–72, Steele 4–61) and 264–8 (Ackerman 95, Birkenshaw 6–95). *Match drawn.* (*N* 4 *bonus points, L* 5 *bonus points.*)

Kent (Northampton)—N 229–4d (Prideaux 104*). K 106–4. *Match drawn.* (*One innings match, no bonus points awarded.*)

Playfair CRICKET MONTHLY provides the most thorough coverage of cricket in the World, with reports on overseas tours

FROM NEWSAGENTS EVERY MONTH **15p**

NOTTINGHAMSHIRE

Formation of present club: 1841, reorganised 1866.
Colours: Green and gold.
Badge: County Badge of Nottinghamshire.
County Champions (6): 1883, 1884, 1885, 1886, 1907 and 1929.
Joint Champions (6): 1873, 1875, 1879, 1880, 1882 and 1889.
Gillette Cup Semi-Finalists: 1969.

Secretary.—R. M. Poulton, County Cricket Ground, Trent Bridge, Nottingham, NG2 6AG.
Captain.—G. S. Sobers.

Stephen Richard BIELBY (Radley College).—B Windsor 9/3/1947. RHB, OB. Played for Buckinghamshire 1965. Debut 1967. HS: 62 v Somerset (Taunton) 1969. Plays hockey. Career record: 542 runs (av 18.06), 2 wkts (av 73.50).

John Brian BOLUS (St. Michael's College, Leeds).—B Whitkirk (Leeds) 31/1/1934. RHB, LM. Debut for Yorkshire 1956. Cap 1960. Not re-engaged at end of 1962 season. Debut for Notts and cap 1963. Vice-captain from 1964 until 1967 and from 1969. Benefit in 1971. Tests: 7 in 1963 and 1963–64. Tour: India 1963–64. 1,000 runs (10)—2,190 runs (av 41.32) in 1963 and 2,143 runs (av 48.70) in 1970 best. Scored two centuries in match (147 and 101) v Northants (Nottingham) 1969. Has twice won "Man of the Match" award in Gillette Cup Competition. HS: 202* v Glamorgan (Nottingham) 1963. BB: 4–40 Yorks v Pakistanis (Bradford) 1962. Career record: 19,716 runs (av 34.65), 31 centuries, 22 wkts (av 38.72).

Graham FROST.—B Old Basford, Nottingham 15/1/1947. RHB, RM. Debut 1967. Scored 856 runs (av 19.45) in 1968. HS: 107 v Surrey (Nottingham) 1970. BB: 3–33 v West Indians (Nottingham) 1969. Career record: 1,879 runs (av 22.91), 1 century, 4 wkts (av 33.00).

Michael John ("Mike") HARRIS.—B St. Just-in-Roseland (Cornwall) 25/5/1944. RHB, LBG. Occasional WK. Debut for Middlesex 1964. Cap 1967. Left staff after 1968 season and joined Notts by special registration in 1969. Cap 1970. 1,000 runs (3)—1,914 runs (av 42.53) in 1970 best. HS: 160 Middlesex v Pakistanis (Lord's) 1967 sharing in 1st wkt partnership record for county, 312 with W. E. Russell. BB: 4–16 v Warwickshire (Nottingham) 1969. Career record: 6,463 runs (av 34.01), 10 centuries, 40 wkts (av 36.45).

Basharat HASSAN.—B Nairobi (Kenya) 24/3/1944. RHB, RM, occasional WK. Debut for East African Invitation XI v M.C.C. 1963–64. Played for Coast Invitation XI v Pakistan International Airways 1964. Also played for Kenya against these and other touring sides. Debut for county 1966. Cap 1970. Scored 1,395 runs (av 32.44) in 1970. HS: 110 v Warwickshire (Birmingham) 1970. Plays hockey. Career record: 2,725 runs (av 27.25), 3 centuries.

John HOWARTH.—B Stockport (Cheshire) 26/3/1945. RHB, RFM. Debut 1966. Left staff after 1967 season. Re-appeared in two John Player League matches in 1970. Plays soccer. BB: 3–30 v Glos (Nottingham) 1967. Career record: 19 wkts (av 33.78).

Peter David JOHNSON (Nottingham H.S. and Cambridge).—B Nottingham 12/11/1949. RHB, LBG. Debut for D. H. Robin's XI v Oxford U (Eastbourne) 1969 whilst still at school and also played for 2nd XI. Debut for University and county 1970. Blue 1970. HS: 82 Cambridge U v Leics (Cambridge) 1970. BB: 3–34 Cambridge U v Glamorgan (Cambridge) 1970. Plays rugby. Career record: 296 runs (av 14.80), 9 wkts (av 74.66).

Peter John PLUMMER (Aylesbury G.S.).—B Nottingham 28/1/1947. RHB, SLA. Good outfield. Joined staff 1968. Debut 1969. HS: 46 v Leics (Leicester) 1970. BB: 4–70 v Hants (Nottingham) 1970. Is a schoolteacher in winter. Career record: 103 runs (av 12.87), 21 wkts (av 25.47).

David Anthony PULLAN.—B Farsley, Yorks 1/5/1944. RHB, WK. Played for Yorks 2nd XI 1961 to 1967 and awarded 2nd XI cap in 1966. Debut 1970. Dismissed 73 batsmen (63 ct 10 st). HS: 13* v Worcs (Kidderminster), 13 v Northants (Nottingham) and 13 v Middlesex (Newark) 1970. Career record: 111 runs (av 11.10), 73 dismissals (63 ct 10 st).

Harold James RHODES.—B Glossop 22/7/1936. Son of A. E. G. Rhodes. RHB, RFM, who started as a spin bowler, but turned to fast-medium in 1957. Debut for Derbyshire 1953. Cap 1958. Testimonial (£8,495) in 1968. Left county after 1969 season to obtain League engagement and played for Notts in John Player League and Gillette Cup matches in 1970. Tests (2): v India, 1959. After being called and reported for throwing, action was officially regarded as fair by Test and County Cricket Board in December 1968. 100 wkts (3)—119 wkts (av 11.04) in 1965 best. "Hat-trick" Derbyshire v Oxford U (Buxton) 1961. HS: 48 Derbyshire v Middlesex (Chesterfield) 1958. BB: 7–38 Derbyshire v Warwickshire (Birmingham) 1965. Career record: 2,427 runs (av 9.48), 1,072 wkts (av 19.69).

Michael John SMEDLEY (Woodhouse G.S., Sheffield).—B Maltby (Yorks) 28/10/1941. RHB. Very good fielder, particularly cover point. Played for Yorkshire 2nd XI 1960 to 1962. Debut 1964. Cap 1966. 1,000 runs in season (4)—1,553 runs (av 36.11) in 1970 best. Shared in 7th wkt partnership record for county, 204 with R. A. White v Surrey (Oval) 1967. HS: 149 v Glamorgan (Cardiff) 1970. Career record: 7,397 runs (av 30.56), 13 centuries.

Garfield St. Aubrun ("Gary") SOBERS.—B Bridgetown 28/7/1936. Outstanding all-rounder. LHB, can bowl all varieties of left-arm bowling —LFM, LM, SLA, SLC. Good close field. Debut for Barbados v Indians 1952–53 aged 16 and has played continuously for Barbados since this date. Played for South Australia in Sheffield Shield Competition from 1961–62 to 1963–64. Has played league cricket for Radcliffe (Central Lancs League) and Norton (N. Staffs and S. Cheshire League). Won single wicket tournament at Lord's in 1967. Debut for county and cap 1968, being appointed county captain. Tests: 81, 76 for West Indies between 1953–54 and 1969, captaining country in 29 Tests and 5 for Rest of World as captain in 1970. Has appeared in 75 consecutive Tests for West Indies since 2nd Test v Australia 1954–55, a record for any country. Has played in more Tests and scored more runs and centuries than any other West Indian cricketer. Tours: West Indies to New Zealand 1955–56, England 1957, 1963, 1966 and 1969 (captain), India and Pakistan 1958–59, Australia 1960–61, India and Ceylon 1966–67 (captain). Australia and New Zealand 1968–69 (captain). 1,000 runs (6)—1,742 runs (av 75.73) in 1970 best. Also scored 1,000 runs in West Indies 1957–58, India and Pakistan 1958–59 Australia 1962–63 and 1963–64 as well as taking over 50 wkts in these two seasons and Australia and New Zealand 1968–69. Hit 6 6's in one over off M. A. Nash v Glamorgan (Swansea) 1968, the first-ever instance in first-class cricket. Has scored two 100's in match twice: 125 and 109* West Indies v Pakistan (Georgetown) 1957–58, and 160 and 103* v Surrey (Oval) 1970. Had match double of 100 runs and 10 wkts v Kent (Dover) 1968 (17, 105* and 11–156), century being scored in 77 minutes—fastest of season. Has won "Man of the Match" award in Gillette Cup Competition on three occasions. HS: 365* West Indies v Pakistan (Kingston) 1957–58—the highest score in Test cricket. HS in England: 219* West Indies v Notts (Nottingham) 1957. BB: 9–49 West Indies v Kent (Canterbury) 1966. Career record: 22,316 runs (av 57.36), 69 centuries, 848 wkts (av 27.33).

Barry STEAD.—B Leeds 21/6/1939. LHB, LFM. Debut for Yorks 1959, taking 7–76 v Indians (Bradford) in his first match. Played for Combined Services in 1960 and 1961. Debut for Notts 1962. Cap 1969 when he took 82 wkts (av 23.63). HS: 35 v Worcs (Kidderminster) 1970. BB: 7–32 v Worcs (Nottingham) 1967. Career record: 535 runs (av 10.49), 267 wkts (av 28.31).

Michael Norman Somerset TAYLOR (Amersham College).—B Amersham (Bucks) 12/11/1942. Twin brother of D. J. S. Taylor of Somerset. RHB, RM. Close field. Played for Buckinghamshire in 1961 and 1962. Debut 1964. Cap 1967. Took 99 wkts (av 21.00) in 1968. "Hat-trick" v Kent (Dover) 1965. HS: 105 v Lancs (Nottingham) 1967. BB: 7–106 v Glamorgan (Nottingham) 1967. Career record: 3,361 runs (av 17.41), 1 century, 416 wkts (av 26.90).

ISN'T IT NICE TO KNOW . . . *Check answers page* 151

12. Who was the Captain of the M.C.C. team on the famous body-line tour?

13. Who was the last County Cricketer to win an F.A. Cup Winners Medal?

Robert Arthur ("Bob") WHITE (Chiswick G.S.).—B Fulham 6/10/1936. LHB, OB. Debut for Middlesex 1958. Cap 1963. Debut for Notts after special registration in 1966 and developed into useful off-break bowler. Cap 1966. Scored 1,355 runs (av 33.87) in 1963. HS: 116* v Surrey (Oval) 1967, sharing in 7th wkt partnership record for county, 204 with M. J. Smedley. BB: 6–56 v Surrey (Nottingham) 1970. Career record: 7,441 runs (av 23.62), 4 centuries, 243 wkts (av 28.22).

N.B. The following players whose particulars appeared in the 1970 Annual are omitted: C. Forbes (left staff), C. R. W. Grant, D. J. Halfyard (not re-engaged).

The career records of Forbes and Halfyard will be found elsewhere in this Annual.

COUNTY AVERAGES

County Championship: Played 24, Won 4, Drawn 12, Lost 8
All First-Class Matches: Played 25, Won 5, Drawn 12, Lost 8

BATTING AND FIELDING

Cap		*M.*	*I.*	*N.O.*	*Runs*	*H.S.*	*Avge.*	100	50	*Ct.*	*St.*
1968	G. S. Sobers	14	23	8	1154	160	76.93	5	4	13	—
1963	J. B. Bolus..............	25	49	9	2073	147*	51.82	2	15	21	—
1970	M. J. Harris	25	49	4	1914	120	42.53	3	14	16	—
1966	M. J. Smedley.........	25	46	3	1553	149	36.11	3	8	28	—
1970	B. Hassan	25	45	2	1395	110	32.44	1	11	21	—
—	G. Frost.................	18	28	8	628	107	31.40	1	1	20	—
1966	R. A. White	24	36	10	671	63*	25.80	—	3	15	—
—	S. R. Bielby............	7	12	0	209	43	17.41	—	—	1	—
1967	M. N. S. Taylor	23	28	7	344	64	16.38	—	1	10	—
1968	D. J. Halfyard	24	26	5	334	47*	15.90	—	—	11	—
—	P. J. Plummer	7	7	0	101	46	14.42	—	—	6	—
1969	B. Stead	14	13	4	116	35	12.88	—	—	2	—
—	D. A. Pullan	25	21	11	111	13*	11.10	—	—	63	10
1965	C. Forbes	17	15	3	118	23	9.83	—	—	5	—

Played in two matches: P. D. Johnson 3, 2, 2, 14 (2 ct).

BOWLING

	Type	*Overs*	*Mdns*	*Runs*	*Wkts*	*Avge.*	*Best*	*5wI.*	*10wM*
P. J. Plummer	SLA	129	28	404	17	23.76	4/70	—	—
G. S. Sobers...	LFMetc	403.3	87	1088	43	25.30	5/39	1	—
R. A. White .	OB	660.1	186	1914	70	25.84	6/56	5	1
B. Stead	LFM	385.3	68	1124	41	27.41	7/36	2	—
C. Forbes	LM	358.1	87	915	33	27.72	4/68	—	—
M.N.S. Taylor	RM	589.2	104	1827	57	32.05	4/24	—	—
D. J. Halfyard	RM	837.4	223	2135	55	38.81	3/29	—	—
M. J. Harris .	LBG	323.3	72	1036	26	39.84	4/80	—	—

Also bowled: S. R. Bielby 1-0-4-0; J. B. Bolus 1.3-0-8-0; P. D. Johnson 11-3-39-0.

County Records

Highest Innings Totals:	For ...739–7d v Leicestershire (Nottingham)	1903
	Agst...706–4d by Surrey (Nottingham)	1947
Lowest Innings Totals:	For ... 13 v Yorkshire (Nottingham)	1901
	Agst... 16 by Derbyshire (Nottinghamshire) and Surrey (The Oval)	1879 & 1880
Highest Individual Inngs.:	For ...312* W. W. Keeton v Middlesex (The Oval)	1939
	Agst...345 C. G. Macartney for Australians (Nottm)	1921
Best bowling figs in an Inngs.	For ...10–66 K. Smales v Gloucestershire (Stroud)	1956
	Agst...10–10 H. Verity for Yorkshire (Leeds)	1932
Best bowling figs in a match	For ...17–89 F. C. L. Matthews v Northants (Nottm)	1923
	Agst...17–89 W. G. Grace for Glos. (Cheltenham)	1877
Most runs in a season	2620 (av 53.46) W. W. Whysall	1929
runs in a career	31327 (av 36.71) G. Gunn	1902–1932
100s in a season	9 by W. W. Whysall	1928
100s in a career	62 by J. Hardstaff	1930–1955
wickets in a season	181 (av 14.96) B. Dooland	1954
wickets in a career	1653 (av 20.40) T. Wass	1896–1914

RECORD WICKET STANDS

1st 391	A. O. Jones & A. Shrewsbury v Gloucestershire (Bristol)	1899
2nd 398	W. Gunn & A. Shrewsbury v Sussex (Nottingham)	1890
3rd 369	J. Gunn & W. Gunn v Leicestershire (Nottingham)	1903
4th 361	A. O. Jones & J. Gunn v Essex (Leyton)	1905
5th 266	A. Shrewsbury & W. Gunn v Sussex (Hove)	1884
6th 303*	H. Winrow & P. F. Harvey v Derbyshire (Nottingham)	1947
7th 204	M. J. Smedley & R. A. White v Surrey (Oval)	1967
8th 220	G. F. H. Heane & R. Winrow v Somerset (Nottingham)	1933
9th 167	W. McIntyre & G. Wootton v Kent (Nottingham)	1869
10th 152	E. Alletson & W. Riley v Sussex (Hove)	1911

Home Matches in Championship

Warwicks (Trent Bridge)—W 235–6d (Kanhai 105, Smith, M. J. K. 83) and 195 (Jameson 61, White 6–72). N 324–5d (Sobers 115*, Bolus 94, Smedley 75) and 201–5 (Bolus 55*) *N* (10 *points*) *won by* 5 *wickets.* (*N* 8 *bonus points, W* 6 *bonus points.*)

Essex (Trent Bridge)—E 143 (Stead 5–46) and 366–2d (Ward 164*, Fletcher 102*, Saville 64). N 282 (Hassan 86, Boyce 5–62) and 223–8. *Match drawn.* (*N* 9 *bonus points, E* 4 *bonus points.*)

Northants (Trent Bridge)—N 381–4d (Ackerman 136, Prideaux 76) and 170–7d. Notts 290 (Harris 70, Bolus 69, Sarfraz 4–71) and 122–3 (Smedley 55*). *Match drawn.* (*Notts* 5 *bonus points, N* 11 *bonus points.*)

Middx (Newark)—M 268 (Parfitt 118, Murray 75, Stead 4–75) and 265–2d (Russell 128*, Parfitt 72). N 292 (Hassan 66, Jones 5–95) and 160 (Harris 74). *M* (10 *points*) *won by* 81 *runs*. (*N* 6 *bonus points*, *M* 6 *bonus points*.)

Surrey (Trent Bridge)—N 313–5d (Frost 107, Bolus 90*) and 115 (Jackman 6–35). S 235 (Roope 95, Storey 76, White 6–56) and 196–4 (Storey 69*). *S* (10 *points*) *won by* 6 *wickets*. (*N* 7 *bonus points*. *S* 4 *bonus points*.)

Glos (Trent Bridge)—G 290–8d (Brown 74, Milton 70) and 245–8d (Brown 104*, Sullivan 53). N 320–8d (Hassan 75, White 63*, Harris 55) and 219–5 (Bolus 54, Smedley 54). *N* (10 *points*) *won by* 5 *wickets*. (*N* 5 *bonus points*, *G* 5 *bonus points*.)

Derbys (Trent Bridge)—D 206 (Gibbs 94, Taylor 4–25). *N* 293–5 (Harris 111). *Match drawn*. (*N* 9 *bonus points*, *D* 3 *bonus points*.)

Hants (Trent Bridge)—H 262 (Reed 52) and 229–8d (Sainsbury 70, Turner 65, Taylor 4–65, Plummer 4–70). N 203 (Harris 84, Cottam 5–53) and 265–9 (Bolus 75, Hassan 66*, Smedley 58, Holder 4–67). *Match drawn*. (*N* 6 *bonus points*, *H* 8 *bonus points*.)

Leics (Trent Bridge)—N 321–7d (Harris 112, Hassan 79, Marner 5–70) and 218–6d (Hassan 87). L 315–7d (Dudleston 93, Birkenshaw 64*, Norman 63) and 149–6. *Match drawn*. (*N* 6 *bonus points*, *L* 7 *bonus points*.)

Yorks (Trent Bridge)—N 288 (Harris 120, Hassan 60, Hutton 6–81) and 191–6d (Bolus 71). Y 269–9d (Hampshire 78, Close 68) and 157–7 (Close 54). *Match drawn*. (*N* 6 *bonus points*, *Y* 6 *bonus points*.)

Som (Trent Bridge)—N 366–5d (Smedley 128, Harris 64, White 60*, Hassan 55) and 195–6d (Bolus 77). S 311 (Kitchen 99, Burgess 54, Harris 4–80) and 206–5 (Virgin 71, Clarkson 63). *Match drawn*. (*N* 8 *bonus points*, *S* 6 *bonus points*.)

Lancs (Trent Bridge)—L 374–8d (Wood 105, Engineer 70, Lloyd, C. H. 67, Hayes 60) and 249–4d (Lloyd, D. 108*). N 338–2d (Bolus 140*, Harris 93, Hassan 87) and 234–5 (Bolus 89, Harris 80, Sobers 52). *Match drawn*. (*N* 7 *bonus points*, *L* 6 *bonus points*.)

ISN'T IT NICE TO KNOW . . . *Check answers page* 151

14. Which player has a surname which is the same as a town in which his county plays?
15. Which player took his first 100 wickets in Test Cricket in the shortest time?
16. Which player has the same christian name as the county he plays for?

SOMERSET

Formation of present club: 1875, reorganised 1885.
Colours: Black, white and maroon.
Badge: Wessex Wyvern.
Best final position in Championship: Third (4), 1892, 1958, 1963 and 1966.
Gillette Cup Finalists: 1967.

Secretary.—A. K. James, County Cricket Ground, St. James's Street, Taunton.
Captain.—B. A. Langford.

Graham Iefvion BURGESS (Millfield School).—B Glastonbury 5/5/1943. RHB, RM. Debut 1966. Cap 1968. HS: 69 v Worcs (Worcester) 1966. BB: 6–71 v Surrey (Taunton) 1969. Plays soccer. Career record: 3,120 runs (av 17.14), 187 wkts (av 28.83).

Thomas William ("Tom") CARTWRIGHT.—B Coventry 22/7/1935. RHB, RM. Debut for Warwickshire 1952, scoring 82 and 22* v Notts (Nottingham) in first match. Cap 1958. Benefit (£9,592) in 1968. Left county after 1969 season to take post as coach at Millfield School. Debut for Somerset by special registration and cap 1970. Tests: 5 between 1964 and 1965. Bowled 77 and 62 overs in Australia's two completed innings in the two tests in 1964. Tour: South Africa 1964–65. 1,000 runs (3)—1,688 runs (av 30.88) in 1961 best. 100 wkts (7)—147 wkts (av 15.52) in 1967 best. Double in 1962. "Hat-trick" Warwickshire v Somerset (Birmingham) 1969. HS: 210 Warwickshire v Middlesex (Nuneaton) 1962. BB: 8–39 Warwickshire v Somerset (Weston-super-Mare) 1962. Had match analysis of 15–89 Warwickshire v Glamorgan (Swansea) 1967. Career record: 11,946 runs (av 22.12), 6 centuries, 1,194 wkts (av 19.43).

Anthony ("Tony") CLARKSON (Harrogate G.S.).—B Killinghall, Harrogate 5/9/1939. RHB, OB. Debut for Yorks 1963. Did not play in 1964 or 1965. Debut for Somerset after special registration in 1966. Cap 1968. 1,000 runs (2)—1,246 runs (av 27.68) in 1970 best. HS: 131 v Northants (Northampton) 1969. BB: 3–51 v Essex (Yeovil) 1967. Career record: 3,698 runs (av 24.65), 2 centuries, 13 wkts (av 28.23).

Dennis Brian CLOSE (Aireborough G.S., Yeadon, Yorks).—B Rawdon (Leeds) 24/2/1931. LHB, RM/OB. Good short-leg field. Debut for Yorks and cap 1949. Benefit (£8,154) in 1961. Appointed county captain in 1963. "Wisden 1963". Testimonial (£5,901) in 1970. Engagement terminated after 1970 season and has joined Somerset for 1971. Tests: 19 between 1949 and 1967 captaining England in 7 Test matches. Made Test debut v New Zealand at age of 18 years 149 days—youngest player ever to appear for England. Tours: Australia 1950–51, Pakistan 1955–56. 1,000 runs (14)—1,985 runs (av 35.44) in 1961 best. 100 wkts (2)—114 wkts (av 254.08) in 1952 best. Doubles (2): 1949 (debut season) and 1952 (next full season after National Service). Only three wkts short in 1955. HS: 198 Yorks v

Surrey (Oval) 1960. BB: 8–41 Yorks v Kent (Leeds) 1959. Played soccer for Leeds United, Arsenal and Bradford City. Career record: 26,340 runs (av 31.96), 38 centuries, 1,079 wkts (av 25.57).

Peter William DENNING (Millfield School).—B Chewton Mendip (Somerset) 16/12/1949. LHB. Debut 1969. HS: 69 v Essex (Taunton) 1969. Is training as a teacher at St. Luke's College, Exeter. Career record: 512 runs (av 15.51).

Maurice HILL.—B Scunthorpe (Lincs) 14/9/1935. RHB, LB. Debut for Notts 1953. Cap 1961. Left staff after 1965 season and made debut for Derbyshire in 1966. Left staff after 1967 season and made debut for Somerset in 1970. 1,000 runs (6)—1,416 runs (av 27.76) in 1964 best. HS: 137* Notts v Lancs (Worksop) 1961. Career record: 10,650 runs (av 24.14), 7 centuries, 5 wkts (av 62.20).

Allan Arthur JONES (St. John's College, Horsham).—B Horley (Surrey) 9/12/1947. RHB, RFM. Debut for Sussex 1966. Left staff in 1969 and made debut for Somerset in 1970. HS: 19 v Glos (Bristol) 1970. BB: 8–25 Sussex v Lancs (Eastbourne) 1968. Career record: 121 runs (av 3.78), 93 wkts (av 29.84).

Mervyn John KITCHEN.—B Nailsea (Somerset) 1/8/1940. LHB, RM. Joined staff 1957. Debut 1960. Cap 1966. 1,000 runs (4)—1,730 runs (av 36.04) in 1968 best. HS: 189 v Pakistanis (Taunton) 1967. Career record: 9,103 runs (av 25.28), 10 centuries, 1 wkt (av 60.00).

Brian Anthony LANGFORD (Dr. Morgan's School, Bridgwater).—B Birmingham 17/12/1935. RHB, OB. Debut 1953. Took 26 wkts for 308 runs in first three matches (all at Bath), including 8–96 (14–156 match) v Kent in his second match. Cap 1957. Testimonial (£4,250) in 1966. Appointed county captain in 1969. Will have second testimonial in 1970. 100 wkts (5)—116 wkts (av 18.28) in 1958 best. HS: 68* v Sussex (Hove) 1960 and 68 v Kent (Gillingham) 1963. BB: 9–26 (15–54 match) v Lancs (Weston-super-Mare) 1958. Career record: 6,859 runs (av 13.44), 1,302 wkts (av 24.34).

Hallam Reynold MOSELEY.—B Christchurch, Barbados 28/5/1948. RHB, RFM. Toured England with Barbados team in 1969 and made debut v Notts (Nottingham). Played for Barbados in Shell Shield 1969–70. Joined county in 1970 and will be qualified in 1971. HS: 17* Barbados v Duke of Norfolk's XI (Bridgetown) 1969–70. Career record: 24 runs (av 24.00), 1 wkt (av 228.00).

Kerry J. O'KEEFE.—Born Sydney 25/11/1949. RHB, LBG. Debut for New South Wales 1968–69. Has joined county for 1971. Tests: 2 for Australia v England 1970–71. Tour: Australia to New Zealand 1969–70. HS: 75 New South Wales v Victoria (Sydney) 1968–69. BB: 6–49 New South Wales v Victoria (Sydney) 9169–70. Career record: 427 runs (av 22.47), 65 wkts (av 28.80).

SOMERSET

John Kelvin ROBERTS (Aireborough G.S., Yeadon, Yorks).—B Liverpool 9/10/1949. RHB, LM. Debut 1969. HS: 2* v Yorks (Leeds) 1969. BB: 4–38 v Yorks (Leeds) 1969. Career record: 3 runs (av 1.00), 15 wkts (av 32.33).

Peter James ROBINSON.—B Worcester 9/2/1943. Nephew of R. O. Jenkins. LHB, SLA. Slip field. Debut for Worcs 1963. Left staff after 1964 season and made debut for Somerset in 1965. Cap 1966. Became opening batsman in 1967 and scored 917 runs (av 26.20), but has subsequently reverted to "middle of order" position. Scored 1,158 runs (av 26.93) in 1970. HS: 140 v Northants (Northampton) 1970. BB: 7–10 v Notts (Nottingham) 1966. Plays soccer as amateur for Worcester City. Career record: 4,026 runs (av 21.64), 2 centuries, 289 wkts (av 27.32).

Brian Charles ROSE (Weston-super-Mare G.S.).—B Dartford, Kent 4/6/1950. LHB, LM. Played for English Schools C.A. at Lord's 1968. Debut 1969. HS: 46 v Northants (Bath) 1969. Career record: 430 runs (av 12.64).

Derek John Somerset TAYLOR (Amersham College).—B Amersham (Bucks) 12/11/1942. Twin brother of M. N. S. Taylor of Notts. RHB, WK. Debut for Surrey 1966. Cap 1969. Left staff after 1969 season and made debut for Somerset in 1970. HS: 56 Surrey v Yorks (Oval) 1967. Has played soccer for Corinthian Casuals. Career record: 580 runs (av 18.12), 76 dismissals (66 ct 10 st).

Roy Thomas VIRGIN (Huish's G.S., Taunton).—B Taunton 26/8/1939. RHB, LB. Joined county staff 1956. Debut 1957. Cap 1960. Testimonial (£4,000) in 1969. 1,000 runs (8)—2,223 runs (av 47.29) in 1970 best. Scored two centuries in match (124 and 125*) v Warwickshire (Birmingham) 1965. Held 42 catches in 1966, a county record. Has won "Man of the Match" award twice in Gillette Cup Competition. HS: 178 v Glamorgan (Glastonbury) 1970. Career record: 13,448 runs (av 28.31), 17 centuries, 4 wkts (av 76.50).

Stephen George WILKINSON (Isleworth G.S.).—B Hounslow 12/1/1949. RHB, SLA. Joined staff in 1970 after being on M.C.C. groundstaff. Will be qualified in 1971. Has not yet appeared in first-class cricket.

N.B. The following players whose particulars appeared in the 1970 Annual have been omitted: D. Cox, J. Galley, B. Lobb, R. Palmer (not re-engaged), R. T. A. Windsor. The career record of Palmer will be found elsewhere in this Annual.

Do you know why a wicket is called a wicket? Your son will know if he's recently bought **I-SPY Cricket** (7½p) from your newsagent. It's full of new cricket facts to discover.

COUNTY AVERAGES

County Championship: Played 24, Won 5, Drawn 9, Lost 10
No other First-Class Matches were played.

BATTING AND FIELDING

Cap		*M.*	*I.*	*N.O.*	*Runs*	*H.S.*	*Avge.*	100	50	*Ct.*	*St.*
1960	R. T. Virgin	24	47	0	2223	178	47.29	7	11	15	—
1968	A. Clarkson	23	45	0	1246	105	27.68	1	8	23	—
1966	P. J. Robinson	24	47	4	1158	140	26.93	1	9	19	—
1966	M. J. Kitchen	24	47	4	977	99	22.72	—	6	12	—
—	M. Hill	17	31	1	660	65	22.00	—	3	7	—
1970	T. W. Cartwright	24	44	9	766	63*	21.88	—	3	21	—
1968	G. I. Burgess	24	46	4	866	67	20.61	—	4	5	—
—	D. J. S. Taylor	24	37	12	443	45	17.72	—	—	50	5
—	P. W. Denning	6	10	0	170	50	17.00	—	1	4	—
1957	B. A. Langford	23	35	5	436	50*	14.53	—	1	16	—
1969	R. Palmer	20	31	12	248	40*	13.05	—	—	12	—
—	B. C. Rose	6	10	0	73	16	7.30	—	—	4	—
—	A. A. Jones	22	26	11	75	19	5.00	—	—	5	—
—	J. K. Roberts	3	2	1	0	0*	0.00	—	—	—	—

BOWLING

	Type	*Overs*	*Mdns*	*Runs*	*Wkts*	*Avge.*	*Best*	*5wI.*	*10wM*
T. W. Cartwright	RM	851.4	318	1891	86	21.98	7/56	6	1
G. I. Burgess	RM	498.5	91	1667	56	29.76	5/45	3	—
P. J. Robinson	SLA	253.3	70	868	28	31.00	4/51	—	—
B. A. Langford	OB	553	141	1634	52	31.42	6/58	3	—
A. A. Jones	RFM	470.5	79	1588	46	34.52	5/35	2	—
R. Palmer	RFM	443.5	72	1517	40	37.92	3/36	—	—

Also bowled: A. Clarkson 6-1-19-0; J. K. Roberts 22-3-84-1.

County Records

Highest Innings Totals:	For	675–9d v Hampshire (Bath)	1924
	Agst	811 by Surrey (The Oval)	1899
Lowest Innings Totals:	For	25 v Gloucestershire (Bristol)	1947
	Agst	22 by Gloucestershire (Bristol)	1920
Highest Individual Inngs.	For	310 H. Gimblett v Sussex (Eastbourne)	1948
	Agst	424 A. C. MacLaren for Lancs (Taunton)	1895
Best bowling figs. in an Inngs.:	For	10–49 E. J. Tyler v Surrey (Taunton)	1895
	Agst	10–35 A. Drake for Yorkshire (Weston-super-Mare)	1914
Best bowling figs. in a match	For	16–83 J. C. White v Worcestershire (Bath)	1919
	Agst	17–137 W. Brearley for Lancashire (Manchester)	1905

Most runs in a season	2761	(av 56.82) W. E. Alley	1961
runs in a career	21108	(av 37.09) H. Gimblett	1935–1954
100s in a season	10	by W. E. Alley	1961
100s in a career	49	by H. Gimblett	1935–1954
wickets in a season	169	(av 19.24) A. W. Wellard	1938
wickets in a career	2153	(av 18.10) J. C. White	1909–1937

RECORD WICKET STANDS

1st	346	H. T. Hewett & L. C. H. Palairet v Yorkshire (Taunton)...1892
2nd	286	J. C. W. MacBryan & M. D. Lyon v Derbyshire (Buxton) 1924
3rd	300	G. Atkinson & P. B. Wight v Glamorgan (Bath)............1960
4th	200	H. Gimblett & G. E. S. Woodhouse v Middlesex (Taunton) 1946
5th	235	J. C. White & C. C. C. Case v Gloucestershire (Taunton).1927
6th	265	W. E. Alley & K. E. Palmer v Northamptonshire (Northampton) 1961
7th	240	S. M. J. Woods & V. T. Hill v Kent (Taunton)..............1898
8th	143*	E. F. Longrigg & C. J. P. Barnwell v Gloucestershire (Bristol) 1938
9th	183	C. Greetham & H. W. Stephenson v Leicestershire (Weston-super-Mare) 1963
10th	143	J. J. Bridges & H. Gibbs v Surrey (Weston-super-Mare)...1919

Home Matches in Championship

Essex (Taunton)—E 230 (Turner 121) and 176–6d. S199 (Burgess 61, Hobbs 4–29, Boyce 4–66) and 127–7. *Match drawn.* (*S* 6 *bonus points, E* 7 *bonus points*).

Middx (Taunton)—S 158 and 230 (Robinson 53, Cartwright 52*, Titmus 4–50). M 347 (Murray 69, Parfitt 54, Smith 50, Burgess 5–74) and 42–1. *M* (10 *points*) *won by* 9 *wickets.* (*S* 2 *bonus points, M* 6 *bonus points.*)

Warwicks (Taunton)—S 300 (Virgin 151, Cartwright 60, Tidy 5–82) and 242–8d (Virgin 59, Clarkson 54, Tidy 4–70). W 237 and 159–3 (Abberley 51, Jameson 50). *Match drawn.* (*S* 3 *bonus points, W* 3 *bonus points.*)

Northants (Taunton)—N 338–6d (Watts 103, Willey 99*) and 225–9d (Watts 69, Steele 57, Langford 5–53). S 316 (Kitchen 71, Hill 65, Virgin 55, Robinson 50) and 148–6. *Match drawn.* (*S* 8 *bonus points, N* 8 *bonus points.*)

Derbys (Bath)—D 198 (Cartwright 4–49) and 211–7d. S 158 (Virgin 52) and 254–7 (Virgin 103, Kitchen 58*, Buxton 6–74). *S* (10 *points*) *won by* 3 *wickets.* (*S* 5 *bonus points, D* 6 *bonus points.*)

Hants (Bath)—S 229–9d (Virgin 87, Clarkson 58, White 7–61) and 132–3d. H 147–5d and 215–3 (Livingstone 56*, Turner 51*, Richards 50). *H* (10 *points*) *won by* 7 *wickets.* (*S* 5 *bonus points, H* 4 *bonus points.*)

Leics (Bath)—L 253–7d (Inman 101*, Marner 71, Cartwright 4–70) and 212 (Dudleston 73, Robinson 4–51). S 225–8d (Virgin 91, Robinson 50, McKenzie 4–51) and 35–5 (Stringer 4–7). *Match drawn.* (*S* 6 *bonus points, L* 8 *bonus points.*)

Glam (Glastonbury)—S 323–9d (Virgin 178) and 183–7d. G 176 (Cartwright 5–57) and 332–5 (Davis, B. A. 91, Khan 68, Lewis, A. R. 54, Davis, R. C. 53). *G (10 points) won by 5 wickets. (S 8 bonus points, G 3 bonus points.)*

Glos (Weston-S-Mare)—S 311–9d (Virgin 137, Davey 4–58) and 144 (Kitchen 73, Davey 4–37, Smith 4–60). G 189 (Nicholls 57, Jones 5–35) and 115 (Cartwright 6–29, Burgess 4–52). *S (10 points) won by 151 runs. (S 8 bonus points, G 4 bonus points.)*

Worcs (Weston-S-Mare)—S 183 (Holder 4–53) and 181–6 (Hill 56*). W 132 (Cartwright 5–47, Burgess 5–48). *Match drawn. (S 6 bonus points, W 5 bonus points.)*

Kent (Weston-S-Mare)—S 211 (Virgin 54, Woolmer 6–53) and 121 (Virgin 50, Underwood 5–40, Johnson 4–31). K 263 (Denness 122, Langford 6–58) and 70–0. *K (10 points) won by 10 wickets. (S 5 bonus points, K 8 bonus points.)*

Yorks (Taunton)—Y 309 (Old 92*, Langford 5–81) and 197–8d (Padgett 59, Robinson 4–68). S 303–9d (Burgess 67, Robinson 62, Cope 6–81) and 204–4 (Burgess 62*, Virgin 56). *S (10 points) won by 6 wickets. (S 4 bonus points, Y 4 bonus points.)*

SURREY

Formation of present club: 1845.
Colours: Chocolate.
Badge: Prince of Wales' Feathers.
County Champions (16): 1887, 1888, 1890, 1891, 1892, 1894, 1895, 1899, 1914, 1952, 1953, 1954, 1955, 1956, 1957 and 1958.
Joint Champions (2): 1889 and 1950.
Gillette Cup Finalists: 1965.

Secretary.—C. G. Howard, Kennington Oval, London, S.E.11.
Captain.—M. J. Stewart.

Geoffrey Graham ("Geoff") ARNOLD.—B Earlsfield (Surrey) 3/9/1944. RHB, RFM. Debut 1963. Cap 1967. Tests: 3 in 1967 and 1969. Tour: Pakistan 1966–67. Took 109 wkts (av 18.22) in 1967. HS: 73 M.C.C. under-25 v Central Zone (Sahiwal) 1966–67. HS in England: 63 v Warwickshire (Birmingham) 1968. BB: 8–41 (13–128 match) v Glos (Oval) 1967. Soccer for Corinthian Casuals. Career record: 1,673 runs (av 15.49), 457 wkts (av 20.61).

John Hugh EDRICH.—B Blofield (Norfolk) 21/6/1937. LHB, RM. Played for Norfolk in 1954 and Surrey 2nd XI in 1955. Debut 1956 for Combined Services. Debut for Surrey 1958. Cap 1959. "Wisden" 1965. Benefit (£9,816) in 1968. Tests: 42 between 1963 and 1970. Scored century (120) on debut v Australia at Lord's 1964. Tours: India 1963–64, Australia and New Zealand 1965–66 and 1970–71, West Indies 1967–68, Ceylon and Pakistan 1968–69. 1,000 runs (12)—2,482 runs (av 51.70) in 1962 best. Also scored 1,060 runs (av 44.16) on 1965–66 tour. Scored 1,799 runs (av 52.91) in 1959 in first full season, despite absence through injury for a few matches. Lowest aggregate in any season since, is 1,586 runs (av 46.64) in 1970. Scored two centuries in match v Notts (Nottingham) 1959 (112 and 124) and v Worcs (Worcester) 1970 (143 and 113*). Scored 1,311 runs in 9 consecutive innings all over 50 including three consecutive centuries, in 1965. Has twice won "Man of the Match award" in Gillette Cup Competition. HS: 310* England v New Zealand (Leeds) 1965 sharing in 2nd wkt partnership of 369 with K. F. Barrington. Career record: 27,192 runs (av 46.01), 70 centuries.

Michael John ("Mike") EDWARDS (Alleyn's School and Cambridge). B Balham 1/3/1940. RHB, OB. Debut for Cambridge U 1960. Debut for Surrey 1961 and joined staff in 1963. Cap 1966. 1,000 runs (5)—1,428 runs (av 36.61) in 1969 best. Held 53 catches in 1967. HS: 137 v M.C.C. (Oval) 1969. Career record: 8,522 runs (av 27.75), 9 centuries, 2 wkts (av 89.50).

John Michael Mackenzie HOOPER (Charterhouse).—B Milford (Surrey) 23/4/1947. RHB, RM. Debut 1967. 2nd XI captain. HS: 41* v Oxford U (Guildford) 1970. Plays soccer and rackets. Career record: 318 runs (av 14.45).

INTIKHAB ALAM.—B Hoshiarpur (India) 28/12/1941. RHB, LBG. Debut for Karachi 1957–58 aged 16 years 9 months and has played continuously for various Karachi sides and Pakistan International Airways since. Professional for West of Scotland Club for some seasons. Debut for county and cap 1969. Tests: 31, 26 for Pakistan between 1959–60 and 1969–70, captaining country in 3 Tests in 1969–70, and 5 for Rest of World in 1970. Took wkt of C. C. McDonald with first ball he bowled in Test cricket. Tours: Pakistan to India 1960–61, England 1962 and 1967, Ceylon 1964, Australia and New Zealand 1964–65, Pakistan Eaglets to England 1963, Pakistan International Airways to East Africa 1964. HS: 106 v Middlesex (Oval) 1970. BB: 8–61 Pakistanis v Minor Counties (Swindon) 1967. Career record: 5,819 runs (av 23.46), 3 centuries, 589 wkts (av 27.16).

Robin David JACKMAN (St. Edmund's School, Canterbury).—B Simla (India) 13/8/1945. RHB, RFM. Debut 1966. Cap 1970. HS: 32* v Hants (Oval) 1969. BB: 7–98 v Yorks (Leeds) 1967. Career record: 482 runs (av 9.26), 250 wkts (av 25.14).

Roy Markham LEWIS (Tulse Hill G.S.).—B Bromley 29/6/1948. RHB, RM. Debut 1968. HS: 87 v Kent (Blackheath) 1969. Plays rugger. Career record: 430 runs (av 30.71).

Arnold LONG.—B Cheam 18/12/1940. LHB, WK. Joined staff 1959. Debut 1960. Cap 1962. Benefit in 1971. Dismissed 7 batsmen in innings and 11 in match (all ct) v Sussex (Hove) 1964, world record for most catches in match and only one short of record for most dismissals in match. Dismissed 89 batsmen (72 ct 17 st) in 1962. HS: 92 v Leics (Leicester) 1970. Soccer for Corinthian Casuals. Career record: 3,428 runs (av 14.71), 592 dismissals (520 ct 72 st).

Dudley Richard OWEN-THOMAS (King's College School, Wimbledon and Cambridge).—B Nairobi, Kenya 20/9/1948. RHB, OB. Played for 2nd XI from 1967 to 1969. Debut for Cambridge U 1969. Blues 1969 and 1970. Debut for county (two matches) 1970. HS: 182* Cambridge U v Middlesex (Cambridge) 1969. BB: 3–20 Cambridge U v Worcs (Halesowen) 1969. Career record: 1,171 runs (av 30.02), 2 centuries, 19 wkts (av 38.31).

Patrick Ian ("Pat") POCOCK (Wimbledon).—B Bangor (Caernarvonshire 24/9/1946. RHB, OB. Debut 1964. Cap 1967. Tests: 4 between 1967–68 and 1968–69. Tours: Pakistan 1966–67, West Indies 1967–68, Ceylon and Pakistan 1968–69. Took 112 wkts (av 18.22) in 1967. HS: 75* v Notts (Oval) 1968. BB: 7–57 v Essex (Romford) 1968. Career record: 1,797 runs (av 11.02), 560 wkts (av 23.66).

Graham Richard James ROOPE (Bradfield).—B Fareham (Hants) 12/7/1946. RHB, RM. Played for Public Schools XI v Comb. Services (Lord's) 1963 and 1964. Played for Berkshire 1963 scoring century against Wiltshire. Joined county staff and debut 1964. Cap 1969. 1,000 runs (2)—1,346 runs (av 34.51) in 1970 best. HS: 111 v Glamorgan (Cardiff) 1970. BB: 5–14 v West Indians (Oval) 1969. Soccer (goalkeeper) for Corinthian Casuals and Wimbledon (Southern League). Career record: 3,881 runs (av 29.62), 2 centuries, 109 wkts (av 30.53).

Lonsdale Ernest SKINNER (Hillcroft Comprehensive School, Tooting). —B Plaisance, British Guiana 7/9/1950. RHB, WK. Joined staff 1969. Has not yet appeared in first-class cricket.

Michael James ("Micky") STEWART (Alleyn's School).—B Herne Hill 16/9/1932. RHB, RM. Fine close to wicket field. Joined staff 1952. Debut 1954, scoring 109 v Pakistan (Oval) in second match. Cap 1955. Elected Best Young Cricketer of the Year in 1957 by the Cricket Writers' Club. "Wisden" 1957. Deputy county captain in 1961 and 1962. Appointed captain in 1963. Benefit (£7,028) in 1965. Has played soccer (IR) for Wimbledon, Hendon and Corinthian Casuals. Turned soccer pro with Charlton Athletic in October 1956. Tests: 8 between 1962 and 1963–64. Tour: India 1963–64 (vice-captain, but returned home early owing to illness).1,000 runs (15)—2,045 runs (av 44.45) in 1962 best. Shares with A. S. Brown of Glos the world record for fielder of holding 7 catches in innings, v Northants (Northampton) 1957. Held 77 catches in 1957 (one short of record of 78 by W. R. Hammond in 1928). HS: 227* v Middlesex (Oval) 1964. Career record: 24,925 runs (av 33.77), 47 centuries, 1 wkt (av 95.00).

SURREY

Stewart James STOREY.—B Worthing 6/1/1941. RHB, RM. Joined county staff 1959. Debut 1960. Cap 1964. 1,000 runs (4)—1,052 runs (av 25.65) in 1965 best. Scored 1,013 runs (av 24.70) ,and took 104 wkts (av 18.39) in 1966 to achieve "double", the first by a Surrey player since F. R. Brown in 1932. "Hat-trick" v Glamorgan (Swansea) 1965. Has twice won "Man of the Match" award in Gillette Cup Competition. HS: 136 v Warwickshire (Oval) 1964. BB: 8–22 v Glamorgan (Swansea) 1965. Career record: 7,022 runs (av 22.72), 8 centuries, 399 wkts (av 25.18).

Christopher Edward WALLER.—B Guildford 3/10/1948. RHB, SLA. Debut 1967. HS: 9* v Yorks (Bradford) 1970. BB: 5–43 v Oxford U (Oxford) 1970. Career record: 26 runs (av 6.50), 24 wkts (av 22.00).

Robert George Dylan ("Bob") WILLIS (Guildford R.G.S.).—B Sunderland 30/5/1949. RHB, RF. Debut 1969. Tour: Australia and New Zealand 1970–71 (flown out as replacement for A. Ward). HS: 27 M.C.C. v South Australia (Adelaide) 1970–71. HS in England: 25 v Warwickshire (Oval) 1970. BB: 5–78 v Notts (Nottingham) 1969. Plays soccer (goal-keeper) for Guildford City. Career record: 72 runs (av 12.00), 62 wkts (av 24.41).

Mohammad YOUNIS AHMED.—B Jullundur (Pakistan) 21/10/1947. LHB, LM/SLA. Younger brother of Saeed Ahmed, who has played for county 2nd XI. Debut 1961–62 for Pakistan Inter Board Schools XI v South Zone at age of 14. Subsequently played in 1963–64 and 1964–65 Quaid-i-Azam Trophy and 1964–65 Ayub Tournament matches, captaining Lahore Board in latter competition. Debut for Surrey 1965. Has subsequently returned to Pakistan to play in winter. Cap 1969. Tests: 2 Pakistan v New Zealand 1969–70. 1,000 runs (2)—1,760 runs (av 47.56) in 1969 best. HS: 147* Pakistan International Airways A v Rawalpindi Blues (Lahore) 1969–70. HS in England: 127* v Derbyshire (Oval) 1969. BB: 3–12 The Rest v Pakistan XI (Sahiwal) 1969–70. Career record: 5,793 runs (av 34.89), 10 centuries, 16 wkts (av 43.25).

N.B. The following players whose particulars appeared in the 1970 Annual have been omitted: V. C. G. Brooks, N. J. Cosh, M. W. W. Selvey, W. A. Smith (left staff) and A. J. Stockley. In addition J. Cumbes was not re-engaged and has re-joined Lancashire, and R. D. V. Knight has joined Gloucestershire; their particulars will be found under these counties. R. G. Humphrey, a wicket-keeper who played in one match in 1964, re-appeared in one match against Oxford University, but has not been included as he is unlikely to play again.

The career records of Smith, Cumbes, Knight and Humphrey will be found elsewhere in this Annual.

Don't forget to take Michelin with you

COUNTY AVERAGES

County Championship: Played 24, Won 6, Drawn 14, Lost 4
All First-Class Matches: Played 26, Won 7, Drawn 15, Lost 4

BATTING AND FIELDING

Cap		*M.*	*I.*	*N.O.*	*Runs*	*H.S.*	*Avge.*	100	50	*Ct.*	*St.*
1959	J. H. Edrich	19	33	3	1490	143	49.66	5	4	9	—
1969	Younis Ahmed	25	46	7	1588	120*	40.71	2	10	14	—
1955	M. J. Stewart	22	39	5	1246	128	36.64	2	7	16	—
1969	G. R. J. Roope	26	45	9	1289	111	35.80	2	4	42	—
1966	M. J. Edwards	22	39	0	1281	117	32.84	1	6	29	—
1964	S. J. Storey	23	37	4	1045	106	31.66	1	8	18	—
1962	A. Long	25	32	8	643	92	26.79	—	2	61	4
1969	Intikhab Alam	19	31	4	683	106	25.29	1	2	8	—
—	R. D. V. Knight	3	5	0	126	59	25.20	—	2	—	—
—	R. M. Lewis	3	6	1	116	55	23.20	—	1	3	—
—	J. M. M. Hooper ...	4	7	3	87	41*	21.75	—	—	2	—
1968	W. A. Smith	7	13	0	203	43	15.61	—	—	—	—
—	R. G. D. Willis.......	13	12	8	61	25	15.25	—	—	3	—
1967	G. G. Arnold	20	21	2	226	46	11.89	—	—	10	—
1967	P. I. Pocock	24	25	5	210	25*	10.50	—	—	6	—
1970	R. D. Jackman	22	20	7	113	16	8.69	—	—	4	—
—	C. E. Waller	6	6	3	20	9*	6.66	—	—	2	—

Played in two matches: D. R. Owen-Thomas 73, 3, 1.
Played in one match: R. G. Humphrey did not bat (1 ct).

BOWLING

	Type	*Overs*	*Mdns*	*Runs*	*Wkts*	*Avge.*	*Best*	*5wI.*	*10wM*
R. D. Jackman	RFM	597	112	1625	69	23.55	6/35	2	—
Intikhab Alam .	LBG	570.1	134	1702	72	23.63	8/74	5	—
G. G. Arnold ...	RFM	577.4	104	1607	64	25.10	6/82	3	—
R. G. D. Willis.	RF	359.3	66	1080	40	27.00	4/57	—	—
P. I. Pocock	OB	772.5	206	1997	69	28.94	6/62	2	1
G. R. J. Roope .	RM	226.3	45	630	19	33.15	3/35	—	—
C. E. Waller	SLA	115.3	32	298	8	37.25	5/43	1	—
S. J. Storey	RM	328	79	826	19	43.47	4/47	—	—

Also bowled: R. D. V. Knight 44.1-9-122-2; Younis Ahmed 4.5-2-15-1.

County Records

Highest Innings Totals:	For	...811 v Somerset (The Oval).......................1899
	Agst	...705–8d by Sussex (Hastings) 1902
Lowest Innings Totals:	For	... 16 v Nottinghamshire (The Oval)............1880
	Agst	... 15 by M.C.C. (Lord's) 1839
Highest Individual Inngs.:	For	...357* R. Abel v Somerset (The Oval).........1899
	Agst	...300* F. Watson for Lancashire (Manchester) 1928
		300 R. Subba Row for Northamptonshire (The Oval) 1958
Best bowling figs in an Inngs.:	For	...10–43 T. Rushby v Somerset (Taunton)......1921
	Agst	...10–28 W. P. Howell for Australians (The Oval) 1899

Best bowling figs in a match:	For ...16–83	G. A. R. Lock v Kent (Blackheath)...1956
	Agst...15–57	W. P. Howell for Australians (The Oval) ...1899
Most runs in a season.........	3246	(av 72.13) T. Hayward............1906
runs in a career............	43703	(av 49.77) J. B. Hobbs 1905–1934
100s in a season	13	by T. Hayward 1906
		J. B. Hobbs..................1925
100s in a career............	144	by J. B. Hobbs...............1905–1934
wickets in a season	250	(av 14.06) T. Richardson 1895
wickets in a career.........	1775	(av 17.91) T. Richardson...1892–1905

RECORD WICKET STANDS

1st	428	J. B. Hobbs & A. Sandham v Oxford U (The Oval).........1926
2nd	371	J. B. Hobbs & E. G. Hayes v Hampshire (The Oval) 1909
3rd	353	A. Ducat & E. G. Hayes v Hampshire (Southampton) ...1919
4th	448	R. Abel & T. Hayward v Yorkshire (The Oval)...............1899
5th	308	J. N. Crawford & F. C. Holland v Somerset (The Oval) ...1908
6th	298	A. Sandham & H. S. Harrison v Sussex (The Oval).........1913
7th	200	T. F. Shepherd & J. W. Hitch v Kent (Blackheath).........1921
8th	204	T. Hayward & L. C. Braund v Lancashire (The Oval)......1898
9th	168	E. R. T. Holmes & E. W. Brookes v Hampshire (The Oval) 1936
10th	**173**	**A. Ducat & A. Sandham v Essex (Leyton)......................1921**

Home Matches in Championship

Northants (The Oval)—**S** 306–6d (Edwards 117, Younis 75*) and 205–4d (Younis 112, Roope 55*) N 258–8d (Steele 58, Breakwell 50*) and 254–7 (Ackerman 108*). *N (10 points) won by 3 wickets. (S 8 bonus points, N 4 bonus points.)*

Yorks (The Oval)—**S** 306–7d (Edwards 93, Storey 81). **Y** 186. *Match drawn. (S 7 bonus points, Y 3 bonus points.)*

Notts (The Oval)—N 281 (Sobers 160, Jackman 6–55) and 218–8d (Sobers 103*). S 278–4d (Edwards 71, Younis 52, Storey 56*) and 225–3 (Edwards 79, Storey 50*) *S (10 points) won by 7 wickets. (S 6 bonus points, N 5 bonus points.)*

Middx (The Oval)—M 212 (Murray 71, Intikhab 8–74) and 341–6d (Parfitt 133, Featherstone 67). S 323 (Intikhab 106, Stewart 65) and 197–7. *Match drawn. (S 8 bonus points, M 5 bonus points.)*

Essex (The Oval)—S 227 (Younis 68) and 192 (Hobbs 4–74). E 203 (Pocock 4–59) and 136 (Intikhab 7–30). *S (10 points) won by 80 runs. (S 7 bonus points, E 6 bonus points.)*

Som (The Oval)—Som 217 (Clarkson 61, Robinson 51, Pocock 6–62) and 100 (Intikhab 5–31, Pocock 4–23). S 382–6d (Younis 120*, Edrich 91, Intikhab 53). *S (10 points) won by an innings and 65 runs. (S 5 bonus points, Som 2 bonus points.)*

Sussex (Guildford)—S 276 (Stewart 79, Roope 66, Greig 4–28) and 254–4d (Stewart 110*). Sussex 262 (Suttle 80, Griffith 74, Willis 4–57) and 133–6 (Langridge 54). *Match drawn.* (*S* 8 *bonus points, Sussex* 8 *bonus points.*)

Warwicks (The Oval)—S 342 (Storey 106, Edwards 81, Blenkiron 4–85) and 181 (Lewis 55, Tidy 5–36). W 258 (Gordon 65, Ibadulla 57) and 265–6 (Jameson 101, Smith, M. J. K. 88). *Match drawn.* (*S* 8 *bonus points, W* 11 *bonus points.*)

Glos (The Oval)—G 256–6d (Green 61, Bissex 51*) and 151–4d (Procter 54*). S 228 (Knight 50, Mortimore 4–66) and 174–4 (Edrich 57*). *Match drawn.* (*S* 6 *bonus points, G* 9 *bonus points.*)

Worcs (The Oval)—W 302–4d (D'Oliveira 105, Yardley 52*, Graveney 50*) and 193–3d (Graveney 82*, Turner 64). S 240 (Owen-Thomas 73, Holder 4–46) and 155 (Gifford 5–35). *W* (10 *points*) *won by* 100 *runs.* (*S* 4 *bonus points, W* 6 *bonus points.*)

Kent (The Oval)—S 151–9d (Woolmer 5–40) and 215–4 (Edrich 100*, Underwood 4–74). K 291–9d (Cowdrey 112, Luckhurst 51, Arnold 6–82). *Match drawn.* (*S* 3 *bonus points, K* 8 *bonus points.*)

Lancs (The Oval)—S 184 (Younis 90, Sullivan 4–44). L 58–7 (Arnold 5–22). *Match drawn.* (*S* 4 *bonus points, L* 5 *bonus points.*)

SUSSEX

Formation of present club: 1839, reorganized 1857.
Colours: Dark blue, light blue and gold.
Badge: County Arms of six Martlets (in shape of inverted pyramid).
Joint Champions: 1875.
County Championship Runners-up (6): 1902, 1903, 1932, 1933, 1934 and 1953.
Gillette Cup Winners (2): 1963 and 1964.
Gillette Cup Finalists (2): 1968 and 1970.

Secretary.—A. A. Dumbrell, County Ground, Eaton Road, Hove, BN3 3AN, Sussex.
Captain.—M. G. Griffith.

John Robert Troutbeck BARCLAY (Eton College).—B Bonn, West Germany 22/1/1954. RHB, OB. Debut 1970 (two matches) age 16½, whilst still at school. Has been in XI at school since age of 14 and scored the record number of runs for school in 1970. Played in M.C.C. Schools matches at Lord's 1969 and 1970. Vice-captain of English Schools Cricket Association team to India 1970–71. HS: 4 v Jamaica XI (Hove) 1970. Career record: 4 runs (av 1.33).

SUSSEX

Donald Lawson ("Don") BATES.—B Hove 10/5/1933. RHB, RFM. Plays in glasses. Joined staff 1949. Debut 1950. Cap 1957. Benefit (£8,000) in 1968. Left staff after 1970 season, but will play occasionally in future. 100 wkts (3)—113 wkts (av 22.65) in 1961 best. HS: 37* v Kent (Tunbridge Wells) 1960. BB: 8–51 v Essex (Hove) 1966. Soccer (RH) for Lewes and Brighton and Hove Albion. Career record: 1,523 runs (av 7.65), 880 wkts (av 25.82).

Antony ("Tony") BUSS (Bexhill G.S.).—B Brightling (Sussex) 1/9/1939. RHB, RFM. Joined county staff 1955. Debut 1958. Cap 1963. Benefit in 1971. 100 wkts (3)—120 wkts (av 20.30) in 1965 and 120 wkts (av 22.55) in 1966 best. "Hat-tricks" (2): v Cambridge U (Cambridge) and Derbyshire (Hove) in 1965. HS: 83 v Northants (Hove) 1969. BB: 8–23 v Notts (Hove) 1966. Career record: 3,861 runs (av 13.54), 874 wkts (av 24.04).

Michael Alan BUSS.—B Brightling (Sussex) 24/1/1944. Brother of A. Buss. LHB, LM. Debut 1961. Developed into opening batsman in 1966, and changed bowling style from SLA to LM in 1967. Cap 1967. Tour: Pakistan 1966–67, flown out as replacement for R. N. Abberley. 1,000 runs (3)—1,379 runs (av 37.27) in 1970 best. Has twice won "Man of the Match" award in Gillette Cup Competition. HS: 159 v Glamorgan (Swansea) 1967. BB: 7–58 v Hants (Bournemouth) 1970. Career record: 6,017 runs (av 23.97), 7 centuries, 223 wkts (av 29.11).

John DENMAN (Ifield G.S., Crawley).—B Horley (Surrey) 13/6/1947. RHB, RM. Debut 1970. HS: 34* v Jamaica XI (Hove) 1970 BB: 4–45 v Derbyshire (Buxton) 1970. Amateur soccer player for Three Bridges in Sussex County League. Career record: 133 runs (av 14.77), 18 wkts (av 44.00).

Peter John GRAVES (Hove Manor School).—B Hove 19/5/1946. LHB, SLA. Close field. Debut 1965. Cap 1969. Played for Orange Free State 1969–70 whilst appointed as coach. Scored 1,142 runs (av 27.85) in 1970. HS: 117* v Kent (Tunbridge Wells) 1970. BB: 3–69 Orange Free State v Australians (Bloemfontein) 1969–70. BB in England: 3–75 v Glos (Cheltenham) 1965. Soccer player. Career record: 3,404 runs (av 23.00), 2 centuries, 9 wkts (av 42.44).

Geoffrey Alan ("Geoff") GREENIDGE.—B Bridgetown (Barbados) 26/5/1948. RHB, LBG. Debut 1966–67 for Barbados in Shell Shield Tournament. Debut for county 1968. Cap 1970. Scored 1,305 runs (av 29.65) in 1970. HS: 205 Barbados v Jamaica (Bridgetown) 1966–67. HS in England: 172 v Middlesex (Hove) 1970. BB: 7–124 Barbados v Jamaica (Bridgetown) 1966–67. Career record: 2,408 runs (av 26.46), 7 centuries, 13 wkts (av 50.15).

Anthony William ("Tony") GREIG (Queen's College, Queenstown). B Queenstown, South Africa. 6/10/1946. Very tall (6 ft 7½ ins). RHB, RM. Good field in any position. Debut for Border in 1965–66 Currie Cup Competition. Debut for Sussex 1966. Cap 1967. Elected Best Young Cricketer of the Year in 1967 by the Cricket Writers' Club. Tests: 3 v

Rest of World 1970. 1,000 runs (4)—1,305 runs (av 26.10) in 1968 best. Scored two centuries in match for L. C. Steven's XI v Cambridge U (Eastbourne) 1966—a match not regarded as first-class. Took 3 wkts in 4 balls v Hants (Hove) 1967. Has won "Man of the Match" award in Gillette Cup Competition on three occasions. HS: 156 v Lancs (Hove) 1967 in debut match in championship. BB: 8–25 v Glos (Hove) 1967. Career record: 5,566 (av 26.25), 6 centuries, 311 wkts (av 27.46).

Mike Grenville GRIFFITH (Marlborough and Cambridge).—B Beaconsfield 25/11/1943. RHB, occasional WK. Son of S. C. Griffith. Debut 1962. Blue 1963, 1964 and 1965. Cap 1967. Appointed county captain during 1968 season following resignation of J. M. Parks. Blues for hockey and racquets 1963 and 1964. Appointed hockey captain for 1965 but was unable to play in University match owing to foot injury sustained on M.C.C. tour to South America. First player to play international hockey (G.B. v Belgium 1967–68) and first-class cricket at Lord's. Scored 1,144 runs (av 30.10) in 1964. HS: 158 v Cambridge U (Hove) 1969. Career record: 6,244 runs (av 23.92), 2 centuries, 214 dismissals (195 ct 19 st), 1 wkt. (av 16.00).

Udaykumar Chhaganlal JOSHI.—B Rajkot, India 23/12/1944. RHB, OB. Debut for Saurashtra in Ranji Trophy 1965–66 taking wicket with first ball in first-class cricket. Subsequently played for Railways and Gujerat, and for West Zone in Duleep Trophy. Debut for county 1970. One match v Jamaica XI (Hove) and also played for Rest of World XI v T. N. Pearce's XI (Scarborough). Is qualified for championship matches in 1971. HS: 61 Gujerat v Saurashtra (Surat) 1968–69. BB: 6–54 Saurashtra v Gujerat (Vallabh Vidyanagar) 1966–67. Career record: 438 runs (av 12.51), 145 wkts (av 22.57).

Richard James LANGRIDGE (Brighton, Hove and Sussex G.S.).—B Brighton 13/4/1939. LHB, OB. Son of late James Langridge. Joined county staff 1955. Debut 1957. Cap 1961. Left staff after 1966 season to train as a teacher. Re-appeared in 1970. 1,000 runs (4)—1,885 runs (av 30.90) in 1962 best. Held 42 catches in 1961 and 41 catches in 1962. HS: 137* v Leics (Leicester) 1963. Career record: 8,194 runs (av 23.21), 5 centuries.

Leslie John LENHAM (Worthing H.S.).—B Worthing 24/5/1936. RHB, OB. Joined staff 1952. Debut 1956. Cap 1957. Joint benefit (£6,300) with G. C. Cooper in 1969. Is now county coach. 1,000 runs (6)—2,016 runs (av 32.51) in 1961 best. HS: 191* v Warwickshire (Birmingham) 1963. Career record: 12,796 runs (av 26.16), 7 centuries, 6 wkts (av 51.00).

Alan William MANSELL.—B Redhill 19/5/1951. RHB, reserve WK. Debut 1969. HS: 8 v Jamaica XI (Hove) 1970. Career record: 17 runs (av 4.25), 11 dismissals (10 ct 1 st).

James Michael ("Jim") PARKS (Hove County G.S.).—B Haywards Heath 21/10/1931. Son of J. H. Parks. RHB, LB, WK. Debut 1949. Cap 1951. Acted as wicket-keeper for some matches in 1958 and took over the position regularly in 1959. Benefit (£9,400) in 1964. Appointed county captain in 1967, but resigned post during 1968 season. "Wisden 1967". Tests: 46 between 1954 and 1967–68. Tours: Pakistan 1955–56, South Africa 1956–57 (returned home ill after first match) and 1964–65, New Zealand 1960–61, India 1963–64, Australia and New Zealand 1965–66, West Indies 1967–68. Went out to West Indies as coach 1959–60 and played in last two matches of M.C.C. tour. 1,000 runs (17) 2,314 runs (av 42.07) in 1955 and 2,313 runs (av 51.40) in 1959 best. Scored century in each innings (101 and 100*) v Worcs (Worcester) 1957. Completed 30,000 runs in 1968. Dismissed 93 batsmen (86 ct 7 st) in 1959 and also (89 ct 4 st) in 1961. Has twice won "Man of the Match" award in Gillette Cup Competition. HS: 205* v Somerset (Hove) 1955. BB: 3–23 v Cambridge U (Hove) 1956. Soccer (IR) for Haywards Heath. Career record: 32,672 runs (av 35.28), 50 centuries, 1,057 dismissals (977 ct 80 st), 51 wkts (av 43.25).

Christopher Paul PHILLIPSON (Ardingly College).—B Brindabar, India 10/2/1952. RHB, RM. Debut 1970. One match v Jamaica XI (Hove) Career record: 1 run (av 0.50), 1 wkt (av 56.00).

John Augustine SNOW (Christ's Hospital).—B Peopleton (Worcs) 13/10/1941. RHB, RF. Debut 1961. Cap 1964. Tests: 30 between 1965 and 1970. Shared in 10th wkt partnership of 128 with K. Higgs v West Indies (Oval) 1966—only 2 runs short of record 10th wkt partnership in Test cricket. Tours: West Indies 1967–68, Ceylon and Pakistan 1968–69, Australia 1970–71. 100 wkts (2)—126 wkts (av 19.09) in 1966 best. HS: 71 v Somerset (Eastbourne) 1966. BB: 7–29 v West Indians (Hove) 1966. Career record: 1,960 runs (av 11.73), 723 wkts (av 21.54).

Eknath Dhondu SOLKAR.—B Bombay 18/3/1948. LHB, LM/SLA. Debut 1965–66 for Vazir Sultan Colts XI v Hyderabad XI in Moin-ud-Dowla Gold Cup Tournament at Hyderabad. Debut for Bombay 1966–67 and has played continuously for state since. Debut for county in one match v New Zealanders (Hove) in 1969. Played only for 2nd XI in 1970, and cannot play in championship or one-day matches until 1973 owing to signing of U. C. Joshi. Tests: 5 for India v New Zealand and Australia 1969–70. Tour: India to West Indies 1970–71. HS: 145* West Zone v North Zone (Bombay) 1968–69. BB: 6–38 Bombay v Saurashtra (Jamnagar) 1966–67 and 6–38 State Bank of India XI v Dungarpur XI (Hyderabad) 1967–68. Career record: 1,607 runs (av 30.32), 2 centuries, 120 wkts (av 24.96).

John SPENCER (Brighton, Hove and Sussex G.S. and Cambridge).—B Brighton 6/10/1949. RHB, RM. Debut 1969. Blue 1970. HS: 13* v Worcs (Eastbourne) 1970. BB: 5–50 v Essex (Eastbourne) 1970. Career record: 80 runs (av 4.70), 73 wkts (av 24.41).

Kenneth George ("Ken") SUTTLE (Worthing H.S.).—B Kensington 25/8/1928. LHB, SLA. Debut 1949. Cap 1952. Benefit (£5,500) in 1966. Developed into useful left-arm bowler in 1956. Played in 423 consecutive

Championship matches between August 1954 and July 1969, exceeding the previous record of 399 by J. Vine of Sussex between 1899 and 1914. Tour: West Indies 1953–54, but did not play in Tests. 1,000 runs (17)—2,326 runs (av 39.42) in 1962 best. Has won "Man of the Match" award in Gillette Cup Competition on three occasions. HS: 204* v Kent (Tunbridge Wells) 1962. BB: 6–64 v Worcs (Worcester) 1970. Played soccer for Chelsea and Brighton and Hove Albion. Later player manager with Arundel. Career record: 29,704 runs (av 31.03), 46 centuries, 262 wkts (av 32.48).

Norman Ian THOMSON.—B Walsall (Staffs) 23/1/1929. RHB, RM. Debut 1952. Cap 1953. Benefit (£6,089) in 1963. Retired after 1965 season. May re-appear in John Player League matches in 1971. Tours: Pakistan 1955–56 (flown out as replacement), South Africa 1964–65. Test: 5 v South Africa 1964–65. 100 wkts (12)—134 wkts (av 20.98) in 1961 best. HS: 77 v Leics (Leicester) 1959. BB: 10–49 (15–75 match) v Warwickshire (Worthing) 1964. Career record: 7,118 runs (av 14.76), 1,596 wkts (av 20.54).

N.B. The following players whose particulars appeared in the 1970 Annual are omitted: C. J. S. Bidwell, E. J. Lewis (left staff) and J. A. Lush. In addition the Nawab of Pataudi who re-appeared in four matches has not been included in view of the uncertainty over his appearing in 1971. R. N. P. Smyth, a right-hand batsman who made his debut in 1970 is also not included as he is unlikely to play again.

The Career records of Pataudi and Smyth will be found elsewhere in this Annual.

COUNTY AVERAGES

County Championship: Played 24, Won 5, Drawn 12, Lost 7
All First-Class Matches: Played 25, Won 5, Drawn 12, Lost 8

BATTING AND FIELDING

Cap		*M.*	*I.*	*N.O.*	*Runs*	*H.S.*	*Avge.*	100	50	*Ct.*	*St.*
1951	J. M. Parks	21	38	7	1300	166*	41.93	2	9	43	3
1967	M. A. Buss	22	42	5	1379	126	37.27	1	8	18	—
1957	L. J. Lenham	3	5	0	155	46	31.00	—	—	—	—
1970	G. A. Greenidge......	24	44	0	1305	172	29.65	5	3	10	—
1967	M. G. Griffith.........	23	38	10	811	74	28.96	—	5	12	—
1969	P. J. Graves	22	41	2	987	117*	25.30	1	6	22	—
1967	A. W. Greig	20	35	3	795	113*	24.84	1	5	26	—
1952	K. G. Suttle	24	39	6	752	80	22.78	—	5	9	—
1961	R. J. Langridge	23	40	4	765	66	21.25	—	4	18	—
1964	J. A. Snow	17	21	11	209	42*	20.90	—	—	11	—
—	J. Denman..............	10	15	6	133	34*	14.77	—	—	2	—
1963	A. Buss	24	31	3	404	57	14.42	—	1	10	—
1963	Nawab of Pataudi ...	4	8	0	113	28	14.12	—	—	3	—
1957	D. L. Bates	19	19	10	97	22*	10.77	—	—	6	—
—	R. N. P. Smyth	3	5	0	42	25	8.40	—	—	—	—
—	A. W. Mansell	3	4	1	16	8	5.33	—	—	8	1
—	J. Spencer	9	10	3	37	13*	5.28	—	—	4	—

Played in two matches: J. R. T. Barclay 4,0,0.
Played in one match: C. P. Phillipson 0, 1; U. C. Joshi 1,2.

BOWLING

	Type	Overs	Mdns	Runs	Wkts	Avge.	Best	5wI.	10wM
J. Spencer	RM	203.3	49	519	26	19.96	5/50	2	—
A. Buss	RFM	713.2	150	2113	88	24.01	6/54	5	—
A. W. Greig	RM	404.2	86	1255	48	26.14	7/74	2	—
J. A. Snow	RF	469.5	94	1274	48	26.54	5/18	2	—
M. A. Buss	LM	511	168	1399	45	31.08	7/58	2	—
K. G. Suttle	SLA	270.4	67	761	19	40.05	6/64	1	—
D. L. Bates	RFM	362.5	94	1058	26	40.69	5/76	1	—
J. Denman.......	RM	199.3	21	792	18	44.00	4/45	—	—

Also bowled: J. R. T. Barclay 17-2-56-0; P. J. Graves 10.4-2-33-0; G. A. Greenidge 53.3-6-220-4; M. G. Griffith 1-0-5-0; U. C. Joshi 29-11-80-0; C. P. Phillipson 16-3-56-1.

County Records

Highest Innings Totals:	For ...705–8d v Surrey (Hastings)......................	1902
	Agst...726 by Nottinghamshire (Nottingham)......	1895
Lowest Innings Totals:	For ... 19 v Surrey (Godalming)........................	1830
	19 v Nottinghamshire (Hove)	1873
	Agst... 18 by Kent (Gravesend)........................	1867
Highest Individual Inngs.:	For ...333 K. S. Duleepsinhji v Northants (Hove)	1930
	Agst...322 E. Paynter for Lancashire (Hove)..........	1937
Best bowling figs. in an Inngs.:	For ...10–48 C. H. G. Bland v Kent (Tonbridge)...	1899
	Agst... 9–11 A. P. Freeman for Kent (Hove)	1922
Best bowling figs. in a match:	For ...17–106 G. R. Cox v Warwicks (Horsham)...	1926
	Agst...17–67 A. P. Freeman for Kent (Hove)......	1922
Most runs in a season.........	2850 (av 64.77) John Langridge	1949
runs in a career............	34152 (av 37.69) John Langridge	1928–1955
100s in a season	12 by John Langridge..................	1949
100s in a career............	76 by John Langridge.........	1928–1955
wickets in a season	198 (av 13.45) M. W. Tate	1925
wickets in a career	2223 (av 16.34) M. W. Tate......	1912–1937

RECORD WICKET STANDS

1st 490	E. H. Bowley & John Langridge v Middlesex (Hove)......	1933
2nd 385	E. H. Bowley & M. W. Tate v Northamptonshire (Hove)	1921
3rd 298	K. S. Ranjitsinhji & E. H. Killick v Lancashire (Hove) ...	1901
4th 326*	G. Cox & James Langridge v Yorkshire (Leeds)............	1949
5th 297	J. H. Parks & H. W. Parks v Hampshire (Portsmouth) ...	1937
6th 255	K. S. Duleepsinhji & M. W. Tate v Northamptonshire (Hove)..	1930
7th 344	K. S. Ranjitsinhji & W. Newham v Essex (Leyton).........	1902
8th 229*	C. L. A. Smith & G. Brann v Kent (Hove).....................	1902
9th 178	H. W. Parks & A. F. Wensley v Derbyshire (Horsham)	1930
10th 156	G. R. Cox & H. R. Butt v Cambridge U (Cambridge)......	1908

Home Matches in Championship

Surrey (Hove)—Surrey 298 (Stewart 128) and 178–3d (Edrich 80, Edwards 72). Sussex 201 (Greig 52) and 170–5 (Suttle 60*, Graves 58). *Match drawn.* (*Surrey* 8 *bonus points, Sussex* 6 *bonus points.*)

Notts (Hove)—S 306–4d (Greenidge 126, Buss, M. 75) and 87 (Stead 7–36). N 237 (Greig 7–74) and 140 (Taylor 64, Snow 5–53). *S* (10 *points*) *won by* 16 *runs.* (*S* 8 *bonus points, N* 4 *bonus points.*)

Glam (Hove)—S 171 (Parks 56, Williams 6–57) and 303–5d (Buss, M. 74, Greenidge 69, Parks 64*). G 208 (Walker 57, Buss, A. 4–40, Greig 4–61) and 157 (Greig 4–33). *S* (10 *points*) *won by* 109 *runs.* (*S* 5 *bonus points, G* 7 *bonus points.*)

Hants (Hove)—H 202 (White 57, Stephenson 50*, Buss, A. 6–80) and 239 (Livingstone 54, Bates 5–76). S 292 (Langridge 66, Graves 61, Buss, A. 57 Cottam 7–106) and 151–3 (Graves 54, Parks 53*). *S* (10 *points*) *won by* 7 *wickets.* (*S* 9 *bonus points, H* 5 *bonus points.*)

Warwicks (Hove)—W 277 (Kanhai 162*, Snow 4–72) and 121 (Buss. A. 6–54). S 352–8d (Parks 166*, Griffith 59, Brown 4–117) and 48–3. *S* (10 *points*) *won by* 7 *wickets.* (*S* 10 *bonus points, W* 7 *bonus points.*)

Worcs (Eastbourne)—S 131 (Graves 65, Holder 6–27) and 211 (Suttle 58, Holder 5–60). W 198 (Yardley 94) and 145–0 (Headley 103*). *W* (10 *points*) *won by* 10 *wickets.* (*S* 3 *bonus points, W* 5 *bonus points.*)

Glos (Hove)—S 172 (Greenidge 58, Procter 4–39) and 326–8d (Greenidge 104, Greig 59, Langridge 54). G 249 (Green 66, Buss, A. 5–74) and 161–5 (Nicholls 60, Green 56). *Match drawn.* (*S* 5 *bonus points, G* 8 *bonus points.*)

Essex (Eastbourne)—S 320–6d (Parks 150, Turner 4–68) and 138–9d. E 194 (Barker 50, Spencer 5–50) and 153–4 (Edmeades 61, Ward 54, Spencer 4–31). *Match drawn.* (*S* 8 *bonus points, E* 2 *bonus points*).

Kent (Hove)—K 308–7d (Luckhurst 80, Cowdrey 77, Brown 52) and 5–0. S 154 (Shepherd 5–45) and 158 (Brown 5–35). *K* (10 *points*) *won by* 10 *wickets.* (*S* 3 *bonus points, K* 10 *bonus points.*)

Lancs (Hove)—L 316–8d (Engineer 89) and 224–4d (Simmons 112, Pilling 63*). S 310 (Graves 75, Griffith 73, Buss, M. A. 51, Hughes 5–81) and 215–8 (Buss, M. A. 91, Lever 4–42). *Match drawn.* (*S* 6 *bonus points, L* 7 *bonus points.*)

Som (Hove)—Som 222 (Virgin 109, Greig 5–64, Buss, M. A. 4–62) and 54 (Snow 5–18, Buss, A. 4–27). S 327–5d (Buss, M. A. 126, Greenidge 111) *S* (10 *points*) *won by an innings and* 51 *runs.* (*S* 12 *bonus points, Som* 4 *bonus points.*)

Middx (Hove)—S 375–5d (Greenidge 172, Suttle 72, Buss, M. A. 70) and 122–6. M 211 (Russell 53) and 379–5d (Smith, M. J. 140, Russell 69, Radley 66*, Featherstone 60). *Match drawn.* (*S* 14 *bonus points, M* 4 *bonus points.*)

WARWICKSHIRE

Formation of present club: 1884.
Colours: Blue, yellow and white.
Badge: Bear and ragged staff.
County Champions (2): 1911 and 1951.
Gillette Cup Winners (2): 1966 and 1968.
Gillette Cup Finalists: 1964.

Secretary.—L. T. Deakins, County Ground, Edgbaston, Birmingham, B5 7QU.
Captain.—A. C. Smith.

Robert Neal ABBERLEY (Saltley G.S.).—B Birmingham 22/4/1944. RHB, OB. Good outfield. Debut 1964. Cap 1966. Tour: Pakistan 1966–67 (returning home early owing to injury). 1,000 runs (3)—1,315 runs (av 28.58) in 1966 best. HS: 117* v Essex (Birmingham) 1966. Career record: 5,455 runs (av 24.90), 2 centuries.

Dennis Leslie AMISS.—B Birmingham 7/4/1943. RHB, SLA. Joined county staff 1958. Debut 1960. Cap 1965. Tests: 6 between 1966 and 1970 Tour: Pakistan 1966–67. 1,000 runs (6)—1,850 runs (av 54.51) in 1967 best. Has won "Man of the Match" award twice in Gillette Cup Competition. HS: 176* v Notts (Coventry) 1967. BB: 3–21 v Middlesex (Lord's) 1970. Career record: 11,624 runs (av 35.01), 16 centuries, 14 wkts (av 34.07).

William ("Bill") BLENKIRON.—B Newfield (Co. Durham) 21/7/1942. RHB, RFM. Debut 1964. Cap 1969. HS: 62 v Worcs (Dudley) 1969. BB: 5–37 v Leics (Leicester) 1968. Soccer for Spennymoor United (Northern League). Career record: 1,072 runs (av 13.74), 233 wkts (av 26.79).

David John ("Dave") BROWN (Queen Mary G.S. Walsall).—B Walsall 30/1/1942. RHB, RFM. Debut 1961. Cap 1964. Tests: 28 between 1965 and 1970. Tours: South Africa 1964–65, Australia and New Zealand 1965–66, Pakistan 1966–67 (vice-captain) West Indies 1967–68, Ceylon and Pakistan 1968–69. Took 86 wkts (av 19.16) in 1964. HS: 69 M.C.C. v Natal (Durban) 1964–65. HS in England: 60 v Glos (Birmingham) 1969. BB: 8–64 v Sussex (Birmingham) 1964. Career record: 2,646 runs (av 12.84), 710 wkts (av 24.18).

Barry John FLICK.—B Coventry 5/3/1952. RHB, WK. Debut 1969 (two matches). Not re-engaged after 1969 season, and did not play in 1970. Has re-joined staff for 1971. Career record: 1 run (av 1.00).

Lancelot Richard ("Lance") GIBBS.—B Georgetown (British Guiana) 29/9/1934. Cousin of C. H. Lloyd. RHB, OB. Good close field. Debut 1953–54 for British Guiana v M.C.C. and played regularly for country (now Guyana) since. Has played as a professional for Burnley and for Whitburn in Durham Senior League. Debut for county in 1967 and also played for Rest of World XI. Qualified for Championship matches in 1968.

Cap 1968. Played for South Australia in Sheffield Shield competition in 1969–70. Returned to Guyana 1970–71 to play against India. Tests: 54, 50 for West Indies between 1957–58 and 1969 and 4 for Rest of World in 1970. Tours: West Indies to India and Pakistan in 1958–59, Australia 1960–61, England 1963, 1966 and 1969 (vice-captain) India and Ceylon 1966–67, Australia and New Zealand 1968–69 (vice-captain). "Hat-trick" West Indies v Australia (Adelaide) 1960–61 after taking 3 wkts in 4 balls in previous Test at Sydney. HS: 43 West Indians v Combined XI (Hobart) 1960–61. HS in England: 31 West Indians v Cambridge U (Cambridge) 1963. BB: 8–37 v Glamorgan (Birmingham) 1970 and 8–38 West Indies v India (Bridgetown) 1961–62. Career record: 1,273 runs (av 8.54), 659 wkts (av 27.37).

Alan GORDON (King Henry VIII School, Coventry).—B Coventry 29/3/1944. RHB. Slip field. Debut 1966. HS: 65 v Surrey (Oval) 1970. Career record: 849 runs (av 16.32).

John Denis GRAY (Woodlands Comprehensive School, Coventry).—B Coventry 9/10/1948. LHB, LM. Played for M.C.C. Schools v Combined Services (Lord's) 1968. Debut 1968 taking 5–2 in first innings of first match v Scotland (Birmingham). Did not play in 1970. HS: 18 v Surrey (Birmingham) 1969. BB: 5–2 as above. Plays rugger. Is student at Loughborough College of Physical Education. Career record: 34 runs (av 11.33), 21 wkts (av 25.42).

Edward Ernest ("Eddie") HEMMINGS (Campion School, Leamington Spa).—B Leamington Spa 20/2/1949. RHB, RM. Debut 1966. HS: 54 v Middlesex (Lord's) 1970. BB: 6–90 v Hants (Basingstoke) 1968. Career record: 756 runs (av 21.60), 58 wkts (av 36.48).

Khalid ("Billy") IBADULLA (Mezang H.S. Lahore).—B Lahore 20/12/1935. RHB, RM/OB. Can keep wicket. Debut for Pakistan touring team in India 1952–53. Debut for Warwicks 1954. Cap 1957. Toured Pakistan with Commonwealth team 1963–64. Tests: 4 for Pakistan between 1964–65 and 1967. Scored 166 on debut in Test cricket v Australia (Karachi) and shared in 1st wkt partnership record for Pakistan in Test cricket. 249 with Abdul Kadir. Played for Otago in Plunket Shield Competition from 1964–65 to 1966–67 whilst coaching in New Zealand. Played for Tasmania v M.C.C. 1970–71 whilst coaching there. Benefit (£7,797) in 1969. 1,000 runs (6)—2,098 runs (av 33.83) in 1962 best. Was dismissed obstructing the field v Hants (Coventry) 1963. Won "Man of the Match" award twice in successive matches in Gillette Cup Competition in 1965, taking 6–32 in second match v Hants (Birmingham). HS: 171 v Oxford U (Oxford) 1961. Scored 170* v Surrey (Oval) 1960, sharing in 1st wkt partnership record for county, 377* with N. F. Horner. Shared in record partnership for county for any wkt, 402 for 4th wkt with R. B. Kanhai v Notts (Nottingham) 1968. BB: 7–22 v Derbyshire (Chesterfield) 1967. Career record: 16,299 runs (av 27.48), 22 centuries, 424 wkts (av 30.73).

John Alexander JAMESON (Taunton School).—B Bombay 30/6/1941.

RHB, OB. Good field in covers, who was outstanding player at school. Debut 1960. Cap 1964. 1,000 runs (7)—1,821 runs (av 38.74) in 1970 best. "Hat-trick" v Glos (Birmingham) 1965. HS: 194 v Cambridge U (Cambridge) 1970. BB: 3-4 v Cambridge U (Cambridge) 1970. Plays rugger, soccer and hockey. Career record: 9,528 runs (av 30.15), 11 centuries, 39 wkts (av 36.87).

Thomas Edward Neville ("Tom") JAMESON (Taunton School and Cambridge).—B Bombay 23/7/1946. LHB, RM. Younger brother of J. A. Jameson. Debut for University and county 1970. Blue 1970. HS: 32 Warwickshire v Cambridge U (Birmingham) 1970. Hockey blue 1970. Career record: 181 runs (av 12.06), 10 wkts (av 53.10).

Alan Keith Colin JONES (Solihull School).—B Solihull 20/4/1951. RHB. Debut 1969 (one match v Scotland) whilst still at school. Played in M.C.C. Schools matches at Lord's in 1969 and 1970. HS: 35 v Scotland (Birmingham) 1969. Career record: 46 runs (av 23.00).

Rohan Babulal KANHAI.—B Port Mourant, Berbice, British Guiana 26/12/1935. RHB, LB. Former WK. Debut for British Guiana (now Guyana) 1954–55. Played for Western Australia in Sheffield Shield Competition in 1961–62. Played league cricket for Aberdeenshire, Blackpool and Ashington. Debut for county and cap 1968. Played for Tasmania 1969–70 whilst coaching. Returned to Guyana 1970–71 to play against India. Tests: 66, 61 for West Indies between 1957 and 1968–69, all consecutive since 1st Test v England 1957, sequence being broken by his returning to England at end of Australian tour to undergo cartilage operation, and 5 for Rest of World 1970. Tours: West Indies to England 1957, 1963 and 1966, India and Pakistan 1958–59, Australia 1960–61, India and Ceylon 1966–67, Australia 1968–69. 1,000 runs (6)—1,894 runs (av 57.39) in 1970 best. Also scored over 1,000 runs in India and Pakistan 1958–59 and in Australia 1960–61. Scored two centuries in Test match (117 and 115) v Australia (Adelaide) 1960–61. HS 256 West Indies v India (Calcutta) 1958–59. HS in England: 253 v Notts (Nottingham) 1968 sharing in record partnership for county for any wkt, 402 with K. Ibadulla. Career record: 18,330 runs (av 48.23), 52 centuries, 9 wkts (av 58.33).

Peter John LEWINGTON.—B Finchampstead, Berks 30/1/1950. RHB, OB. Played for Berkshire from 1967 to 1969. Debut 1970. HS: 7 v Surrey (Oval) 1970. BB: 4-39 v Glos (Gloucester) 1970. Plays soccer. Career record: 12 runs (av 12.00), 19 wkts (av 24.31).

James Ian ("Jamie") McDOWALL (Rugby School and Cambridge).—B Sutton Coldfield 9/12/1947. Son of Hon. Treasurer of County Club. RHB, WK. Debut 1969 for both university and county. Blue 1969. HS: 62 Cambridge U v Leics (Cambridge) 1969. Career record: 627 runs (av 16.50), 42 dismissals (40 ct 2 st).

Norman Michael McVICKER (Stand G.S., Whitefield, Manchester).—B Manchester 4/11/1940. RHB, RFM. Played for Lincolnshire from 1963 to 1968, and was captain in 1967–68. Debut for Minor Counties v South

Africans (Jesmond) 1965. Debut for county 1969. HS: 44* v Glamorgan (Swansea) 1969. BB: 7–29 v Northants (Birmingham) 1969. Career record: 431 runs (av 14.36), 114 wkts (av 27.94).

Stephen John ("Mic") ROUSE (Moseley County School).—B Merthyr Tydfil, Glamorgan 20/1/1949. LHB, LM. Debut 1970 (two matches). HS: 9 v Middlesex (Lord's) 1970. BB: 4–34 v Oxford U (Oxford) 1970. Plays rugger, hockey and basketball. Career record: 9 runs (av 9.00), 4 wkts (av 16.75).

Alan Christopher SMITH (King Edward's, Birmingham and Oxford).—B Hall Green, Birmingham 25/10/1936. RHB, WK. Occasional RM. Played for county 2nd XI while still at school. Debut 1958. Cap 1961. Blue 1958, 1959 and 1960 (captain in 1959 and 1960). Appointed county captain in 1968 and Test Selector in 1969. Tests (6): 4 v Australia and 2 v New Zealand 1962–63. Tours: Canada 1959, Australia and New Zealand 1962–63. Scored 1,201 runs (av 31.60) and dismissed 82 batsmen (79 ct 3 st) in 1962. Scored two centuries in match (145 and 124) for Oxford U v Hants (Bournemouth) 1959. Shared in 9th wkt partnership of 163* with M. C. Cowdrey v New Zealand (Wellington) 1962–63—record 9th wkt partnership for England in Test cricket. "Hat-trick" v Essex (Clacton) 1965—probably the only instance in first class cricket by a wicket-keeper taking off his pads and going on to bowl. HS: 145 as above. BB: 5–32 (9–77 in match) Oxford U v Free Foresters (Oxford) 1960. Career record: 9 631 runs (av 21.26), 3 centuries, 713 dismissals (655 ct 58 st). 37 wkts (av 22.00).

Michael John Knight ("Mike") SMITH (Stamford School and Oxford).—B Broughton Astley (Leics) 30/6/1933. RHB. Good close field. Plays in glasses. Debut for Leicestershire 1951. Cap 1955. Blue 1954, 1955 and 1956 (captain in last year). Created record by scoring three centuries in University match including 201* in 1954. Debut for Warwicks 1956. Cap 1957. County captain from 1957 to 1967. Retired after 1967 season but returned to play regularly in 1970. "Wisden 1959". Tests: 47 between 1958 and 1966 captaining England in 25 Test matches. Tours: West Indies 1959–60. India and Pakistan 1961–62 (vice-captain) India 1963–64 (captain) South Africa 1964–65 (captain) Australia and New Zealand 1965–66 (captain). 1,000 runs (15)—3,245 runs (av 57.94) in 1959 best. Also scored 1,000 runs (1,079 runs, av 46.91) in Australia and New Zealand 1965–66. Scored 1,209 runs in July 1959. Held 6 catches in innings v Leics (Hinckley) 1962. Held 52 catches for Warwicks in 1961—county record. Won "Man of the Match" award in Gillette Cup Competition twice in 1964. Blue and England cap for rugger. HS: 204 Commonwealth XI v Natal (Durban) 1960–61. HS in England: 201* Oxford U v Cambridge U (Lord's) 1954. Career record: 33.524 runs (av 42.01), 58 centuries, 5 wkts (av 59.60).

Chilton Richard Vernon TAYLOR (Birkenhead School).—B Birkenhead 3/10/1951. RHB, WK. Played for M.C.C. Schools at Lord's and for Cheshire in both 1969 and 1970. Debut 1970. One match v Cambridge U (Birmingham). Is now studying at Trinity College, Cambridge. Career record: 2 dismissals (2 ct).

Warwick Nigel TIDY (John Wilmott G.S., Sutton Coldfield).—B Birmingham 10/2/1953. RHB, LBG. Named after, but not related to, Warwick Armstrong, the former Australian cricketer. Debut 1970, aged 17¼. HS: 7* v Sussex (Hove), v Surrey (Oval) and v Middlesex (Lord's) 1970. BB: 5–24 v Leics (Nuneaton) 1970. Career record: 52 runs (av 4.33), 48 wkts (av 31.12).

Bryan Stanley Valentine TIMMS.—B Ropley (Hants) 17/12/1940. RHB, WK. Debut for Hants 1959. Cap 1963. Left staff after 1968 season and made debut for Warwickshire in 1969. Dismissed 77 batsmen (58 ct 19 st) in 1964 and 79 batsmen (73 ct 6 st) in 1965. HS: 120 Hants v Oxford U (Oxford) 1966. Career record: 3,519 runs (av 15.70), 1 century, 499 dismissals (435 ct 64 st).

Graham Sydney WARNER (Darlaston G.S.).—B Darlaston (Staffs) 21/11/1945. RHB, OB. Outfield. Debut 1966. HS: 118* v Scotland (Birmingham) 1968. Career record: 900 runs (av 24.32), 2 centuries.

N.B. The following players who appeared in the 1970 Annual have been omitted: R. W. Barber, M. G. Bayley, T. W. Cartwright (joined Somerset by special registration in 1970 and his particulars will be found under that county), D. R. Cook, A. J. Cross, K. F. Flaherty and W. J. Stewart (joined Northants by special registration in 1970 and his particulars will be found under that county).

The career records of Cartwright and Stewart will be found elsewhere in this Annual.

COUNTY AVERAGES

County Championship: Played 24, Won 7, Drawn 11, Lost 6
All First-Class Matches: Played 27, Won 8, Drawn 13, Lost 6

BATTING AND FIELDING

Cap		*M.*	*I.*	*N.O.*	*Runs*	*H.S.*	*Avge.*	100	50	*Ct.*	*St.*
1968	R. B. Kanhai	15	26	3	1529	187*	66.47	6	4	20	—
1965	D. L. Amiss	24	42	9	1476	110	44.72	1	8	24	—
1957	M. J. K. Smith	26	48	7	1644	153*	40.09	2	11	22	—
1964	J. A. Jameson	27	50	3	1821	194	38.74	4	9	16	—
—	G. S. Warner	6	10	3	249	102	35.57	1	—	1	—
—	E. E. Hemmings	12	17	7	354	54	35.40	—	1	8	—
1966	R. N. Abberley	25	47	1	1212	108	26.34	1	6	15	—
1957	K. Ibadulla	21	35	4	725	81	23.38	—	3	22	—
—	A. Gordon	10	18	1	366	65	21.52	—	3	10	—
1969	W. Blenkiron	24	32	9	379	52*	16.47	—	1	12	—
—	B. S. V. Timms	8	11	0	151	35	13.72	—	—	10	2
—	N. M. McVicker	15	17	6	148	38	13.45	—	—	5	—
1961	A. C. Smith	19	29	6	309	42*	13.43	—	—	38	3
—	P. J. Lewington	4	2	1	12	7	12.00	—	—	1	—
1964	D. J. Brown	19	27	2	247	33	9.88	—	—	14	—
1968	L. R. Gibbs	18	19	5	76	20*	5.42	—	—	14	—
—	W. N. Tidy	20	21	9	52	7*	4.33	—	—	10	—

Played in two matches: S. J. Rouse 9.

Played in one match: T. E. N. Jameson 31, 32 (1 ct); C. R. V. Taylor did not bat (2 ct).

BOWLING

	Type	Overs	Mdns	Runs	Wkts	Avge.	Best	5wI.	10wM
D. J. Brown	RFM	580.1	117	1693	70	24.18	5/58	1	—
P. J. Lewington	OB	175	52	462	19	24.31	4/39	—	—
W. Blenkiron ...	RFM	806.5	219	2038	76	26.81	5/89	1	—
W. N. Tidy	LBG	535.2	120	1494	48	31.12	5/24	3	—
K. Ibadulla	RM/OB	319.3	51	949	30	31.63	4/21	—	—
L. R. Gibbs......	OB	698.3	229	1600	50	32.00	8/37	2	—
J. A. Jameson .	OB	145	26	435	11	39.54	3/4	—	—
N. M. McVicker	RFM	441.2	86	1459	34	42.91	5/16	1	—
E. E. Hemmings	RM	228	70	634	14	45.28	4/88	—	—

Also bowled: R. N. Abberley 10-0-32-0; D. L. Amiss 24-8-70-4; A. Gordon 0.4-0-1-0; T. E. N. Jameson 20-7-75-0; R. B. Kanhai 1.2-0-15-0; S. J. Rouse 33-10-67-4; A. C. Smith 25-2-84-1; M. J. K. Smith 3.3-1-12-0; G. S. Warner 3-0-10-0.

County Records

Highest Innings Totals: For ...657–6d v Hampshire (Birmingham).........1899
Agst...887 by Yorkshire (Birmingham)...............1896

Lowest Innings Totals: For ... 16 v Kent (Tonbridge) 1913
Agst... 15 by Hampshire (Birmingham) 1922

Highest Individual Inngs.: For ...305* F. R. Foster v Worcestershire (Dudley) 1914
Agst...316 R. H. Moore for Hants (Bournemouth) 1937

Best bowling figs in an Inngs.: For ...10–41 J. D. Bannister v Combined Services (Birmingham) 1959
Agst...10–36 H. Verity for Yorkshire (Leeds) 1931

Best bowling figs. in a match: For ...15–76 S. Hargreave v Surrey (The Oval)......1903
Agst...17–92 A. P. Freeman for Kent (Folkestone) 1932

Most runs in a season......... 2417 (av 60.42) M. J. K. Smith.........1959
runs in a career............34172 (av 35.31) W. G. Quaife ...1894–1928
100s in a season .... 8 by R. E. S. Wyatt..................1937
100s in a career .... 71 by W. G. Quaife............1894–1928
wickets in a season ...... 180 (av 15.13) W. E. Hollies 1946
wickets in a career ...... 2201 (av 20.45) W. E. Hollies ...1932–1957

RECORD WICKET STANDS

1st	377*	N. F. Horner & K. Ibadulla v Surrey (The Oval)............1960
2nd	344	J. Devey & S. P. Kinneir v Derbyshire (Birmingham)......1900
3rd	327	S. P. Kinneir & W. G. Quaife v Lancashire (Birmingham) 1901
4th	402	R. B. Kanhai & K. Ibadulla v Notts (Nottingham) 1968
5th	268	W. Quaife & W. G. Quaife v Essex (Leyton)..................1900
6th	220	H. E. Dollery & J. Buckingham v Derbyshire (Derby)...1938
7th	250	H. E. Dollery & J. S. Ord v Kent (Maidstone)...............1953
8th	228	A. J. Croom & R. E. S. Wyatt v Worcestershire (Dudley) 1925
9th	154	G. W. Stephens & A. J. Croom v Derbyshire (Birmingham) 1925
10th	128	F. R. Santall & W. Sanders v Yorkshire (Birmingham) ...1930

Home Matches in Championship

Essex (Edgbaston)—W 327–6d (Jameson 73, Kanhai 69, Amiss 67) and 134–6d (Jameson 60*). E 268–5d (Edmeades 102, Fletcher 58*, Saville 50) and 185–9 (Taylor 85, Barker 51*, Blenkiron 4–44, Gibbs 4–72). *Match drawn.* (*W* 7 *bonus points, E* 5 *bonus points*).

Glam (Edgbaston)—W 227 (Smith, M. J. K. 84, Amiss 67, Shepherd 5–41) and 188 (Kanhai 91, Shepherd 7–48). G 205 (Jones, A. 74, McVicker 4–37) and 135 (Gibbs 8–37). *W* (10 *points*) *won by* 75 *runs.* (*W* 7 *bonus points, G* 6 *bonus points.*)

Glos (Edgbaston)—G 318–6d (Phillips 82, Bissex 78*) and 167–1d (Nicholls 86*, Green 67). W 244–8d (Kanhai 55, Procter 4–73) and 66–2. *Match drawn.* (*W* 4 *bonus points. G* 7 *bonus points.*)

Leics (Nuneaton)—W 90 (Birkenshaw 5–33) and 178 (Smith, M. J. K. 59, Steele 5–43). L 143 (Marner 57, Tidy 5–24) and 128–2 (Marner 51*). *L* (10 *points*) *won by* 8 *wickets.* (*W* 5 *bonus points, L* 5 *bonus points.*)

Yorks (Edgbaston)—W 120 and 263 (Amiss 89*, Gordon 56). Y 203 (Padgett 61, Brown 4–50) and 181–7 (Padgett 75, Woodford 51, Ibadulla 4–21). *Y* (10 *points*) *won by* 3 *wickets.* (*W* 5 *bonus points, Y* 7 *bonus points.*)

Som (Edgbaston)—S 268–8d (Cartwright 63*) and 291–4d (Virgin 111, Clarkson 105, Robinson 50*, Lewington 4–82). W 279–5d (Abberley 108, Jameson 93) and 168–5 (Amiss 66). *Match drawn.* (*W* 8 *bonus points, S* 4 *bonus points.*)

Worcs (Edgbaston)—Warwicks 150 (Abberley 52, Holder 4–41) and 217–4 (Jameson 94). W 368 (Headley 108, Turner 106, Yardley 61, Blenkiron 5–89). *Match drawn.* (*Warwicks* 1 *bonus point, W* 9 *bonus points.*)

Notts (Edgbaston)—N 324–3d (Bolus 147*, Hassan 110) and 91–0 (Harris 54*). W 175–6d and 241–5 (Jameson 74, Smith, M. J. K. 74*). *W* (10 *points*) *won by* 5 *wickets.* (*W* 2 *bonus points, N* 7 *bonus points.*)

Derbys (Coventry)—W 295 (Kanhai 187*, Ward 6–69) and 177 (Amiss 58, Swarbrook 6–48). D 286 (Page 80) and 190–4. *D* (10 *points*) *won by* 6 *wickets.* (*W* 8 *bonus points, D* 7 *bonus points.*)

Lancs (Edgbaston)—W 186 (Blenkiron 52*, Shuttleworth 6–60) and 299–4d (Jameson 141*, Smith, M. J. K. 109). L 307 (Bond 76, Simmons 58, Lloyd, D. 54, Brown 4–66, Tidy 4–79) and 147. *W* (10 *points*) *won by* 31 *runs.* (*W* 4 *bonus points, L* 6 *bonus points*).

Hants (Edgbaston)—W 140 (Castell 4–24) and 229 (Kanhai 72, Abberley 53, Holder 5–36). H 218 (Greenidge 51, Brown 4–48) and 155–1 (Greenidge 62*, Richards 57). *H* (10 *points*) *won by* 9 *wickets.* (*W* 5 *bonus points, H* 7 *bonus points.*)

Northants (Edgbaston)—N 331–6d (Prideaux 64, Sharp 55*, Watts 55, Ackerman 53) and 195–4d (Lightfoot 77, Crump 65*). W 265 (Abberley 65, Crump 4–43, Sarfraz 4–48) and 262–6 (Smith, M. J. K. 70*). *W* (10 *points*) *won by* 4 *wickets.* (*W* 4 *bonus points, N* 5 *bonus points.*)

WORCESTERSHIRE

Formation of present club: 1865.
Colours: Dark green and black.
Badge: Shield, *Argent* bearing *Fess* between three *Pears Sable.*
County Champions (2): 1964 and 1965.
Gillette Cup Finalists (2): 1963 and 1966.

Secretary.—J. Lister, County Ground, New Road, Worcester, WR2 4QQ
Captain.—N. Gifford.

Roy BOOTH.—B Marsden (Yorks) 1/10/1926. RHB, WK. Played for Yorks 1951 to 1955, and gained regular place 1954 but was replaced by J. G. Binks in 1955. Debut for Worcs and cap 1956. Benefit (£6,240) in 1966. Retired after 1968 season, but re-appeared in four matches in 1970 through injury to G. R. Cass. Scored 1,042 runs (av 27.42) in 1959. Dismissed 101 batsmen (85 ct 16 st) in 1960 and 100 batsmen (91 ct 9 st) in 1964. HS: 113* v Sussex (Hove) 1959. Career record: 10,139 runs (av 18.91), 2 centuries, 1,124 dismissals (948 ct 176 st).

Brian Maurice BRAIN.—B Worcester 13/9/1940. RHB, RFM. Debut 1959. Left staff in 1960. Rejoined staff in 1963 and re-appeared in 1964. Cap 1966. HS: 38 v Glos (Cheltenham) 1964. BB: 6–38 v Notts (Nottingham) 1969. Career record: 497 runs (av 6.80), 288 wkts (av 26.06).

Robert George Mallaby CARTER (Nunthorpe G.S., York).—B Horden (Co. Durham) 11/7/1937. LHB, RFM. Debut 1961. Cap 1965. "Hat-trick" v Lancs (Worcester) 1965. HS: 23 v Leics (Leicester) 1967. BB: 6–7 v Lancs (Worcester) 1965. Career record: 260 runs (av 4.48), 410 wkts (av 24.74).

George Rodney CASS.—B Overton (Yorks) 23/4/1940. LHB, WK. Joined Essex staff in 1963 and made debut in 1964. Left staff after 1967 season and joined Worcs. Debut for county 1969. Cap 1970. Played for Tasmania against M.C.C. in 1970–71. HS: 104* Essex v Warwickshire (Birmingham) 1967. Career record: 2,601 runs (av 21.14), 1 century, 122 dismissals, (103 ct 19 st).

Basil Lewis D'OLIVEIRA.—B Cape Town 4/10/1931. RHB, RM/OB. Played for Middleton in Central Lancashire League from 1960 to 1963. Made first-class debut in Commonwealth tour of 1961–62 playing in two matches in Rhodesia. Took part in further tour of Rhodesia in 1962–63. Toured Pakistan with Commonwealth XI 1963–64. Joined Worcestershire in 1964, becoming eligible for Championship matches in 1965. Cap 1965. "Wisden 1966". Played for Kidderminster in Birmingham League whilst qualifying. Awarded M.B.E. in 1969 Birthday Honours List. Tests: 29 between 1966 and 1970. Tours: West Indies 1967–68 Ceylon and Pakistan 1968–69, Australia and New Zealand 1970–71. 1,000 runs (5)—1,691 runs (av 43.35) in 1965 best. HS: 174* v Indians (Worcester) 1967. BB: 6–29 v Hants (Portsmouth) 1968. Career record: 10,049 runs (av 40.19), 26 centuries, 292 wkts (av 27.22).

Norman GIFFORD.—B Ulverston (Lancs) 30/3/1940. LHB, SLA.

Joined staff 1958 and made debut 1960. Cap 1961. Appointed county captain in 1971 after being vice-captain since 1969. Tests: 2 v Australia 1964. 100 wkts (3)—133 wkts (av 19.66) in 1961 best. "Hat-trick" v Derbyshire (Chesterfield) 1965. HS: 89 v Oxford U (Oxford) 1963. BB: 8–28 v Yorks (Sheffield) 1968. Career record: 3,290 runs (av 12.60), 953 wkts (av 19.39).

Kevin GRIFFITH (Worcester R.G.S.).—B Warrington (Lancs) 17/1/1950. RHB, OB. Cover field. Debut 1967.HS: 27 v Hants (Worcester) 1969. BB: 7–41 v Oxford U (Oxford) 1969. Career record: 182 runs (av 9.57), 16 wkts (av 23.93).

Ronald George Alphonso ("Ron") HEADLEY.—B Kingston (Jamaica) 29/6/1939. Son of George Headley, leading West Indian batsman before the war. LHB, LB. Debut 1958. Cap 1961. Played for Jamaica in Shell Shield Competition in 1965–66. 1,000 runs (10)—2,040 runs (av 31.87) in 1961 best. HS: 150* v Somerset (Dudley) 1961. BB: 4–40 v Glamorgan (Worcester) 1963. Career record: 16,607 runs (av 29.70), 22 centuries, 12 wkts (av 48.16).

Edward John Orton HEMSLEY (Bridgnorth G.S.).—B Stoke-on-Trent 1/9/1943. RHB, RM. Cover point. Debut 1963. Cap 1969. HS: 138* v Oxford U (Oxford) 1969. BB: 3–23 v Essex (Worcester) 1968. Soccer (wing-half) for Shrewsbury Town and Sheffield United. Career record: 2,223 runs (av 26.46), 1 century, 25 wkts (av 29.60).

Vanburn Alonza ("Van") HOLDER.—B St. Michael (Barbados) 8/10/1945. RHB, RFM. Debut 1966–67 for Barbados in one match in Shell Shield Tournament. Debut for county 1968. Cap 1970. Returned to Barbados 1970–71 to play against India. Tests: 3 West Indies v England 1969. Tour: West Indies to England 1969. HS: 52 v Glos (Dudley) 1970. BB: 6–21 v Glamorgan (Neath) 1970. Career record: 562 runs (av 8.78), 234 wkts (av 23.36).

Joseph Alan ORMROD (Kirkcaldy H.S.).—B Ramsbottom (Lancs) 22/12/1942. RHB, OB. Slip field. Debut 1962. Cap 1966. Tour: Pakistan 1966–67. 1,000 runs (5)—1,466 runs (av 30.54) in 1968 best. HS: 155* v Notts (Kidderminster) 1970. Career record: 8,046 runs (av 27.00), 6 centuries, 4 wkts (av 76.50).

Douglas Norman Frank SLADE.—B Feckenham (Worcs) 24/8/1940. RHB, SLA. Joined county staff 1956. Debut 1958. Cap 1960. Benefit in 1971. Tour: Pakistan with Commonwealth team 1963–64. Took 97 wkts (av 19.83) in 1960. HS: 125 v Leics (Leicester) 1969. BB: 7–47 v Middlesex (Lord's) 1960. Career record: 4,753 runs (av 17.80), 1 century, 477 wkts (av 22.75).

David Ernest Robertson STEWART (Cathedral Boys H.S., Bombay).—B Bombay 22/5/1948. RHB, RM. Slip or cover field. Debut for Scotland 1969. Debut for county (two matches) 1970. HS: 51 Scotland v Warwickshire (Birmingham) 1969. Has been a skiing instructor in Scotland. Career record: 106 runs (av 15.14).

Glenn Maitland TURNER (Otago Boys' H.S.).—B Dunedin (New Zealand) 26/5/1947. RHB, OB. Slip or cover field. Debut for Otago in Plunket Shield Competition 1964–65 whilst still at school. Debut for county 1967. Cap 1968. Tests: 9 for New Zealand between 1968–69 and 1969–70. Tours: New Zealand to England 1969, India and Pakistan 1969–70, Australia 1969–70. Carried bat (43*) through second innings (131) of 2nd Test v England (Lord's) 1969. 1,000 runs (3)—2,379 runs (av 61.00) in 1970 best. Scored 10 centuries in 1970, a county record. HS: 167 Otago v Wellington (Dunedin) 1968–69. HS in England: 154* v Glos (Bristol) 1970. BB: 3–18 v Pakistanis (Worcester) 1967. Has played hockey for Worcs and had trial for Midlands. Career record: 6,941 runs (av 37.92), 15 centuries, 5 wkts (av 33.60).

Keith William WILKINSON.—B Stoke-on-Trent 15/1/1950. LHB, SLA. Debut 1969 (two matches). Did not play in 1970. HS: 3* v Glos (Cheltenham) 1969. Career record: 5 runs (av 2.50).

Thomas James YARDLEY.—B Chaddesley Corbett (Worcs) 27/10/1946. LHB, RM. Outfield. Debut 1967. HS: 94 v Sussex (Eastbourne) 1970. Career record: 1,307 runs (av 23.76).

N.B. The following players whose particulars appeared in the 1970 Annual are omitted: T. W. Graveney (retired and is now coach to Queensland Cricket Association) and J. Standen (not re-engaged).

The career records of both Graveney and Standen will be found elsewhere in this Annual.

COUNTY AVERAGES

County Championship: Played 24, Won 7, Drawn 16, Lost 1
All First-Class Matches: Played 25, Won 8, Drawn 16, Lost 1

BATTING AND FIELDING

Cap		*M.*	*I.*	*N.O.*	*Runs*	*H.S.*	*Avge.*	100	50	*Ct.*	*St.*
1962	T. W. Graveney	21	34	13	1316	114	62.66	2	9	18	—
1968	G. M. Turner	25	46	7	2379	154*	61.00	10	9	25	—
1965	B. L. D'Oliveira	15	24	3	934	111	44.47	3	3	4	—
1961	R. G. A. Headley	24	44	4	1670	148*	41.75	5	6	17	—
—	T. J. Yardley	18	26	7	762	94	40.10	—	6	9	—
1966	J. A. Ormrod	22	39	2	1228	155*	33.18	2	5	28	—
1969	E. J. O. Hemsley	11	19	4	404	52	26.93	—	1	7	—
1970	G. R. Cass	21	26	4	398	53	18.09	—	1	32	10
1960	D. N. F. Slade	19	21	3	286	38	15.88	—	—	9	—
1961	N. Gifford	25	24	9	218	38*	14.53	—	—	18	—
1962	J. A. Standen	18	18	2	209	92*	13.06	—	1	7	—
1970	V. A. Holder	23	20	5	158	52	10.53	—	1	10	—
1956	R. Booth	4	4	0	24	21	6.00	—	—	21	—
1965	R. G. M. Carter	19	10	6	16	7*	4.00	—	—	7	—
1966	B. M. Brain	7	6	6	7	5*	—	—	—	3	—

Played in two matches: D. E. R. Stewart 3,1,8.
Played in one match: K. Griffith did not bat.

WORCESTERSHIRE

BOWLING

	Type	Overs	Mdns	Runs	Wkts	Avge.	Best	5wI.	10wM
N. Gifford ...	SLA	965.5	331	2092	105	19.92	6/43	7	—
V. A. Holder.	RFM	707.3	141	1773	84	21.10	6/21	6	1
E.J.O.Hemsley	RM	68	13	204	7	29.14	2/26	—	—
D. N. F. Slade	SLA	296.4	94	732	24	30.50	4/25	—	—
B. M. Brain...	RFM	210	38	587	19	30.89	3/49	—	—
R.G.M.Carter	RFM	590.2	94	1850	53	34.90	6/49	2	—
J. A. Standen	RM	539.5	128	1432	40	35.80	3/44	—	—
B.L.D'Oliveira	RM/OB	230.4	79	488	11	44.36	2/20	—	—

Also bowled: T. W. Graveney 14-1-53-2; K. Griffith 27-5-86-1; J. A. Ormrod 32-8-101-1; G. M. Turner 4-1-19-1; T. J. Yardley 2-0-8-0.

County Records

Highest Innings Totals:	For ...633 v Warwickshire (Worcester)	1906
	Agst...701–4d by Leicestershire (Worcester)	1906
Lowest Innings Totals:	For ... 24 v Yorkshire (Huddersfield)	1903
	Agst... 30 by Hampshire (Worcester)	1903
Highest Individual Inngs.:	For ...276 F. L. Bowley v Hampshire (Dudley)	1914
	Agst...331* J.D.Robertson for Middx (Worcester)	1949
Best bowling figs in an Inngs.:	For ... 9–23 C. F. Root v Lancashire (Worcester)	1931
	Agst...10–51 J.Mercer for Glamorgan (Worcester)	1936
Best bowling figs. in a match:	For ...15–87 A. J. Conway v Gloucestershire (Moreton-in-the-Marsh)	1914
	Agst...17–212 J. C. Clay for Glamorgan (Swansea)	1937
Most runs in a season	2654 (av 52.03) H. H. Gibbons	1934
runs in a career	34490 (av 34.04) D. Kenyon	1946–1967
100s in a season	10 by G. M. Turner	1970
100s in a career	70 by D. Kenyon	1946–1967
wickets in a season	207 (av 17.52) C. F. Root	1925
wickets in a career	2143 (av 23.73) R. T. D. Perks	1930–1955

RECORD WICKET STANDS

1st 309	F. L. Bowley & H. K. Foster v Derbyshire (Derby)	1901
2nd 274	H. H. Gibbons & Nawab of Pataudi v Kent (Worcester)	1933
	H. H. Gibbons & Nawab of Pataudi v Glamorgan (Worcester)	1934
3rd 315	W. V. Fox & L. G. Crawley v Northamptonshire (Worcester)	1923
4th 277	H. H. Gibbons & B. W. Quaife v Middlesex (Worcester)	1931
5th 393	E. G. Arnold & W. B. Burns v Warwickshire (Birmingham)	1909
6th 195	G. N. Foster & J. A. Cuffe v Leicestershire (Worcester)	1913
7th 197	H. H. Gibbons & R. Howorth v Surrey (The Oval)	1938
8th 145*	F. Chester & W. H. Taylor v Essex (Worcester)	1914
9th 181	J. A. Cuffe & R. O. Burrows v Gloucestershire (Worcester)	1907
10th 119	W. B. Burns & G. A. Wilson v Somerset (Worcester)	1906

Home Matches in Championship

Surrey (Worcester)—S 370 (Edrich 143, Younis 73, Gifford 4–60) and 216–4d (Edrich 113*). W 368–5d (D'Oliveira 101, Turner 66, Yardley 57) and 213–8 (Turner 52, Storey 4–47). *Match drawn.* (*W* 6 *bonus points, S* 4 *bonus points.*)

Glam (Worcester)—G 328–7d (Jones, A. 144, Nash 61) and 136–3. W 176 (Headley 53, Nash 4–59) and 390–3d (Headley 133, Graveney 94*, Ormrod 76). *Match drawn.* (*W* 3 *bonus points, G* 9 *bonus points.*)

Derbys (Worcester)—D 325–6d (Smith, D. H. K. 98, Buxton 72) and 246–2d (Gibbs 112*, Buxton 61). W 342–7d (D'Oliveira 111, Turner 63, Graveney 62) and 158 (Ward 4–17). *D* (10 *points*) *won by* 71 *runs.* (*W* 5 *bonus points, D* 4 *bonus points.*)

Essex (Worcester)—E 237 (Barker 124, Holder 5–55) and 181–3d (Edmeades 66, Saville 65*). W 226–4d (Turner 122) and 193–4 (Turner 72, Graveney 53*). *W* (10 *points*) *won by* 6 *wickets.* (*W* 6 *bonus points. E* 3 *bonus points.*)

Notts (Kidderminster)—W 86 (White 5–39) and 311 (Ormrod 155*, White 4–81). N 171 (Carter 6–49) and 106 (Gifford 5–30, Slade 4–25). *W* (10 *points*) *won by* 120 *runs.* (*W* 5 *bonus points, N* 5 *bonus points.*)

Sussex (Worcester)—W 318–6d (Headley 148*, Bates 4–74) and 185–8d (Cass 53, Headley 52, Suttle 6–64). S 311–9d (Parks 79, Suttle 52, Gifford 4–71) and 48–2. *Match drawn.* (*W* 5 *bonus points, S* 5 *bonus points.*)

Glos (Dudley)—W 212 (Holder 52, Procter 4–47) and 147–2 (D'Oliveira 70*, Headley 55*). G 364 (Green 146, Shepherd 61, Carter 5–95). *Match drawn.* (*W* 4 *bonus points, G* 10 *bonus points.*)

Leics (Worcester)—L 328 (Inman 82, Marner 51, Gifford 4–53) and 233–7d (Dudleston 112, Booth 50). W 296–3d (Turner 112, Ormrod 67) and 101–1. *Match drawn.* (*W* 6 *bonus points, L* 5 *bonus points.*)

Som (Worcester)—S 184 (Holder 5–39) and 270–7d (Clarkson 63). W 154 (Burgess 5–45, Cartwright 4–44) and 301–3 (Turner 118*, Yardley 60*). *W* (10 *points*) *won by* 7 *wickets.* (*W* 5 *bonus points, S* 6 *bonus points.*)

Yorks (Worcester)—Y 213 and 164–8 (Gifford 6–43). W 432–8d (Turner 140, Graveney 100*, Headley 91). *Match drawn.* (*W* 8 *bonus points, Y* 3 *bonus points.*)

Lancs (Worcester)—W 168 (Turner 73, D'Oliveira 51, Hughes 5–60) and 194–3d (Turner 99, D'Oliveira 72*). L 143–6d (Gifford 4–46) and 86–7 *Match drawn.* (*W* 3 *bonus points, L* 5 *bonus points.*)

Warwicks (Worcester)—Warwicks 168 (Carter 4–60) and 322–4d (Kanhai 132*, Jameson 59, Abberley 56). W 253–2d (Turner 133*, Ormrod 60) and 179–5 (Headley 70). *Match drawn.* (*W* 9 *bonus points, Warwicks* 1 *bonus point.*)

YORKSHIRE

Formation of present club: 1863, reorganized 1891.
Colours: Oxford Blue, Cambridge blue and gold.
Badge: White Rose.
County Champions (29): 1893, 1896, 1898, 1900, 1901, 1902, 1905, 1908, 1912, 1919, 1922, 1923, 1924, 1925, 1931, 1932, 1933, 1935, 1937, 1938, 1939, 1946, 1959, 1960, 1962, 1963, 1966, 1967 and 1968.
Joint Champions (1) 1949.
Gillette Cup Winners (2): 1965 and 1969.

Secretary.—J. H. Nash, Headingley Cricket Ground, Leeds, LS6 3BU.
Captain.—G. Boycott.

David Leslie ("Blue") BAIRSTOW (Hanson G.S., Bradford).—B Bradford 1/9/1951. RHB, WK. Debut 1970 whilst still at school. Played for M.C.C. Schools at Lord's in 1970. HS: 36 v Somerset (Taunton) 1970. Soccer for Bradford City. Career record: 334 runs (av 17.57), 49 dismissals (43 ct 6 st).

John Christopher ("Chris") BALDERSTONE.—B Huddersfield 16/11/1940. RHB, SLA. Debut 1961. Played in only two John Player League matches in 1970. HS: 82 v Indians (Sheffield) 1967. BB: 4–31 v Warwickshire (Birmingham) 1965. Soccer for Huddersfield Town and Carlisle United. Career record: 1,332 runs (av 17.76), 37 wkts (av 21.35).

Michael Kenneth BORE.—B Hull 2/6/1947. RHB, LFM. Debut 1969 HS: 21* v Northants (Northampton) 1970. BB: 5–51 v Northants (Northampton) 1970. Career record: 85 runs (av 12.14), 31 wkts (av 26.87).

Geoffrey ("Geoff") BOYCOTT (Hemsworth G.S.).—B Fitzwilliam (Yorks) 21/10/1940. RHB, RM. Plays in contact lenses. Debut 1962. Cap 1963. Elected Best Young Cricketer of the Year in 1963 by the Cricket Writers' Club. "Wisden 1964". Appointed county captain for 1971. Tests: 43 between 1964 and 1970. Tours: South Africa 1964–65 Australia and New Zealand 1965–66 and 1970–71 (returned home early through broken arm injury), West Indies 1967–68. 1,000 runs (8)—2,110 runs (av 52.75) in 1964 best. Also scored 1,000 runs in South Africa 1964–65, (1,135 runs, av 56.73), West Indies 1967–68 (1,154 runs av 82.42), Australia 1970–71 (1,535 runs, av 95.93). Scored two centuries in match (103 and 105) v Notts (Sheffield) 1966. Holds record for highest score in Gillette Cup Competition—146 v Surrey in Final (Lord's) 1965 sharing in partnership of 192 for 2nd wkt with D. B. Close. HS: 260* v Essex (Colchester) 1970. BB: 3–47 England v South Africa (Cape Town) 1964–65. Career record: 17,000 runs (av 47.88), 42 centuries, 20 wkts (av 45.65).

Phillip ("Fergus") CARRICK.—B Leeds 16/7/1952. RHB, SLA. Debut 1970 (three matches). HS: 32 v Somerset (Taunton) 1970. BB: 6–85 v M.C.C. (Scarborough) 1970. Career record: 36 runs (av 18.00), 14 wkts (av 22.28).

Geoffrey Alan ("Geoff") COPE.—B Leeds 23/2/1947. RHB, OB. Wears glasses. Debut 1966. Cap 1970. "Hat-trick" v Essex (Colchester) 1970. HS: 66 v Northants (Northampton) 1970. BB: 7–36 v Essex (Colchester) 1970. Career record: 539 runs (av 10.36), 186 wkts (av 22.67).

Andrew John DALTON (Leeds G.S. and Newcastle University).—B Horsforth (Yorks) 14/3/1947. RHB. Debut 1969. HS: 47* (retired hurt) v M.C.C. (Scarborough) 1970. Career record: 193 runs (av 17.54).

John Harry ("Jackie") HAMPSHIRE.—B Thurnscoe (Yorks) 10/2/1941. RHB, LB. Debut 1961. Cap 1963. Played for Tasmania v Indians 1967–68 and v West Indians 1968–69 whilst on coaching engagement in Tasmania. Tests: 2 v West Indies 1969. Scored 107 in his first Test and is only player to have scored a century on debut in Test cricket when this has occurred at Lord's. Tour: Australia and New Zealand 1970–71. 1,000 runs (8)—1,513 runs (av 32.19) in 1965 best. HS: 156* M.C.C. v Tasmania (Hobart) 1970–71. HS in England: 150 v Leics (Bradford) 1964. BB: 7–52 v Glamorgan (Cardiff) 1963. Career record: 11,394 runs (av 30.06), 14 centuries, 15 wkts (av 80.46).

Richard Anthony HUTTON (Repton and Cambridge).—B Pudsey 6/9/1942. Son of Sir Leonard Hutton. RHB, RFM. Debut 1962. Blue 1962, 1963 and 1964. Cap 1964. Is a chartered accountant. Tour: Pakistan 1966–67. Scored 1,122 runs (av 27.36) in 1963. "Hat-trick" M.C.C. v North Zone (Peshawar) 1966–67. HS: 163* Cambridge U v Surrey (Guildford) 1963. BB: 8–50 Cambridge U v Derbyshire (Burton-on-Trent) 1963. Holds record for BB in John Player League—7–15 v Worcs (Leeds) 1969. Career record: 5,465 runs (av 21.51), 2 centuries, 451 wkts (av 23.77).

Colin JOHNSON (Pocklington School).—B Pocklington (Yorks) 5/9/1947. RHB, OB. Played in M.C.C. Schools matches at Lord's 1966. Debut 1969. HS: 61* v New Zealanders (Bradford) 1969. Career record: 275 runs (av 19.64), 1 wkt (av 104.00).

Barry LEADBEATER.—B Leeds 14/8/1943. RHB. Debut 1966. Cap 1969. HS: 89* v Cambridge U (Cambridge) 1970. Won "Man of the Match" award in Gillette Cup Final 1969. Career record: 1,321 runs (av 23.17).

Richard Graham LUMB (Mexborough G.S.).—B Doncaster 26/2/1950. RHB. Played in M.C.C. Schools matches at Lord's 1968. Played in one John Player League match in 1969 and one in 1970. Debut 1970. One match v Worcs. HS: 17 v Worcs (Worcester) 1970. Career record: 21 runs (av 10.50).

Anthony George ("Tony") NICHOLSON (Wheelwright G.S., Dewsbury).—B Dewsbury 25/6/1938. RHB, RFM. Former policeman in Rhodesia. Debut 1962. Cap 1963. Selected to tour South Africa 1964–65 but had to withdraw owing to back injury. 100 wkts (2)—113 wkts (av 15.50) in 1966 best. HS: 43 v Kent (Bradford) 1968. BB: 9–62 v Sussex (Eastbourne) 1967. Career record: 992 runs (av 10.55), 639 wkts (av 18.94).

Christopher Middleton ("Chris") OLD (Acklam Hall Secondary G.S., Middlesbrough).—B Middlesbrough 22/12/1948. LHB, RFM. Good field in any position. Debut 1966. Cap 1969. Elected Best Young Cricketer of the Year in 1970 by the Cricket Writers' Club. Tests: 2 v Rest of World 1970. HS: 92* v Somerset (Taunton) 1970. BB: 7–20 v Glos (Middlesbrough) 1969. Career record: 913 runs (av 15.47), 169 wkts (av 20.78).

Douglas Ernest Vernon ("Doug") PADGETT.—B Bradford 20/7/1934. RHB, RM. Debut 1951. Cap 1958. Benefit (£5,920) in 1969. Appointed joint coach with A. Mitchell for 1971. Tests: 2 v S. A. 1960. Tour: New Zealand 1960–61. 1,000 runs (12)—2,181 runs (av 41.15) in 1959 best. HS: 161* v Oxford U (Oxford) 1959. Career record: 20,258 runs (av 28.73), 31 centuries, 6 wkts (av 35.33).

Dennis SCHOFIELD.—B Holmfirth 9/10/1947. RHB, RM. Debut 1970. One match v Leics (Sheffield) 1970. Career record: 1 run.

Philip John ("Phil") SHARPE (Worksop College).—B Shipley 27/12/1936. RHB, OB. Outstanding slip field. Debut 1956 for Combined Services. Debut for Yorks 1958. Cap 1960. Elected Best Young Cricketer of the Year in 1962 by the Cricket Writers' Club. "Wisden 1962". Benefit in 1971. Tests: 13 between 1963 and 1970. Tour: India 1963–64. 1,000 runs (10)—2,252 runs (av 40.94) in 1962 best. Held 71 catches in 1962. Won "Man of the Match" award twice in Gillette Cup Competition in 1969. HS: 203* v Cambridge U (Cambridge) 1960. Scored 202 for Minor Counties v Indians (Stoke) 1959. Good hockey player. Career record: 17,512 runs (av 31.16), 22 centuries, 2 wkts (av 84.00).

Neil SMITH (Ossett G.S.)—B Dewsbury 1/4/1949. RHB, WK. Debut 1970. HS: 20 v Glamorgan (Middlesbrough) 1970. Career record: 82 runs (av 13.66), 16 dismissals (13 ct 3 st).

Rodney SMITH.—B Batley 6/4/1944. RHB, SLA. Debut 1969. Played in only one match in 1970. HS: 37* v Glos (Gloucester) 1969. Career record: 99 runs (av 19.80).

Donald ("Don") WILSON.—B Settle (Yorks) 7/8/1937. LHB, SLA. Good badminton player. Debut 1957. Cap 1960. Appointed county vice-captain for 1971. Tests: 7 in 1963–64 and 1970. Tours: New Zealand 1960–61, India 1963–64, Australia and New Zealand 1970–71. 100 wkts (5)—109 wkts (av 13.95) in 1968 best. Scored 30 runs (466266) in one over off R. Hobbs v M.C.C. (Scarborough) 1966. Hat-tricks (3): v Notts (Middlesbrough) 1959, v Notts (Worksop) 1966 and v Kent (Harrogate) 1966. HS: 112 M.C.C. v South Zone (Hyderabad) 1963–64. HS in England: 83 v Surrey (Sheffield) 1960. BB: 8–36 (14–71 match) M.C.C. v Ceylon (Colombo) 1969–70. BB in England: 7–19 v M.C.C. (Scarborough) 1969. Career record: 5,814 runs (av 14.79), 1 century, 1,075 wkts (av 20.46).

John Douglas WOODFORD (Carlton G.S., Bradford).—B Bradford 9/9/1943. RHB, RM. Debut 1968. HS: 56 v Worcs (Sheffield) 1969. Is a schoolteacher. Plays soccer in Yorkshire League. Career record: 734 runs (av 20.97).

N.B. The following player whose particulars appeared in the 1970 Annual has been omitted: D. B. Close (has joined Somerset). His career record is included elsewhere in this Annual.

COUNTY AVERAGES

County Championship: Played 24, Won 8, Drawn 11, Lost 5
All First-Class Matches: Played 26, Won 10, Drawn 11, Lost 5

BATTING AND FIELDING

Cap		*M.*	*I.*	*N.O.*	*Runs*	*H.S.*	*Avge.*	100	50	*Ct.*	*St.*
1963	G. Boycott	21	34	4	1558	260*	51.93	2	11	9	—
1969	B. Leadbeater	6	9	1	299	89*	37.37	—	2	5	—
1963	J. H. Hampshire......	21	34	5	1079	120*	37.20	2	4	20	—
1949	D. B. Close	20	28	2	949	128	36.50	1	6	20	—
1960	P. J. Sharpe............	24	38	1	1149	120	31.05	2	7	33	—
1958	D. E. V. Padgett	24	38	4	1042	108	30.64	2	6	14	—
1964	R. A. Hutton	26	38	7	875	104	28.22	1	4	26	—
1969	C. M. Old	19	22	5	433	92*	25.47	—	1	10	—
—	A. J. Dalton	6	9	1	174	47*	21.75	—	—	2	—
—	P. Carrick	3	3	1	36	32	18.00	—	—	2	—
—	D. L. Bairstow	19	24	5	334	36	17.57	—	—	43	6
—	J. D. Woodford	10	17	0	275	51	16.17	—	1	4	—
1970	G. A. Cope	26	29	8	327	66	15.57	—	2	11	—
1960	D. Wilson	16	18	2	238	48	14.87	—	—	5	—
1963	A. G. Nicholson......	23	21	9	173	24*	14.41	—	—	5	—
—	N. Smith	7	11	5	82	20	13.66	—	—	13	3
—	M. K. Bore	10	9	4	50	21*	10.00	—	—	5	—

Played in two matches: C. Johnson 15, 3*, 2 (1 ct).
Played in one match: R. G. Lumb 17, 4; D. Schofield 1*; R. Smith 2.

BOWLING

	Type	*Overs*	*Mdns*	*Runs*	*Wkts*	*Avge.*	*Best*	5w*I.*	10w*M*
C. M. Old	RFM	489.4	118	1252	65	18.95	5/14	2	—
R. A. Hutton ...	RFM	619.1	152	1597	74	21.58	6/81	2	1
P. Carrick	SLA	84.3	14	312	14	22.28	6/85	1	—
G. A. Cope	OB	878.5	282	2111	83	25.43	7/36	4	1
D. Wilson	SLA	553.5	195	1255	47	26.70	5/41	1	—
M. K. Bore	LFM	279	94	648	23	28.17	5/51	1	—
A. G. Nicholson	RFM	792.2	227	1939	65	29.83	5/82	2	—

Also bowled: D. B. Close 34-10-95-2; J. H. Hampshire 15-4-69-0; C. Johnson 7-2-20-0; D. E. V. Padgett 1-0-3-0; D. Schofield 20-9-53-0; P. J. Sharpe 2-0-4-0; J. D. Woodford 19-5-47-0.

County Records

Highest Innings Totals:	For ...887 v Warwickshire (Birmingham)............	1896
	Agst...630 by Somerset (Leeds)	1901
Lowest Innings Totals:	For ... 23 v Hampshire (Middlesbrough)	1965
	Agst... 13 by Nottinghamshire (Nottingham)	1901
Highest Individual Inngs.:	For ...341 G. H. Hirst v Leicestershire (Leicester)	1905
	Agst...318* W. G. Grace for Glos (Cheltenham)...	1876

YORKSHIRE

Best bowling figs in an Inngs.:	For ...10–10 H. Verity v Nottinghamshire (Leeds)	1932
	Agst...10–37 C. V. Grimmett for Australians (Sheffield)	1930
Best bowling figs in a match:	For ...17–91 H. Verity v Essex (Leyton)	1933
	Agst...17–91 H. Dean for Lancashire (Liverpool)	1913
Most runs in a season	2883 (av 80.08) H. Sutcliffe	1932
runs in a career	38561 (av 50.21) H. Sutcliffe	1919–1945
100s in a season	12 by H. Sutcliffe	1932
100s in a career	112 by H. Sutcliffe	1919–1945
wickets in a season	240 (av 12.72) W. Rhodes	1900
wickets in a career	3608 (av 16.00) W. Rhodes	1898–1930

RECORD WICKET STANDS

1st 555	P. Holmes & H. Sutcliffe v Essex (Leyton)	1932
2nd 346	W. Barber & M. Leyland v Middlesex (Sheffield)	1932
3rd 323*	H. Sutcliffe & M. Leyland v Glamorgan (Huddersfield)	1928
4th 312	G. H. Hirst & D. Denton v Hampshire (Southampton)	1914
5th 340	E. Wainwright & G. H. Hirst v Surrey (The Oval)	1899
6th 276	M. Leyland & E. Robinson v Glamorgan (Swansea)	1926
7th 254	D. C. F. Burton & W. Rhodes v Hampshire (Dewsbury)	1919
8th 292	Lord Hawke & R. Peel v Warwickshire (Birmingham)	1896
9th 192	G. H. Hirst & S. Haigh v Surrey (Bradford)	1898
10th 148	Lord Hawke & D. Hunter v Kent (Sheffield)	1898

Home Matches in Championship

Derbys (Bradford)—D 107 (Old 5–14) and 111 (Cope 4–44). Y 238 (Hutton 104, Smith, E. 7–84). *Y (10 points) won by an innings and 20 runs. (Y 7 bonus points, D 4 bonus points.)*

Glam (Middlesbrough)—Y 124 (Close 56*, Williams 4–32, Nash 4–49) and 159 (Boycott 68, Nash 4–62). G 161 (Lewis 56) and 124–5. *G (10 points) won by 5 wickets. (Y 5 bonus points, 4 bonus points.)*

Lancs (Headingley)—L 381 (Wood 105, Engineer 70, Lloyd, D. 64, Nicholson 5–116) and 25–0. Y 121 (Lever 4–51) and 281 (Boycott 71, Hutton 51). *L (10 points) won by 10 wickets. (Y 1 bonus point, L 8 bonus points.)*

Glos (Bradford)—Y 267 (Leadbeater 70, Sharpe 62, Procter 6–38) and 152 (Bissex 5–34). G 304 (Green 69, Bissex 53) and 116–1 (Nicholls 79*). *G (10 points) won by 9 wickets. (Y 8 bonus points, G 10 bonus points.)*

Hants (Sheffield)—H 144 and 139 (Wilson 4–49). Y 288–9d (Padgett 106, Cope 50, White 4–84). *Y (10 points) won by an innings and 5 runs. (Y 5 bonus points, H 1 bonus point.)*

Notts (Sheffield)—Y 252 (Stead 4–43) and 189–7d. N 106 and 259–6 (Sobers 144*, Wilson 4–99). *Match drawn. (Y 7 bonus points, N 2 bonus points.)*

Leics (Sheffield)—L 184 (Booth 84, Birkenshaw 57, Bore 4–33, Hutton 4–35) and 265–3d (Marner 110, Inman 103*). Y 131 (Stringer 5–43) and 187–2 (Boycott 82*, Sharpe 53). *Match drawn.* (*Y* 4 *bonus points, L* 6 *bonus points.*)

Sussex (Headingley)—S 175 (Buss, M. A. 78) and 216–4 (Greenidge 70, Grieg 53*). Y 307–8d (Sharpe 64, Boycott 62, Hutton 58*, Close 55, Buss, A. 4–86). *Match drawn.* (*Y* 8 *bonus points, S* 3 *bonus points.*)

Kent (Sheffield)—K 132 (Hutton 4–27, Old 4–48) and 292 (Denness 96, Ealham 85). Y 349 (Boycott 148, Sharpe 108, Shepherd 5–123). *Match drawn.* (*Y* 8 *bonus points, K* 1 *bonus point.*)

Surrey (Bradford)—S 193 (Knight 59, Old 5–44) and 171 (Cope 6–55). Y 244 (Boycott 77, Intikhab 5–93) and 122–5. *Y* (10 *points*) *won by* 5 *wickets.* (*Y* 7 *bonus points, S* 6 *bonus points.*)

Middx (Scarborough)—Y 304–7d (Sharpe 120, Boycott 64). M 183–7 (Brearley 67*, Parfitt 51). *Match drawn.* (*Y* 7 *bonus points, M* 3 *bonus points.*)

Som (Hull)—Y 306 (Hampshire 85, Close 68). S 111 and 165 (Virgin 53, Cope 4–33). *Y* (10 *points*) *won by an innings and* 30 *runs.* (*Y* 9 *bonus points, S* 3 *bonus points.*)

ISN'T IT NICE TO KNOW . . . CHECK ANSWERS

1. In a document relating to a plot of land at Guildford in 1598.
2. Leicestershire—ten.
3. None.
4. Stuart Surridge, who was captain of Surrey for five years—1952–1956, and Surrey won the Championship in all five.
5. A. Sandham (Surrey)—325 in West Indies in 1929–30.
6. Charles Palmer took 8 for 7 against Surrey at Leicester in 1955.
7. 'Tich' Freeman (Kent)—304 in 1928.
8. 555—Holmes and Sutcliffe, Yorkshire v Essex at Leyton, 1932.
9. Trevor Bailey 361 minutes (68) England v Australia at Brisbane 1958–59.
10. The Australians—721 v Essex at Southend in 1948.
11. He scored a hundred in his first Test Match—140 v West Indies at Trinidad, 1947–48.
12. D. R. Jardine.
13. G. Hurst Essex, J. Standen (Worcestershire), West Ham United 1963–64
14. I. R. Buxton (Derbyshire).
15. G. D. McKenzie (Australia) 3 years 165 days.
16. D. J. S. Taylor (Somerset).
17. A. Long (Surrey) v Sussex 1964 took 11 catches in a match, the most by a wicket keeper.
18. F. W. Swarbrook aged 16 years 6 months.
19. A. C. Smith the Warwickshire wicket keeper who took off his pads in the match v Essex in 1965.

THE FIRST-CLASS UMPIRES FOR 1971

N.B. The abbreviations used are identical with those used in "The Counties and their Players."

William Edward ("Bill") ALLEY.—B Sydney (Australia) 3/2/1919. LHB, RM. Played for New South Wales 1945–46 to 1947–48. Subsequently came to England to play League cricket and then for Somerset from 1957 to 1968. "Wisden 1961". Testimonial (£2,700) in 1961. Tours: India and Pakistan 1949–50, Pakistan 1963–64 with Commonwealth team. Scored 3,019 runs (av 56.96) in 1961 including 2,761 runs and 10 centuries for county, both being records. HS: 221* v Warwickshire (Nuneaton) 1961. BB: 8–65 v Surrey (Oval) 1962. Career record: 19,612 runs (av 31.88), 31 centuries, 768 wkts (av 22.68). Appointed 1969.

John ("Johnny") ARNOLD.—B Cowley (Oxford) 30/11/1907. Opening RHB and fine field at cover. Played for Oxfordshire and Hampshire in 1929 and continued to play for Hampshire until 1950 when career was terminated by serious illness. Shared joint benefit (£1,470) with four other players 1948–50. Tests (1): 1 v New Zealand 1931. HS: 227 v Glamorgan (Cardiff) 1932. Career record: 21,831 runs (av 32.82), 37 centuries, 17 wkts (av 69.52). Soccer (OL) for Southampton and Fulham becoming a double-international when he played against Scotland in 1932–33. Appointed 1961.

Ronald ("Ron") ASPINALL.—B Almondbury (Yorks) 26/10/1918, RHB, RFM. Played for Yorkshire from 1946 to 1950 (retiring early through injury) and for Durham from 1951 to 1957. HS: 75* v Notts (Nottingham) 1948. BB: 8–42 v Northants (Rushden) 1949. Career record: 763 runs (av 19.07), 131 wkts (av 20.38). Appointed 1960.

Harold Denis BIRD.—B Barnsley 19/4/1933. RHB, RM. Played for Yorks from 1956 to 1959 and for Leics from 1960 to 1964. Has since been professional at Paignton C.C. HS: 181* Yorks v Glamorgan (Bradford) 1959. Career record: 3,315 runs (av 20.71), 2 centuries. Appointed 1970.

William Lloyd BUDD.—B Hawkley (Hants) 20/10/1913. RHB, RFM. Played for Hampshire from 1934 to 1946. HS: 77* v Surrey (Oval) 1937. BB: 4–22 v Essex (Southend) 1937. Career record: 941 runs (av 11.47), 64 wkts (av 39.15). Was on Minor Counties list for some years. Appointed 1969.

David John CONSTANT.—B Bradford-on-Avon (Wilts) 9/11/1941. LHB, SLA. Played for Kent from 1961 to 1963 and for Leics from 1965 to 1968. HS: 80 v Glos (Bristol) 1966. Career record: 1,517 runs (av 19.20), 1 wkt (av 36.00). Appointed 1969.

Cecil ("Sam") COOK.—B Tetbury (Glos) 23/8/1921. RHB, SLA. Played for Gloucestershire from 1946 to 1964. Benefit (£3,067) in 1957. Took wicket with first ball in first-class cricket. Tests: 1 v S.A. 1947. HS: 35* v Sussex (Hove) 1957. BB: 9–42 v Yorks (Bristol) 1947. Career record: 1,964 runs (av 5.39), 1,782 wkts (av 20.52). Appointed 1971, after having withdrawn from appointment in 1966.

John Frederick ("Jack") CRAPP.—B St. Colomb (Cornwall) 14/10/1912. LHB. Played for Gloucestershire from 1936 to 1956 captaining county in 1953 and 1954. Benefit (£3,611) in 1951. Tests: 7 in 1948 and 1948–49. Tours: South Africa 1948–49, India 1953–54 with Commonwealth Team. HS: 175 v Cambridge U (Cambridge) 1947. Career record: 23,615 runs (av 35.03), 38 centuries, 6 wkts (av 51.00). Appointed 1957. Umpired in 4 Tests in 1964 and 1965.

Charles Standish ("Charlie") ELLIOTT.—B Bolsover (Derbyshire) 24/4/1912. Opening RHB. Played for Derbyshire from 1932 to 1953. Testimonial (£1,667) in 1950. HS: 215 v Notts (Nottingham) 1947. Career record: 11,965 runs (av 27.25), 9 centuries, 11 wkts (av 47.81). Appointed 1956. Has umpired in 34 Tests from 1957 to 1970, a total exceeded only by F. Chester (48) and J. S. Buller (35).

David Gwilliam Lloyd EVANS.—B Lambeth (London) 27/7/1933. RHB, WK. Played for Glamorgan from 1956 to 1969. Benefit (£3,500) in 1969. HS: 46* v Oxford U (Oxford) 1961. Career record: 2,875 runs (av 10.53), 558 dismissals (502 ct 56 st). Appointed 1971.

Arthur Edward FAGG.—B Chartham (Kent) 15/6/1915. Opening RHB, slip field. Played for Kent from 1932 to 1957. Benefit (£3,456) in 1951. Tests: 5 between 1936 and 1939. Tour: Australia 1936–37 returning home early through illness. Holds world record of two double-centuries in match (244 and 202*) v Essex (Colchester) 1938. HS: 269* v Notts (Nottingham) 1953. Career record: 27,291 runs (av 36.05) 58 centuries. Appointed 1959. Has umpired in 11 Tests between 1967 and 1970.

Oswald William ("Lofty") HERMAN.—B Headington, Oxford 18/9/1907. Father of R. S. Herman of Middlesex. RHB, RFM. Played for Hampshire from 1929 to 1948. Shared joint benefit (£1,470) with four other players 1948–50. HS: 92 v Leics (Leicester) 1948. BB: 8–49 v Yorks (Bournemouth) 1930. Career record: 4,336 runs (av 11.06), 1,045 wkts (av 27.00). Appointed 1963.

Frederick ("Freddie") JAKEMAN.—B Holmsfirth (Yorks) 10/1/1921. LHB. Played for Yorkshire in 1946 and 1947 and for Northamptonshire from 1949 to 1954. HS: 258* v Essex (Northampton) 1951 as part of four innings when he scored 558 runs before being dismissed. Career record: 5,952 runs (av 32.00), 11 centuries, 5 wkts (av 32.40). Appointed 1961.

Arthur JEPSON.—B Selston (Notts) 12/7/1915. RHB, RFM. Played for Notts from 1938 to 1959. Benefit (£2,000) in 1951. HS: 130 v Worcs (Nottingham) 1950. BB: 8–45 v Leics (Nottingham) 1958. Career record: 6,369 runs (av 14.31), 1 century, 1,051 wkts (av 29.08). Soccer (goalkeeper) for Port Vale, Stoke City and Lincoln City. Appointed 1960. Has umpired in 4 Tests between 1966 and 1969.

John George LANGRIDGE.—B Chailey (Sussex) 10/2/1910. Younger brother of late James Langridge. Opening RHB and outstanding slip field. Played for Sussex from 1928 to 1955. "Wisden 1949". Shared joint benefit (£1,930) with H. W. Parks in 1948. Testimonial (£3,825) in 1953. Scored more runs and centuries in first-class cricket than any other player who never appeared in a Test match. Only F. E. Woolley, W. G. Grace, W. R. Hammond and G. A. R. Lock have held more catches than his total of 786. HS: 250* v Glamorgan (Hove) 1933. Career record: 34,380 runs (av 37.45), 76 centuries, 44 wkts (av 42.00). Appointed 1956. Umpired in 7 Tests between 1960 and 1963.

Cecil George ("Cec") PEPPER.—B Forbes, New South Wales (Australia) 15/9/1918. RHB, LBG. Played for New South Wales 1938–39 to 1940–41, Australian Services 1945 and 1945–46. Returned to England to play in League cricket from 1947 and appeared in the Hastings Festivals in 1956 and 1957. Tours: India and Ceylon 1945–46 with Australian Services Team and India and Pakistan 1949–50 with Commonwealth Team. HS: 168 Australian Services v H. D. G. Leveson-Gower's XI (Scarborough) 1945. BB: 6–33 Commonwealth XI v Holkar Cricket Association (Indore) 1949–50. Career record: 1,927 runs (av 29.64), 1 century, 169 wkts (av 29.31). Appointed 1964.

William Edward ("Eddie") PHILLIPSON.—B North Reddish (Lancs) 3/12/1910. RHB, RFM. Played for Lancashire from 1933 to 1948. Grant (£1,750) in 1948. Tour: New Zealand with Sir Julian Cahn's Team 1938–39. HS: 113 v Glamorgan (Preston) 1939. BB: 8–100 v Kent (Dover) 1934. Career record: 4,096 runs (av 25.76), 2 centuries 555 wkts (av 24.72). Appointed 1956. Umpired in 12 Tests between 1958 and 1965.

George Henry POPE.—B Tibshelf (Derbyshire) 27/1/1911. Younger brother of A. V. Pope. RHB RFM. Played for Derbyshire from 1933 to 1948. Tests: 1 v S.A. 1947. Tours: India 1937–38 with Lord Tennyson's Team. India, Pakistan and Ceylon 1949–50 with Commonwealth Team. HS: 207* v Hants (Portsmouth) 1948. BB: 8–38 v Sussex (Burton-on Trent) 1948. Career record: 7,518 runs (av 28.05), 8 centuries, 677 wkts (av 19.92). Appointed 1966.

Albert Ennion Growcott ("Dusty") RHODES.—B Tintwhistle (Cheshire) 10/10/1916. Father of H. J. Rhodes, RHB, LBG. Played for Derbyshire from 1937 to 1954. Testimonial (£2,096) in 1952. Tour: India 1951–52 returning home early owing to injury. Achieved 5 "Hat-tricks". HS: 127 v Somerset (Taunton) 1949. BB: 8–162 v Yorks (Scarborough) 1947. Career record: 7,363 runs (av 18.97), 3 centuries, 661 wkts (av 28.22). Appointed 1959. Has umpired in 5 Tests between 1963 and 1970.

Edmund John ("Eddie") ROWE.—B Netherfield, Notts 21/7/1920. RHB, WK. Played for Notts from 1949 to 1957. HS: 16 v Kent (Blackheath) 1955. Career record: 295 runs (av 5.46), 205 dismissals (152 ct 53 st). Appointed 1971.

Thomas William ("Tom") SPENCER.—B Deptford 22/3/1914. RHB, RM. Played for Kent from 1935 to 1946. HS: 96 v Sussex (Tunbridge Wells) 1946. Career record: 2,152 runs (av 20.11), 1 wkt (av 19.00). Appointed 1950 (longest serving umpire on list). Has umpired in 2 Tests in 1954 and 1969.

Alan Geoffrey Thomas WHITEHEAD.—B Butleigh (Somerset) 28/10/1940. LHB, SLA. Played for Somerset from 1957 to 1961. HS: 15 v Hants (Southampton) 1959 and 15 v Leics (Leicester) 1960. BB: 6–74 v Sussex (Eastbourne) 1959. Career record: 137 runs (av 5.70), 67 wkts (av 34.41). Served on Minor Counties list in 1969. Appointed 1970.

Peter Bernard WIGHT.—B Georgetown (British Guiana) 25/6/1930. RHB, OB. Played for British Guiana in 1950–51 and for Somerset from 1953 to 1965. Benefit (£5,000) in 1963. HS: 222* v Kent (Taunton) 1959. BB: 6–29 v Derbyshire (Chesterfield) 1957. Career record: 17,773 runs (av 33.09), 28 centuries, 68 wkts (av 33.26). Appointed 1966.

Hugo YARNOLD.—B Worcester 6/7/1917. RHB, WK. Played for Worcs from 1938 to 1955. Stumped 6 batsmen in innings (world record) v Scotland (Broughty Ferry) 1951 and caught a seventh. Dismissed 110 batsmen (63 ct 47 st) in 1949. HS: 68 North v South (Kingston) 1947. Career record: 3,741 runs (av 10.75), 695 dismissals (462 ct 233 st). Appointed 1959. Umpired in 3 Tests in 1967 and 1968.

N.B. The Test Match panel for 1971 *is D. Constant, C. S. Elliott, A. E. Fagg, A. E. G. Rhodes and T. W. Spencer.*

CHAMPIONSHIP TABLE, 1970

	P.	*W.*	*L.*	*D.*	*Bonus Pts. Bt.*	*Bonus Pts. Bw.*	*Pts.*
1. Kent (10)	24	9	5	10	70	77	237
2. Glamorgan (1)	24	9	6	9	48	82	220
3. Lancashire (15)	24	6	2	16	78	78	216
4. Yorkshire (13)	24	8	5	11	49	86	215
5. Surrey (3)	24	6	4	14	60	83	203
6. Worcestershire (12)	24	7	1	16	46	84	200
7. Derbyshire (16)	24	7	7	10	51	78	199
Warwickshire (4)	24	7	6	11	53	71	199
9. Sussex (7)	24	5	7	12	62	87	199
10. Hampshire (5)	24	4	6	14	69	88	197
11. Notts (8)	24	4	8	12	71	73	184
12. Essex (6)	24	4	6	14	64	76	180
13. Somerset (17)	24	5	10	9	40	86	176
14. Northamptonshire (9)	24	4	6	14	60	74	174
15. Leicestershire (14)	24	5	6	13	46	77	173
16. Middlesex (11)	24	5	5	14	47	69	166
17. Gloucestershire (2)	24	3	8	13	56	80	166

Warwickshire's record includes 5 points in drawn match when scores finished level and they were batting. Figures in brackets 1969 positions.

HIGHLIGHTS OF LAST SEASON

HIGHEST TOTALS

563—9d.	Rest of the World v. England at Birmingham.
546	Rest of the World v. England at Lord's.
498—9d.	Kent v. Sussex at Tunbridge Wells.
496—7d.	Worcestershire v. Oxford University at Oxford.
468—5d.	Derbyshire v. Lancashire at Derby.
468—7d.	Warwickshire v. Derbyshire at Derby.
450—4d.	Yorkshire v. Essex at Colchester.
432—8d.	Worcestershire v. Yorkshire at Worcester.
432—9d.	Northamptonshire v. Leicestershire at Leicester.
430—7d.	Lancashire v. Yorkshire at Manchester.
421—7d.	Kent v. Leicestershire at Folkestone.
418	Lancashire v. Sussex at Blackpool.
412—8d.	Hampshire v. Glamorgan at Portsmouth.
411	Leicestershire v. Nottinghamshire at Leicester.
411	Yorkshire v. Northamptonshire at Northampton.
409	England v. Rest of the World at Birmingham.
400—7d.	Lancashire v. Gloucestershire at Manchester.

LOWEST TOTALS

47	Cambridge University v. Essex at Harlow.
54	Somerset v. Sussex at Hove.
75	Sussex v. Derbyshire at Buxton.
84	Glamorgan v. Worcestershire at Neath.
85	Glamorgan v. Derbyshire at Derby.
85	Sussex v. Northamptonshire at Kettering (two retired hurt).
86	Worcestershire v. Nottinghamshire at Kidderminster.
87	Derbyshire v. Glamorgan at Swansea.
87	Sussex v. Nottinghamshire at Hove.
90	Warwickshire v. Leicestershire at Nuneaton.
93	Ireland v. Scotland at Perth.
95	Middlesex v. Kent at Canterbury.
96	Sussex v. Jamaican XI at Hove.

This is the smallest number of totals under 100 *in a season since* 1894, *the previous lowest being* 23 *in* 1928.

BATTING

DOUBLE CENTURIES

260*	G. Boycott for Yorkshire v. Essex at Colchester.
208	H. M. Ackerman for Northamptonshire v. Leicestershire at Leicester.
203*	B. W. Luckhurst for Kent v. Cambridge University at Cambridge.
200	M. J. Khan for Cambridge University v. Oxford University at Lord's.

CENTURY IN EACH INNINGS

143 and 113* J. H. Edrich for Surrey v. Worcestershire at Worcester.
119* and 104* H. Pilling for Lancashire v. Warwickshire at Manchester.
160 and 103* G. S. Sobers for Nottinghamshire v. Surrey at the Oval.

OPENING BATSMAN CARRYING BAT

70* (142) R. M. Ridley for Oxford University v. Nottinghamshire at Oxford.

CENTURY BEFORE LUNCH

113* (153) B. A. Richards for Hampshire v. Derbyshire at Chesterfield (2nd day).
110* M. J. Stewart for Surrey v. Sussex at Guildford (3rd day).

WICKET PARTNERSHIPS

FIRST WICKET

265 D. Lloyd and B. Wood for Lancashire v. Sussex at Blackpool.
241 M. A. Buss and G. A. Greenidge for Sussex v. Somerset at Hove.
209 W. E. Russell and M. J. Smith for Middlesex v. Sussex at Hove.
207 R. T. Virgin and A. Clarkson for Somerset v. Warwickshire at Birmingham.
201 B. A. Richards and C. G. Greenidge for Hampshire v. Leicestershire at Southampton.
201 R. M. Prideaux and H. M. Ackerman for Northamptonshire v. Nottinghamshire at Nottingham.

SECOND WICKET

239 G. M. Turner and J. A. Ormrod for Worcestershire v Gloucestershire at Bristol.
225 P. G. Carling and M. J. Khan for Cambridge University v. Glamorgan at Cambridge.
205 G. Boycott and P. J. Sharpe for Yorkshire v. Kent at Sheffield.
205 J. B. Bolus and B. Hassan for Nottinghamshire v. Warwickshire at Birmingham.

THIRD WICKET

231 H. Pilling and C. H. Lloyd for Lancashire v. Kent at Dartford.
222 M. J. Smith and C. T. Radley for Middlesex v. Sussex at Lord's.
208* B. Ward and K. W. R. Fletcher for Essex v. Nottinghamshire at Nottingham.
200 G. A. Greenidge and K. G. Suttle for Sussex v. Middlesex at Hove.

FOURTH WICKET

263 R. E. Marshall and D. A. Livingstone for Hampshire v. Middlesex at Lord's (county record).
230 J. A. Jameson and M. J. K. Smith for Warwickshire v. Lancashire at Birmingham.

217 J. A. Jameson, D. L. Amiss and K. Ibadulla for Warwickshire v. Cambridge University at Cambridge (Amiss retired at 170).
212 G. Boycott and J. H. Hampshire for Yorkshire v. Essex at Colchester.
210 M. J. K. Smith and D. L. Amiss for Warwickshire v. Oxford University at Oxford.
208* P. J. Graves and A. W. Greig for Sussex v. Kent at Tunbridge Wells.
208 G. J. Saville and B. Taylor for Essex v. Cambridge University at Harlow.
205 G. Barker and B. Taylor for Essex v. Northamptonshire at Northampton.
203 M. J. Smedley and G. S. Sobers for Nottinghamshire v. Kent at Folkestone.

CENTURY PARTNERSHIP FOR FIRST WICKET IN EACH INNINGS

131 and 140* W. E. Russell and M. J. Smith for Middlesex v. Oxford University at Oxford.
100 and 101 D. M. Green and R. B. Nicholls for Gloucestershire v. Sussex at Hove.
172 and 154 M. J. Harris and J. B. Bolus for Nottinghamshire v. Lancashire at Nottingham.

FIELDING

MOST DISMISSALS IN AN INNINGS BY WICKET-KEEPER

7 (6ct 1st) E. W. Jones for Glamorgan v. Cambridge University at Cambridge.
6 (6ct) F. M. Engineer for Lancashire v. Northamptonshire at Liverpool.
6 (6ct) F. M. Engineer for Lancashire v. Surrey at the Oval.

FIVE CATCHES IN AN INNINGS BY A FIELDER

R. C. Davis for Glamorgan v. Northamptonshire at Cardiff.
P. M. Walker for Glamorgan v. Derbyshire at Swansea.

EIGHT CATCHES IN A MATCH BY A FIELDER

P. M. Walker for Glamorgan v. Derbyshire at Swansea.

BOWLING

HAT TRICKS

E. J. Barlow for Rest of the World v. England at Leeds (he went on to take 4 wickets in 5 balls).
G. A. Cope for Yorkshire v. Essex at Colchester.

BEST BOWLING IN AN INNINGS

8—37 L. R. Gibbs for Warwickshire v. Glamorgan at Birmingham.
8—39 D. Breakwell for Northants v Kent at Dover.
8—56 J. S. E. Price for Middlesex v. Kent at Lord's.
8—74 Intikhab Alam for Surrey v. Middlesex at the Oval.

ALL-ROUND CRICKET

FIRST TO TARGETS

1,000 runs	R. B. Kanhai (Wa) on June 13th.
2,000 runs	G. M. Turner (Wo) on August 25th.
100 wickets	D. J. Shepherd (Gm) on August 31st.

COMPARATIVE TABLE

	1970	1969	1968	1967	1966	Record
2,000 runs	4	1	3	3	2	23 (1959)
1,000 runs	76	58	64	70	65	111 (1961)
Centuries	234	190	174	209	158	414 (1928)
100 wickets	4	5	7	18	23	31 (1961)
Doubles	—	—	—	1	1	12 (1923)

COUNTY CAPS AWARDED DURING SEASON (20)

Derbyshire	C. P. Wilkins.
Essex	D. L. Acfield, J. K. Lever, G. J. Saville, S. Turner B. Ward.
Glamorgan	None.
Gloucestershire	M. Bissex.
Hampshire	D. R. Turner.
Kent	A. G. E. Ealham, G. W. Johnson, R. A. Woolmer.
Lancashire	D. P. Hughes.
Leicestershire	None.
Middlesex	None.
Northamptonshire	None.
Nottinghamshire	M. J. Harris, B. Hassan.
Somerset	T. W. Cartwright.
Surrey	R. D. Jackman.
Sussex	G. A. Greenidge.
Warwickshire	None.
Worcestershire	G. R. Cass, V. A. Holder.
Yorkshire	G. A. Cope.

ISN'T IT NICE TO KNOW . . . *Check answers page* 151

17. Which Wicket Keeper performed a world record at Hove?

18. Who is the youngest player ever to appear for Derbyshire?

19. Which Wicket Keeper went on to bowl and did the hat-trick?

THE 1970 UNIVERSITY MATCH

PLAYED AT LORD'S, JULY 11, 13 and 14
MATCH DRAWN

CAMBRIDGE UNIVERSITY

P. G. Carling c Millener b Burton	44	not out	25
M. T. Barford b Heard	13	not out	26
M. J. Khan c Johns b Millener	200		
R. D. V. Knight c Burton b Millener	33		
D.R.Owen-ThomascBurchnall bBurton	6		
P. D. Johnson c May b Heard	8		
‡R. C. Bromley c Heal b Heard	13		
T. E. N. Jameson not out	8		
†A. M. Jorden b Millener	5		
C. L. Wilkin did not bat			
J. Spencer did not bat			
Extras (B2, LB4, W1)	7	(B2)	2
Total (8 wkts. dec.)	337	(0 wkts.)	53

OXFORD UNIVERSITY

R. M. Ridley c Jameson b Knight	31
R. L. Burchnall lbw b Spencer	9
B. May b Knight	13
P. R. B. Wilson c & b Wilkin	8
A. N. Campbell c Khan b Jorden	57
M. G. Heal b Johnson	18
R. Johns not out	61
†M. St. J. Burton b Jorden	8
H. Heard c Khan b Owen-Thomas	2
D. J. Millener c Bromley b Knight	24
‡D. F. Allison c Bromley b Spencer	0
Extras (B11, LB8, W3, NB1)	23
Total	254

BOWLING

OXFORD	*O.*	*M.*	*R.*	*W.*	*O.*	*M.*	*R.*	*W.*
Millener	28.3	5	86	3	9	0	30	0
Heard	28	5	101	3	4	0	19	0
Burton	24	7	66	2	4	3	2	0
Johns	19	4	59	0				
Wilson	1	0	18	0				
CAMBRIDGE								
Jorden	23	11	38	2				
Spencer	15.5	4	48	2				
Knight	19	10	37	3				
Owen-Thomas	13	0	23	1				
Wilkin	14	5	35	1				
Johnson	13	2	46	1				
Jameson	2	1	4	0				

Fall of Wickets

	C. *1st*	*O.* *1st*
1st	15	34
2nd	181	48
3rd	249	65
4th	272	65
5th	300	106
6th	322	162
7th	322	170
8th	337	205
9th		249
10th		254

OXFORD UNIVERSITY

Played 10, Won 0, Drawn 4, Lost 6

BATTING AND FIELDING

	M.	*I.*	*N.O.*	*Runs*	*H.S.*	*Avge.*	100	50	*Ct.*	*St.*
†A. N. Campbell	4	7	0	220	73	31.42	—	3	2	—
†R. M. Ridley	9	17	1	411	70*	25.68	—	3	5	—
†M. S. Burton	10	18	2	356	84	22.25	—	1	5	—
†R. L. Johns	8	15	2	273	61*	21.00	—	1	6	—
†B. May	6	11	0	217	103	19.72	1	—	4	—
†P. R. B. Wilson	5	9	0	173	41	19.22	—	—	3	—
†M. G. Heal	6	11	0	180	64	16.36	—	1	2	—
†R. L. Burchnall	10	19	0	288	79	15.15	—	1	4	—
P. R. Carroll	6	12	1	162	49	14.72	—	—	1	—
†H. Heard	4	6	2	58	31	14.50	—	—	3	—
†D. J. Millener	4	6	1	70	24	14.00	—	—	2	—
J. Ward	3	6	0	81	38	13.50	—	—	—	—
D. Williams	5	9	3	72	21	12.00	—	—	2	—
M. J. J. Faber	5	10	1	88	25	9.77	—	—	3	—
R. D. Lees	3	6	2	29	17*	7.25	—	—	—	—
†D. F. Allison	6	9	2	48	21	6.85	—	—	4	—
A. Douglas-Home	4	6	1	33	23	6.60	—	—	1	—
D. J. Hone	3	5	0	26	13	5.20	—	—	1	—

Played in two matches: D. Bryant 0*, 0*, 0, 3; P. Mucklow 32, 1, 2, 13 (1 ct); G. A. Robinson 27, 0, 0, 0 (4 ct); S. A. Verity 11, 9*, 2. *Played in one match:* S. C. Corlett 19, 6.

BOWLING

	Overs	*Mdns*	*Runs*	*Wkts.*	*Avge.*	*Best*	*5wI*	*10wM*
A. Douglas-Home	95	25	273	9	30.33	3–71	—	—
P. R. B. Wilson	32	3	182	6	30.33	4–60	—	—
D. J. Millener	150.3	38	382	11	34.72	3–61	—	—
H. Heard	104	20	323	9	35.88	4–59	—	—
M. S. Burton	283.4	73	898	21	42.76	5–96	1	—
R. L. Johns	240	63	671	13	51.61	4–76	—	—

Also bowled: D. Bryant 38-7-148-4; S. C. Corlett 7-1-26-0; D. J. Hone 69.2-11-284-1; R. D. Lees 46-8-144-1; R. M. Ridley 1-1-0-0; S. A. Verity 37-6-121-0; D. Williams 39-7-248-2.

†1970 Blue

UNIVERSITY RECORDS—OXFORD

Highest Innings Totals:	For	651 v Sussex (Hove)	1895
	Agst	679–6d by Australians (Oxford)	1938
Lowest Innings Totals:	For	12 v M.C.C. (Oxford)	1877
	Agst	36 by M.C.C. (Oxford)	1867
Highest Individual Inngs.:	For	281 K. J. Key v Middlesex (Chiswick)	1887
	Agst	338 W. W. Read for Surrey (The Oval)	1888
Best Bowling Figs in a Inngs:	For	10-38 S. E. Butler v Cambridge U. (Lord's)	1871
	Agst	10-49 W. G. Grace for M.C.C. (Oxford)	1886

Best Bowling Figs in a Match	For	...15-95 S. E. Butler v Cambridge U. (Lord's) . 1871
	Agst	...16-225 J. E. Walsh for Leicestershire (Oxfd.) . 1953
Most runs in a season	....	1307 (av. 93.35) Nawab of Pataudi (Snr.) 1931
runs in a career	......	3319 (av. 47.41) N. S. Mitchell—Innes 1934–1937
100s in a season	....	6 by Nawab of Pataudi (Senior)......1931
100s in a career	......	9 by A. M. Crawley 1927–1930
		Nawab of Pataudi (Senior) . 1928–31
		N. S. Mitchell-Innes 1934–37
		M. P. Donnelly 1946–47
wickets in a season	.	70 (av. 18.15) I. A. R. Peebles 1930

RECORD WICKET STANDS

1st	338	T. Bowring & H. Teesdale v Gentlemen (Oxford)	1908
2nd	226	W. G. Keighley & H. A. Pawson v Cambridge U. (Lord's)	1947
3rd	273	F. C. de Saram & N. S. Mitchell-Innes v Gloucestershire (Oxford)	1934
4th	276	P. G. T. Kingsley & N. M. Ford v Surrey (The Oval)	1930
5th	256*	A. A. Baig & C. A. Fry v Free Foresters (Oxford)	1959
6th	270	D. R. Walsh & S. A. Westley v Warwickshire (Oxford)	1969
7th	340	K. J. Key & H. Philipson v Middlesex (Chiswick)	1887
8th	133	J. V. Richardson & T. B. Raikes v Free Foresters (Oxford)	1924
9th	160	H. Philipson & A. C. M. Croome v M.C.C. (Lord's)	1889
10th	149	F. H. Hollins & B. A. Collins v M.C.C. (Oxford)	1901

CAMBRIDGE UNIVERSITY

Played 12, Won 1, Drawn 4, Lost 7

BATTING AND FIELDING

	M.	*I.*	*N.O.*	*Runs*	*H.S.*	*Avge.*	100	50	*Ct.*	*St.*
†M. J. Khan	12	23	1	1216	200	55.27	5	5	9	—
†R. D. V. Knight	11	21	2	603	164*	31.73	1	3	10	—
†P. G. Carling	11	22	1	598	104	28.47	1	2	7	—
†D. R. Owen-Thomas	11	20	1	499	80	26.26	—	3	6	—
†M. T. Barford	5	9	2	182	48	26.00	—	—	3	—
†P. D. Johnson	9	15	1	249	82	17.78	—	1	5	—
R. L. Short	3	5	0	87	37	17.40	—	—	2	—
J. I. McDowall	9	17	2	197	31	13.13	—	—	11	—
J. E. Hall	6	12	0	149	42	12.41	—	—	1	—
N. P. G. Ross	3	5	2	35	12*	11.66	—	—	—	—
J. R. A. Cragg	7	13	0	149	55	11.46	—	1	2	—
†C. L. A. Wilkin	10	16	4	131	22	10.91	—	—	2	—
†T. E. N. Jameson	9	15	2	118	31*	9.07	—	—	11	—
†R. C. Bromley	5	9	0	78	18	8.66	—	—	6	—
†A. M. Jorden	7	12	3	73	13	8.11	—	—	1	—
†J. Spencer	11	16	9	35	10*	5.00	—	—	4	—

Played in two matches: H. K. Steele 0, 0, 1. *Played in one match:* R. J. Wiggs 6, 0*.

BOWLING

	Ovrs	Mdns	Runs	Wkts.	Avge.	Best	5wI	10wM
R. D. V. Knight ...	284.4	67	664	29	22.89	6–65	1	—
A. M. Jorden	163.2	38	442	14	31.57	3–72	—	—
J. Spencer	325.4	73	856	27	31.70	4–130	—	—
D.R. Owen-Thomas	196.1	49	517	13	39.76	2–26	—	—
T. E. N. Jameson .	195.1	65	456	10	45.60	2–21	—	—
C. L. A. Wilkin	267.1	60	700	15	46.66	3–74	—	—
P. D. Johnson.......	172.5	36	564	9	62.66	3–34	—	—

Also bowled: P. G. Carling 1-0-8-0; M. J. Khan 13-3-34-2; N. P. G. Ross 17-1-62-2; H. K. Steele 49-7-141-2; R. J. Wiggs 19-0-44-1.

†1970 Blue

UNIVERSITY RECORDS—CAMBRIDGE

Highest Innings Totals:	For ...703–9d v Sussex (Hove)	1890
	Agst...730–3d by West Indians (Cambridge)	1950
Lowest Innings Totals:	For ... 30 v Yorkshire (Cambridge)	1928
	Agst... 32 by Oxford U. (Lord's)	1878
Highest Individual Inngs.:	For ...254* K. S. Duleepsinhji v Middx. (Cambridge)	1927
	Agst...304* E. D. Weekes for West Indies (Cambridge)	1950
Best Bowling Figs in a Inngs.	For ...10-69 S. M. J. Woods v C. I. Thorton's XI (Cambridge)	1890
	Agst...10-38 S. E. Butler for Oxford U. (Lord's) ...	1871
Best Bowling Figs in a Match	For ...15-88 S. M. J. Woods v C. I. Thorton's XI (Cambridge)	1890
	Agst...15-95 S. E. Butler for Oxford U. (Lord's)......	1871
Most runs in a season	1581 (av. 79.05) D. S. Sheppard	1952
runs in a career	4310 (av. 38.48) J. M. Brearley....	1961–1968
100s in a season	7 by D. S. Sheppard	1952
100s in a career	14 by D. S. Sheppard	1950–1952
wickets in a season .	80 (av. 17.63) O. S. Wheatley	1958

RECORD WICKET STANDS

1st	349	J. G. Dewes & D. S. Sheppard v Sussex (Hove)...............	1950
2nd	429*	J. G. Dewes & G. H. G. Doggart v Essex (Cambridge)......	1949
3rd	284	E. T. Killick & G. C. Grant v Essex (Cambridge)............	1929
4th	275	R. de W. K. Winlaw & J. H. Human v Essex (Cambridge).	1934
5th	220	R. Subba Row & F. C. M. Alexander v Nottinghamshire (Nottingham)	1953
6th	245	J. L. Bryan & C. T. Ashton v Surrey (The Oval).............	1921
7th	289	G. Goonesena & G. W. Cook v Oxford U. (Lord's).........	1957
8th	145	H. Ashton & A. E. R. Gilligan v Free Foresters (Cambridge)	1920
9th	200	G. W. Cook & C. S. Smith v Lancashire (Liverpool).......	1957
10th	177	A. E. R. Gilligan & J. H. Naumann v Sussex (Hove)......	1919

FIRST-CLASS AVERAGES, 1970

The following averages are published in alphabetical order and include everyone who appeared in matches officially designated by the T.C.C.B. as first-class, viz.:

(a) England v. Rest of the World (5).
(b) County Championship (204).
(c) M.C.C. v. Glamorgan (1).
(d) Matches played by Oxford and Cambridge Universities v. first-class counties and the University match (21).
(e) Jamaican XI v. Essex, Glamorgan, Lancashire and Sussex (4).
(f) Scarborough Festival (3).
(g) Scotland v. Ireland (1).

No other three-day matches were accorded first-class status.

† = left-handed batsman; E = England; Ex = Essex; Sca = Scarborough Festival.

BATTING AND FIELDING

	Cap	*M.*	*I.*	*N.O.*	*Runs*	*H.S.*	*Avge.*	100	50	*Ct.*	*St.*
Abberley, R. N. (Wa).	1966	25	47	1	1212	108	26.34	1	6	15	—
Acfield, D. L. (Ex) ...	1970	19	20	10	137	34	13.70	—	—	6	—
†Ackerman, H. M. (No/Sca)	1969	26	48	1	1565	208	33.29	3	6	33	—
Allan, J. M. (Sc)	—	1	—	—	—	—	—	—	—	—	—
†Alldis, J. S. (M)	—	2	4	1	7	4*	2.33	—	—	—	—
Allen, D. A. (Gs)	1959	20	26	7	337	41	17.73	—	—	12	—
Allison, D. F. (OU) .	—	6	9	2	48	21	6.85	—	—	4	—
Amiss, D. L. (Wa/Sca)	1965	27	48	10	1757	110	46.23	2	9	26	—
Anderson, I. J. (Ire)...	—	1	2	1	40	40*	40.00	—	—	—	—
Arnold, G. G. (Sy) ...	1967	20	21	2	226	46	11.89	—	—	10	—
Asif Iqbal (K)	1968	24	40	5	1379	109	39.40	3	7	23	—
Bairstow, D. L. (Y) .	—	19	24	5	334	36	17.57	—	—	43	6
Barclay, J. R. T. (Sx)	—	2	3	0	4	4	1.33	—	—	—	—
Barford, M. T. (CU),	—	5	9	2	182	48	26.00	—	—	3	—
Barker, G. (Ex)	1955	25	45	6	1111	124	28.48	2	6	5	—
Barlow, E. J. (RW) ...	—	5	9	0	353	142	39.22	2	—	10	—
†Barlow, G. D. (M)....	—	4	7	0	129	38	18.42	—	—	—	—
Barr, D. (Sc)	—	1	1	0	14	14	14.00	—	—	2	—
†Barratt, R. J. (Le)	—	3	6	2	42	14*	10.50	—	—	6	—
Barrett, A. (Jam)	—	4	4	1	87	37*	29.00	—	—	4	—
Bates, D. L. (Sx)	1957	19	19	10	97	22*	10.77	—	—	6	—
Bevan, D. G. (Gs)	—	3	5	0	53	17	10.60	—	—	1	—
Bielby, S. R. (Nt)	—	7	12	0	209	43	17.41	—	—	1	—
†Birkenshaw, J. (Le) ...	1965	25	39	6	570	64*	17.27	—	2	16	—
Bissex, M. (Gs).........	1970	24	44	9	1316	104	37.60	1	9	19	—
Black, C. J. R. (M) ...	—	2	2	0	15	9	7.50	—	—	—	—
Blenkiron, W. (Wa/Sca)	1969	25	34	9	391	52*	15.64	—	1	12	—
Bolus, J. B. (Nt/Sca) .	1963	27	53	9	2143	147*	48.70	2	15	22	—
Bond, J. D. (La).......	1961	25	33	9	780	89	32.50	—	5	25	—
Booth, B. J. (Le)	1964	20	35	4	820	84	26.45	—	5	6	—
Booth, R. (Wo)	1956	4	4	0	24	21	6.00	—	—	21	—

	Cap	M.	I.	N.O.	Runs	H.S.	Avge.	100	50	Ct.	St.
Booton, W. T. (Ire)	—	1	1	0	12	12	12.00	—	—	—	—
Bore, M. K. (Y)	—	10	9	4	50	21*	10.00	—	—	5	—
Boyce, K. D. (Ex/Sca)	1967	28	48	1	750	70	15.95	—	4	24	—
Boycott, G. (Y/Sca/E)	1963	25	42	5	2051	260*	55.43	4	12	12	—
Bradfield, G. W. (No)	—	1	1	0	50	50	50.00	—	1	—	—
Brain, B. M. (Wo)	1966	7	6	6	7	5*	—	—	—	3	—
†Breakwell, D. (No/Sca)	—	27	34	8	496	97	19.07	—	2	10	—
Brearley, J. M. (M)	1964	10	17	1	471	85	29.43	—	4	4	—
†Bromley, R. C. (CU)	—	5	9	0	78	18	8.66	—	—	6	—
†Brooks, V. C. G. (Ex)	—	1	1	0	15	15	15.00	—	—	—	—
Brown, A. (K)	1961	13	16	5	129	52	11.72	—	1	3	—
Brown, A. S. (Gs)	1957	24	39	10	878	104*	30.27	1	2	19	—
Brown, D. J. (E/Wa)	1964	21	30	2	295	33	10.53	—	—	16	—
Brown, J. (Sc)	—	1	—	—	—	—	—	—	—	2	—
Bryant, D. J. (OU)	—	2	4	2	3	3	1.50	—	—	—	—
Burchnall, R. L. (OU)	—	10	19	0	288	79	15.15	—	1	4	—
Burgess, G. I. (So)	1968	24	46	4	866	67	20.61	—	4	5	—
Burton, M. S. W. (OU)	—	10	18	2	356	84	22.25	—	1	5	—
Buss, A. (Sx)	1963	24	31	3	404	57	14.42	—	1	10	—
†Buss, M. A. (Sx)	1967	22	42	5	1379	126	37.27	1	8	18	—
Buxton, I. R. (D)	1962	25	42	7	863	72	24.65	—	5	10	—
Campbell, A. (Jam)	—	2	2	1	6	5	6.00	—	—	2	—
†Campbell, A. N. (OU)	—	4	7	0	220	73	31.42	—	3	2	—
†Carling, P. G. (CU)	—	11	22	1	598	104	28.47	1	2	7	—
Carrick, P. (Y)	—	3	3	1	36	32	18.00	—	—	2	—
Carroll, P. R. (OU)	—	6	12	1	162	49	14.72	—	—	1	—
†Carter, R. G. M. (Wo)	1965	19	10	6	16	7*	4.00	—	—	7	—
Cartwright, T. W. (So)	1970	24	44	9	766	63*	21.88	—	3	21	—
†Cass, G. R. (Wo)	1970	21	26	4	398	53	18.09	—	1	32	10
Castell, A. T. (H)	—	21	24	5	370	73	19.47	—	1	20	—
Chisholm, R. H. E. (Sc)	—	1	2	0	111	105	55.50	1	—	—	—
Clarkson, A. (So)	1968	23	45	0	1246	105	27.68	1	8	23	—
†Close, D. B. (Y)	1949	20	28	2	949	128	36.50	1	6	20	—
Colhoun, O. D. (Ire)	—	1	1	0	1	1	1.00	—	—	2	—
Connolly, A. N. (M)	1969	20	21	3	123	26	6.83	—	—	5	—
Cope, G. A. (Y)	1970	26	29	8	327	66	15.57	—	2	11	—
Cordle, A. E. (Gm)	1967	26	41	7	564	48	16.58	—	—	8	—
Corlett, S. C. (OU)	—	1	2	0	25	19	12.50	—	—	—	—
Cottam, R. M. H. (H)	1965	22	21	11	79	16	7.90	—	—	12	—
Cowdrey, M. C. (E/K)	1951	21	35	6	1254	126	43.24	3	8	19	—
Cragg, J. R. A. (CU)	—	7	13	0	149	55	11.46	—	1	2	—
Cross, G. F. (Le)	—	8	15	2	188	53	14.46	—	1	3	—
Crump, B. S. (No)	1962	22	29	13	612	75	38.25	—	3	6	—
Dalton, A. J. (Y)	—	6	9	1	174	47*	21.75	—	—	2	—
†Davey, J. (Gs)	—	8	10	7	25	11	8.33	—	—	4	—
Davis, B. A. (Gm)	1969	27	52	3	1532	91	31.26	—	14	29	—
Davis, R. C. (Gm)	1969	27	47	6	823	69	20.07	—	4	36	—
Davison, B. F. (Le)	—	7	11	0	285	76	25.90	—	3	4	—
Denman, J. (Sx)	—	10	15	6	133	34*	14.77	—	—	2	—
Denness, M. H. (E/K)	1964	24	41	2	1531	167*	39.25	2	10	33	—
†Denning, P. W. (So)	—	6	10	0	170	50	17.00	—	1	4	—
†Dineen, P. J. (Ire)	—	1	2	1	27	17	27.00	—	—	—	—
†Dinsdale, S. C. (Ex)	—	5	7	0	97	29	13.85	—	—	4	—

	Cap	M.	I.	N.O.	Runs	H.S.	Avge.	100	50	Ct.	St.
Dixon, A. L. (K)	1960	9	13	5	211	44	26.37	—	—	1	—
D'Oliveira, B. L. (E/Wo)	1965	19	31	3	1242	111	44.35	4	5	6	—
†Douglas-Home, A.(OU)	—	4	6	1	33	23	6.60	—	—	1	—
Dudleston, B. (Le/Sca)	1969	25	48	4	1374	112	31.22	4	5	24	—
Dye, J. C. J. (K)	1966	15	12	5	52	27*	7.42	—	—	2	—
Ealham, A. G. E. (K)	1970	15	19	5	544	88	38.85	—	4	7	—
East, R. E. (Ex)	1967	25	31	8	424	50*	18.43	—	1	19	—
Edmeades, B.E.A.(Ex)	1965	26	49	3	1620	120*	35.21	4	10	7	—
†Edrich, J. H. (E/Sy) .	1959	21	37	3	1586	143	46.64	5	4	10	—
Edwards, M. J. (Sy)...	1966	22	39	0	1281	117	32.84	1	6	29	—
Ellis, G. P. (Gm)	—	9	15	3	318	55	26.50	—	2	1	—
Elms, R. (K)	—	1	—	—	—	—	—	—	—	—	—
Engineer, F. M. (La/RW)	1968	24	36	4	800	89	25.00	—	5	86	5
†Eyre, T. J. P. (D)	1967	11	11	2	87	31	9.66	—	—	6	—
Faber, M. J. J. (OU)	—	5	10	1	88	25	9.77	—	—	3	—
Featherstone, N. G. (M)	—	26	43	4	1096	94	28.10	—	9	26	—
Fletcher, K. W. R. (E/Ex/MCC/Sca) ...	1963	25	44	6	1732	169*	45.57	4	11	22	—
Folkes, C. (Jam).......	—	4	1	1	1	1*	—	—	—	—	—
†Forbes, C. (Nt).........	1965	17	15	3	118	23	9.83	—	—	5	—
Foster, M. L. C. (Jam)	—	4	5	1	243	110	60.75	1	1	1	—
Frost, G. (Nt)	—	18	28	8	628	107	31.40	1	1	20	—
Gibbs, L. R. (Wa/RW/Sca)	1968	23	25	9	87	20*	5.43	—	—	18	—
Gibbs, P. J. K. (D) ...	1968	21	38	3	1441	112*	41.17	2	11	19	—
†Gifford, N. (Wo)	1961	25	24	9	218	38*	14.53	—	—	18	—
†Gilliat, R. M. C. (H/MCC)............	1969	3	4	1	18	10	6.00	—	—	2	—
Goddard, G. F. (Sc) .	—	1	—	—	—	—	—	—	—	—	—
†Gooch, P. A. (La)	—	4	3	1	0	0*	0.00	—	—	3	—
Goodwin, D. (Ire)	—	1	1	0	0	0	0.00	—	—	—	—
Goodwin, K. (La)	1965	4	6	2	16	6	4.00	—	—	14	2
Gordon, A. (Wa)	—	10	18	1	366	65	21.52	—	3	10	—
Graham, J. N. (K) ...	1967	12	13	4	36	11*	4.00	—	—	5	—
Graveney, T. W. (Wo)	1962	21	34	13	1316	114	62.66	2	9	18	—
†Graves, P. J. (Sx/Sca)	1969	23	43	2	1142	117*	27.85	1	8	22	—
Green, D. M. (Gs/MCC)	1968	25	48	0	1429	146	29.77	2	9	12	—
Greenidge, C. G. (H)	—	7	11	1	351	73	35.10	—	4	6	—
Greenidge, G. A. (Sx)	1970	24	44	0	1305	172	29.65	5	3	10	—
Greig, A. W. (E/Sx/MCC/Sca) ...	1967	26	46	4	1008	113*	24.00	1	7	31	—
Griffith, K. (Wo)	—	1	—	—	—	—	—	—	—	—	—
Griffith, M. G. (Sx) .	1967	23	38	10	811	74	28.96	—	5	12	—
Halfyard, D. J. (Nt) .	1968	24	26	5	334	47*	15.90	—	—	11	—
Hall, I. W. (D)	1961	19	32	6	701	107	26.96	1	1	20	—
Hall, J. E. (CU)	—	6	12	0	149	42	12.41	—	—	1	—
Hallam, M. R. (Le) .	1954	1	1	0	11	11	11.00	—	—	1	—
Halliday, M. (Ire)	—	1	1	0	6	6	6.00	—	—	—	—
Hampshire, J. H. (Y/Sca)...............	1963	22	36	6	1130	120*	37.66	2	4	20	—

	Cap	M.	I.	N.O.	Runs	H.S.	Avge.	100	50	Ct.	St.
Hardie, B. R. (Sc)	—	1	1	1	36	36*	—	—	—	—	—
Harris, M. J. (Nt)	1970	25	49	4	1914	120	42.53	3	14	16	—
Harrison, J. (Sc)	—	1	2	0	85	65	42.50	—	1	1	—
Harvey, J. F. (D)	1968	16	26	4	726	80	33.00	—	6	3	—
Hassan, B. (Nt)	1970	25	45	2	1395	110	32.44	1	11	21	—
Hatteea, S. A. (Sca) .	—	1	1	0	0	0	0.00	—	—	2	—
Haye, W. (Jam)	—	1	—	—	—	—	—	—	—	1	—
Hayes, F. C. (La/Sc) .	—	17	24	4	780	99	39.00	—	6	18	—
Haywood, P. R. (Le)	—	13	26	1	503	65	20.12	—	3	4	—
†Headley, R.G.A.(Wo)	1961	24	44	4	1670	148*	41.75	5	6	17	—
Heal, M. G. (OU)	—	6	11	0	180	64	16.36	—	1	2	—
Heard, H. (OU)	—	4	6	2	58	31	14.50	—	—	3	—
Hemmings, E. E. (Wa)	—	12	17	7	354	54	35.40	—	1	8	—
Hemsley, E. J. O. (Wo)	1969	11	19	4	404	52	26.93	—	1	7	—
Hendrick, M. (D)......	—	5	5	3	6	3*	3.00	—	—	2	—
Herman, R. S. (M) ...	1969	9	7	2	57	24*	11.40	—	—	—	—
Hill, L. W. (Gm)	—	7	12	2	244	80	24.40	—	1	8	—
Hill, M. (So)	—	17	31	1	660	65	22.00	—	3	7	—
Hobbs, R. N. S. (Ex/Sca)	1964	27	41	12	595	83*	20.51	—	1	26	—
†Hodgson, A. (No)	—	1	—	—	—	—	—	—	—	—	—
Holder, J. W. (H)	—	15	14	4	144	28*	14.40	—	—	4	—
Holder, V. A. (Wo) .	1970	23	20	5	158	52	10.53	—	1	10	—
Hone, D. J. (OU)......	—	3	5	0	26	13	5.20	—	—	1	—
Hooper, J. M. M. (Sy)	—	4	7	3	87	41*	21.75	—	—	2	—
Hopkins, J. A. (Gm)	—	1	2	0	6	4	3.00	—	—	—	—
Hopkins, J. D. (M) ...	—	1	1	0	4	4	4.00	—	—	5	—
Hughes, D. P. (La) ...	1970	26	28	9	343	55	18.05	—	1	16	—
Humphrey, R. G. (Sy)	—	1	—	—	—	—	—	—	—	1	—
Hutton, R. A. (Y)	1964	26	38	7	875	104	28.22	1	4	26	—
Ibadulla, K. (Wa/Sca)	1957	22	37	5	793	81*	24.78	—	4	22	—
Illingworth, R. (E/Le/MCC)	1969	23	38	4	1047	102*	30.79	1	6	7	—
†Inman, C. (Le)	1963	24	44	5	1280	105	32.82	3	7	9	—
Intikhab Alam (Sy/RW)	1969	24	39	5	923	106	27.14	1	4	9	—
Jackman, R. D. (Sy) .	1970	23	20	7	113	16	8.69	—	—	5	—
Jameson, J. A. (Wa) .	1964	27	50	3	1821	194	38.74	4	9	16	—
†Jameson, T. E. N. (CU/Wa)	—	10	17	2	181	32	12.06	—	—	12	—
†Jenkins, H. (Gm)	—	1	2	1	81	65	81.00	—	1	1	—
Jesty, T. E. (H).........	—	22	32	9	572	73*	24.86	—	3	12	—
Johns, R. L. (OU)	—	8	15	2	273	61*	21.00	—	1	6	—
Johnson, C. (Y)	—	2	3	1	20	15	10.00	—	—	1	—
Johnson, G. W. (K)...	1970	25	40	1	927	116	23.76	3	3	24	—
Johnson, L. A. (No) .	1960	18	21	6	159	41	10.60	—	—	29	7
Johnson, P. D. (Nt/CU)	—	11	19	1	270	82	15.00	—	1	7	—
†Jones, A. (E/Gm)	1962	20	38	2	1394	161*	38.72	5	5	11	—
Jones, A. A. (So)	—	22	26	11	75	19	5.00	—	—	5	—
Jones, E. W. (Gm) ...	1967	28	49	12	626	56*	16.91	—	2	85	9
Jones, K. V. (M)	—	22	32	14	417	56*	23.16	—	2	14	—
Jorden, A. M. (CU/Ex)	—	8	13	3	81	13	8.10	—	—	1	—
Joshi, U. C. (Sx/Sca)	—	2	3	0	12	9	4.00	—	—	—	—

	Cap	M.	I.	N.O.	Runs	H.S.	Avge.	100	50	Ct.	St.
Julian, R. (Le)	1961	1	2	0	19	19	9.50	—	—	1	—
Julien, B. (K)	—	1	1	0	5	5	5.00	—	—	1	—
Kanhai, R. B. (Wa/RW/Sca)	1968	21	37	4	1894	187*	57.39	7	6	25	—
†Kennedy, A. (La)	—	1	2	1	26	25	26.00	—	—	—	—
Kennedy, J. H. (Sc) .	—	1	—	—	—	—	—	—	—	—	—
Kettle, M. K. (No) ...	—	2	3	1	12	7*	6.00	—	—	1	—
Khan, M. J. (CU/Gm)	1968	22	42	2	1862	200	46.55	7	8	25	—
Kingston, G. C. (Gm)	—	5	8	1	84	22	12.00	—	—	1	—
†Kitchen, M. J. (So) ...	1966	24	47	4	977	99	22.72	—	6	12	—
†Knight, R. D. V. (CU/Sy)	—	14	26	2	729	164*	30.37	1	5	10	—
Knott, A. P. E. (E/K)	1965	22	29	7	519	51*	23.59	—	2	62	2
Laing, J. G. B. (Sc) ...	—	1	2	1	93	93	93.00	—	1	—	—
Langford, B. A. (So)	1957	23	35	5	436	50*	14.53	—	1	16	—
†Langridge, R. J. (Sx) .	1961	23	40	4	765	66	21.25	—	4	18	—
Latchman, H. C. (M)	1968	13	13	2	137	43	12.45	—	—	7	—
Laycock, D. A. (K) .	—	1	1	0	8	8	8.00	—	—	1	—
Leadbeater, B. (Y) ...	1969	6	9	1	299	89*	37.37	—	2	5	—
Leary, S. E. (K)	1957	19	30	5	669	88	26.76	—	3	19	—
Lee, P. (No)	—	5	2	0	4	4	2.00	—	—	2	—
Lees, R. D. (OU)	—	3	6	2	29	17*	7.25	—	—	—	—
Lenham, L. J. (Sx) ...	1957	3	5	0	155	46	31.00	—	—	—	—
Lever, J. K. (Ex)	1970	16	17	11	189	91	31.50	—	1	2	—
Lever, P. (E/La)	1965	22	14	8	125	26*	20.83	—	—	12	—
Lewington, P. J. (Wa)	—	4	2	1	12	7	12.00	—	—	1	—
Lewis, A. R. (Gm/Sca)	1960	26	49	6	1693	128	39.37	2	11	24	—
Lewis D. (Jam)	—	4	5	0	64	24	12.80	—	—	9	—
Lewis, R. M. (Sy)	—	3	6	1	116	55	23.20	—	1	3	—
Lewis, R. V. (H)	—	11	22	1	311	74	14.80	—	1	10	—
†Lightfoot, A. (No) ...	1961	13	24	2	837	96	38.04	—	5	9	—
†Livingstone, D. A. (H)	1961	23	37	4	1020	103	30.90	1	6	15	2
†Llewellyn, M. J. (Gm)	—	1	2	0	15	15	7.50	—	—	2	—
†Lloyd, C. H. (La/RW)	1969	23	37	3	1603	163	47.14	5	7	12	—
†Lloyd, D. (La)	1968	22	39	4	1039	124	29.68	3	4	19	—
†Long, A. (Sy)	1962	25	32	8	643	92	26.79	—	2	61	4
Luckhurst, B. W. (E/K/MCC)..........	1963	23	38	4	1633	203*	48.02	4	8	26	—
Lumb, R. G. (Y)	—	1	2	0	21	17	10.50	—	—	—	—
Lyons, K. J. (Gm) ...	—	15	28	4	452	58*	18.83	—	1	5	—
McDowall, J. I. (CU)	—	9	17	2	197	31	13.13	—	—	11	—
McIlwaine, R. J. (H)	—	2	1	0	10	10	10.00	—	—	1	—
McKenzie, G. D. (Le/RW)	1969	22	29	3	291	37	11.19	—	—	11	—
McMorris, E. D. S. A. (Jam)	—	3	4	1	36	25	12.00	—	—	2	—
McVicker, N. M. (Wa)	—	15	17	6	148	38	13.45	—	—	5	—
Mansell, A. W. (Sx)...	—	3	4	1	16	8	5.33	—	—	8	1
Marner, P. T. (Le) ...	1965	23	41	2	1409	115	36.12	2	10	28	—
Marshall, R. E. (H) .	1955	25	41	2	1590	189*	40.76	2	10	10	—
May, B. (OU)	—	6	11	0	217	103	19.72	1	—	4	—
Meyer, B. J. (Gs)	1958	24	27	13	163	34	11.64	—	—	43	8
Miles, O. (Jam)	—	4	1	0	10	10	10.00	—	—	4	—

	Cap	M.	I.	N.O.	Runs	H.S.	Avge.	100	50	Ct.	St.
Millener, D. J. (OU) .	—	4	6	1	70	24	14.00	—	—	2	—
Milton, C. A. (Gs) ...	1949	14	26	5	600	149*	28.57	1	2	12	—
Moan, R. (Ire)	—	1	1	1	0	0*	—	—	—	—	—
More, H. K. (Sc)	—	1	2	1	23	13*	23.00	—	—	—	—
Morgan, S. (Jam)	—	3	4	1	84	61*	28.00	—	1	1	—
Mortimore, J. B. (Gs)	1954	18	26	5	318	46	15.14	—	—	10	—
Mucklow, P. (OU) ...	—	2	4	0	48	32	12.00	—	—	1	—
Murray, D. L. (RW/Sca).............	—	4	6	0	223	95	37.16	—	2	17	—
Murray, J. T. (M/Sca)	1956	27	44	5	1106	97	28.35	—	6	32	17
Mushtaq Mohammad (No/RW/Sca)	1967	23	43	2	1482	151*	36.14	1	10	14	—
†Nash, M. A. (Gm) ...	1969	26	42	7	606	61	17.31	—	2	13	—
†Nicholls, D. (K)	1969	8	12	0	154	41	12.83	—	—	20	—
Nicholls, R. B. (Gs)...	1957	24	46	2	1341	100	30.47	1	7	7	—
Nicholson, A. G. (Y)	1963	23	21	9	173	24*	14.41	—	—	5	—
Norman, M.E.J.C. (Le)	1966	9	16	1	429	88	28.60	—	2	2	—
†Old, C. M. (E/Y/MCC/Sca)	1969	24	28	6	501	92*	22.77	—	1	17	—
O'Riordan, A. J. (Ire)	—	1	1	0	31	31	31.00	—	—	—	—
Ormrod, J. A. (Wo)...	1966	22	39	2	1228	155*	33.18	2	5	28	—
†Osman, W. M. (No) .	—	1	1	0	9	9	9.00	—	—	2	—
Owen-Thomas, D. R. (CU/Sy)	—	13	23	1	576	80	26.18	—	4	6	—
Padgett, D. E. V. (Y/Sca)................	1958	26	42	5	1127	108	30.45	2	7	17	—
Page, M. H. (D)	1964	20	35	2	1344	113	40.72	1	9	19	—
Palmer, R. (So)	1969	20	31	12	248	40*	13.05	—	—	12	—
†Parfitt, P. H. (M/Sca)	1960	24	42	6	1403	133	38.97	3	10	32	—
Parks, J. M. (Sx)	1951	21	38	7	1300	166*	41.93	2	9	43	3
Pataudi, Nawab of (Sx)	1963	4	8	0	113	28	14.12	—	—	3	—
Payne, C. J. (M).......	—	3	5	0	37	22	7.40	—	—	—	—
Pearman, H. (M)	—	3	3	1	51	43*	25.50	—	—	3	—
Pember, J. D. D. (Le)	—	10	11	6	104	53	20.80	—	1	5	—
Phillips, R. W. (Gs) .	—	9	15	0	281	82	18.73	—	1	8	—
Phillipson, P. C. (Sx).	—	1	2	0	1	1	0.50	—	—	—	—
Pigot, D. R. (Ire)	—	1	2	0	92	88	46.00	—	1	—	—
Pilling, H. (La/MCC)	1965	26	43	7	1319	120*	36.63	4	5	8	—
Pinnock, R. (Jam)	—	4	4	0	321	176	80.25	1	2	2	—
Plummer, P. J. (Nt) .	—	7	7	0	101	46	14.42	—	—	6	—
Pocock, P. I. (Sy/Sca)	1967	25	25	5	210	25*	10.50	—	—	6	—
Pollock, P.M. (RW) .	—	1	1	1	23	23*	—	—	—	—	—
†Pollock, R. G. (RW)	—	5	8	0	250	114	31.25	1	1	1	—
Pont, K. R. (Ex).......	—	1	1	0	5	5	5.00	—	—	—	—
Presland, E. R. (Ex) .	—	10	17	2	300	45	20.00	—	—	11	—
†Price, J. S. E. (M/Sca)	1963	27	20	13	39	12	5.57	—	—	12	—
Prideaux, R.M. (No/Sca)	1962	26	47	6	1679	176*	40.95	4	7	11	—
Procter, M. J. (Gs/RW)	1968	20	33	7	934	115	35.92	1	5	16	—
Pullan, D. A. (Nt)	—	25	21	11	111	13*	11.10	—	—	63	10
†Pullar, G. (Gs).........	—	6	10	1	227	73	25.22	—	1	2	—
Racionzer, T. B. (Sc)	—	1	1	0	10	10	10.00	—	—	1	—
Radley, C. T. (M)	1967	26	44	4	1329	116	33.22	1	9	19	—
Reed, B. L. (H)	1967	12	21	0	816	138	38.85	1	5	7	—

	Cap	M.	I.	N.O.	Runs	H.S.	Avge.	100	50	Ct.	St.
†Reith, M. R. (Ire)	—	1	2	0	82	82	41.00	—	1	—	—
Reynolds, B. L. (No).	1956	10	19	3	358	83	22.37	—	1	5	—
†Reynolds, G.E.A. (Gm)	—	1	1	1	9	9*	—	—	—	—	—
Richards, B.A.(H/RW)	1968	20	33	2	1667	153	53.77	3	12	15	—
Richards, R. (Ex)	—	1	—	—	—	—	—	—	—	—	—
Ridley, R. M. (OU)...	—	9	17	1	411	70*	25.68	—	3	5	—
Roberts, J. K. (So) ...	—	3	2	1	0	0*	0.00	—	—	—	—
†Robinson, G. A. (OU)	—	2	4	0	27	27	6.75	—	—	4	—
†Robinson, P. J. (So) .	1966	24	47	4	1158	140	26.93	1	9	19	—
Roope, G.R.J. (Sy/Sca)	1969	28	48	9	1346	111	34.51	2	4	44	—
†Rose, B. C. (So)	—	6	10	0	73	16	7.30	—	—	4	—
†Ross, N. P. G. (CU) .	—	3	5	2	35	12*	11.66	—	—	—	—
†Rouse, S. J. (Wa)	—	2	1	0	9	9	9.00	—	—	—	—
Rowe, L. A. (Jam) ...	—	4	5	0	125	52	25.00	—	1	5	—
Rumsey, F. E. (D) ...	—	1	1	1	2	2*	—	—	—	—	—
Russell, P. E. (D)	—	18	20	4	234	72	14.62	—	1	10	—
Russell, W. E. (M)....	1959	22	37	2	1580	128*	45.14	3	9	18	—
†Sadiq Mohammad (Ex/Sca)	—	2	3	0	97	56	32.33	—	1	—	—
Sainsbury, P. J. (H) .	1955	23	36	7	688	70	23.72	—	2	20	—
Sarfraz Nawaz (No) .	—	22	20	9	229	44*	20.81	—	—	13	—
Saville, G. J. (Ex)......	1970	25	45	7	1133	103	29.81	1	7	24	—
Schofield, D. (Y)	—	1	1	1	1	1*	—	—	—	—	—
Sharp, G. (No)	—	7	9	5	165	55*	41.25	—	1	11	3
Sharpe, P. J. (E/Y) ...	1960	25	40	1	1155	120	29.61	2	7	34	—
Shepherd, D. J. (Gm)	1952	27	30	12	180	36*	10.00	—	—	9	—
Shepherd, D. R. (Gs)	1969	23	42	2	1079	111	26.97	1	6	6	—
Shepherd, J. N. (K) .	1967	25	36	4	734	105	22.93	1	2	23	—
Short, R. L. (CU)	—	3	5	0	87	37	17.40	—	—	2	—
Shuttleworth, K. (La/E)	1968	21	16	9	115	20	16.42	—	—	5	—
Simmons, J. (La)	—	25	28	8	423	112	21.15	1	2	9	—
Slade, D. N. F. (Wo)	1960	19	21	3	286	38	15.88	—	—	9	—
Smedley, M. J. (Nt) .	1966	25	46	3	1553	149	36.11	3	8	28	—
Smith, A. C. (Wa)	1961	19	29	6	309	42*	13.43	—	—	38	3
†Smith, D. H. K. (D) .	1968	25	46	3	1241	136	28.86	1	3	20	—
Smith, D. R. (Gs)	1957	23	28	3	400	61*	16.00	—	1	27	—
Smith, E. (D)	1954	24	28	10	303	28	16.83	—	—	10	—
Smith, M. J. (M)	1967	25	45	2	1705	151	39.65	6	6	13	—
Smith, M. J. K. (Wa)	1957	26	48	7	1644	153*	40.09	2	11	22	—
Smith, N. (Y)	—	7	11	5	82	20	13.66	—	—	13	3
Smith, R. (Y)	—	1	1	0	2	2	2.00	—	—	—	—
†Smith, W. A. (Sy)	1968	7	13	0	203	43	15.61	—	—	—	—
Smyth, R. N. P. (Sx) .	—	3	5	0	42	25	8.40	—	—	—	—
Snellgrove, K. L. (La)	—	8	14	1	474	138	36.46	1	1	3	—
Snow, J. A. (Sx/E)	1964	22	30	14	324	42*	20.25	—	—	13	—
†Sobers, G. S. (Nt/RW)	1968	19	32	9	1742	183	75.73	7	7	20	—
Spencer, J. (CU/Sx) .	—	20	26	12	72	13*	5.14	—	—	8	—
Standen, J. A. (Wo)...	1962	18	18	2	209	92*	13.06	—	1	7	—
Staziker, M. W. (La)	—	2	2	2	1	1*	—	—	—	—	—
†Stead, B. (Nt)	1969	14	13	4	116	35	12.88	—	—	2	—
Steele, D. S. (No)	1965	22	39	3	913	90*	25.36	—	6	26	—
Steele, H. K. (CU) ...	—	2	3	0	1	1	0.33	—	—	—	—
Steele, J. F. (Le)	—	19	22	6	167	22	10.43	—	—	22	—

	Cap	M.	I.	N.O.	Runs	H.S.	Avge.	100	50	Ct.	St.
Stephenson, G. R. (H)	1969	24	32	8	422	82	17.58	—	2	73	7
Stewart, D. E. R. (Wo)	—	2	3	0	12	8	4.00	—	—	—	—
Stewart, M. J. (Sy)....	1955	22	39	5	1246	128	36.64	2	7	16	—
Storey, S. J. (Sy)	1964	23	37	4	1045	106	31.66	1	8	18	—
†Stringer, P. M. (Le) .	—	19	26	9	109	17	6.41	—	—	5	—
Sullivan, J. (La)	1969	21	32	3	669	72	23.06	—	3	17	—
Sullivan, J. P. (Gs)....	—	5	9	0	168	53	18.66	—	1	2	—
†Suttle, K. G. (Sx)	1952	24	39	6	752	80	22.78	—	5	9	—
†Swarbrook, F. W. (D)	—	24	30	8	367	90	16.68	—	1	16	—
Swinburne, J. W. (No)	—	10	11	1	36	13	3.60	—	—	4	—
†Taylor, B. (Ex/Sca) ...	1956	28	48	7	1190	113*	29.02	2	5	52	20
Taylor, C. R. V. (Wa)	—	1	—	—	—	—	—	—	—	2	—
Taylor, D. J. S. (So) .	—	24	37	12	443	45	17.72	—	—	50	5
Taylor, M. N. S. (Nt)	1967	23	28	7	344	64	16.38	—	1	10	—
Taylor, R.W. (D/MCC)	1962	26	35	5	546	56	18.20	—	2	51	11
Thompson, E. R. (Sc)	—	1	1	1	8	8*	—	—	—	—	—
Tidy, W. N. (Wa)	—	20	21	9	52	7*	4.33	—	—	10	—
Timms, B. S. V. (Wa)	—	8	11	0	151	35	13.72	—	—	10	2
Titmus, F. J. (M/Sca)	1953	28	39	12	467	38	17.29	—	—	16	—
Tolchard, J. G. (Le) .	—	9	14	3	189	43	17.18	—	—	2	—
Tolchard, R. W. (Le/Sca)	1966	25	40	7	998	126*	30.24	2	4	53	8
†Turner, D. R. (H)	1970	23	39	3	1165	116	32.36	1	7	12	—
Turner, G. M. (Wo) ...	1968	25	46	7	2379	154*	61.00	10	9	25	—
Turner, S. (Ex)	1970	25	40	6	545	121	16.02	1	—	26	—
Underwood, D. L. (K/E)	1964	21	23	6	147	32	8.64	—	—	10	—
Verity, S. A. (OU) ...	—	2	3	1	22	11	11.00	—	—	—	—
Virgin, R. T. (So)......	1960	24	47	0	2223	178	47.29	7	11	15	—
Walker, P. M. (Gm) .	1958	27	49	6	1049	114	24.39	1	6	39	—
Wallace, K. W. (Ex) .	—	1	1	0	4	4	4.00	—	—	—	—
Waller, C. E. (Sy)	—	6	6	3	20	9*	6.66	—	—	2	—
Ward, A. (D/E/MCC)	1969	18	21	4	126	26	7.41	—	—	10	—
Ward, B. (Ex)	1970	18	32	1	774	164*	24.96	1	2	6	—
Ward, J. (OU)	—	3	6	0	81	38	13.50	—	—	—	—
Warner, G. S. (Wa) .	—	6	10	3	249	102	35.57	1	—	1	—
†Watts, P. J. (No)	1962	24	41	6	966	103	27.60	1	4	22	—
Wellington, L. (Jam)	—	4	2	1	77	47	77.00	—	—	1	—
Wheatley, K. J. (H) .	—	14	26	5	538	73	25.61	—	2	8	—
†White, D. W. (H)......	1960	14	12	9	150	57	50.00	—	1	3	—
†White, R. A. (Nt)	1966	24	36	10	671	63*	25.80	—	3	15	—
Wiggs, R. J. (CU)	—	1	2	1	6	6	6.00	—	—	—	—
Wilkin, C. L. A. (CU)	—	10	16	4	131	22	10.91	—	—	2	—
Wilkins, C. P. (D/Sca)	1970	26	46	5	1638	102*	39.95	3	9	17	—
Willey, P. (No/Sca) ...	—	26	42	10	923	99*	28.84	—	7	16	—
Williams, D. (OU) ...	—	5	9	3	72	21	12.00	—	—	2	—
†Williams, D. L. (Gm)	—	26	22	10	35	5*	2.91	—	—	4	—
Willis, R.G.D. (Sy/Sca)	—	14	12	8	61	25	15.25	—	—	4	—
†Wilson, D. (Y/E/MCC)	1960	19	23	4	260	48	13.68	—	—	7	—
Wilson, P.R.B. (OU)	—	5	9	0	173	41	19.22	—	—	3	—
Wood, B. (La)	1968	26	44	7	1457	144	39.37	5	5	15	—
Woodford, J. D. (Y) .	—	10	17	0	275	51	16.17	—	1	4	—
Woolmer, R. A. (K) .	1970	15	20	5	270	58	18.00	—	1	10	—

	Cap	M.	I.	N.O.	Runs	H.S.	Avge.	100	50	Ct.	St.
Wright, L. (Jam)	—	3	1	0	13	13	13.00	—	—	5	—
†Yardley, T. J. (Wo) .	—	18	26	7	762	94	40.10	—	6	9	—
†Younis Ahmed (Sy)...	1969	25	46	7	1588	120*	40.71	2	10	14	—

BOWLING

N.B.—Players who did not bowl in first-class cricket last season are omitted from the following list.

	Type	O.	M.	Runs	Wkts.	Avge.	Best	5wI	10 wM
Abberley, R. N. (Wa)	OB	10	0	32	0	—	—	—	—
Acfield, D. L. (Ex) .	OB	532.1	150	1263	51	24.76	5–39	2	—
Ackerman, H. M. (No/Sca)	RM	2.2	0	8	0	—	—	—	—
Allan, J. M. (Sc)	SLA	19	8	51	1	51.00	1–51	—	—
Alldis, J. S. (M)	SLA	15	5	37	1	37.00	1–33	—	—
Allen, D. A. (Gs) ...	OB	501.4	128	1460	48	30.41	4–53	—	—
Amiss, D. L. (Wa/Sca)	SLA	27.5	9	80	5	16.00	3–21	—	—
Arnold, G. G. (Sy) .	RFM	577.4	104	1607	64	25.10	6–82	3	—
Asif Iqbal (K)	RM	137	29	363	10	36.30	3–46	—	—
Barclay, J. R. T. (Sx)	OB	17	2	56	0	—	—	—	—
Barlow, E. J. (RW) .	RM	152	33	396	20	19.80	7–64	3	1
Barr, D. (Sc)	RFM	33	13	56	2	28.00	1–28	—	—
Barratt, R. J. (Le) ...	SLA	51	16	119	3	39.66	1–8	—	—
Barrett, A. (Jam)	LBG	47.1	14	119	5	23.80	3–82	—	—
Bates, D. L. (Sx)	RFM	362.5	94	1058	26	40.69	5–76	1	—
Bielby, S. R. (Nt) ...	OB	1	0	4	0	—	—	—	—
Birkenshaw, J. (Le)...	OB	721.1	191	1769	63	28.07	6–72	5	1
Bissex, M. (Gs).......	SLA	393	88	1242	35	35.48	5–34	2	—
Black, C. J. R. (M) .	RM	20	5	62	0	—	—	—	—
Blenkiron, W. (Wa/Sca)	RFM	825.5	222	2093	76	27.53	5–89	1	—
Bolus, J. B. (Nt/Sca)	LM	4.3	0	14	1	14.00	1–6	—	—
Booth, B. J. (Le)	LBG	34	6	115	3	38.33	2–45	—	—
Booton, W. T. (Ire)	RM	16	1	72	2	36.00	2–72	—	—
Bore, M. K. (Y)	LFM	279	94	648	23	28.17	5–51	1	—
Boyce, K. D. (Ex/Sca)	RFM	772.1	115	2351	88	26.71	5–39	4	—
Brain, B. M. (Wo) .	RFM	210	38	587	19	30.89	3–49	—	—
Breakwell, D. (No/Sca)	SLA	696.4	214	1843	72	25.59	8–39	2	1
Brown, A. (K)	RFM	369	84	1065	34	31.32	5–35	1	—
Brown, A. S. (Gs) ...	RM	469.3	92	1308	38	34.42	6–48	1	—
Brown, D. J. (E/Wa)	RFM	630.1	122	1886	73	25.83	5–58	1	—
Bryant, D. J. (OU) .	RFM	38	7	148	4	37.00	2–73	—	—
Burgess, G. I. (So) .	RM	498.5	91	1667	56	29.76	5–45	3	—
Burton, M.S.W. (OU)	OB	283.4	73	898	21	42.76	5–96	1	—
Buss, A. (Sx)	RFM	713.2	150	2113	88	24.01	6–54	5	—
Buss, M. A. (Sx)	LM	511	168	1399	45	31.08	7–58	2	—
Buxton, I. R. (D) ...	RM	422.2	142	1018	46	22.13	6–34	2	—
Carling, P. G. (CU) .	—	1	0	8	0	—	—	—	—
Carrick, P. (Y)	SLA	84.3	14	312	14	22.28	6–85	1	—
Carter, R.G.M. (Wo)	RFM	590.2	94	1850	53	34.90	6–49	2	—
Cartwright, T.W.(So)	RM	851.4	318	1891	86	21.98	7–56	6	1

	Type	O.	M.	Runs	Wkts.	Avge.	Best	5wI	10 wM
Castell, A. T. (H) ...	RM/LBG	570.4	109	1714	43	39.86	4–24	—	—
Chisholm, R.H.E.(Sc)	LBG	9	0	33	0	—	—	—	—
Clarkson, A. (So) ...	OB	6	1	19	0	—	—	—	—
Close, D. B. (Y)	RM/OB	34	10	95	2	47.50	1–15	—	—
Connolly, A. N. (M)	RFM	598.2	145	1610	52	30.96	5–32	1	—
Cope, G. A. (Y)	OB	878.5	282	2111	83	25.43	7–36	4	1
Cordle, A. E. (Gm) .	RM	451.3	114	1179	37	31.86	4–35	—	—
Corlett, S. C. (OU) .	OB	7	1	26	0	—	—	—	—
Cottam, R. M. H. (H)	RFM	763.1	173	1988	77	25.81	7–106	3	—
Cowdrey, M. C. (E/K)	LBG	11	0	47	1	47.00	1–44	—	—
Cross, G. F. (Le)	RM	93.1	19	293	11	26.63	4–28	—	—
Crump, B. S. (No) .	RM	589.1	154	1562	47	33.23	5–48	1	—
Davey, J. (Gs)	LFM	208.2	35	736	22	33.45	4–37	—	—
Davis, B. A. (Gm) .	OB	24	6	85	1	85.00	1–27	—	—
Davis, R. C. (Gm) .	OB	520.5	145	1373	54	25.42	6–82	1	—
Davison, B. F. (Le) .	RM	105	22	285	7	40.71	4–99	—	—
Denman, J. (Sx)	RM	199.3	21	792	18	44.00	4–45	—	—
Dixon, A. L. (K)	RM/OB	130.4	32	371	6	61.83	3–24	—	—
D'Oliveira, B. L. (E/Wo)	RM/OB	351.2	120	766	20	38.30	4–43	—	—
Douglas-Home, A. (OU)..................	RM	95	25	273	9	30.33	3–71	—	—
Dudleston, B. (Le/Sca)	SLA	19.4	0	120	2	60.00	2–48	—	—
Dye, J. C. J. (K)......	LFM	417.4	104	1064	38	28.00	5–69	1	—
Ealham, A. G. E. (K)	OB	1	0	4	0	—	—	—	—
East, R. E. (Ex)	SLA	677	229	1458	53	27.50	6–22	1	—
Edmeades, B.E.A.(Ex)	RM	70	18	143	5	28.60	2–21	—	—
Elms, R. (K)	LFM	27	9	88	4	22.00	2–38	—	—
Engineer, F. M. (La/RW)	LB	4	1	10	0	—	—	—	—
Eyre, T. J. P. (D) ...	RFM	236.2	65	749	15	49.93	4–57	—	—
Featherstone, N. G. (M)	OB	31	6	121	0	—	—	—	—
Fletcher, K. W. R. (E/Ex/MCC/Sca) .	LB	18.5	1	91	2	45.50	2–36	—	—
Folkes, C. (Jam)......	RFM	90.3	24	190	10	19.00	5–22	1	—
Forbes, C. (Nt).......	LM	358.1	87	915	33	27.72	4–68	—	—
Foster, M.L.C.(Jam)	OB	28	6	88	5	17.60	3–24	—	—
Gibbs, L. R. (Wa/RW/Sca)	OB	871.3	282	1928	54	35.70	8–37	2	—
Gibbs, P. J. K. (D) .	OB	3	1	14	0	—	—	—	—
Gifford, N. (Wo)	SLA	965.5	331	2092	105	19.92	6–43	7	—
Goddard, G. F. (Sc)	OB	32	7	60	1	60.00	1–9	—	—
Gooch, P. A. (La) ...	RFM	83.1	18	252	6	42.00	4–52	—	—
Goodwin, D. (Ire) ...	RFM	28	15	35	0	—	—	—	—
Gordon, A. (Wa) ...	—	0.4	0	1	0	—	—	—	—
Graham, J. N. (K) .	RM	384.1	86	1036	40	25.90	6–67	2	—
Graveney, T. W. (Wo)	LB	14	1	53	2	26.50	2–10	—	—
Graves, P. J. (Sx/Sca)	SLA	18.4	5	43	2	21.50	2–10	—	—
Green, D. M. (Gs/MCC)	RM	32	9	86	0	—	—	—	—

	Type	O.	M.	Runs	Wkts.	Avge.	Best	5wI	10 wM
Greenidge, C. G. (H)	RM	1	1	0	0	—	—	—	—
Greenidge, G. A. (Sx)	LBG	53.3	6	220	4	55.00	2–62	—	—
Greig, A. W. (E/Sx/MCC/Sca) .	RM	528.2	108	1634	59	27.69	7–74	2	—
Griffith, K. (Wo)	OB	27	5	86	1	86.00	1–86	—	—
Griffith, M. G. (Sx)	—	1	0	5	0	—	—	—	—
Halfyard, D. J. (Nt)	RM	837.4	223	2135	55	38.81	3–29	—	—
Halliday, M. (Ire) ...	OB	10	2	32	0	—	—	—	—
Hampshire, J. H. (Y/Sca)...............	LB	15	4	69	0	—	—	—	—
Harris, M. J. (Nt) ...	LBG	323.3	72	1036	26	39.84	4–80	—	—
Hatteea, S. A. (Sca) .	RFM	17	2	62	4	15.50	2–30	—	—
Haye, W. (Jam)	RFM	7	1	20	1	20.00	1–20	—	—
Hayes, F. C. (La/Sca)	RM	7	3	10	0	—	—	—	—
Haywood, P. R. (Le)	LB	2	1	5	0	—	—	—	—
Heard, H. (OU)	RM	104	20	323	9	35.88	4–59	—	—
Hemmings, E. E. (Wa)	RM	228	70	634	14	45.28	4–88	—	—
Hemsley, E. J. O.(Wo)	RM	68	13	204	7	29.14	2–26	—	—
Hendrick, M. (D)....	RFM	97	14	343	9	38.11	4–77	—	—
Herman, R. S. (M) .	RFM	187	34	556	14	39.71	4–57	—	—
Hobbs, R. N. S. (Ex/Sca)	LBG	736	178	2183	102	21.40	7–59	5	—
Hodgson, A. (No) ...	RFM	12	5	12	2	6.00	2–4	—	—
Holder, J. W. (H) ...	RFM	471	99	1280	55	23.27	5–36	1	—
Holder, V. A. (Wo)	RFM	707.3	141	1773	84	21.10	6–21	6	1
Hone, D. J. (OU)....	RM	69.2	11	284	1	284.00	1–82	—	—
Hughes, D. P. (La) .	SLA	803.3	248	2377	82	28.98	7–24	4	1
Hutton, R. A. (Y) ...	RFM	619.1	152	1597	74	21.58	6–81	2	1
Ibadulla, K.(Wa/Sca)	RM/OB	340.3	56	1011	33	30.63	4–21	—	—
Illingworth, R. (E/Le/MCC)	OB	539.1	155	1261	47	26.82	5–35	1	—
Inman, C. (Le)	OB	3	0	14	0	—	—	—	—
Intikhab Alam (Sy/RW)	LBG	854	233	2339	86	27.19	8–74	6	—
Jackman, R. D. (Sy)	RFM	610.2	115	1666	71	23.46	6–35	2	—
Jameson, J. A. (Wa)	OB	145	26	435	11	39.54	3–4	—	—
Jameson, T. E. N. (CU/Wa)	RM	215.1	72	531	10	53.10	2–21	—	—
Jesty, T. E. (H).......	RM	496	101	1403	32	43.84	4–37	—	—
Johns, R. L. (OU) ...	OB	240	63	671	13	51.61	4–76	—	—
Johnson, C. (Y)	OB	7	2	20	0	—	—	—	—
Johnson, G. W. (K) .	OB	225.1	47	671	26	25.80	6–35	2	1
Johnson, L. A. (No)	—	12	0	60	1	60.00	1–60	—	—
Johnson, P. D. (Nt/CU)	LBG	183.5	39	603	9	67.00	3–34	—	—
Jones, A. (E/Gm) ...	OB	9	1	44	1	44.00	1–41	—	—
Jones, A. A. (So)	RFM	470.5	79	1588	46	34.52	5–35	2	—
Jones, K. V. (M)	RM	462.5	108	1329	42	31.64	5–64	2	—
Jorden, A. M. (CU/Ex)	RFM	178.2	39	481	16	30.06	3–72	—	—
Joshi, U. C. (Sx/Sca)	OB	44	14	135	1	135.00	1–53	—	—
Julien, B. (K)	LMetc.	24	10	58	2	29.00	2–15	—	—

	Type	O.	M.	Runs	Wkts.	Avge.	Best	5w I	10 wM
Kanhai, R. B. (Wa/RW/Sca)	LB	2.2	0	19	0	—	—	—	—
Kennedy, J. H. (Sc)	LFM	20	3	66	1	66.00	1–17	—	—
Kettle, M. K. (No) ...	LM	31	8	93	4	23.25	4–16	—	—
Khan, M. J. (CU/Gm)	RM	93	28	207	11	18.81	3–17	—	—
Kingston, G. C. (Gm)	RM	33	6	126	3	42.00	2–18	—	—
Knight, R. D. V. (CU/Sy)	RM	292.5	76	786	31	25.35	6–65	1	—
Langford, B. A. (So)	OB	553	141	1634	52	31.42	6–58	3	—
Latchman, H. C. (M)	LBG	324	67	1139	30	37.96	5–46	1	—
Leary, S. E. (K)......	LB	15	0	67	0	—	—	—	—
Lee, P. (No)	RFM	93	11	299	7	42.71	2–21	—	—
Lees, R. D. (OU) ...	RM	46	8	144	1	144.00	1–53	—	—
Lever, J. K. (Ex)	LFM	356	65	1078	31	34.77	4–32	—	—
Lever, P. (E/La)	RFM	690.2	175	1774	83	21.37	7–83	3	1
Lewington, P. J. (Wa)	OB	175	52	462	19	24.31	4–39	—	—
Llewellyn, M. J. (Gm)	OB	43.2	13	129	6	21.50	4–35	—	—
Lloyd, C. H. (La/RW)	RM	323	85	818	28	29.21	4–48	—	—
Lloyd, D. (La)	SLA	93	27	316	7	45.14	2–14	—	—
Luckhurst, B. W. (E/K/MCC).........	SLA	4	0	23	0	—	—	—	—
Lyons, K. J. (Gm) .	RM	26	0	93	0	—	—	—	—
McIlwaine, R. J. (H)	RM	25	3	98	2	49.00	2–40	—	—
McKenzie, G. D. (Le/RW)	RFM	736.4	186	1860	91	20.43	7–67	4	1
McVicker, N. M. (Wa)	RFM	441.2	86	1459	34	42.91	5–16	1	—
Marner, P. T. (Le) ...	RM	269.4	47	790	24	32.91	5–70	1	—
Marshall, R. E. (H) .	RM/OB	16	10	7	1	7.00	1–5	—	—
Miles, O. (Jam)	OB	98.5	14	320	20	16.00	5–67	1	—
Millener, D. J. (OU)	RFM	150.3	38	382	11	34.72	3–61	—	—
Moan, R. (Ire)	OB	16	4	58	1	58.00	1–58	—	—
Mortimore, J. B. (Gs)	OB	577.1	116	1561	54	28.90	5–43	2	—
Murray, J. T. (M/Sca)	RM	6.3	0	29	1	29.00	1–7	—	—
Mushtaq Mohammad (No/RW/Sca)	LBG	516.5	102	1653	58	28.50	4–56	—	—
Nash, M. A. (Gm) ...	LM	705.2	202	1761	79	22.29	6–42	5	—
Nicholls, R. B. (Gs) .	OB	5	2	16	0	—	—	—	—
Nicholson, A. G. (Y)	RFM	792.2	227	1939	65	29.83	5–82	2	—
Norman, M. E. J. C. (Le)..................	RM	9	0	44	0	—	—	—	—
Old, C. M. (E/Y/MCC/Sca) .	RFM	629.4	138	1674	74	22.62	5–14	2	—
O'Riordan, A. J. (Ire)	LFM	39	7	98	2	49.00	2–91	—	—
Ormrod, J. A. (Wo) .	OB	32	8	101	1	101.00	1–71	—	—
Owen-Thomas, D.R. (CU/Sy)	OB	196.1	49	517	13	39.76	2–26	—	—
Padgett, D. E. V. (Y/Sca)...............	RM	1	0	3	0	—	—	—	—
Page, M. H. (D)	OB	23	9	53	2	26.50	1–8	—	—
Palmer, R. (So)	RFM	443.5	72	1517	40	37.92	3–36	—	—
Parfitt, P. H. (M/Sca)	OB	255	50	930	29	32.06	3–38	—	—
Pearman, H. (M)	SLA	25	5	85	0	—	—	—	—

	Type	O.	M.	Runs	Wkts.	Avge.	Best	5wI	10 wM
Pember, J. D. D. (Le)	RM	171.4	40	473	12	39.41	2–18	—	—
Phillipson, C. P. (Sx).	RM	16	3	56	1	56.00	1–56	—	—
Pilling, H. (La/MCC)	OB	0.2	0	4	0	—	—	—	—
Plummer, P. J. (Nt)	SLA	129	28	404	17	23.76	4–70	—	—
Pocock, P. I. (Sy/Sca)	OB	791.5	209	2097	69	30.39	6–62	2	1
Pollock, P. M. (RW)	RFM	33	6	110	2	55.00	1–48	—	—
Pollock, R. G. (RW)	LB	0.2	0	5	0	—	—	—	—
Pont, K. R. (Ex)......	RM	4	1	9	0	—	—	—	—
Presland, E. R. (Ex)	RM	16	0	78	1	78.00	1–78	—	—
Price, J. S. E. (M/Sca)	RF	700.4	145	2046	80	25.57	8–56	3	1
Prideaux, R. M. (No/Sca)	RM	3	1	3	0	—	—	—	—
Procter, M. J. (Gs/RW)	RF	647	181	1398	65	21.50	6–38	2	—
Pullar, G. (Gs)	LB	1	1	0	0	—	—	—	—
Reynolds, B. L. (No)	OB	11	0	47	0	—	—	—	—
Reynolds, G. E. A. (Gm)	RM	17	11	24	2	12.00	2–24	—	—
Richards, B. A. (H/RW)	OB	39	8	138	3	46.00	2–77	—	—
Ridley, R. M. (OU)		1	1	0	0	—	—	—	—
Roberts, J. K. (So) .	LM	22	3	84	1	84.00	1–14	—	—
Robinson, P.J. (So) .	SLA	253.3	70	868	28	31.00	4–51	—	—
Roope, G. R. J. (Sy/Sca).............	RM	262.3	50	746	25	29.84	5–62	1	—
Ross, N. P. G. (CU)	LB	17	1	62	2	31.00	2–38	—	—
Rouse, S. J. (Wa)	LM	33	10	67	4	16.75	4–34	—	—
Rowe, L. A. (Jam) .	RM	10	4	23	0	—	—	—	—
Rumsey, F. E. (D) .	LFM	30.5	5	97	2	48.50	1–34	—	—
Russell, P. E. (D) ...	RM/OB	547.4	179	1325	50	26.50	6–61	2	—
Sainsbury, P. J. (H)	SLA	803.5	310	1885	71	26.54	5–40	2	—
Sarfraz Nawaz (No)	RFM	656.3	147	1841	63	29.22	5–43	1	—
Schofield, D. (Y)	RM	20	9	53	0	—	—	—	—
Sharpe, P. J. (E/Y) .	OB	2	0	4	0	—	—	—	—
Shepherd, D. J. (Gm)	RM/OB	1123.3	420	2031	106	19.16	7–48	6	2
Shepherd, J. N. (K)	RM	894.5	231	2320	86	26.97	6–33	6	—
Shuttleworth, K. (La/E)	RFM	617.5	147	1684	74	22.75	6–60	5	1
Simmons, J. (La)	OB	559.2	153	1478	40	36.95	5–45	1	—
Slade, D. N. F. (Wo)	SLA	296.4	94	732	24	30.50	4–25	—	—
Smith, A. C. (Wa)...	RM	25	2	84	1	84.00	1–26	—	—
Smith, D. H. K. (D)	RM	4.2	3	3	1	3.00	1–1	—	—
Smith, D. R. (Gs) ...	RM	622.1	115	2020	61	33.11	6–86	1	—
Smith, E. (D)	OB	794.1	246	2227	73	30.50	7–84	1	—
Smith, M. J. (M)	SLA	1	0	4	0	—	—	—	—
Smith, M. J. K. (Wa)	—	3.3	1	12	0	—	—	—	—
Snow, J. A. (Sx/E) .	RF	692.1	142	1955	67	29.17	5–18	2	—
Sobers, G. S. (Nt/RW)	LFMetc	676.1	193	1540	64	24.06	6–21	2	—
Spencer, J. (CU/Sx) .	RM	529.1	122	1375	53	25.94	5–50	2	—
Standen, J. A. (Wo).	RM	539.5	128	1432	40	35.80	3–44	—	—
Staziker, M. W. (La)	RM	57	11	269	1	269.00	1–114	—	—

	Type	O.	M.	Runs	Wkts.	Avge.	Best	5wI	10 wM
Stead, B. (Nt)	LFM	385.3	68	1124	41	27.41	7–36	2	—
Steele, D. S. (No)	SLA	60.4	26	139	8	17.37	3–17	—	—
Steele, H. K. (CU) ...	RM	49	7	141	2	70.50	1–47	—	—
Steele, J. F. (Le)	SLA	399.4	146	928	29	32.00	5–43	1	—
Storey, S. J. (Sy)	RM	328	79	826	19	43.47	4–47	—	—
Stringer, P. M. (Le) .	RFM	482.4	133	1288	43	29.95	5–43	1	—
Sullivan, J. (La)........	RM	183.2	51	470	22	21.36	4–44	—	—
Suttle, K. G. (Sx) ...	SLA	270.4	67	761	19	40.05	6–64	1	—
Swarbrook, F. W. (D)	SLA	613.4	184	1694	57	29.71	6–48	3	—
Swinburne, J. W. (No)	OB	345.5	81	1056	34	31.05	5–81	2	—
Taylor, M. N. S. (Nt)	RM	589.2	104	1827	57	32.05	4–24	—	—
Taylor, R. W. (D/MCC)............	RM	1	0	4	0	—	—	—	—
Thompson, E. R. (Sc)	RFM	46.4	8	110	6	18.33	5–37	1	—
Tidy, W. N. (Wa) ...	LBG	535.2	120	1494	48	31.12	5–24	3	—
Titmus, F. J. (M/Sca)	OB	1106.3	320	2804	105	26.70	7–81	6	1
Tolchard, J. G. (Le)	RM	1	0	5	0	—	—	—	—
Turner, D. R. (H) ...	RM	1	0	4	1	4.00	1–4	—	—
Turner, G. M. (Wo) .	OB	4	1	19	1	19.00	1–6	—	—
Turner, S. (Ex)	RM	720.1	184	1646	70	23.51	4–53	—	—
Underwood, D. L. (K/E)	LM	851.2	307	2043	89	22.95	7–103	7	2
Verity, S. A. (OU) .	RM	37	6	121	0	—	—	—	—
Walker, P. M. (Gm)	LM/SLA	686	224	1599	60	26.65	6–33	3	—
Waller, C. E. (Sy) ...	SLA	115.3	32	298	8	37.25	5–43	1	—
Ward, A. (D/E/MCC)	RF	479.1	101	1444	61	23.67	6–30	2	1
Warner, G. S. (Wa) .	OB	3	0	10	0	—	—	—	—
Watts, P. J. (No)	RM	257	72	679	18	37.72	3–2	—	—
Wellington, L. (Jam)	RFM	58	13	159	4	39.75	2–33	—	—
Wheatley, K. J. (H) .	OB	106.5	31	253	15	16.86	4–38	—	—
White, D. W. (H)....	RFM	439.4	113	1074	45	23.86	7–61	2	—
White, R. A. (Nt) ...	OB	660.1	186	1914	70	27.34	6–56	5	1
Wiggs, R. J. (CU) ...	SLA	19	10	44	1	44.00	1–44	—	—
Wilkin, C. L. A. (CU)	SLA	267.1	60	700	15	46.66	3–74	—	—
Wilkins, C. P. (D/Sca)	RM	152	27	484	12	40.33	4–21	—	—
Willey, P. (No/Sca)...	RM	411.3	107	987	38	25.97	5–14	2	—
Williams, D. (OU) .	SLA	39	7	248	2	124.00	2–84	—	—
Williams, D. L. (Gm)	RFM	619.1	164	1604	61	26.29	7–60	4	—
Willis, R. G. D. (Sy/Sca).............	RF	373.3	67	1135	40	28.37	4–57	—	—
Wilson, D. (Y/E/MCC)	SLA	682.4	242	1542	59	26.13	5–25	2	—
Wilson, P. R. B. (OU)	LB	32	3	182	6	30.33	4–60	—	—
Wood, B. (La)	RM	287	80	601	31	19.38	5–54	1	—
Woodford, J. D. (Y)	RM	19	5	47	0	—	—	—	—
Woolmer, R. A. (K)	RM	286	84	777	32	24.28	6–53	3	—
Wright, L. (Jam)	LB	18	6	46	5	9.20	3–25	—	—
Yardley, T. J. (Wo)...	RM	2	0	8	0	—	—	—	—
Younis Ahmed (Sy)	LM/SLA	4.5	2	15	1	15.00	1–7	—	—

CAREER FIGURES FOR THE LEADING PLAYERS

THE FOLLOWING are the abbreviated figures of the leading batsmen and bowlers based on their career averages, and fielders and wicket-keepers based on the number of their catches and dismissals. The figures are complete to 30th September 1970 and the full career records will be found in the main table on pages 179 to 193. The qualification for inclusion for batsmen and bowlers is 100 innings and 100 wickets respectively.

Only those players likely to play first-class county cricket in 1971 have been included.

BATSMEN	*Runs*	*Avge.*	*100's*
G. S. Sobers	22,316	57.36	69
B. A. Richards	9,307	53.48	25
R. B. Kanhai	18,330	48.23	52
G. Boycott	17,000	47.88	42
C. H. Lloyd	6,543	47.75	16
J. H. Edrich	27,192	46.01	70
M. C. Cowdrey	37,060	43.70	94
Mushtaq Mohammad	16,170	42.32	37
M. J. Khan	9,313	42.14	25
M. J. K. Smith	33,524	42.01	58
B. L. D'Oliveira	10,049	40.19	26
G. M. Turner	6,941	37.92	15
B. W. Luckhurst	13,736	36.82	27
P. H. Parfitt	23,756	35.93	51
C. P. Wilkins	3,474	35.81	5

BOWLERS	*Wkts*	*Avge.*
D. L. Underwood	965	17.90
M. J. Procter	414	18.05
A. G. Nicholson	639	18.94
A. Ward	177	19.13
J. N. Graham	341	19.14
R. Illingworth	1,674	19.26
N. Gifford	953	19.39
T. W. Cartwright	1,194	19.43
F. E. Rumsey	580	20.29
D. Wilson	1,075	20.46
G. G. Arnold	457	20.61
C. M. Old	169	20.78
R. M. H. Cottam	642	20.90
D. J. Shepherd	2,127	21.01
J. A. Snow	723	21.54

FIELDERS	*Ct.*
C. A. Milton	713
P. M. Walker	633
M. J. Stewart	601
M. C. Cowdrey	547
P. J. Sainsbury	530
M. J. K. Smith	514
P. J. Sharpe	504
P. H. Parfitt	500
F. J. Titmus	420
K. G. Suttle	381
A. S. Brown	370
S. E. Leary	346
R. Illingworth	337
K. Ibadulla	322

WICKET-KEEPERS	*Total*	*Ct.*	*St.*
J. T. Murray	1,274	1,063	211
B. Taylor	1,149	966	183
R. Booth	1,124	948	176
J. M. Parks	1,057	977	80
B. J. Meyer	781	669	112
A. C. Smith	713	655	58
R. W. Taylor	689	630	59
A. Long	592	520	72
A. P. E. Knott	551	476	75
B. S. V. Timms	499	435	64
F. M. Engineer	465	373	92
R. Julian	418	379	39
E. W. Jones	342	314	28
R. W. Tolchard	322	285	37

CAREER RECORDS

THE FOLLOWING career records are for all players appearing in first-class cricket in the 1970 season. A few cricketers who did not re-appear for their counties this season, but who may do so next season are also included. Since the corresponding figures were compiled after the 1969 season, the Test and County Cricket Board have decided that the match between Ireland and Pakistan International Airlines should not count as first-class. The necessary adjustments have been made to the figures of the players concerned.

BATTING AND FIELDING

	M.	*I.*	*N.O.*	*Runs*	*H.S.*	*Avge.*	100	*Ct.*	*St.*
Abberley, R. N.	136	233	14	5455	117*	24.90	2	75	—
Acfield, D. L.	108	137	59	632	42	8.10	—	41	—
Ackerman, H. M.	106	186	13	5648	208	32.64	10	84	—
Allan, J. M.	176	265	45	4981	153	22.64	5	120	—
Alldis, J. S.	2	4	1	7	4*	2.33	—	—	—
Allen, D. A.	438	614	137	9016	121*	18.90	1	244	—
Allison, D. F.	6	9	2	48	21	6.85	—	4	—
Amiss, D. L.	222	376	44	11624	176*	35.01	16	171	—
Anderson, I. J.	6	11	4	273	44	39.00	—	2	—
Arnold, G. G............	140	137	29	1673	73	15.49	—	58	—
Asif Iqbal	169	264	27	7990	159	33.71	10	131	—
Bailey, D.	27	36	1	845	136	24.14	1	10	—
Bailey, R. R.	32	30	14	147	18*	9.18	—	16	—
Bairstow, D. L.	19	24	5	334	36	17.57	—	43	6
Balderstone, J. C.	68	81	6	1332	82	17.76	—	23	—
Barclay, J. R. T.	2	3	0	4	4	1.33	—	—	—
Barford, M. T.	5	9	2	182	48	26.00	—	3	—
Barker, G.	442	796	46	22122	181*	29.49	30	231	—
Barlow, E. J.	131	227	13	9141	212	42.71	25	127	—
Barlow, G. D.............	6	10	0	194	38	19.40	—	2	—
Barr, D.	41	70	9	1199	86	19.65	—	33	—
Barratt, R. J.	70	88	16	604	39	8.38	—	50	—
Barrett, A.	15	18	5	343	102*	26.38	1	16	—
Bates, D. L.	314	356	157	1523	37*	7.65	—	119	—
Bevan, D. G.	33	52	3	605	63	12.34	—	11	—
Bielby, S. R.	29	36	6	542	62	18.06	—	14	—
Birkenshaw, J.	258	386	63	7199	131	22.28	3	135	—
Bissex, M.	181	300	32	5603	104*	20.90	2	118	—
Black, C. J. R.	2	2	0	15	9	7.50	—	—	—
Blenkiron, W.	87	103	25	1072	62	13.74	—	43	—
Bolus, J. B.	355	628	59	19716	202*	34.65	31	164	—
Bond, J. D.	301	475	67	11018	157	27.00	13	191	—

	M.	I.	N.O.	Runs	H.S.	Avge.	100	Ct.	St.
Booth, B. J.	309	538	44	13787	183*	27.90	16	111	—
Booth, R.	468	671	135	10139	113*	18.91	2	948	176
Booton, W. T.	1	1	0	12	12	12.00	—	—	—
Bore, M. K.	14	13	6	85	12*	12.14	—	7	—
Boyce, K. D.	123	197	13	3735	147*	20.29	3	107	—
Boycott, G.	246	405	50	17000	260*	47.88	42	101	—
Boyers, M. J. H.	1	2	0	2	2	1.00	—	—	—
Bradfield, G. W.	1	1	0	50	50	50.00	—	—	—
Brain, B. M.	92	98	25	497	38	6.80	—	18	—
Breakwell, D.	41	47	10	580	97	15.67	—	17	—
Brearley, J. M.	167	296	33	8937	312*	33.98	13	174	12
Bromley, R. C.	5	9	0	78	18	8.66	—	6	—
Brooks, V. C. G.	1	1	0	15	15	15.00	—	—	—
Brown, A.	251	312	87	2189	81	9.72	—	106	—
Brown, A. S.	367	605	74	9407	109*	17.71	2	370	—
Brown, D. J.	233	272	66	2646	69	12.84	—	86	—
Brown, J.	55	80	18	1287	90	20.75	—	79	21
Bryant, D. J.	2	4	2	3	3	1.50	—	—	—
Burchnall, R. L.	25	44	2	685	85	16.30	—	8	—
Burgess, G. I.	109	193	11	3120	69	17.14	—	39	—
Burton, M. S. W.	29	46	5	675	84	16.46	—	9	—
Buss, A.	267	353	68	3861	83	13.54	—	112	—
Buss, M. A.	156	275	24	6017	159	23.97	7	128	—
Buxton, I. R.	284	467	64	9566	118*	23.73	5	164	—
Campbell, A.	3	4	1	44	24	14.66	—	4	3
Campbell, A. N.	15	27	1	530	73	20.38	—	5	—
Carling, P. G.	30	55	3	1160	104	22.30	1	13	—
Carrick, P.	3	3	1	36	32	18.00	—	2	—
Carroll, P. R.	9	17	1	193	49	12.06	—	5	—
Carter, R. G. M.	136	133	75	260	23	4.48	—	41	—
Cartwright, T. W.	394	624	84	11946	210	22.12	6	287	—
Cass, G. R.	92	141	18	2601	104*	21.14	1	103	19
Castell, A. T.	99	124	37	1443	76	16.58	—	82	—
Chisholm, R. H. E.	60	104	5	2275	105	22.97	1	18	—
Clarkson, A.	87	155	5	3698	131	24.65	2	40	—
Close, D. B.	615	943	119	26340	198	31.96	38	641	1
Colhoun, O. D.	19	26	13	43	9*	3.30	—	25	1
Connolly, A. N.	194	206	93	1009	40	8.92	—	69	—
Cope, G. A.	68	79	27	539	66	10.36	—	31	—
Cordle, A. E.	135	194	25	2556	56*	15.12	—	63	—
Corlett, S. C.	1	2	0	25	19	12.50	—	—	—
Cottam, R. M. H.	175	161	65	575	35	5.98	—	80	—
Cowdrey, M. C.	583	953	105	37060	307	43.70	94	547	—
Cragg, J. R. A.	7	13	0	149	55	11.46	—	2	—
Cross, G. F.	60	103	12	1596	78	17.53	—	50	—
Crump, B. S.	279	408	90	7266	120	22.84	2	130	—
Cumbes, J.	34	25	16	76	25*	8.44	—	12	—
Dalton, A. J.	8	12	1	193	47*	17.54	—	3	—
Davey, J.	52	60	33	149	17	5.51	—	12	—
Davis, B. A.	105	183	13	5944	188*	34.96	5	122	—
Davis, F. J.	28	47	13	552	63	16.23	—	17	—
Davis, R. C.	110	187	13	3231	116	18.56	1	141	—

	M.	I.	N.O.	Runs	H.S.	Avge.	100	Ct.	St.
Davison, B. F.	20	29	2	602	76	22.29	—	15	—
Denman, J.	10	15	6	133	34*	14.77	—	2	—
Denness, M. H.	255	433	33	12232	174	30.58	12	231	—
Denning, P. W..........	19	35	2	512	69	15.51	—	9	—
Dineen, P. J.	6	10	1	158	84	17.55	—	2	—
Dinsdale, S. C.	6	9	0	113	29	12.55	—	5	—
Dixon, A. L.	380	578	71	9575	125*	18.88	3	155	—
D'Oliveira, B. L.	192	296	46	10049	174*	40.19	26	153	—
Douglas-Home, A.......	4	6	1	33	23	6.60	—	1	—
Dudleston, B.	83	137	14	3309	171*	26.90	7	63	—
Dye, J. C. J.	136	117	59	314	27*	5.41	—	34	—
Ealham, A. G. E.	88	123	24	2387	103*	24.11	1	69	—
East, R. E.	126	161	52	1300	58	11.92	—	81	—
Edmeades, B. E. A. ...	226	362	58	7390	148	24.30	10	71	—
Edrich, J. H.	379	657	66	27192	310*	46.01	70	210	—
Edwards, M. J.	187	326	19	8522	137	27.75	9	231	—
Ellis, G. P.	9	15	3	318	55	26.50	—	1	—
Elms, R.	1	—	—	—	—	—	—	—	—
Engineer, F. M.	196	297	24	7886	162	28.88	6	373	92
Eyre, T. J. P.	179	247	42	3314	102	16.16	1	70	—
Faber, M. J. J.	5	10	1	88	25	9.77	—	3	—
Featherstone, N. G.....	52	85	7	2054	94	26.33	—	51	—
Fletcher, K. W. R.......	269	463	55	13893	228*	34.05	19	261	—
Flick, B. J.	2	1	0	1	1	1.00	—	—	—
Folkes, C.	12	8	1	36	9	5.14	—	1	—
Forbes, C.	238	311	69	3453	86	14.26	—	141	—
Foster, M. L. C..........	44	73	8	2243	147	34.50	5	16	—
Francis, B. C.	15	30	0	841	126	28.03	2	9	—
Frost, G.	61	97	15	1879	107	22.91	1	49	—
Gibbs, L. R.	218	242	93	1273	43	8.54	—	130	—
Gibbs, P. J. K.	134	235	11	6459	138*	28.83	8	76	—
Gifford, N.	305	370	109	3290	89	12.60	—	141	—
Gilliat, R. M. C.	113	186	12	4905	223*	28.18	9	65	—
Goddard, G. F.	10	17	2	245	39	16.33	—	—	—
Gooch, P. A.	4	3	1	0	0*	0.00	—	3	—
Goodwin, D..............	8	11	2	124	23*	13.77	—	2	—
Goodwin, K..............	108	136	38	575	23	5.86	—	211	20
Gordon, A.	32	56	4	849	65	16.32	—	33	—
Graham, J. N.	95	96	37	243	23	4.11	—	21	—
Graveney, T. W.	727	1214	157	47670	258	45.09	122	547	1
Graves, P. J.	99	166	18	3404	117*	23.00	2	77	—
Gray, J. D.	7	6	3	34	18	11.33	—	1	—
Green, D. M.	263	474	15	13325	233	29.03	14	94	—
Greenidge, C. G.	7	11	1	351	73	35.10	—	6	—
Greenidge, G. A.	56	95	4	2408	205	26.46	7	23	—
Greig, A. W.	137	228	16	5566	156	26.25	6	118	—
Griffith, K.	15	20	1	182	27	9.57	—	4	—
Griffith, M. G.	195	317	56	6244	158	23.92	2	195	19
Halfyard, D. J.	264	348	51	3242	79	10.91	—	115	—
Hall, I. W.................	234	415	26	9552	136	24.55	7	163	—
Hall, J. E.	14	26	0	385	69	14.80	—	3	—
Hallam, M. R.	504	905	56	24488	210*	28.84	32	452	—

	M.	*I.*	*N.O.*	*Runs*	*H.S.*	*Avge.*	100	*Ct.*	*St.*
Halliday, M.	1	1	0	6	6	6.00	—	—	—
Hampshire, J. H.	264	421	42	11394	150	30.06	14	212	—
Hardie, B. R.	1	1	1	36	36*	—	—	—	—
Harris, M. J.	124	212	22	6463	160	34.01	10	67	—
Harrison, J.	2	4	0	119	65	29.75	—	2	—
Harvey, J. F..............	166	277	26	5948	168	23.69	4	60	—
Hassan, B.	72	110	10	2725	110	27.25	3	45	—
Hatteea, S. A.	5	3	0	1	1	0.33	—	5	—
Haye, W.	1	—	—	—	—	—	—	1	—
Hayes, F. C.	17	24	4	780	99	39.00	—	18	—
Haywood, P. R.	14	27	1	512	65	19.69	—	5	—
Headley, R. G. A.	338	614	55	16607	150*	29.70	22	310	—
Heal, M. G.	8	15	0	187	64	12.46	—	4	—
Heard, H.	30	45	14	273	31	8.80	—	5	—
Hemmings, E. E.	34	52	17	756	54	21.60	—	13	—
Hemsley, E. J. O.	61	103	19	2223	138*	26.46	1	39	—
Hendrick, M.	7	6	4	15	9*	7.50	—	3	—
Herman, R. S.	87	79	27	417	40*	8.01	—	34	—
Hill, L. W.	34	55	8	967	80	20.57	—	18	1
Hill, M.	267	479	38	10650	137*	24.14	7	150	—
Hobbs, R. N. S.	284	356	86	3087	100	11.43	1	202	—
Hodgson, A.	1	—	—	—	—	—	—	—	—
Holder, J. W.	27	24	7	211	28*	12.41	—	7	—
Holder, V. A.	76	81	17	562	52	8.78	—	24	—
Hone, D. J.	3	5	0	26	13	5.20	—	1	—
Hooper, J. M. M.	17	29	7	318	41*	14.45	—	13	—
Hopkins, J. A.	1	2	0	6	4	3.00	—	—	—
Hopkins, J. D.	2	3	0	4	4	1.33	—	9	—
Howarth, J.	13	7	3	0	0*	0.00	—	3	—
Hughes, D. P.	77	89	17	1009	55	14.01	—	35	—
Humphrey, R. G.........	2	2	1	63	58	63.00	—	4	1
Hutton, R. A.	198	293	39	5465	163*	21.51	2	146	—
Ibadulla, K.	389	663	70	16299	171	27.48	22	322	—
Illingworth, R.	576	813	155	18511	162	28.13	19	337	—
Inman, C.	232	384	37	11708	178	33.74	17	104	—
Intikhab Alam	187	277	29	5819	106	23.46	3	106	—
Jackman, R. D.	91	87	35	482	32*	9.26	—	26	—
Jameson, J. A.	215	350	34	9528	194	30.15	11	138	—
Jameson, T. E. N.	10	17	2	181	32	12.06	—	12	—
Jenkins, H.	1	2	1	81	65	81.00	—	1	—
Jesty, T. E.	53	74	20	1246	73*	23.07	—	29	—
Johns, R. L.	8	15	2	273	61*	21.00	—	6	—
Johnson, C.	10	16	2	275	61*	19.64	—	6	—
Johnson, G. W.	60	93	11	1709	116	20.84	3	53	—
Johnson, L. A.	138	166	31	1366	50	10.11	—	234	59
Johnson, P. D.	12	21	1	296	82	14.80	—	7	—
Jones, A.	339	616	42	18253	187*	31.79	26	188	—
Jones, A. A.	40	47	15	121	19	3.78	—	6	—
Jones, A. K. C.	1	2	0	46	35	23.00	—	—	—
Jones, E. W.	130	200	44	2886	146*	18.50	2	314	28
Jones, K. V.	41	57	19	717	56*	18.86	—	18	—
Jorden, A. M.	89	130	31	1112	67*	11.23	—	47	—

	M.	I.	N.O.	Runs	H.S.	Avge.	100	Ct.	St.
Joshi, U. C.	29	42	7	438	61	12.51	—	14	—
Julian, R.	191	288	23	2581	51	9.73	—	379	39
Julien, B.	10	11	0	209	54	19.00	—	9	—
Kanhai, R. B.	254	415	35	18330	256	48.23	52	183	7
Kennedy, A.	1	2	1	26	25	26.00	—	—	—
Kennedy, J. H.	1	—	—	—	—	—	—	—	—
Kettle, M. K.	88	105	20	1117	88	13.14	—	62	—
Khan, M. J.	146	242	21	9313	241	42.14	25	150	—
Kingston, G. C.	7	11	2	124	22	13.77	—	2	—
Kitchen, M. J.	217	379	19	9103	189	25.28	10	93	—
Knight, R. D. V.	66	122	6	3126	164*	26.94	2	40	—
Knott, A. P. E.	198	283	52	5580	102	24.15	2	476	75
Laing, J. G. B.	18	30	4	630	93	24.23	—	9	—
Langford, B. A.	450	645	135	6859	68*	13.44	—	216	—
Langridge, R. J.	206	380	27	8194	137*	23.21	5	187	—
Latchman, H. C.	120	122	30	913	43	9.92	—	55	—
Laycock, D. A.	5	8	1	151	58	21.57	—	2	—
Leadbeater, B.	39	64	7	1321	89*	23.17	—	20	—
Leary, S. E.	369	604	89	16087	158	31.23	18	346	—
Lee, P.	25	19	6	145	26	11.15	—	7	—
Lees, R. D.	3	6	2	29	17*	7.25	—	—	—
Lenham, L. J.	300	539	50	12796	191*	26.16	7	109	—
Lever, J. K.	78	92	40	526	91	10.11	—	37	—
Lever, P.	176	209	41	2577	83	15.33	—	61	—
Lewington, P. J.	4	2	1	12	7	12.00	—	1	—
Lewis, A. R.	336	584	55	17225	223	32.56	26	163	—
Lewis, D.	4	5	0	64	24	12.80	—	9	—
Lewis, R. M.	10	18	4	430	87	30.71	—	5	—
Lewis, R. V.	40	73	4	1176	114	17.04	1	33	—
Lightfoot, A.	294	495	61	12000	174*	27.64	12	160	—
Livingstone, D. A.	288	495	61	12150	200	27.99	16	237	2
Llewellyn, M. J.	1	2	0	15	15	7.50	—	2	—
Lloyd, C. H.	98	156	19	6543	205*	47.75	16	59	—
Lloyd, D.	124	202	34	4378	148*	26.05	5	86	—
Long, A.	258	299	66	3428	92	14.71	—	520	72
Luckhurst, B. W.	256	428	55	13736	203*	36.82	27	267	—
Lumb, R. G.	1	2	0	21	17	10.50	—	—	—
Lyons, K. J.	29	49	7	658	58*	15.66	—	13	—
McDowall, J. I.	23	43	5	627	62	16.50	—	40	2
McIlwaine, R. J.	4	3	1	29	17	14.50	—	1	—
McKenzie, G. D.	248	324	59	4092	76	15.44	—	143	—
McMorris, E. D. S. A.	85	143	17	5505	218	43.69	18	31	—
McVicker, N. M.	40	48	18	431	44*	14.36	—	14	—
Mansell, A. W.	4	5	1	17	8	4.25	—	10	1
Marner, P. T.	414	680	62	17513	142*	28.33	18	376	—
Marshall, R. E.	558	975	46	33143	228*	35.67	63	283	—
May, B.	6	11	0	217	103	19.72	1	4	—
Meyer, B. J.	388	547	181	5164	63	14.10	—	669	112
Miles, O.	13	13	4	146	43*	16.22	—	13	—
Millener, D. J.	26	30	12	176	24	9.77	—	9	—
Milton, C. A.	577	1006	120	30269	170	34.16	55	713	—
Moan, R.	1	1	1	0	0*	—	—	—	—

	M.	I.	N.O.	Runs	H.S.	Avge.	100	Ct.	St.
More, H. K.	10	20	2	399	89	22.16	—	4	—
Morgan, S.	7	12	2	238	68	23.80	—	6	—
Mortimore, J. B.	551	869	88	14513	149	18.58	4	304	—
Moseley, H. R...........	3	5	4	24	17*	24.00	—	1	—
Mucklow, P.	2	4	0	48	32	12.00	—	1	—
Murray, D. L.	177	277	38	6834	166*	28.59	7	312	51
Murray, J. T.	516	764	117	15207	142	23.50	14	1063	211
Mushtaq Mohammad .	266	439	57	16170	303*	42.32	37	186	—
Nash, M. A..............	93	127	23	1754	69	16.86	—	47	—
Nicholls, D.	99	171	7	3062	211	18.67	1	118	5
Nicholls, R. B..........	461	822	47	20380	217	26.29	17	257	1
Nicholson, A. G........	202	187	93	992	43	10.55	—	67	—
Norman, M. E. J. C. .	329	584	39	16276	221*	29.86	23	149	—
Old, C. M.	68	74	15	913	92*	15.47	—	42	—
O'Riordan, A. J.	19	34	4	407	59	13.56	—	9	—
Ormrod, J. A.	206	342	44	8046	155*	27.00	6	156	—
Osman, W. M.	1	1	0	9	9	9.00	—	2	—
Owen-Thomas, D. R. .	23	42	3	1171	182*	30.02	2	13	—
Padgett, D. E. V.	483	771	66	20258	161*	28.73	31	242	—
Page, M. H.	160	283	34	6790	162	27.26	6	179	—
Palmer, R.	74	110	32	1037	84	13.29	—	25	—
Parfitt, P. H.	448	756	95	23756	200*	35.93	51	500	—
Parks, J. M.	646	1073	147	32672	205*	35.28	50	977	80
Pataudi, Nawab of......	261	430	34	13456	203*	33.97	27	194	—
Payne, C. J...............	5	8	0	40	22	5.00	—	—	—
Pearman, H.	11	16	1	233	43*	15.53	—	6	—
Pember, J. D. D.	22	24	9	251	53	16.73	—	8	—
Phillips, R. W.	18	28	0	529	92	18.89	—	11	—
Phillipson, C. P..........	1	2	0	1	1	0.50	—	—	—
Pigot, D. R.	6	12	0	278	88	23.16	—	3	—
Pilling, H.	178	296	33	7886	133*	29.98	13	32	—
Pinnock, R.	26	44	4	1902	176	47.55	6	24	5
Plummer, P. J.	9	9	1	103	46	12.87	—	6	—
Pocock, P. I.	186	207	44	1797	75*	11.02	—	54	—
Pollock, P. M.	109	150	37	2470	79	21.85	—	42	—
Pollock, R. G.	110	189	20	9025	274	53.40	28	110	—
Pont, K. R................	1	1	0	5	5	5.00	—	—	—
Presland, E. R.	30	41	4	625	51	16.89	—	24	—
Price, J. S. E.	212	177	78	710	53*	7.17	—	79	—
Prideaux, R. M.	369	668	62	20593	202*	33.98	34	240	—
Procter, M .J.	109	174	17	4402	155	28.03	7	86	—
Pullan, D. A.	25	21	11	111	13*	11.10	—	63	10
Pullar, G.	400	672	63	21528	175	35.34	41	126	—
Racionzer, T. B.	33	57	7	1106	91	22.12	—	28	—
Radley, C. T.	155	241	40	6237	139	31.02	8	134	—
Reed, B. L................	123	215	11	4962	138	24.32	2	61	—
Reith, M. R.	1	2	0	82	82	41.00	—	—	—
Reynolds, B. L.	429	737	65	18824	169	28.01	21	302	20
Reynolds, G. E. A.	1	1	1	9	9*	—	—	—	—
Rhodes, H. J.............	321	399	143	2427	48	9.48	—	85	—
Richards, B. A.	117	194	20	9307	206	53.48	25	97	—
Richards, R.	1	—	—	—	—	—	—	—	—

	M.	I.	N.O.	Runs	H.S.	Avge.	100	Ct.	St.
Ridley, R. M.	23	42	1	994	79	24.24	—	9	—
Roberts, J. K.	8	9	6	3	2*	1.00	—	2	—
Robinson, G. A.	2	4	0	27	27	6.75	—	4	—
Robinson, P. J...........	154	236	50	4026	140	21.64	2	149	—
Roope, G. R. J.	109	168	37	3881	111	29.62	2	127	—
Rose, B. C.	22	37	3	430	46	12.64	—	8	—
Ross, N. P. G.	8	14	6	224	68	28.00	—	5	—
Rouse, S. J.	2	1	0	9	9	9.00	—	—	—
Rowe, L. A.	14	23	1	655	109	29.77	1	14	—
Rumsey, F. E.	180	204	84	1015	45	8.45	—	91	—
Russell, P. E.	49	56	11	705	72	15.66	—	36	—
Russell, W. E.............	405	719	58	23033	193	34.84	37	281	—
Sadiq Mohammad	36	58	7	1869	167	36.64	3	20	—
Sainsbury, P. J.	492	762	152	15882	163	26.03	5	530	—
Sarfraz Nawaz	31	29	13	298	44*	18.62	—	16	—
Saville, G. J.	73	128	21	2554	116	23.86	2	46	—
Schofield, D.	1	1	1	1	1*	—	—	—	—
Selwood, T.	6	9	1	105	35	13.12	—	2	—
Shackleton, D............	647	852	197	9561	87*	14.59	—	223	—
Sharp, G....................	9	9	5	165	55*	41.25	—	14	3
Sharpe, P. J.	386	631	69	17512	203*	31.16	22	504	—
Shepherd, D. J.	627	794	237	5410	73	9.71	—	243	—
Shepherd, D. R.	119	215	18	4641	153	23.55	8	37	—
Shepherd, J. N.	106	153	17	3365	170	24.74	4	101	—
Short, R. L.	11	20	1	355	58	18.68	—	4	—
Shuttleworth, K.	113	128	41	1394	71	16.02	—	48	—
Simmons, J.	49	51	14	631	112	17.05	1	14	—
Slade, D. N. F...........	257	361	94	4753	125	17.80	1	177	—
Smedley, M. J.	166	281	39	7397	149	30.56	13	116	—
Smith, A. C.	353	524	71	9631	145	21.26	3	655	58
Smith, D. H. K.	112	198	14	4915	136	26.71	4	83	—
Smith, D. R.	386	520	116	4970	74	12.30	—	294	—
Smith, E.	490	662	140	6926	90	13.26	—	203	—
Smith, M. J.	203	320	57	7768	181	29.53	14	141	—
Smith, M. J. K.	527	909	111	33524	204	42.01	58	514	—
Smith, N....................	7	11	5	82	20	13.66	—	13	3
Smith, R.	5	8	3	99	37*	19.80	—	—	—
Smith, W. A.	144	242	18	5024	103	22.42	2	52	—
Smyth, R. N. P.	3	5	0	42	25	8.40	—	—	—
Snellgrove, K. L.	44	75	4	1523	138	21.45	2	13	—
Snow, J. A.	202	248	81	1960	71	11.73	—	68	—
Sobers, G. S...............	290	458	69	22316	365*	57.36	69	316	—
Solkar, E. D.	46	66	13	1607	145*	30.33	2	64	—
Spencer, C. T.............	468	657	134	5712	90	10.92	—	358	—
Spencer, J.	26	34	17	80	13*	4.70	—	9	—
Standen, J. A.	133	174	28	2092	92*	14.32	—	84	—
Staziker, M. W.	2	2	2	1	1*	—	—	—	—
Stead, B.	103	92	41	535	35	10.49	—	29	—
Steele, D. S.	182	287	36	6532	118*	26.02	4	210	—
Steele, H. K.	2	3	0	1	1	0.33	—	—	—
Steele, J. F.	19	22	6	167	22	10.43	—	22	—
Stephenson, G. R.	59	80	14	1049	82	15.89	—	146	12

	M.	I.	N.O.	Runs	H.S.	Avge.	100	Ct.	St.
Stewart, D. E. R.	4	7	0	106	51	15.14	—	3	—
Stewart, M. J.	488	825	87	24925	227*	33.77	47	601	—
Stewart, W. J.	289	489	56	14773	182*	34.11	25	132	—
Storey, S. J...............	230	342	33	7022	136	22.72	8	236	—
Stringer, P. M.	38	43	17	210	17	8.07	—	12	—
Sullivan, J.	112	179	23	3049	80*	19.54	—	69	—
Sullivan, J. P.	9	14	1	225	53	17.30	—	6	—
Suttle, K. G.	603	1048	91	29704	204*	31.03	46	381	3
Swarbrook, F. W.	35	44	13	528	90	17.03	—	22	—
Swinburne, J. W.	10	11	1	36	13	3.60	—	4	—
Taylor, B.	513	862	66	17575	135	22.07	9	966	183
Taylor, C. R. V.	1	—	—	—	—	—	—	2	—
Taylor, D. J. S.	34	45	13	580	56	18.12	—	66	10
Taylor, M. N. S.	180	248	55	3361	105	17.41	1	112	—
Taylor, R. W.	267	373	73	4467	65	14.89	—	630	59
Thompson, E. R.	12	14	4	100	29*	10.00	—	11	—
Thomson, N. I.	423	581	99	7118	77	14.76	—	137	—
Tidy, W. N.	20	21	9	52	7*	4.33	—	10	—
Timms, B. S. V.	223	295	71	3519	120	15.70	1	435	64
Titmus, F. J.	636	949	151	19215	137*	24.07	5	420	—
Tolchard, J. G.	9	14	3	189	43	17.18	—	2	—
Tolchard, R. W.	151	206	56	3457	126*	23.04	2	285	37
Turner, D. R.	73	116	16	2433	181*	24.33	2	52	—
Turner, G. M.	118	210	27	6941	167	37.92	15	113	—
Turner, S.	64	94	18	1141	121	15.01	2	49	—
Underwood, D. L.	235	256	60	1655	80	8.44	—	96	—
Verity, S. A.	4	7	2	55	15	11.00	—	—	—
Virgin, R. T.	280	496	21	13448	178	28.31	17	257	—
Walker, P. M.............	423	717	99	16160	152*	26.14	11	633	—
Wallace, K. W...........	8	12	0	148	55	12.33	—	1	—
Waller, C. E..............	10	7	3	26	9*	6.50	—	3	—
Ward, A.	53	51	15	356	44	9.88	—	18	—
Ward, B.	83	146	9	3074	164*	22.43	3	39	—
Ward, J. M.	3	6	0	81	38	13.50	—	—	—
Warner, G. S.	27	43	6	900	118*	24.32	2	12	—
Watts, P. J.	238	399	47	9492	145	26.96	7	184	—
Wellington, L.	9	11	4	181	49	25.85	—	5	—
Westley, S. A.	27	42	12	454	93*	15.13	—	56	7
Wheatley, K. J.	79	110	14	1781	79*	18.55	—	32	—
White, D. W.	323	378	102	3002	58*	10.87	—	102	—
White, R. A.	235	376	61	7441	116*	23.62	4	108	—
Wiggs, R. J.	1	2	1	6	6	6.00	—	—	—
Wilkin, C. L. A.	11	18	4	148	22	10.57	—	2	—
Wilkins, C. P.	58	104	7	3474	133	35.81	5	80	6
Wilkinson, K. W........	2	3	1	5	3*	2.50	—	3	—
Willey, P..................	85	134	29	2171	99*	20.67	—	40	—
Williams, D.	15	24	8	176	32*	11.00	—	9	—
Williams, D. L.	52	45	17	151	37*	5.39	—	11	—
Willis, R. G. D.	20	18	12	72	25	12.00	—	6	—
Wills, R.	33	54	6	824	151*	17.16	1	27	—
Wilson, D.................	371	474	81	5814	112	14.79	1	221	—
Wilson, P. R. B.	23	39	1	664	94	17.47	—	9	—

	M.	I.	N.O.	Runs	H.S.	Avge.	100	Ct.	St.
Wood, B.	101	167	21	3987	144	27.30	7	97	—
Woodford, J. D..........	23	36	1	734	56	20.97	—	9	—
Woolmer, R. A.	38	50	14	588	58	16.33	—	19	—
Worrell, L. R............	1	—	—	—	—	—	—	—	—
Wright, L.	10	11	3	91	33	11.37	—	14	—
Yardley, T. J.	45	68	13	1307	94	23.76	—	28	—
Younis Ahmed	119	197	31	5793	147*	34.89	10	62	—

BOWLING

N.B.—Players who have not bowled in first-class cricket are omitted from the following list.

	Runs	Wkts.	Avge.	B.B.	5w Inns.	10w match	100w season
Abberley, R. N........	65	0	—	—	—	—	—
Acfield, D. L...........	7188	254	28.29	6–28	9	—	—
Ackerman, H. M.	623	14	44.50	2–18	—	—	—
Allan, J. M.	11012	420	26.21	6–17	17	1	—
Alldis, J. S...............	37	1	37.00	1–33	—	—	—
Allen, D. A.	27538	1173	23.47	8–34	56	8	1
Amiss, D. L.	477	14	34.07	3–21	—	—	—
Anderson, I. J.	71	6	11.83	3–12	—	—	—
Arnold, G. G...........	9421	457	20.61	8–41	20	1	1
Asif Iqbal	5862	198	29.60	6–45	4	—	—
Bailey, R. R.	1764	72	24.50	5–25	5	—	—
Balderstone, J. C.......	790	37	21.35	4–31	—	—	—
Barclay, J. R. T.........	56	0	—	—	—	—	—
Barker, G.	181	4	45.25	2–34	—	—	—
Barlow, E. J.	6183	228	27.11	7–26	8	1	—
Barr, D.	2747	88	31.21	6–89	2	—	—
Barratt, R. J.	4007	141	28.41	7–35	7	1	—
Barrett, A.	1312	55	23.85	7–90	5	1	—
Bates, D. L.	22726	880	25.82	8–51	34	2	3
Bielby, S. R.............	147	2	73.50	1–32	—	—	—
Birkenshaw, J.	14728	535	27.52	7–28	23	3	2
Bissex, M................	5059	180	28.10	7–70	8	1	—
Black, C. J. R.	62	0	—	—	—	—	—
Blenkiron, W.	6243	233	26.79	5–37	5	—	—
Bolus, J. B...............	852	22	38.72	4–40	—	—	—
Bond, J. D.	60	0	—	—	—	—	—
Booth, B. J..............	4476	140	31.97	7–143	1	—	—
Booth, R.	3	0	—	—	—	—	—
Booton, W. T.	72	2	36.00	2–72	—	—	—
Bore, M. K.	833	31	26.87	5–51	1	—	—
Boyce, K. D.............	9165	363	25.24	9–61	13	3	—
Boycott, G.	913	20	45.65	3–47	—	—	—
Brain, B. M.............	7508	288	26.06	6–38	12	2	—
Breakwell, D.	2679	105	25.51	8–39	4	1	—
Brearley, J. M.	91	1	91.00	1–21	—	—	—
Brown, A................	18309	743	24.64	8–47	26	4	1

	Runs	Wkts.	Avge.	B.B.	5w Inns.	10w match	100w season
Brown, A. S.	25000	962	25.98	8–80	45	8	2
Brown, D. J.	17171	710	24.18	8–64	25	4	—
Bryant, D. J.	148	4	37.00	2–73	—	—	—
Burgess, G. I.	5393	187	28.83	6–71	7	—	—
Burton, M. S. W.	2536	49	51.75	5–96	1	—	—
Buss, A.	21013	874	24.04	8–23	43	3	3
Buss, M. A.	6492	223	29.11	7–58	7	—	—
Buxton, I. R.	10023	396	25.31	7–33	11	2	—
Carling, P. G.	25	0	—	—	—	—	—
Carrick, P.	312	14	22.28	6–85	1	—	—
Carroll, P. R.	64	0	—	—	—	—	—
Carter, R. G. M.	10146	410	24.74	6–7	14	1	—
Cartwright, T. W.	23209	1194	19.43	8–39	69	14	7
Castell, A. T.	6260	202	30.99	6–22	8	1	—
Chisholm, R. H. E. ...	839	26	32.26	4–9	—	—	—
Clarkson, A.	367	13	28.23	3–51	—	—	—
Close, D. B.	27597	1079	25.57	8–41	42	3	2
Connolly, A. N.	17418	657	26.51	9–67	24	4	—
Cope, G. A.	4217	186	22.67	7–36	9	2	—
Cordle, A. E.	6834	295	23.16	9–49	7	2	—
Corlett, S. C.	26	0	—	—	—	—	—
Cottam, R. M. H.	13419	642	20.90	9–25	36	2	3
Cowdrey, M. C.	2893	54	53.57	4–22	—	—	—
Cross, G. F.	2154	73	29.50	4–28	—	—	—
Crump, B. S.	18874	787	23.98	7–29	30	5	2
Cumbes, J.	2238	103	21.72	6–35	5	—	—
Davey, J.	4028	133	30.28	6–95	2	—	—
Davis, B. A.	432	9	48.00	4–79	—	—	—
Davis, F. J.	1694	52	32.57	5–67	2	—	—
Davis, R. C.	2924	113	25.87	6–82	2	—	—
Davison, B. F.	966	34	28.41	5–52	1	—	—
Denman, J.	792	18	44.00	4–45	—	—	—
Denness, M. H.	36	1	36.00	1–36	—	—	—
Denning, P. W.........	4	0	—	—	—	—	—
Dinsdale, S. C.	24	1	24.00	1–24	—	—	—
Dixon, A. L.	24037	935	25.70	8–61	46	10	3
D'Oliveira, B. L.	7950	292	27.22	6–29	11	2	—
Douglas-Home, A.....	273	9	30.33	3–71	—	—	—
Dudleston, B.	269	5	53.80	2–48	—	—	—
Dye, J. C. J.	8354	337	24.78	6–37	11	1	—
Ealham, A. G. E.	21	1	21.00	1–1	—	—	—
East, R. E.	7384	303	24.36	8–63	15	2	—
Edmeades, B. E. A. .	8030	319	25.17	7–37	9	1	1
Edrich, J. H.	49	0	—	—	—	—	—
Edwards, M. J.	179	2	89.50	2–53	—	—	—
Elms, R.	88	4	22.00	2–38	—	—	—
Engineer, F. M.	117	1	117.00	1–40	—	—	—
Eyre, T. J. P.	9065	327	27.72	8–65	8	—	—
Featherstone, N. G....	365	7	52.14	2–1	—	—	—
Fletcher, K. W. R.....	608	11	55.27	4–50	—	—	—
Folkes, C.	714	25	28.56	5–22	2	—	—

	Runs	*Wkts.*	*Avge.*	*B.B.*	*5w Inns.*	*10w match*	*100w season*
Forbes, C.	17696	697	25.38	7–19	23	2	3
Foster, M. L. C........	1413	51	27.70	5–76	1	—	—
Frost, G.	132	4	33.00	3–33	—	—	—
Gibbs, L. R.	18042	659	27.37	8–37	30	4	—
Gibbs, P. J. K.	321	4	80.25	2–54	—	—	—
Gifford, N.	18484	953	19.39	8–28	49	8	3
Gilliat, R. M. C.	32	1	32.00	1–8	—	—	—
Goddard, G. F.	271	9	30.11	3–36	—	—	—
Gooch, P. A.	252	6	42.00	4–52	—	—	—
Goodwin, D.............	421	14	30.07	5–46	1	—	—
Gordon, A.	1	0	—	—	—	—	—
Graham, J. N.	6529	341	19.14	8–20	20	3	1
Graveney, T. W.	3037	80	37.96	5–28	1	—	—
Graves, P. J.	382	9	42.44	3–69	—	—	—
Gray, J. D.	534	21	25.42	5–2	1	—	—
Green, D. M.	4410	115	38.34	5–61	1	—	—
Greenidge, C. G.	0	0	—	—	—	—	—
Greenidge, G. A.	652	13	50.15	7–124	1	—	—
Greig, A. W.	8541	311	27.46	8–25	10	3	—
Griffith, K.	383	16	23.93	7–41	1	—	—
Griffith, M. G.	16	1	16.00	1–4	—	—	—
Halfyard, D. J.	24822	963	25.77	9–39	55	13	5
Hall, I. W.	23	0	—	—	—	—	—
Hallam, M. R.	142	4	35.00	1–12	—	—	—
Halliday, M.	32	0	—	—	—	—	—
Hampshire, J. H.	1207	15	80.46	7–52	1	—	—
Harris, M. J.	1458	40	36.45	4–16	—	—	—
Harvey, J. F.	21	1	21.00	1–0	—	—	—
Hassan, B.	126	0	—	—	—	—	—
Hatteea, S. A.	528	24	22.00	5–33	1	—	—
Haye, W.	20	1	20.00	1–20	—	—	—
Hayes, F. C.	10	0	—	—	—	—	—
Haywood, P. R.	5	0	—	—	—	—	—
Headley, R. G. A.	578	12	48.16	4–40	—	—	—
Heard, H.	2048	49	41.79	6–78	1	—	—
Hemmings, E. E.	2116	58	36.48	6–90	1	—	—
Hemsley, E. J. O.	740	25	29.60	3–23	—	—	—
Hendrick, M.	419	12	34.91	4–77	—	—	—
Herman, R. S.	5552	192	28.91	6–32	4	—	—
Hill, L. W.	36	0	—	—	—	—	—
Hill, M.	311	5	62.20	2–60	—	—	—
Hobbs, R. N. S.	19275	765	25.19	8–63	35	7	2
Hodgson, A.	12	2	6.00	2–4	—	—	—
Holder, J. W.	1920	80	24.00	5–36	2	—	—
Holder, V. A.	5467	234	23.36	6–21	10	1	—
Hone, D. J.	284	1	284.00	1–82	—	—	—
Howarth, J.	642	19	33.78	3–30	—	—	—
Hughes, D. P.	4498	163	27.59	7–24	7	1	—
Hutton, R. A.	10722	451	23.77	8–50	14	2	—
Ibadulla, K.	13032	424	30.73	7–22	5	—	—
Illingworth, R.	32245	1674	19.26	9–42	90	11	10

	Runs	Wkts.	Avge.	B.B.	5w Inns.	10w match	100w season
Inman, C.	76	1	76.00	1–30	—	—	—
Intikhab Alam	16001	589	27.16	8–61	29	5	—
Jackman, R. D.	6285	250	25.14	7–98	10	1	—
Jameson, J. A.	1438	39	36.87	3–4	—	—	—
Jameson, T. E. N.	531	10	53.10	2–21	—	—	—
Jesty, T. E.	2400	65	36.92	4–25	—	—	—
Johns, R. L.	671	13	51.61	4–76	—	—	—
Johnson, C.	104	1	104.00	1–53	—	—	—
Johnson, G. W.	1341	44	30.47	6–35	2	1	—
Johnson, L. A.	61	1	61.00	1–60	—	—	—
Johnson, P. D.	672	9	74.66	3–34	—	—	—
Jones, A.	208	2	104.00	1–24	—	—	—
Jones, A. A.	2776	93	29.84	8–25	3	1	—
Jones, K. V.	1976	70	28.22	6–78	4	—	—
Jorden, A. M.	5347	176	30.38	5–95	1	—	—
Joshi, U. C.	3274	145	22.57	6–54	15	3	—
Julien, B.	742	31	23.93	7–63	1	—	—
Kanhai, R. B.	525	9	58.33	2–54	—	—	—
Kennedy, J. H.	66	1	66.00	1–17	—	—	—
Kettle, M. K.	4800	179	26.81	6–67	5	—	—
Khan, M. J.	3061	120	25.50	6–67	3	—	—
Kingston, G. C.	126	3	42.00	2–18	—	—	—
Kitchen, M. J.	60	1	60.00	1–4	—	—	—
Knight, R. D. V.	2690	74	36.35	6–65	1	—	—
Knott, A. P. E.	43	1	43.00	1–40	—	—	—
Langford, B. A.	31699	1302	24.34	9–26	78	16	5
Langridge, R. J.	91	0	—	—	—	—	—
Latchman, H. C.	7146	274	26.08	7–91	11	—	—
Leary, S. E.	4901	145	33.80	5–22	2	—	—
Lee, P.	1620	45	36.00	6–86	2	—	—
Lees, R. D.	144	1	144.00	1–53	—	—	—
Lenham, L. J.	306	6	51.00	2–24	—	—	—
Lever, J. K.	4840	170	28.47	6–72	2	—	—
Lever, P.	11910	458	26.00	7–83	15	1	—
Lewington, P. J.	462	19	24.31	4–39	—	—	—
Lewis, A. R.	425	6	70.83	3–18	—	—	—
Lewis, R. M.	2	0	—	—	—	—	—
Lewis, R. V.	13	0	—	—	—	—	—
Lightfoot, A.	6192	172	36.00	7–25	4	—	—
Livingstone, D. A. ...	92	1	92.00	1–31	—	—	—
Llewellyn, M. J.	129	6	21.50	4–35	—	—	—
Lloyd, C. H.	2141	61	35.09	4–48	—	—	—
Lloyd, D.	2377	86	27.63	7–38	2	1	—
Luckhurst, B. W.	2268	44	51.54	4–32	—	—	—
Lyons, K. J.	126	0	—	—	—	—	—
McIlwaine, R. J.	273	4	68.25	2–40	—	—	—
McKenzie, G. D.	23230	819	28.36	8–71	33	4	—
McMorris, E. D. S. A.	78	0	—	—	—	—	—
McVicker, N. M.	3186	114	27.94	7–29	5	—	—
Marner, P. T.	11385	360	31.62	7–29	13	1	—
Marshall, R. E.	5092	176	28.93	6–36	5	—	—

	Runs	Wkts.	Avge.	B.B.	5w Inns.	10w match	100w season
Meyer, B. J.	28	0	—	—	—	—	—
Miles, O.	1095	46	23.80	7–71	2	—	—
Millener, D. J.	1958	57	34.35	4–97	—	—	—
Milton, C. A.	3630	79	45.94	5–64	1	—	—
Moan, R.	58	1	58.00	1–58	—	—	—
Mortimore, J. B.	34879	1550	22.50	8–59	65	7	3
Moseley, H. R.	228	1	228.00	1–110	—	—	—
Murray, D. L.	204	4	51.00	2–50	—	—	—
Murray, J. T.	226	6	37.66	2–10	—	—	—
Mushtaq Mohammad	10760	477	22.55	7–18	20	2	—
Nash, M. A.	5477	241	22.72	7–15	12	1	—
Nicholls, D.	4	1	4.00	1–4	—	—	—
Nicholls, R. B.	521	7	74.42	2–19	—	—	—
Nicholson, A. G.	12107	639	18.94	9–62	28	3	2
Norman, M. E. J. C.	164	2	82.00	2–0	—	—	—
Old, C. M.	3513	169	20.78	7–20	4	1	—
O'Riordan, A. J.	1465	68	21.54	6–35	2	—	—
Ormrod, J. A.	306	4	76.50	2–14	—	—	—
Owen-Thomas, D. R.	728	19	38.31	3–20	—	—	—
Padgett, D. E. V.	212	6	35.33	1–2	—	—	—
Page, M. H.	453	6	75.50	1–8	—	—	—
Palmer, R.	5439	172	31.62	6–45	4	—	—
Parfitt, P. H.	7617	248	30.71	6–45	4	—	—
Parks, J. M.	2206	51	43.25	3–23	—	—	—
Pataudi, Nawab of....	695	8	86.87	1–0	—	—	—
Pearman, H.	567	16	35.43	4–56	—	—	—
Pember, J. D. D.	1260	40	31.50	5–45	1	—	—
Phillips, R. W.	6	0	—	—	—	—	—
Phillipson, C. P.	56	1	56.00	1–56	—	—	—
Pilling, H.	46	0	—	—	—	—	—
Pinnock, R.	11	0	—	—	—	—	—
Plummer, P. J.	535	21	25.47	4–70	—	—	—
Pocock, P. I.	13252	560	23.66	7–57	19	5	1
Pollock, P. M.	9220	432	21.34	7–19	25	2	—
Pollock, R. G.	1976	40	49.40	3–46	—	—	—
Pont, K. R.	9	0	—	—	—	—	—
Presland, E. R.	761	13	58.53	2–19	—	—	—
Price, J. S. E.	14716	621	23.69	8–48	17	2	—
Prideaux, R. M.	34	0	—	—	—	—	—
Procter, M. J.	7475	414	18.05	7–25	16	3	1
Pullar, G.	387	10	38.70	3–91	—	—	—
Racionzer, T. B.	5	0	—	—	—	—	—
Radley, C. T.	18	2	9.00	1–7	—	—	—
Reed, B. L.	0	0	—	—	—	—	—
Reynolds, B. L.	284	4	71.00	1–0	—	—	—
Reynolds, G. E. A. ...	24	2	12.00	2–24	—	—	—
Rhodes, H. J.	21113	1072	19.69	7–38	42	4	3
Richards, B. A.	1163	34	34.20	7–63	1	—	—
Ridley, R. M.	0	0	—	—	—	—	—
Roberts, J. K.	485	15	32.33	4–38	—	—	—
Robinson, P. J..........	7897	289	27.32	7–10	10	1	—

	Runs	Wkts.	Avge.	B.B.	5w Inns.	10w match	100w season
Roope, G. R. J.	3328	109	30.53	5–14	4	—	—
Ross, N. P. G.	261	9	29.00	2–22	—	—	—
Rouse, S. J.	67	4	16.75	4–34	—	—	—
Rowe, L. A.	23	0	—	—	—	—	—
Rumsey, F. E.	11773	580	20.29	8–26	30	5	3
Russell, P. E.	2724	97	28.08	6–61	3	—	—
Russell, W. E............	977	22	44.40	3–20	—	—	—
Sadiq Mohammad ...	1118	41	27.26	5–29	2	—	—
Sainsbury, P. J.	24406	951	25.66	7–25	20	—	1
Sarfraz Nawaz	2532	82	30.87	5–43	1	—	—
Saville, G. J.	17	0	—	—	—	—	—
Schofield, D.	53	0	—	—	—	—	—
Selwood, T.	1	0	—	—	—	—	—
Shackleton, D.	53303	2857	18.65	9–30	194	38	20
Sharpe, P. J.	168	2	84.00	1–1	—	—	—
Shepherd, D. J.	44707	2127	21.01	9–47	120	28	12
Shepherd, D. R.	5	1	5.00	1–1	—	—	—
Shepherd, J. N.	6646	281	23.65	8–40	20	—	—
Shuttleworth, K.	6828	312	21.88	7–41	12	1	—
Simmons, J.	2480	75	33.06	5–45	1	—	—
Slade, D. N. F..........	10853	477	22.75	7–47	14	1	—
Smedley, M. J.	4	0	—	—	—	—	—
Smith, A. C.	814	37	22.00	5–32	1	—	—
Smith, D. H. K.	23	1	23.00	1–1	—	—	—
Smith, D. R.	29655	1250	23.72	7–20	51	6	5
Smith, E.	30411	1186	25.64	9–46	50	4	1
Smith, M. J.	1742	53	32.86	4–13	—	—	—
Smith, M. J. K.	298	5	59.60	1–0	—	—	—
Smith, W. A.	1	0	—	—	—	—	—
Snow, J. A.	15577	723	21.54	7–29	36	4	2
Sobers, G. S............	23181	848	27.33	9–49	33	1	—
Solkar, E. D.	2996	120	24.96	6–38	4	—	—
Spencer, C. T...........	35202	1319	26.68	9–63	46	6	1
Spencer, J.	1782	73	24.41	5–50	2	—	—
Standen, J. A.	7934	313	25.34	7–30	13	—	—
Staziker, M. W.	269	1	269.00	1–114	—	—	—
Stead, B.	7561	267	28.31	7–32	10	—	—
Steele, D. S.	3513	151	23.26	8–29	2	—	—
Steele, H. K.	141	2	70.50	1–47	—	—	—
Steele, J. F.	928	29	32.00	5–43	1	—	—
Stewart, M. J.	95	1	95.00	1–4	—	—	—
Stewart, W. J.	15	2	7.50	2–4	—	—	—
Storey, S. J.............	10050	399	25.18	8–22	11	2	1
Stringer, P. M.	1984	75	26.45	5–43	1	—	—
Sullivan, J.	1094	41	26.68	4–44	—	—	—
Suttle, K. G.	8510	262	32.48	6–64	1	—	—
Swarbrook, F. W. ...	2267	80	28.33	6–48	3	—	—
Swinburne, J. W.	1056	34	31.05	5–81	2	—	—
Taylor, B.	29	1	29.00	1–16	—	—	—
Taylor, M. N. S.	11194	416	26.90	7–106	11	—	—
Taylor, R. W.	12	0	—	—	—	—	—

	Runs	Wkts.	Avge.	B.B.	5w Inns.	10w match	100w season
Thompson, E. R.	953	23	41.43	5–11	2	—	—
Thomson, N. I.	32785	1596	20.54	10–49	73	8	12
Tidy, W. N.	1494	48	31.12	5–24	3	—	—
Titmus, F. J.	50158	2292	21.88	9–52	141	23	15
Tolchard, J. G.	5	0	—	—	—	—	—
Turner, D. R.	5	1	5.00	1–4	—	—	—
Turner, G. M.	168	5	33.60	3–18	—	—	—
Turner, S.	3199	131	24.41	4–10	—	—	—
Underwood, D. L. ...	17278	965	17.90	9–28	67	20	6
Verity, S. A.	260	4	65.00	3–42	—	—	—
Virgin, R. T.	306	4	76.50	1–6	—	—	—
Walker, P. M...........	21351	766	27.87	7–58	25	2	1
Waller, C. E............	528	24	22.00	5–43	1	—	—
Ward, A.	3387	177	19.13	6–30	7	3	—
Ward, B.	7	3	2.33	2–5	—	—	—
Warner, G. S.	13	0	—	—	—	—	—
Watts, P. J.	7769	313	24.82	6–18	7	—	—
Wellington, L.	411	11	37.36	3–29	—	—	—
Wheatley, K. J.	1954	69	28.31	4–1	—	—	—
White, D. W.	26164	1124	23.27	9–44	56	5	4
White, R. A.	6859	243	28.22	6–56	11	1	—
Wiggs, R. J.	44	1	44.00	1–44	—	—	—
Wilkin, C. L. A.	751	15	50.06	3–74	—	—	—
Wilkins, C. P.	589	15	39.26	4–21	—	—	—
Willey, P..................	2462	85	28.96	5–14	3	—	—
Williams, D.	645	16	40.31	5–19	1	—	—
Williams, D. L.	2948	122	24.16	7–60	5	—	—
Willis, R. G. D.	1514	62	24.41	5–78	1	—	—
Wilson, D................	22005	1075	20.46	8–36	46	8	5
Wilson, P. R. B.	233	7	33.28	4–60	—	—	—
Wood, B.	1905	74	25.74	7–52	3	—	—
Woodford, J. D.........	61	0	—	—	—	—	—
Woolmer, R. A.	1300	53	24.52	7–47	4	—	—
Worrell, L. R............	25	0	—	—	—	—	—
Wright, L.	198	12	16.50	4–25	—	—	—
Yardley, T. J.	8	0	—	—	—	—	—
Younis Ahmed	692	16	43.25	3–12	—	—	—

For the widest coverage of world cricket
by the games top writers

PLAYFAIR CRICKET MONTHLY

Price 15p Obtainable from all newsagents or from

THE DICKENS PRESS

161, Queen Victoria Street, London E.C.4

MINOR COUNTIES COMPETITION

	P.	W.	L.	*1st Innings* W.	L.	N.R.	Pts.	Avge
Bedfordshire	10	6	—	3	1	—	70	7.00
Lincolnshire	12	5	—	3	3	1	64	5.33
Staffordshire	10	3	2†	1	2	2	45	4.50
Northumberland	12	4	2	3	2	1	53	4.41
Hertfordshire	10	3	1	3	3	—	42	4.20
Oxfordshire	10	3	1	2	2	2	42	4.20
Somerset II	10	3	2	3	1	1	42	4.20
Buckinghamshire	12	2	4‡	4	2	—	46	3.83
Yorkshire II	10	2	1	5	1	1	38	3.80
Durham	8	2	1	2	2	1	30	3.75
Devon	10	2	—	4	4	—	36	3.60
Norfolk	12	3	3	2	1	3	43	3.58
Cumberland	8	2	3	—	2	1	24	3.00
Cheshire	12	2	4†	1	4	1	35	2.91
Berkshire	12	1	1	6	4	—	32	2.66
Lancashire II	8	1	4*	2	—	1	21	2.62
Dorset	10	1	2*	2	3	2	26	2.60
Wiltshire	10	1	3	5	1	—	26	2.60
Shropshire	8	—	3†	3	2	—	17	2.12
Cornwall	10	1	3*	—	5	1	20	2.00
Suffolk	10	1	5*	—	4	—	17	1.70
Cambridgeshire	10	—	3	1	6	—	9	0.90

* 1st innings points (3) in *ONE* match lost.
† 1st innings points (3) in *TWO* matches lost.
‡ 1st innings points (3) in *FOUR* matches lost.

2nd XI FINAL TABLE, 1970

	P.	W.	L.	*1st Inns.* W.	L.	N.R.	Tie	Pts.	Avge.
Kent	11	5	—	5	1	—	—	66	6.00
*Gloucester	10	4	2	2	2	1	1	55	5.50
Hampshire	12	5	4	1	1	1	—	54	4.50
‡†Surrey	15	5	3	1	3	3	—	67	4.46
Leicester	11	3	3	3	2	—	—	41	3.72
Essex	6	2	2	—	1	1	—	21	3.50
*Glamorgan	12	3	4	2	2	1	—	41	3.41
Lancashire	11	2	—	4	4	1	—	36	3.27
Warwickshire	16	3	3	3	5	1	1	49	3.05
‡Northants	18	2	—	7	6	3	—	49	2.61
Worcester	15	2	2	4	5	2	—	37	2.46
*Notts	12	1	4	3	4	—	—	26	2.16
*Derbyshire	12	1	2	3	3	3	—	25	2.08
Sussex	9	1	3	2	2	1	—	18	2.00
*Middlesex	10	1	8	0	1	—	—	14	1.40

*First Innings points in one game lost.
†First Innings points in three games lost.
‡Tie on First Innings—unfinished match.

CRICKET RECORDS

COMPLETE TO SEPTEMBER 30, 1970

Highest Innings Totals

1107	Victoria v New South Wales (Melbourne)	1926–27
1059	Victoria v Tasmania (Melbourne)	1922–23
918	New South Wales v South Australia (Sydney)	1900–01
912-8d	Holkar v Mysore (Indore)	1945–46
910-6d	Railways v Dera Ismail Khan (Lahore)	1964–65
903-7d	England v Australia (Oval)	1938
887	Yorkshire v Warwickshire (Birmingham)	1896
849	England v West Indies (Kingston)	1929–30
843	Australians v Ox. & Camb. Univ. P & P (Portsmouth)	1893
839	New South Wales v Tasmania (Sydney)	1898–99
826-4	Maharashtra v Kathiawar (Poona)	1948–49
824	Lahore Greens v Bahawalpur (Lahore)	1965–66
821-7d	South Australia v Queensland (Adelaide)	1939–40
815	New South Wales v Victoria (Sydney)	1908–09
811	Surrey v Somerset (Oval)	1899
807	New South Wales v South Australia (Adelaide)	1899–1900
805	New South Wales v Victoria (Melbourne)	1905–06
803-4d	Kent v Essex (Brentwood)	1934
803	Non-Smokers v Smokers (East Melbourne)	1886–87
802	New South Wales v South Australia (Sydney)	1920–21
801	Lancashire v Somerset (Taunton)	1895

Lowest Innings Totals

12†	Oxford University v M.C.C. and Ground (Oxford)	1877
12	Northamptonshire v Gloucestershire (Gloucester)	1907
13	Wellington v Nelson (Nelson)	1862–63
13	Auckland v Canterbury (Auckland)	1877–78
13	Nottinghamshire v Yorkshire (Nottingham)	1901
15	M.C.C. v Surrey (Lord's)	1839
15†	Victoria v M.C.C. (Melbourne)	1903–04
15†	Northamptonshire v Yorkshire (Northampton)	1908
15	Hampshire v Warwickshire (Birmingham)	1922
16	M.C.C. and Ground v Surrey (Lord's)	1872
16	Derbyshire v Nottinghamshire (Nottingham)	1879
16	Surrey v Nottinghamshire (Oval)	1880
16	Warwickshire v Kent (Tonbridge)	1913
16	Trinidad v Barbados (Bridgetown)	1941–42
16	Border v Natal (East London)	1959–60

† *Batted one man short.*

Highest Aggregates in a First-class Match

2376	(38)	Bombay v Maharashtra (Poona)	1948–49
2078	(40)	Bombay v Holkar (Bombay)	1944–45
1981	(35)	England v South Africa (Durban)	1938–39
1929	(39)	New South Wales v South Australia (Sydney)	1925–26
1911	(34)	New South Wales v Victoria (Sydney)	1908–09
1905	(40)	Otago v Wellington (Dunedin)	1923–24

In England the highest are:

1723 (31) England v Australia (Leeds) 5 day match 1948
1601 (29) England v Australia (Lord's) 4 day match 1930
1502 (28) M.C.C. v New Zealanders (Lord's) 1927
1499 (31) T. N. Pearce's XI v Australians (Scarborough) 1961
1496 (24) England v Australia (Nottingham) 4 day match 1938
1494 (37) England v Australia (Oval) 4 day match....................1934
1492 (33) Worcestershire v Oxford U. (Worcester)....................1904
1477 (32) Hampshire v Oxford U. (Southampton) 1913
1477 (33) England v South Africa (Oval) 4 day match 1947
1475 (27) Northamptonshire v Surrey (Northampton) 1920

(Wickets that fell given in parentheses.)

Tie Matches

Due to the change of law made in 1948 for tie matches, a tie is now a rarity. The law states that only if the match is played out and the scores are equal is the result a tie.

The most recent tie matches are as follows:

Yorks (351-4d & 113) v Leics (328 & 136) at Huddersfield....................1954
Sussex (172 & 120) v Hants (153 & 139) at Eastbourne....................1955
Victoria (244 & 197) v New South Wales (281 & 160) at Melbourne (St. Kilda)....................1956–57
(The first tie in Sheffield Shield cricket)
T. N. Pearce's XI (313-7d & 258) v New Zealanders (268 & 303-8d) at Scarborough....................1958
Essex (364-6d & 176-8d) v Glos (329 & 211) at Leyton....................1959
Australia (505 & 232) v West Indies (453 & 284) at Brisbane......1960–61
(The first tie in Test cricket)
Bahawalpur (123 & 282) v Lahore B (127 & 278) at Bahawalpur...1961–62
Middlesex (327-5d) & 123-9d) v Hants (277 & 173) at Portsmouth ...1967
England XI (312-8d & 190-3d) v England Under-25 XI (320-9d & 182) at Scarborough....................1968

Highest Individual Scores

499 Hanif Mohammad, Karachi v Bahawalpur (Karachi)......1958–59
452* D. G. Bradman, New South Wales v Queensland (Sydney) 1929–30
443* B. B. Nimbalkar, Maharashtra v Kathiawar (Poona).........1948–49
437 W. H. Ponsford, Victoria v Queensland (Melbourne)......1927–28
429 W. H. Ponsford, Victoria v Tasmania (Melbourne).........1922–23
424 A. C. MacLaren, Lancashire v Somerset (Taunton)....................1895
385 B. Sutcliffe, Otago v Canterbury (Christchurch)............1952–53
383 C. W. Gregory, New South Wales v Queensland (Brisbane) 1906–07
369 D. G. Bradman, South Australia v Tasmania (Adelaide)...1935–36
365* C. Hill, South Australia v New South Wales (Adelaide)...1900–01
365* G. S. Sobers, West Indies v Pakistan (Kingston) 1957–58
364 L. Hutton, England v Australia (Oval)....................1938
359* V. M. Merchant, Bombay v Maharashtra (Bombay).........1943–44
359 R. B. Simpson, New South Wales v Queensland (Brisbane) 1963–64
357* R. Abel, Surrey v Somerset (Oval)....................1899
357 D. G. Bradman, South Australia v Victoria (Melbourne)...1935–36
356 B. A. Richards, South Australia v Western Australia (Perth) 1970–71
355 B. Sutcliffe, Otago v Auckland (Dunedin)....................1949–50
352 W. H. Ponsford, Victoria v New South Wales (Melbourne) 1926–27

Most Centuries in a Season

18 D. C. S. Compton 1947
16 J. B. Hobbs 1925
15 W. R. Hammond..1938
14 H. Sutcliffe 1932

Most Centuries in an Innings

6 for Holkar v Mysore (Indore) 1945–46
5 for New South Wales v South Australia (Sydney) 1900–01
5 for Australia v West Indies (Kingston)..........................1954–55

Most Centuries in Succession

6 C. B. Fry..1901
6 D. G. Bradman..1938–39
6 M. J. Procter..1970–71
5 E. D. Weekes 1955–56

Most Centuries in Succession in Test Matches

5 E. D. Weekes, West Indies ....1947–48 and 1948–49
4 J. H. Fingleton, Australia...........................1935–36 and 1936–37
4 A. Melville, South Africa ....1938–39 and 1947

Two Double Centuries in a Match

A. E. Fagg, 244 and 202* for Kent v Essex (Colchester)..................1938

A Double Century and a Century in a Match

C. B. Fry, 125 and 229, Sussex v Surrey (Hove)..........................1900
W. W. Armstrong, 157* and 245, Victoria v South Australia (Melbourne) 1920–21
H. T. W. Hardinge, 207 and 102* for Kent v Surrey (Blackheath)......1921
C. P. Mead, 113 and 224, Hampshire v Sussex (Horsham)...............1921
K. S. Duleepsinhji, 115 and 246, Sussex v Kent (Hastings)............1929
D. G. Bradman, 124 and 225, Woodfull's XI v Ryder's XI (Sydney) 1929–30
B. Sutcliffe, 243 and 100*, New Zealanders v Essex (Southend) 1949
M. R. Hallam, 210* and 157 Leics v Glamorgan (Leicester).........1959
M. R. Hallam, 203* and 143*, Leics v Sussex (Worthing)...............1961
Hanumant Singh, 109 and 213*, Rajasthan v Bombay (Bombay) 1966–67
Salahuddin, 256 and 102* Karachi v East Pakistan (Karachi) 1968–69
K. D. Walters, 242 and 103, Australia v West Indies (Sydney) 1968–69

Most Centuries in First-class Cricket

J. B. Hobbs, 197 (175 in England); E. Hendren, 170 (151); W. R. Hammond, 167 (134); C. P. Mead, 153 (145); H. Sutcliffe, 149 (135); F. E. Woolley, 145 (135); L. Hutton 129 (105); W. G. Grace, 126 (125); D. C. S. Compton 123 (92); T. W. Graveney, 122 (91); D. G. Bradman, 117 (41); A. Sandham, 107 (87); T. Hayward, 104 (100); E. Tyldesley, 102 (94); L. E. G. Ames, 102 (89).

N.B.—In his "amended" career record W. G. Grace scored 124 centuries (123 in England).

Highest Individual Batting Aggregates in a Season

Runs		Season	Innings	Times not out	Highest Score	Avge.	100s
3,816	D. C. S. Compton ...	1947	50	8	246	90.85	18
3,539	W. J. Edrich	1947	52	8	267*	80.43	12
3,518	T. Hayward	1906	61	8	219	66.37	13
3,429	L. Hutton...............	1949	56	6	269*	68.58	12
3,352	F. E. Woolley	1928	59	4	198	60.94	12
3,336	H. Sutcliffe	1932	52	7	313	74.13	14
3,323	W. R. Hammond ...	1933	54	5	264	67.81	13
3,311	E. Hendren	1928	54	7	209*	70.44	13
3,309	R. Abel..................	1901	68	8	247	55.15	7
3,252	W. R. Hammond......	1937	55	5	217	65.04	13
3,245	M. J. K. Smith.........	1959	67	11	200*	57.94	8
3,186	E. Hendren	1933	65	9	301*	56.89	11
3,179	C. P. Mead	1921	52	6	280*	69.10	10
3,170	T. Hayward	1904	63	5	205	54.65	11
3,159	K. S. Ranjitsinhji ...	1899	58	8	197	63.18	8
3,147	C. B. Fry	1901	43	3	244	78.67	13
3,065	K. S. Ranjitsinhji......	1900	40	5	275	87.57	11
3,058	L. E. G. Ames	1933	57	5	295	58.80	9
3,041	J. T. Tyldesley	1901	60	5	221	55.29	9
3,027	C. P. Mead	1928	50	10	180	75.67	13
3,024	J. B. Hobbs	1925	48	5	266*	70.32	16
3,024	E. Tyldesley	1928	48	10	242	79.57	10
3,019	W. E. Alley	1961	64	11	221*	56.96	11
3,011	W. R. Hammond......	1938	42	2	271	75.27	15
3,010	E. Hendren	1923	51	12	200*	77.17	13
3,006	H. Sutcliffe	1931	42	11	230	96.96	13
3,003	J. H. Parks	1937	63	4	168	50.89	11
3,002	H. Sutcliffe	1928	44	5	228	76.97	13

Partnerships for First Wicket

555 H. Sutcliffe and P. Holmes, Yorks v Essex (Leyton)...............1932
554 J. T. Brown and J. Tunnicliffe, Yorks v Derby (Chesterfield)...1898
490 E. H. Bowley and John Langridge, Sussex v Middlesex (Hove) 1933
456 W. H. Ponsford and E. R. Mayne, Victoria v Queensland (Melbourne) 1923–24
428 J. B. Hobbs and A. Sandham, Surrey v Oxford U (Oval)......1926
424 J. F. W. Nicholson and I. J. Siedle, Natal v Orange Free State (Bloemfontein) 1926–27
413 V. Mankad and P. Roy, India v New Zealand (Madras)......1955–56
395 D. M. Young and R. B. Nicholls, Glos v Oxford U (Oxford)...1962

Partnerships for Second Wicket

455 K. V. Bhandarkar and B. B. Nimbalkar, Maharashtra v Kathiawar (Poona) 1948–49
451 D. G. Bradman and W. H. Ponsford, Australia v England (Oval) 1934
446 C. C. Hunte and G. S. Sobers, West Indies v Pakistan (Kingston)...1957–58
429* J. G. Dewes and G. H. G. Doggart, Camb U v Essex (Camb.) 1949
398 W. Gunn and A. Shrewsbury, Notts v Sussex (Nottingham)...1890

Partnerships for Third Wicket

445 P. E. Whitelaw and W. N. Carson, Auckland v Otago (Dunedin) 1936–37
434 J. B. Stollmeyer and G. E. Gomez, Trinidad v British Guiana (Port of Spain) 1946–47
424* W. J. Edrich and D. C. S. Compton, Middlesex v Somerset (Lord's) 1948
410 R. S. Modi and L. Amarnath, India v Rest (Calcutta)......1946–47
399 R. T. Simpson and D. C. S. Compton, M.C.C. v N.E. Transvaal (Benoni) 1948–49

Partnerships for Fourth Wicket

577 Gul Mahomed and V. S. Hazare, Baroda v Holkar (Baroda) 1946–47
574* C. L. Walcott and F. M. Worrell, Barbados v Trinidad (Port of Spain)........1945–46
502* F. M. Worrell and J. D. C. Goddard, Barbados v Trinidad (Bridgetown)........1943–44
448 R. Abel and T. Hayward, Surrey v Yorks (Oval) 1899
424 I. S. Lee and S. O. Quin, Victoria v Tasmania (Melbourne) 1933–34
411 P. B. H. May and M. C. Cowdrey, England v West Indies (Birmingham) 1957
410 G. Abraham and B. Pandit, Kerala v Andhra (Pulghat)...1959–60
402 W. Watson and T. W. Graveney, M.C.C. v British Guiana (Georgetown) 1953–54
402 R. B. Kanhai and K. Ibadulla, Warwicks v Notts (Nottingham) 1968

Partnerships for Fifth Wicket

405 D. G. Bradman and S. G. Barnes, Australia v England (Sydney)........1946–47
397 W. Bardsley and C. Kellaway, New South Wales v South Australia (Sydney) 1920–21
393 E. G. Arnold and W. B. Burns, Worcs v Warwicks (Birmingham) 1909
360 V. M. Merchant and M. N. Raiji, Bombay v Hyderabad (Bombay) 1947–48
347 D. Brookes and D. Barrick, Northants v Essex (Northampton) 1952

Partnerships for Sixth Wicket

487* G. Headley and C. C. Passailaigue, Jamaica v Lord Tennyson's XI (Kingston) 1931–32
428 W. W. Armstrong and M. A. Noble, Australians v Sussex (Hove) 1902
411 R. M. Poore and E. G. Wynyard, Hants v Somerset (Taunton) 1899
376 R. Subba Row and A. Lightfoot, Northants v Surrey (Oval)...1958
371 V. M. Merchant and R. S. Modi, Bombay v Maharashtra (Bombay) 1943–44

Partnerships for Seventh Wicket

347 D. Atkinson and C. Depeiza, West Indies v Australia (Bridgetown)........1954–55

344 K. S. Ranjitsinhji and W. Newham, Sussex v Essex (Leyton)...1902
340 K. J. Key and H. Philipson, Oxford U v Middlesex (Chiswick Park) 1887
336 F. C. W. Newman and C. R. Maxwell, Cahn's XI v Leics (Nottingham) 1935
335 C. W. Andrews and E. C. Bensted, Queensland v New South Wales (Sydney)....................1934–35

Partnerships for Eighth Wicket

433 V. T. Trumper and A. Sims, Australians v Canterbury (Christchurch) 1913–14
292 R. Peel and Lord Hawke, Yorks v Warwicks (Birmingham)...1896
270 V. T. Trumper and E. P. Barbour, New South Wales v Victoria (Sydney)....................1912–13
263 D. R. Wilcox and R. M. Taylor, Essex v Warwicks (Southend) 1946
255 E. A. V. Williams and E. A. Martindale, Barbados v Trinidad (Bridgetown)....................1935–36

Partnerships for Ninth Wicket

283 A. R. Warren and J. Chapman, Derbyshire v Warwickshire (Blackwell) 1910
251 J. W. H. T. Douglas and S. N. Hare, Essex v Derbyshire (Leyton) 1921
245 V. S. Hazare and N. D. Nagarwalla, Maharashtra v Baroda (Poona) 1939–40
239 H. B. Cave and I. B. Leggat, Central Districts v Otago (Dunedin) 1952–53
232 C. Hill and E. Walkley, South Australia v New South Wales (Adelaide) 1900–01

Partnerships for Tenth Wicket

307 A. F. Kippax and J. E. H. Hooker, New South Wales v Victoria (Melbourne) 1928–29
249 C. T. Sarwate and S. N. Bannerjee, Indians v Surrey (Oval)...1946
235 F. E. Woolley and A. Fielder, Kent v Worcs (Stourbridge)......1909
230 R. W. Nicholls and W. Roche, Middlesex v Kent (Lord's)......1899
218 F. H. Vigar and T. P. B. Smith, Essex v Derbyshire (Chesterfield) 1947

Most Wickets in a Season

W.		Season	O.	M.	R.	Avge.
304	A. P. Freeman............	1928	1,976.1	423	5,489	18.05
298	A. P. Freeman............	1933	2,039	651	4,549	15.26
290	T. Richardson............	1895	1,690.1	463	4,170	14.37
283	C. T. B. Turner	1888	2,427.2	1,127	3,307	11.68
276	A. P. Freeman............	1931	1,618	360	4,307	15.60
275	A. P. Freeman............	1930	1,014.3	472	4,632	16.84
273	T. Richardson	1897	1,603.4	495	3,945	14.45
267	A. P. Freeman............	1929	1,670.5	381	4,879	18.27
261	W. Rhodes	1900	1,553	455	3,606	13.81
257	J. T. Hearne...............	1896	2,003.1	818	3,670	14.28
253	A. P. Freeman............	1932	1,565.5	404	4,149	16.39
251	W. Rhodes	1901	1,565	505	3,797	15.12

All Ten Wickets in an Innings

On three occasions: A. P. Freeman, 1929, 1930 and 1931

On two occasions: J. C. Laker, 1956, H. Verity, 1931 and 1932, V. E. Walker 1859 and 1865.

Instances since the war:

W. E. Hollies, Warwicks v Notts (Birmingham), 1946; J. M. Sims of Middlesex playing for East v West (Kingston), 1948; J. K. Graveney, Gloucestershire v Derbyshire (Chesterfield), 1949; T. E. Bailey, Essex v Lancashire (Clacton), 1949, R. Berry, Lancashire v Worcestershire (Blackpool), 1953; S. P. Gupte, Bombay v Pakistan Services (Bombay), 1954–55; J. C. Laker, Surrey v Australians (Oval), 1956; J. C. Laker, England v Australia (Manchester), 1956; G. A. R. Lock, Surrey v Kent, (Blackheath), 1956; K. Smales, Nottingham v Gloucestershire (Stroud), 1956; P. Chatterjee, Bengal v Assam (Jorhat), 1956–57; J. D. Bannister, Warwickshire v Combined Services (Birmingham), 1959; A. J. G. Pearson, Cambridge University v Leicestershire (Loughborough), 1961; N. I. Thomson, Sussex v Warwickshire (Worthing) 1964; P. Allan, Queensland v Victoria (Melbourne) 1965–66; I. Brayshaw, Western Australia v Victoria (Perth), 1967–68.

Nineteen Wickets in a Match

J. C. Laker 19–90 (9–37 and 10–53), England v Australia (Manchester), 1956.

Eighteen Wickets in a Match

H. A. Arkwright 18–96 (9–43 and 9–53), M.C.C. v Gentlemen of Kent (Canterbury), 1861, (twelve-a-side match).

Seventeen Wickets in a Match

Instances between the two wars were: A. P. Freeman (for 67 runs), Kent v Sussex (Brighton), 1922; F. C. L. Matthews (89 runs), Notts v Northants (Nottingham) 1923; C. W. L. Parker (56 runs) Glos. v Essex (Gloucester), 1925; G. R. Cox (106 runs), Sussex v Warwicks (Horsham), 1926; A. P. Freeman (92 runs), Kent v Warwicks (Folkestone), 1932; H. Verity (91 runs), Yorks v Essex (Leyton), 1933; J. C. Clay (212) runs, Glamorgan v Worcs (Swansea), 1937; T. W. Goddard (106 runs), Glos. v Kent (Bristol), 1939. There has been no instance since the last war.

Most hat-tricks in a Career

7 D. V. P. Wright.
6 T. W. Goddard, C. W. L. Parker.
5 S. Haigh, V. W. C. Jupp, A. E. G. Rhodes, F. A. Tarrant.

The "Double" Event

3,000 runs and 100 wickets: J. H. Parks, 1937.
2,000 runs and 200 wickets: G. H. Hirst, 1906.
2,000 runs and 100 wickets: F. E. Woolley (4), J. W. Hearne (3), G. H. Hirst (2), W. Rhodes (2), T. E. Bailey, E. Davies, W. G. Grace, G. L. Jessop, V. W. C. Jupp, James Langridge, F. A. Tarrant, C. L. Townsend, L. F. Townsend.
1,000 runs and 200 wickets: M. W. Tate (3), A. E. Trott (2), A. S. Kennedy.
Most "Doubles": W. Rhodes (16), G. H. Hirst (14), V. W. C. Jupp (10)
"Double" in first season: D. B. Close, 1949. At the age of 18, Close is the youngest player ever to perform this feat.

Fielding

Most catches in a season:	78 W. R. Hammond......1928
	77 M. J. Stewart 1957
Most catches in a match:	10 W. R. Hammond, Gloucestershire v Surrey (Cheltenham)......1928
Most catches in a innings:	7 M. J. Stewart, Surrey v Northants (Northampton) 1957
	7 A. S. Brown, Gloucestershire v Nottinghamshire (Nottingham) 1966

Wicket-keeping

Most Dismissals in a Season

127 (ct 79, st 48), L. E. G. Ames (Kent) 1929
121 (ct 69, st 52), L. E. G. Ames (Kent) 1928
110 (ct 63, st 47), H. Yarnold (Worcestershire) 1949
107 (ct 77, st 30), G. Duckworth (Lancashire) 1928
107 (ct 96, st 11), J. G. Binks (Yorkshire) 1960
104 (ct 82, st 22), J. T. Murray (Middlesex) 1957
102 (ct 70, st 32), F. H. Huish (Kent) 1913
102 (ct 95, st 7), J. T. Murray (Middlesex) 1960
101 (ct 85, st 16), R. Booth (Worcestershire) 1960
100 (ct 36, st 64), L. E. G. Ames (Kent) 1932
100 (ct 62, st 38), F. H. Huish (Kent) 1911
100 (ct 91, st 9), R. Booth (Worcestershire) 1964

Most dismissals in a match:	12 E. Pooley (8ct 4st) Surrey v Sussex (Oval)......1868
	12 D. Tallon (9ct 3st), Queensland v New South Wales (Sydney)...1938–39
	12 H. B. Taber (9ct 3st), New South Wales v South Australia (Adelaide)......1968–69
Most catches in a match:	11 A. Long, Surrey v Sussex (Hove) 1964
	10 A. E. Wilson, Gloucestershire v Hants (Portsmouth) 1953
	10 L. A. Johnson, Northants v Sussex (Worthing)......1963
	10 R. W. Taylor, Derbyshire v Hants (Chesterfield) 1963
Most dismissals in an innings:	8 A. T. W. Grout (8ct) Queensland v W. Australia (Brisbane) 1959–60

Did you know that Lord's dispensed with a sightscreen at the Pavilion end until 1964? This is one of many fascinating details to be found in **I-SPY Cricket**, on sale at newsagents for 7½p.

TEST CRICKET RECORDS

(Including Matches between England and Rest of World 1970)
Up to 9th March, 1971, but excluding matches between West Indies and India.

HIGHEST INNINGS TOTALS

903—7d	England v Australia (Oval)	1938
849	England v West Indies (Kingston)	1929–30
790—3d	West Indies v Pakistan (Kingston)	1957–58
758—8d	Australia v West Indies (Kingston)	1954–55
729—6d	Australia v England (Lord's)	1930
701	Australia v England (Oval)	1934
695	Australia v England (Oval)	1930
681—8d	West Indies v England (Port of Spain)	1953–54
674	Australia v India (Adelaide)	1947–48
668	Australia v West Indies (Bridgetown)	1954–55
659—8d	Australia v England (Sydney)	1946–47
658—8d	England v Australia (Nottingham)	1938
657—8d	Pakistan v West Indies (Bridgetown)	1957–58
656—8d	Australia v England (Manchester)	1964
654—5	England v South Africa (Durban)	1938–39
650—6d	Australia v West Indies (Bridgetown)	1964–65

The highest innings for the countries not mentioned above are:

622-9d	South Africa v Australia (Durban)	1969–70
539-9d	India v Pakistan (Madras)	1960–61
505	New Zealand v South Africa (Cape Town)	1953–54

LOWEST INNINGS TOTALS

26	New Zealand v England (Auckland)	1954–55
30	South Africa v England (Port Elizabeth)	1895–96
30	South Africa v England (Birmingham)	1924
35	South Africa v England (Cape Town)	1898–99
36	Australia v England (Birmingham)	1902
36	South Africa v Australia (Melbourne)	1931–32
42	Australia v England (Sydney)	1887–88
42	New Zealand v Australia (Wellington)	1945–46
43	South Africa v England (Cape Town)	1888–89
44	Australia v England (Oval)	1896
45	England v Australia (Sydney)	1886–87
45	South Africa v Australia (Melbourne)	1931–32
47	South Africa v England (Cape Town)	1888–89
47	New Zealand v England (Lord's)	1958

The lowest innings for the countries not mentioned above are:

58	India v Australia (Brisbane)	1947–48
58	India v England (Manchester)	1952
76	West Indies v Pakistan (Dacca)	1958–59
87	Pakistan v England (Lord's)	1954

HIGHEST INDIVIDUAL INNINGS

365*	G. S. Sobers: West Indies v Pakistan (Kingston)	1957–58
364	L. Hutton: England v Australia (Oval)	1938
337	Hanif Mohammad: Pakistan v West Indies (Bridgetown)	1957–58
336*	W. R. Hammond: England v New Zealand (Auckland)	1932–33

334 D. G. Bradman: Australia v England (Leeds) 1930
325 A. Sandham: England v West Indies (Kingston) 1929–30
311 R. B. Simpson: Australia v England (Manchester) 1964
310* J. H. Edrich: England v New Zealand (Leeds) 1965
307 R. M. Cowper: Australia v England (Melbourne) 1965–66
304 D. G. Bradman: Australia v England (Leeds) 1934
299* D. G. Bradman: Australia v South Africa (Adelaide) 1931–32
287 R. E. Foster: England v Australia (Sydney) 1903–04
285* P. B. H. May: England v West Indies (Birmingham) 1957
278 D. C. S. Compton: England v Pakistan (Nottingham) 1954
274 R. G. Pollock: South Africa v Australia (Durban) 1969–70
270* G. A. Headley: West Indies v England (Kingston) 1934–35
270 D. G. Bradman: Australia v England (Melbourne) 1936–37
266 W. H. Ponsford: Australia v England (Oval) 1934
261 F. M. Worrell: West Indies v England (Nottingham) 1950
260 C. C. Hunte: West Indies v Pakistan (Kingston) 1957–58
258 T. W. Graveney: England v West Indies (Nottingham) 1957
258 S. M. Nurse: West Indies v New Zealand (Christchurch) 1968–69
256 R. B. Kanhai: West Indies v India (Calcutta) 1958–59
256 K. F. Barrington: England v Australia (Manchester) 1964
255* D. J. McGlew: South Africa v New Zealand (Wellington) 1952–53
254 D. G. Bradman: Australia v England (Lord's) 1930
251 W. R. Hammond: England v Australia (Sydney) 1928–29

The highest individual innings for the countries not mentioned above are:

239 G. T. Dowling: New Zealand v India (Christchurch) 1967–68
231 V. Mankad: India v New Zealand (Madras) 1955–56

HIGHEST RUN AGGREGATES IN A TEST RUBBER

R.		*Season*	*T.*	*I.*	*N.O.*	*H.S.*	*Av.*	100s	50s
974	D. G. Bradman (A. v E.)	1930	5	7	0	334	139.14	4	—
905	W. R. Hammond (E. v A.)	1928–29	5	9	1	251	113.12	4	—
834	R. N. Harvey (A. v S.A.)	1952–53	5	9	0	205	92.66	4	3
827	C. L. Walcott (W.I. v A.)	1954–55	5	10	0	155	82.70	5	2
824	G. S. Sobers (W.I. v P.)	1957–58	5	8	2	365*	137.33	3	3
810	D. G. Bradman (A. v E.)	1936–37	5	9	0	270	90.00	3	1
806	D. G. Bradman (A. v S.A.)	1931–32	5	5	1	299*	201.50	4	—
779	D. E. Weekes (W.I. v I.)	1948–49	5	7	0	194	111.28	4	2
758	D. G. Bradman (A. v E.)	1934	5	8	0	304	94.75	2	1
753	D. C. S. Compton (E. v S.A.)	1947	5	8	0	208	94.12	4	2

RECORD WICKET PARTNERSHIPS—ALL TEST CRICKET

1st 413 V. Mankad & P. Roy: I. v N.Z. (Madras) 1955–56
2nd 451 W. H. Ponsford & D. G. Bradman: A. v E. (Oval) 1934
3rd 370 W. J. Edrich & D. C. S. Compton: E. v S.A. (Lord's) 1947
4th 411 P. B. H. May & M. C. Cowdrey: E. v W.I. (Birm'ham) ... 1957
5th 405 S. G. Barnes & D. G. Bradman: A. v E. (Sydney) 1946–47
6th 346 J. H. Fingleton & D. G. Bradman: A. v E. (Melbourne) 1936–37
7th 347 D. Atkinson & C. Depeiza: W.I. v A. (Bridgetown) ... 1954–55
8th 246 L. E. G. Ames & G. O. Allen: E. v N.Z. (Lord's) 1931
9th 190 Asif Iqbal & Intikhab Alam: P. v E. (Oval) 1967
10th 130 R. E. Foster & W. Rhodes: E. v A. (Sydney) 1903–04

WICKET PARTNERSHIPS OF OVER 300

451 2nd W. H. Ponsford & D. G. Bradman: A. v E. (Oval)............1934
446 2nd C. C. Hunte & G. S. Sobers: W. I. v P. (Kingston).........1957–58
413 1st V. Mankad & P. Roy: I. v N.Z. (Madras)......................1955–56
411 4th P. B. H. May & M. C. Cowdrey: E. v W.I. (Birm.)............1957
405 5th S. G. Barnes & D. G. Bradman: A. v E. (Sydney).........1946–47
399 4th G. S. Sobers & F. M. Worrell: W.I. v E. (Bridgetown)...1959–60
388 4th W. H. Ponsford & D. G. Bradman: A. v E. (Leeds)............1934
382 2nd L. Hutton & M. Leyland: E. v A. (Oval)........................1938
382 1st W. M. Lawry & R. B. Simpson: A. v W.I. (Bridgetown) 1964–65
370 3rd W. J. Edrich & D. C. S. Compton: E. v S.A. (Lord's).........1947
369 2nd J. H. Edrich & K. F. Barrington: E. v N.Z. (Leeds).........1965
359 1st L. Hutton & C. Washbrook: E. v S.A. (Johannesburg)...1948–49
347 7th D. Atkinson & C. Depeiza: W.I. v A. (Bridgetown)......1954–55
346 6th J. H. Fingleton & D. G. Bradman: A. v E. (Melbourne) 1936–37
341 3rd E. J. Barlow & R. G. Pollock: S.A. v A. (Adelaide)........1963–64
338 3rd E. D. Weekes & F. M. Worrell: W.I. v. E. (Port of Spain) 1953–54
336 4th W. M. Lawry & K. D. Walters: A. v W.I. (Sydney) ...1968–69
323 1st J. B. Hobbs & W. Rhodes: E. v A. (Melbourne)............1911–12
319 3rd A. Melville & A. D. Nourse, Jun.: S.A. v E. (Notts)............1947
308 7th Waqar Hasan & Imtiaz Ahmed: P. v N.Z. (Lahore)......1955–56
301 2nd A. R. Morris & D. G. Bradman: A. v E. (Leeds)...............1948

'HAT-TRICKS'

F. R. Spofforth......Australia v England (Melbourne)...............1878–79
W. Bates ....England v Australia (Melbourne)...............1882–83
J. Briggs...............England v Australia (Sydney) 1891–92
G. A. Lohmann......England v South Africa (Port Elizabeth)......1895–96
J. T. Hearne ....England v Australia (Leeds) 1899
H. Trumble ....Australia v England (Melbourne)...............1901–02
H. Trumble ....Australia v England (Melbourne)...............1903–04
T. J. Matthews(2)† Australia v South Africa (Manchester)............1912
M. J. C. Allom‡ ...England v New Zealand (Christchurch)......1929–30
T. W. Goddard......England v South Africa (Johannesburg)......1938–39
P. J. Loader ....England v West Indies (Leeds) 1957
L. Kline...............Australia v South Africa (Cape Town).........1957–58
W. W. Hall ....West Indies v Pakistan (Lahore)...............1958–59
G. Griffin ....South Africa v England (Lord's).......................1960
L. R. Gibbs ....West Indies v Australia (Adelaide)............1960–61
E. J. Barlow‡ ....Rest of World v England (Leeds) 1970

† *Matthews achieved the 'hat-trick' in each innings.*
‡ *Allom and Barlow took four wickets with five consecutive balls.*

NINE OR TEN WICKETS IN AN INNINGS

10—53 J. C. Laker: England v Australia (Manchester)...............1956
9—28 G. A. Lohmann: England v South Africa (Johannesb'g) 1895–96
9—37 J. C. Laker: England v Australia (Manchester)...............1956
9—69 J. M. Patel: India v Australia (Kanpur)......................1959–60
9—102 S. P. Gupte: India v West Indies (Kanpur)...............1958–59
9—103 S. F. Barnes: England v South Africa (Johannesburg)...1913–14
9—113 H. J. Tayfield: South Africa v England (Johannesburg) 1956–57
9—121 A. A. Mailey: Australia v England (Melbourne).........1920–21

FIFTEEN OR MORE WICKETS IN A MATCH

19—90	J. C. Laker: England v Australia (Manchester)	1956
17—159	S. F. Barnes: England v South Africa (Johannesburg)	1913–14
15—28	J. Briggs: England v South Africa (Cape Town)	1888–89
15—45	G. A. Lohmann: England v South Africa (Pt. Elizabeth)	1895–96
15—99	C. Blythe: England v South Africa (Leeds)	1907
15—104	H. Verity: England v Australia (Lord's)	1934
15—124	W. Rhodes: England v Australia (Melbourne)	1903–04

HIGHEST WICKET AGGREGATES IN A TEST RUBBER

W.		*Season*	*Tests*	*Balls*	*Mdns*	*Runs*	*Av.*	*5wI.*	*10wM*
49	S. F. Barnes (E. v S.A.)	1913–14	4	1356	56	536	10.93	7	3
46	J. C. Laker (E. v A.)	1956	5	1703	127	442	9.60	4	2
44	C. V. Grimmett (A. v S.A.)	1935–36	5	2077	140	642	14.59	5	3
39	A. V. Bedser (E. v A.)	1953	5	1591	58	682	17.48	5	1
38	M. W. Tate (E. v A.)	1924–25	5	2528	62	881	23.18	5	1
37	W. J. Whitty (A. v S.A.)	1910–11	5	1395	55	632	17.08	2	—
37	H. J. Tayfield (S.A. v E.)	1956–57	5	2280	105	636	17.18	4	1
36	A. E. E. Vogler (S.A. v E.)	1909–10	5	1349	33	783	21.75	4	1
36	A. A. Mailey (A. v E.)	1920–21	5	1463	27	946	26.27	4	2
35	G. A. Lohmann (E. v S.A.)	1895–96	3	520	38	203	5.80	4	2

MOST WICKET-KEEPING DISMISSALS IN AN INNINGS

6 (6 ct.) A. T. W. Grout, Australia v South Africa (Johannesburg) 1957–58
6 (6 ct.) D. Lindsay, South Africa v Australia (Johannesburg) 1966–67
6 (6 ct.) J. T. Murray, England v India (Lord's) 1967

MOST WICKET-KEEPING DISMISSALS IN A MATCH

9 (8 ct. 1 st.) G. R. Langley, Australia v England (Lord's) 1956

MOST WICKET-KEEPING DISMISSALS IN A SERIES

26 (23 ct. 3 st.) J. H. B. Waite, South Africa v New Zealand ...1961–62
24 (22 ct. 2 st.) D. L. Murray, West Indies v England 1963
24 (21 ct. 3 st.) A. P. E. Knott, England v Australia 1970–71

HIGHEST WICKET-KEEPING DISMISSAL AGGREGATES

Total			*Tests*	*Ct.*	*St.*
219	T. G. Evans	(E.)	91	173	46
187	A. T. W. Grout	(A.)	51	163	24
141	J. H. B. Waite	(S.A.)	50	124	17
130	W. A. Oldfield	(A.)	54	78	52
114	J. M. Parks	(E.)	46	103	11

N.B. Parks figures include 2 catches as a fielder.

HIGHEST RUN AGGREGATES

Runs			*Tests*	*Inns.*	*N.O.*	*H.S.*	*Avge.*	*100s*	*50s*
7650	M. C. Cowdrey	(E)	112	185	15	182	45.00	22	41
7364	G. S. Sobers	(W.I., R.O.W.)	81	141	18	365*	59.86	23	29
7249	W. R. Hammond	(E.)	85	140	16	336*	58.45	22	24
6996	D. G. Bradman	(A.)	52	80	10	334	99.94	29	13
6971	L. Hutton	(E.)	79	138	15	364	56.67	19	33
6806	K. F. Barrington	(E.)	82	131	15	256	58.67	20	35
6149	R. N. Harvey	(A.)	79	137	10	205	48.41	21	24
5807	D. C. S. Compton	(E.)	78	131	15	278	50.06	17	28

5410	J. B. Hobbs (E.)	61	102	7	211	56.94	15	28
5340	R. B. Kanhai (W.I., R.O.W.)	66	117	3	256	46.84	13	23
5234	W. M. Lawry (A.)	67	123	12	210	47.15	13	27
4882	T. W. Graveney (E.)	79	123	13	258	44.38	11	20
4555	H. Sutcliffe (E.)	54	84	9	194	60.73	16	23
4537	P. B. H. May (E.)	66	106	9	285*	46.77	13	22
4502	E. R. Dexter (E.)	62	102	8	205	47.89	9	27
4455	E. D. Weekes (W.I.)	48	81	5	207	58.61	15	19
4131	R. B. Simpson (A.)	52	92	7	311	48.60	8	24
3915	Hanif Mohammad (P.)	55	97	8	337	43.98	12	15
3860	F. M. Worrell (W.I.)	51	87	9	261	49.48	9	22
3798	C. L. Walcott (W.I.)	44	74	7	220	56.68	15	14
3631	P. R. Umrigar (I.)	59	94	8	223	42.22	12	14
3533	A. R. Morris (A.)	46	79	3	206	46.48	12	12
3526	G. Boycott (E.)	48	84	12	246*	48.97	9	19
3525	E. Hendren (E.)	51	83	9	205*	47.63	7	21
3494	J. H. Edrich (E.)	50	82	6	310*	45.97	10	14
3471	B. Mitchell (S.A.)	42	80	9	189*	48.88	8	21
3431	J. R. Reid (N.Z.)	58	108	5	142	33.31	6	22
3412	C. Hill (A.)	49	89	2	191	39.21	7	19
3283	F. E. Woolley (E.)	64	98	7	154	36.07	5	23
3245	C. C. Hunte (W.I.)	44	78	6	260	45.06	8	13
3209	V. L. Manjrekar (I.)	55	92	10	189*	39.13	7	15
3164	V. T. Trumper (A.)	48	89	8	214*	39.06	8	13
3106	C. C. McDonald (A.)	47	83	4	170	39.31	5	17
3104	B. F. Butcher (W.I.)	44	78	6	209*	43.11	7	16
3073	A. L. Hassett (A.)	43	69	3	198*	46.56	10	11
3062	C. G. Borde (I.)	55	97	11	177*	35.60	5	18

HIGHEST WICKET AGGREGATES

Wkts.		*Tests*	*Balls*	*Mdns.*	*Runs*	Av.	5w*I.*	10w*M.*
307	F. S. Trueman (E.)	67	15178	521	6625	21.57	17	3
255	G. D. McKenzie (A.) (R.O.W.)	63	18415	578	7611	29.84	16	3
252	J. B. Statham (E.)	70	16026	590	6257	24.82	9	1
248	R. Benaud (A.)	63	19090	805	6704	27.03	16	1
236	A. V. Bedser (E.)	51	15941	572	5876	24.89	15	5
228	R. R. Lindwall (A.)	61	13666	418	5257	23.05	12	—
216	C. V. Grimmett (A.)	37	14573	734	5231	24.21	21	7
214	G. S. Sobers (W.I., R.O.W.)	81	19002	838	7129	33.31	7	—
212	L. R. Gibbs (W.I., R.O.W.)	54	18235	877	6064	28.60	13	2
193	J. C. Laker (E.)	46	12009	673	4099	21.23	9	3
192	W. W. Hall (W.I.)	48	10415	312	5066	26.38	9	1
189	S. F. Barnes (E.)	27	7873	358	3106	16.43	24	7
186	A. K. Davidson (A.)	44	11665	432	3838	20.58	14	2
174	G. A. R. Lock (E.)	49	13063	806	4452	25.58	9	3
170	K. R. Miller (A.)	55	10474	338	3905	22.97	7	1
170	H. J. Tayfield (S.A.)	37	13565	602	4405	25.91	14	2
162	V. Mankad (I.)	44	14686	777	5235	32.31	8	2
160	W. A. Johnston (A.)	40	11048	370	3825	23.90	7	—
158	S. Ramadhin (W.I.)	43	13939	813	4577	28.96	10	1
155	M. W. Tate (E.)	39	12571	579	4051	26.13	7	1

MOST TEST APPEARANCES FOR EACH COUNTRY

N.B. The abandoned match at Melbourne in 1970–71 *is excluded from these figures.*

England

M. C. Cowdrey	112
T. G. Evans	91
W. R. Hammond	85
K. F. Barrington	82
T. W. Graveney	79
L. Hutton	79

Australia

R. N. Harvey	79
W. M. Lawry	67
R. Benaud	63
R. R. Lindwall	61
G. D. McKenzie	60
S. E. Gregory	58

South Africa

J. H. B. Waite	50
A. D. Nourse, Senior	45
B. Mitchell	42
H. W. Taylor	42
T. L. Goddard	41
R. A. McLean	40

West Indies

G. S. Sobers	76
R. B. Kanhai	61
F. M. Worrell	51
L. R. Gibbs	50
W. W. Hall	48
E. D. Weekes	48

New Zealand

J. R. Reid	58
B. Sutcliffe	42
G. T. Dowling	37
R. C. Motz	32
B. E. Congdon	31
V. Pollard	28

India

P. R. Umrigar	59
C. G. Borde	55
V. L. Manjrekar	55
V. Mankad	44
P. Roy	43
R. G. Nadkarni	41

Pakistan

Hanif Mohammad	55
Imtiaz Ahmed	41
Saeed Ahmed	38
Fazal Mahmood	34
Nasim-ul-Ghani	28
Mahmood Hussain	27

Young Cricketer of the Year

The selections to date are:

1950	R. Tattersall (Lancashire)
1951	P. B. H. May (Surrey)
1952	F. S. Trueman (Yorkshire)
1953	M. C. Cowdrey (Kent)
1954	P. J. Loader (Surrey)
1955	K. F. Barrington (Surrey)
1956	B. Taylor (Essex)
1957	M. J. Stewart (Surrey)
1958	A. C. D. Ingleby-Mackenzie (Hampshire)
1959	G. Pullar (Lancashire)
1960	D. A. Allen (Gloucestershire)
1961	P. H. Parfitt (Middlesex)
1962	P. J. Sharpe (Yorkshire)
1963	G. Boycott (Yorkshire)
1964	J. M. Brearley (Middlesex)
1965	A. P. Knott (Kent)
1966	D. L. Underwood (Kent)
1967	A. W. Greig (Sussex)
1968	R. M. H. Cottam (Hants)
1969	A. Ward (Derbyshire)
1970	C. M. Old (Yorkshire)

TEST CAREER RECORDS

N.B.—Players who have not bowled in test cricket are omitted from the bowling list.

ENGLAND

BATTING AND FIELDING

	M.	*I.*	*N.O.*	*Runs*	*H.S.*	*Avge*	100	50	*Ct.*	*St.*
†D. L. Amiss	6	10	1	184	45	20.44	—	—	5	—
†G. Boycott	48	84	12	3526	246*	48.97	9	19	16	—
†D. J. Brown	28	37	5	390	44*	12.18	—	—	9	—
†M. C. Cowdrey	112	185	15	7650	182	45.00	22	41	120	—
†M. H. Denness	2	4	1	94	55*	31.33	—	1	3	—
†B. L. D'Oliveira	37	58	6	2230	158	42.88	6	13	25	—
†J. H. Edrich	50	82	6	3494	310*	45.97	10	14	29	—
†K. W. R. Fletcher	16	28	2	798	89	30.69	—	6	14	—
†A. W. Greig	3	5	0	96	55	19.20	—	1	2	—
J. H. Hampshire	6	12	1	327	107	29.72	1	2	7	—
†R. Illingworth	49	72	9	1668	113	26.47	1	9	34	—
†A. Jones	1	2	0	5	5	2.50	—	—	—	—
†A. P. Knott	30	46	8	1295	101	34.07	1	9	87	11
†P. Lever	7	11	1	164	64	16.40	—	1	5	—
†B. W. Luckhurst	12	23	3	931	131	46.55	3	4	8	—
†C. M. Old	2	4	0	42	37	10.50	—	—	—	—
†P. J. Sharpe	13	23	4	792	111	41.68	1	4	18	—
†K. Shuttleworth	5	7	2	26	11	5.20	—	—	1	—
†J. A. Snow	36	49	15	529	59*	15.55	—	1	13	—
R. W. Taylor	1	1	0	4	4	4.00	—	—	2	1
†D. L. Underwood	26	33	14	230	45*	12.10	—	—	20	—
†A. Ward	4	5	1	51	21	12.75	—	—	2	—
R. G. D. Willis	5	7	3	47	15*	11.75	—	—	3	—
†D. Wilson	8	11	2	82	42	9.11	—	—	2	—

BOWLING

	Balls	*Runs*	*Wkts*	*Avge.*	*Best*	*5wI*	*10wM*
G. Boycott	792	346	7	49.22	3–47	—	—
†D. J. Brown	5398	2430	82	29.63	5–42	2	—
M. C. Cowdrey	119	104	0	—	—	—	—
†B. L. D'Oliveira	4990	1716	40	42.90	4–43	—	—
J. H. Edrich	30	23	0	—	—	—	—
†K. W. R. Fletcher	238	158	1	158.00	1–48	—	—
†A. W. Greig	546	288	11	26.18	4–59	—	—
†R. Illingworth	9977	3257	107	30.43	6–29	2	—
†P. Lever	1735	636	21	30.28	7–83	1	—
B. W. Luckhurst	16	6	0	—	—	—	—
†C. M. Old	408	184	2	92.00	2–70	—	—
†K. Shuttleworth	1059	429	12	35.75	5–47	1	—
†J. A. Snow	9116	4113	149	27.60	7–40	6	1
†D. L. Underwood	6873	2136	107	19.96	7–32	9	3
†A. Ward	641	331	14	23.64	4–61	—	—
R. G. D. Willis	864	398	14	28.42	3–58	—	—
†D. Wilson	1952	671	15	44.73	2–17	—	—

† figures for players marked thus include performances v Rest of the World in 1970

Note: The abandoned Third Test in 1970–71 v Australia has not been included as a match played by the players selected

AUSTRALIA

BATTING AND FIELDING

	M.	*I.*	*N.O.*	*Runs*	*H.S.*	*Avge.*	100	50	*Ct.*	*St.*
G. S. Chappell	5	8	1	243	108	34.71	1	1	3	—
I. M. Chappell	37	66	4	2219	165	35.79	6	10	53	—
A. N. Connolly	29	45	20	260	37	10.40	—	—	17	—
A. R. Dell	1	2	2	6	3*	—	—	—	—	—
J. R. F. Duncan.......	1	1	0	3	3	3.00	—	—	—	—
K. H. Eastwood	1	2	0	5	5	2.50	—	—	—	—
J. W. Gleeson	26	42	7	358	45	10.22	—	—	17	—
T. J. Jenner	2	4	0	36	30	9.00	—	—	2	—
W. M. Lawry	67	123	12	5234	210	47.15	13	27	30	—
D. K. Lillee.............	2	3	0	16	10	5.33	—	—	2	—
G. D. McKenzie	60	89	12	945	76	12.27	—	2	34	—
A. A. Mallett	10	16	5	161	43*	14.63	—	—	4	—
R. W. Marsh	6	9	1	215	92*	26.87	—	1	11	3
K. J. O'Keeffe	2	3	0	42	27	14.00	—	—	—	—
I. R. Redpath	43	76	8	2656	171	39.05	2	19	53	—
A. P. Sheahan...........	25	43	3	1261	114	31.52	1	7	15	—
K. R. Stackpole	27	50	3	1753	207	37.29	4	7	34	—
A. L. Thomson.........	4	5	4	22	12*	22.00	—	—	—	—
K. D. Walters	31	54	6	2623	242	54.64	8	16	12	—

BOWLING

	Balls	*Runs*	*Wkts.*	*Avge.*	*Best*	*5wI*	*10wM*
G. S. Chappell	744	255	5	51.00	2–54	—	—
I. M. Chappell	2055	964	12	80.33	2–21	—	—
A. N. Connolly	7818	2981	102	29.22	6–47	4	—
A. R. Dell	343	97	5	19.40	3–65	—	—
J. R. F. Duncan.......	112	30	0	—	—	—	—
K. H. Eastwood	40	21	1	21.00	1–21	—	—
J. W. Gleeson	8397	3210	90	35.66	5–61	3	—
T. J. Jenner	526	176	6	29.33	3–42	—	—
W. M. Lawry	14	6	0	—	—	—	—
D. K. Lillee.............	499	199	8	24.87	5–84	1	—
G. D. McKenzie	17681	7328	246	29.78	8–71	16	3
A. A. Mallett	3280	1178	46	25.60	6–64	4	1
K. J. O'Keeffe	800	260	6	43.33	3–48	—	—
I. R. Redpath	56	31	0	—	—	—	—
K. R. Stackpole	2111	925	14	66.07	2–33	—	—
A. L. Thomson.........	1519	654	12	54.50	3–79	—	—
K. D. Walters	1761	758	23	32.95	4–53	—	—

Are you a regular reader of Playfair Cricket Monthly? A year's subscription costs only £2.10 and you'll be sure of all-the-year-round cricket reading

WEST INDIES

BATTING AND FIELDING

	M.	I.	N.O.	Runs	H.S.	Avge.	100	50	Ct.	St.
B. F. Butcher	44	78	6	3104	209*	43.11	7	16	15	—
G. S. Camacho	9	18	0	572	87	31.77	—	4	3	—
M. C. Carew	13	25	3	863	109	39.22	1	5	7	—
C. A. Davis	4	8	0	236	103	29.50	1	—	2	—
T. M. Findlay	2	4	0	51	23	12.75	—	—	9	—
M. L. C. Foster	1	2	0	7	4	3.50	—	—	—	—
R. C. Fredericks.......	10	19	0	525	76	27.63	—	4	11	—
L. R. Gibbs..............	50	73	22	337	22	6.60	—	—	34	—
J. L. Hendriks	20	32	8	447	64	18.62	—	2	42	5
V. A. Holder............	3	6	0	80	35	13.33	—	—	1	—
R. B. Kanhai	61	108	3	5056	256	48.15	12	22	32	—
C. H. Lloyd	18	33	3	1159	129	38.63	3	5	9	—
J. N. Shepherd	3	5	0	65	32	13.00	—	—	1	—
G. C. Shillingford	2	3	1	11	5*	5.50	—	—	—	—
G. S. Sobers	76	132	17	6776	365*	58.92	21	26	96	—

BOWLING

	Balls	Runs	Wkts	Avge.	Best	5wI	10wM
B. F. Butcher	256	90	5	18.00	5–34	1	—
G. S. Camacho	18	12	0	—	—	—	—
M. C. Carew	964	364	8	45.50	1–11	—	—
C. A. Davis	312	126	2	63.00	1–27	—	—
M. L. C. Foster	12	7	0	—	—	—	—
L. R. Gibbs..............	17233	5757	209	27.54	8–38	13	2
V. A. Holder............	893	335	9	37.22	4–48	—	—
R. B. Kanhai	50	21	0	—	—	—	—
C. H. Lloyd	524	202	4	50.50	2–17	—	—
J. N. Shepherd	827	266	12	22.16	5–104	1	—
G. C. Shillingford	358	160	6	26.66	2–30	—	—
G. S. Sobers	17366	6677	193	34.59	6–73	6	—

NEW ZEALAND

BATTING AND FIELDING

	M.	I.	N.O.	Runs	H.S.	Avge	100	50	Ct.	St.
M. G. Burgess	15	28	2	851	119*	32.73	2	5	10	—
R. O. Collinge	15	20	4	259	54	16.18	—	1	6	—
B. E. Congdon	31	61	2	1569	104	26.59	1	11	26	—
R. S. Cunis	15	26	7	202	35	10.63	—	—	1	—
G. T. Dowling	37	73	3	2261	239	32.30	3	11	22	—
H. J. Howarth	11	17	8	70	25	7.77	—	—	11	—
R. W. Morgan	17	31	1	726	97	24.20	—	5	9	—
B. A. G. Murray	13	26	1	598	90	23.92	—	5	21	—
V. Pollard	28	52	5	900	81*	19.14	—	5	18	—
M. J. F. Shrimpton ...	8	15	0	199	46	13.26	—	—	2	—
G. M. Turner	11	22	3	710	110	37.36	1	5	14	—
K. J. Wadsworth	11	18	0	141	21	7.83	—	—	30	3
M. Webb	1	—	—	—	—	—	—	—	—	—

BOWLING

	Balls	Runs	Wkts	Avge.	Best	5wI	10wM
M. G. Burgess	408	163	5	32.60	3–23	—	—
R. O. Collinge	2813	1295	47	27.55	4–41	—	—
B. E. Congdon	946	403	12	33.58	3–33	—	—
R. S. Cunis	3151	1269	45	28.20	6–76	1	—
G. T. Dowling	36	19	1	19.00	1–19	—	—
H. J. Howarth	3029	995	41	24.26	5–34	2	—
R. W. Morgan	831	479	4	119.75	1–16	—	—
B. A. G. Murray	6	0	1	0.00	1–0	—	—
V. Pollard	4035	1695	36	47.08	3–3	—	—
M. J. F. Shrimpton ...	201	119	3	39.66	3–35	—	—
M. Webb	232	144	2	72.00	1–50	—	—

PAKISTAN

BATTING AND FIELDING

	M.	I.	N.O.	Runs	H.S.	Avge.	100	50	Ct.	St.
Aftab Baluch	1	1	0	25	25	25.00	—	—	—	—
Aftab Gul	3	4	0	76	30	19.00	—	—	3	—
Asif Iqbal................	17	29	1	872	146	31.14	1	5	15	—
Asif Masood	3	2	0	28	17	14.00	—	—	1	—
Hanif Mohammad ...	55	97	8	3915	337	43.98	12	15	40	—
Intikhab Alam	26	44	8	754	61	20.94	—	4	14	—
Javed Burki	25	48	4	1341	140	30.47	3	4	7	—
Mohammad Nazir ...	3	4	3	61	29*	61.00	—	—	—	—
Mushtaq Mohammad	22	39	4	1194	101	34.11	2	7	7	—
Pervez Sajjad	11	13	7	67	18	11.16	—	—	5	—
Sadiq Mohammad ...	3	6	0	163	69	27.16	—	1	2	—
Salahuddin	5	8	2	117	34*	19.50	—	—	3	—
Salim Altaf	4	5	2	10	7*	3.33	—	—	—	—
Shafqat Rana	5	7	0	221	95	31.57	—	2	5	—
Wasim Bari	9	12	2	115	19	11.50	—	—	13	3
Younis Ahmed	2	4	0	89	62	22.25	—	1	—	—
Zahir Abbas	1	2	0	39	27	19.50	—	—	—	—

BOWLING

	Balls	Runs	Wkts	Avge.	Best	5wI	10wM
Aftab Baluch	12	2	0	—	—	—	—
Asif Iqbal	2612	963	40	24.07	5–48	2	—
Asif Masood	474	246	6	41.00	3–68	—	—
Hanif Mohammad ...	206	93	1	93.00	1–1	—	—
Intikhab Alam	5159	2205	49	45.00	5–91	2	1
Javed Burki	42	23	0	—	—	—	—
Mohammad Nazir ...	756	226	10	22.60	7–99	1	—
Mushtaq Mohammad	975	416	14	29.71	4–80	—	—
Pervez Sajjad	2892	925	48	19.27	7–74	3	—
Sadiq Mohammad ...	24	6	0	—	—	—	—
Salahuddin	546	187	7	26.71	2–36	—	—
Salim Altaf	762	269	9	29.88	3–33	—	—
Shafqat Rana	36	9	1	9.00	1–2	—	—

SOUTH AFRICA

	M.	*I.*	*N.O.*	*Runs*	*H.S.*	*Avge.*	100	50	*Ct.*	*St.*
A. Bacher	12	22	1	679	73	32.33	—	6	10	—
E. J. Barlow	30	57	2	2516	201	45.74	6	15	35	—
G. A. Chevalier	1	2	1	0	0*	0.00	—	—	1	—
D. Gamsy	2	3	1	39	30*	19.50	—	—	5	—
T. L. Goddard	41	78	5	2516	112	34.46	1	18	48	—
B. L. Irvine	4	7	0	353	102	50.42	1	2	2	—
H. R. Lance	13	22	1	591	70	28.14	—	5	7	—
D. Lindsay	19	31	1	1130	182	37.66	3	5	57	2
P. M. Pollock	28	41	13	607	75*	21.67	—	2	9	—
R. G. Pollock	23	41	4	2256	274	60.97	7	11	17	—
M. J. Procter	7	10	1	226	48	25.11	—	—	4	—
B. A. Richards	4	7	0	508	140	72.57	2	2	3	—
M. A. Seymour	7	10	3	84	36	12.00	—	—	2	—
A. J. Traicos	3	4	2	8	5*	4.00	—	—	4	—
P. H. J. Trimborn	4	4	2	13	11*	6.50	—	—	7	—

BOWLING	*Balls*	*Runs*	*Wkts*	*Avge.*	*Best*	*5wI*	*10wM*
E. J. Barlow	3045	1362	40	34.05	5–85	1	—
G. A. Chevalier	253	100	5	20.00	3–68	—	—
T. L. Goddard	11735	3226	123	26.22	6–53	5	—
H. R. Lance	948	479	12	39.91	3–30	—	—
P. M. Pollock	6522	2806	116	24.18	6–38	9	1
R. G. Pollock	414	204	4	51.00	2–50	—	—
M. J. Procter	1514	616	41	15.02	6–73	1	—
B. A. Richards	72	26	1	26.00	1–12	—	—
M. A. Seymour	1458	588	9	65.33	3–80	—	—
A. J. Traicos	470	207	4	51.75	2–70	—	—
P. H. J. Trimborn	747	257	11	23.36	3–12	—	—

INDIA

	M.	*I.*	*N.O.*	*Runs*	*H.S.*	*Avge.*	100	50	*Ct.*	*St.*
S. Abid Ali	12	24	0	530	81	22.08	—	3	13	—
M. Amarnath	1	2	1	16	16*	16.00	—	—	—	—
B. S. Bedi	19	32	8	204	22	8.50	—	—	9	—
C. G. Borde	55	97	11	3062	177*	35.60	5	18	38	—
C. Chauhan	3	6	0	105	34	17.50	—	—	6	—
S. A. Durani	23	40	2	935	104	24.60	1	5	11	—
F. M. Engineer	30	57	1	1607	109	28.69	1	8	42	12
A. Gandotra	2	4	0	54	18	13.50	—	—	1	—
S. Guha	4	7	2	17	6	3.40	—	—	2	—
Hanumant Singh	14	24	2	686	105	31.18	1	5	11	—
K. S. Indrajitsinh,	4	7	1	51	23	8.50	—	—	6	3
M. L. Jaisimha	36	66	4	2013	129	32.46	3	12	17	—
A. V. Mankad	7	14	1	422	97	32.46	—	4	1	—
A. M. Pai	1	2	0	10	9	5.00	—	—	—	—
Nawab of Pataudi	39	71	2	2552	203*	36.98	6	14	24	—
E. A. S. Prasanna	22	38	6	362	26	11.31	—	—	9	—
A. Roy	4	7	0	91	48	13.00	—	—	—	—
D. N. Sardesai	21	39	3	1189	200*	33.02	2	7	4	—
E. D. Solkar	5	9	2	191	44	27.28	—	—	11	—
R. F. Surti	26	48	4	1263	99	28.70	—	9	27	—
S. Venkataraghavan	14	23	6	254	36*	14.94	—	—	13	—
G. R. Viswanath	4	8	1	334	137	47.71	1	2	3	—
A. L. Wadekar	21	42	2	1366	143	34.15	1	10	29	—

BOWLING

	Balls	Runs	Wkts	Avge.	Best	5wI	10wM
S. Abid Ali	1527	626	21	29.80	6–55	1	—
M. Amarnath	186	52	2	26.00	2–31	—	—
B. S. Bedi	5540	1798	70	25.68	7–98	4	—
C. G. Borde	5707	2416	52	46.46	5–88	1	—
S. A. Durani	5918	2437	71	34.32	6–73	3	1
A. Gandotra	6	5	0	—	—	—	—
S. Guha	674	311	3	103.66	2–55	—	—
Hanumant Singh	66	51	0	—	—	—	—
M. L. Jaisimha	1947	765	9	85.00	2–54	—	—
A. V. Mankad	11	10	0	—	—	—	—
A. M. Pai	114	31	2	15.50	2–29	—	—
Nawab of Pataudi	120	84	1	84.00	1–10	—	—
E. A. S. Prasanna	7592	3057	113	27.05	6–74	8	1
D. N. Sardesai	48	33	0	—	—	—	—
E. D. Solkar	405	170	3	56.66	1–8	—	—
R. F. Surti	3875	1962	42	46.71	5–74	1	—
S. Venkataraghavan	3650	1183	47	25.17	8–72	2	1
G. R. Viswanath	12	8	0	—	—	—	—
A. L. Wadekar	43	43	0	—	—	—	—

REST OF THE WORLD

BATTING AND FIELDING

	M.	I.	N.O.	Runs	H.S.	Avge.	100	50	Ct.	St.
E. J. Barlow (SA)	35	66	2	2869	201	44.82	8	15	45	—
F. M. Engineer (I)	32	60	1	1610	109	27.28	1	8	50	13
L. R. Gibbs (WI)	54	78	25	344	22	6.49	—	—	36	—
Intikhab Alam (P)	31	52	9	994	61	23.11	—	6	15	—
R. B. Kanhai (WI)	66	117	3	5340	256	46.84	13	23	35	—
C. H. Lloyd (WI)	23	42	4	1559	129	41.02	5	6	12	—
G. D. McKenzie (A)	63	93	14	955	76	12.08	—	2	34	—
D. L. Murray (WI)	13	21	3	369	95	20.50	—	2	50	3
Mushtaq Mohd. (P)	24	43	4	1223	101	31.35	2	7	9	—
P. M. Pollock (SA)	29	42	14	630	75*	22.50	—	2	9	—
R. G. Pollock (SA)	28	49	4	2506	274	55.68	8	12	18	—
M. J. Procter (SA)	12	19	4	518	62	34.53	—	2	6	—
B. A. Richards (SA)	9	15	1	765	140	54.64	2	3	6	—
G. S. Sobers (WI)	81	141	18	7364	365*	59.86	23	29	103	—

BOWLING

	Balls	Runs	Wkts	Avge.	Best	5wI.	10wM
E. J. Barlow (SA)	3957	1758	60	29.30	7–64	4	1
L. R. Gibbs (WI)	18235	6064	212	28.60	8–38	13	2
Intikhab Alam (P)	6862	2842	63	45.11	6–113	3	1
R. B. Kanhai (WI)	56	25	0	—	—	—	—
C. H. Lloyd (WI)	842	322	10	32.20	3–34	—	—
G. D. McKenzie (A)	18415	7611	255	29.84	8–71	16	3
Mushtaq Mohd. (P)	1305	551	15	36.73	4–80	—	—
P. M. Pollock (SA)	6720	2916	118	24.71	6–38	9	1
R. G. Pollock (SA)	416	209	4	52.25	2–50	—	—
M. J. Procter (SA)	2781	975	56	17.41	6–73	2	—
B. A. Richards (SA)	72	26	1	26.00	1–12	—	—
G. S. Sobers (WI)	19002	7129	214	33.31	6–21	7	—

PRINCIPAL FIXTURES, 1971

*Indicates that second day's play is on a Sunday

Wednesday, April 21st

Oxford: Oxford U v Warwickshire

Saturday, April 24th

Oxford: Oxford U v Kent
Cambridge: Cambridge U v Warwickshire.

Wednesday, April 28th

Lord's: M.C.C. v Kent
Oxford: Oxford U v Hampshire
Cambridge: Cambridge U v Leics

Saturday, May 1st

Worcester: Worcs v Pakistan
Derby: Derbyshire v Middlesex
Bristol: Gloucestershire v Lancashire
Southampton: Hants v Northants
Leicester: Leicestershire v Somerset
Trent Bridge: Notts v Glamorgan
The Oval: Surrey v Essex
Hove: Sussex v. Warwickshire
Bradford: Yorkshire v Kent

Wednesday, May 5th

Edgbaston: Warwicks v Pakistan
Chesterfield: Derbyshire v Leics
Old Trafford: Lancashire v Hants
Oxford: Oxford U v Sussex
Cambridge:CambridgeU vMiddlesex

Saturday, May 8th

Northampton: Northants v Pakistan
Chelmsford: Essex v Glamorgan
Bristol: Glos v Derbyshire
Dartford: Kent v Leicestershire
Old Trafford: Lancashire v Surrey
Lord's: Middlesex v Notts
Taunton: Somerset v Sussex
Middlesbrough: Yorks v Warwicks

Wednesday, May 12th

Portsmouth: Hampshire v Pakistan
Chelmsford: Essex v Northants
Cardiff: Glamorgan v Worcs
Leicester: Leicestershire v Notts
The Oval: Surrey v Warwickshire
Oxford: Oxford U v Yorkshire
Cambridge: Cambridge U v Lancs

Saturday, May 15th

Cambridge: Cambridge U v Pakistan
Lord's: Middlesex v Leicestershire
Hove: Sussex v Yorkshire
Edgbaston: Warwicks v Derbyshire

Gillette Cup—First Round

Chelmsford: *Essex v Bedfordshire*
Canterbury: *Kent v Northants*
Jesmond: *Northumberland v Lincs*
Taunton: *Somerset v Lancashire*
Longton: *Staffordshire v Glamorgan*
The Oval: *Surrey v Hertfordshire*

Wednesday, May 19th

Trent Bridge: Notts v Pakistan
Canterbury: Kent v Surrey
Lord's: Middlesex v Glamorgan
Northampton: Northants v Hants
Taunton: Somerset v Worcestershire
Oxford: Oxford U v Warwickshire
Hove: Sussex v Essex

Saturday, May 22nd

Lord's: M.C.C. v Pakistan
Chesterfield: Derbyshire v Yorkshire
Swansea: Glamorgan v Lancashire
Leicester: Leicestershire v Glos
Nottingham: Notts v Hampshire
The Oval: Surrey v Kent
Edgbaston: Warwickshire v Susssex
Oxford: Oxford U v Worcestershire

Wednesday, May 26th

Gravesend: Kent v Pakistan
Derby: Derbyshire v Somerset
Colwyn Bay: Glamorgan v Glos
The Oval: Surrey v Sussex
Worcester: Worcestershire v Lancs
Headingley: Yorkshire v Middlesex
Oxford: Oxford U v Leicestershire

Saturday, May 29th

Bristol: Gloucestershire v Pakistan
Burton-on-Trent: Derbys v Essex
Cardiff: Glamorgan v Warwickshire
Southampton: Hants v Leics
Old Trafford: Lancashire v Yorks
Lord's: Middlesex v Sussex
Northampton: Northamptonshire v Somerset
Trent Bridge: Notts v Surrey
Worcester: Worcestershire v Kent
*Oxford: Oxford U v Free Foresters

Wednesday, June 2nd

Old Trafford: Lancs v Warwicks
Lord's: Middlesex v Gloucestershire
Trent Bridge: Notts v Leicestershire
Bath: Somerset v Essex
Sheffield: Yorkshire v Worcs
*Oxford: Oxford U v M.C.C.

Thursday, June 3rd

EDGBASTON — ENGLAND v PAKISTAN
(First Test, five days)

Saturday, June 5th

Ilford: Essex v Warwickshire
Swansea: Glamorgan v Hampshire
Blackheath: Kent v Derbyshire
Leicester: Leicestershire v Worcs
Lord's: Middlesex v Northants
Bath: Somerset v Gloucestershire
Hove: Sussex v Lancashire
Headingley: Yorkshire v Notts
Cambridge: Cambridge U v Surrey

Wednesday, June 9th

Bradford: Yorkshire v Pakistan
Ilford: Essex v Derbyshire
Bristol: Glos v Glamorgan
Bath: Somerset v Lancashire
The Oval: Surrey v Leicestershire
Worcester: Worcs v Middlesex
Cambridge: Cambridge U v Notts

Saturday, June 12th

Oxford: Oxford U v Pakistan
*Cambridge: Cambridge U v M.C.C.

Gillette Cup—Second Round

Ilford or Luton: *Essex or Bedfordshire v Staffordshire or Glamorgan*
Portsmouth: *Hampshire v Notts*
Canterbury or Northampton: *Kent or Northamptonshire v Yorkshire*
Leicester: *Leicestershire v Derbyshire*
The Oval or Hitchin: *Surrey or Hertfordshire v Middlesex*
Hove: *Sussex v Gloucestershire*
Edgbaston: *Warwickshire v Northumberland or Lincolnshire*
Worcester: *Worcs v Somerset or Lancashire*

Wednesday, June 16th

Chesterfield: Derbyshire v Worcs
Neath: Glamorgan v Middlesex
Southampton: Hampshire v Kent
Leicester: Leicestershire v Essex
Trent Bridge: Notts v Lancashire
Edgbaston: Warwickshire v Surrey
Oxford: Oxford U v Northants

Thursday, June 17th

LORD'S—ENGLAND v PAKISTAN
(Second Test, five days)

Saturday, June 19th

Derby: Derbyshire v Hampshire
Cardiff: Glamorgan v Leicestershire
Tunbridge Wells: Kent v Sussex
Liverpool: Lancashire v Essex
Northampton: Northamptonshire v Gloucestershire
Taunton: Somerset v Yorkshire
Guildford: Surrey v Worcestershire
Edgbaston: Warwickshire v Notts
Eastbourne: D. Robin's XI v Oxford U
Belfast: Ireland v Scotland

Wednesday, June 23rd

Swansea: Glamorgan v Pakistan
Lord's: Middlesex v India
Colchester: Essex v Yorkshire
Tunbridge Wells: Kent v Glos
Northampton: Northants v Lancs
Hove: Sussex v Surrey
Kidderminster: Worcs v Hampshire
Burton-on-Trent: Derby v Oxford U
Eastbourne: D. Robins XI v Cambridge U

Saturday, June 26th

Old Trafford: Lancashire v Pakistan
Colchester: Essex v India
Bristol: Gloucestershire v Somerset
Bournemouth: Hants v Warwicks
Leicester: Leicestershire v Sussex
Lord's: Middlesex v Kent
Trent Bridge: Notts v Derbyshire
Worcester: Worcs v Northants
Sheffield: Yorkshire v Surrey
Pontypridd: Glam v Cambridge U
*Aldershot: Army v Oxford U

Wednesday, June 30th

Selkirk: Scotland v Pakistan
Eastbourne: D. Robin's XI v India

Gillette Cup—Third Round

Saturday, July 3rd

Chesterfield: Derbyshire v Pakistan
Canterbury: Kent v India
Old Trafford: Lancashire v Notts
Lord's: Middlesex v Yorkshire
Northampton: Northants v Leics
Taunton: Somerset v Surrey
Hove: Sussex v Hampshire
Worcester: Worcs v Warwicks
*Camberley: Combined Services v Cambridge U

Wednesday, July 7th

Leicester: Leicestershire v India
Derby: Derbyshire v Kent
Newark: Notts v Gloucestershire
Edgbaston: Warwicks v Northants
Llandarcy: Glamorgan v Oxford U
Horsham: Sussex v Cambridge U

Thursday, July 8th

HEADINGLEY — ENGLAND v PAKISTAN
(Third Test, five days)

Saturday, July 10th

Lord's: Oxford U v Cambridge U
Edgbaston: Warwickshire v India
Westcliff: Essex v Hampshire
Cardiff: Glamorgan v Sussex
Gloucester: Glos v Middlesex
Southport: Lancashire v Kent
Leicester: Leics v Derbyshire
Trent Bridge: Notts v Worcestershire
The Oval: Surrey v Somerset

Wednesday, July 14th

The Oval: Surrey v Pakistan
Cardiff: Glamorgan v India
Westcliff: Essex v Sussex
Gloucester: Gloucestershire v Notts
Maidstone: Kent v Somerset
Southport: Lancashire v Northants
Lord's: Middlesex v Hampshire
Scarborough: Yorks v Derbyshire
Aberdeen: Scotland v M.C.C.

Saturday, July 17th

Bournemouth: Hampshire v India
Buxton: Derbyshire v Lancashire
Maidstone: Kent v Nottinghamshire
Northampton: Northants v Glam
Glastonbury: Somerset v Warwicks
The Oval: Surrey v Middlesex
Hove: Sussex v Leicestershire
Worcester: Worcestershire v Essex
Sheffield: Yorkshire v Glos
*Cork: Ireland v Wales

Wednesday, July 21st

Portsmouth: Hants v Glamorgan
Northampton: Northamptonshire v Warwickshire
Worksop: Notts v Middlesex

Thursday, July 22nd

LORD'S—ENGLAND v INDIA
(First Test, five days)

Saturday, July 24th

Swansea: Glamorgan v Northants
Bristol: Gloucestershire v Essex
Basingstoke: Hants v Derbyshire
Old Trafford: Lancashire v Somerset
Leicester: Leicestershire v Surrey
Trent Bridge: Notts v Sussex
Edgbaston: Warwickshire v Kent
Dudley: Worcestershire v Yorkshire

Wednesday, July 28th

Lakenham, Norfolk: Minor Counties v India

Gillette Cup—Semi-Final Round

Saturday, July 31st

The Oval: Surrey v India
Ilkeston: Derbyshire v Notts
Portsmouth: Hampshire v Sussex
Canterbury: Kent v Middlesex
Leicester: Leicestershire v Warwicks
Northampton: Northants v Essex
Weston-super-Mare: Somerset v Glamorgan
Worcester: Worcestershire v Glos
Sheffield: Yorkshire v Lancashire

Wednesday, August 4th

Swansea: Glamorgan v Notts
Portsmouth: Hampshire v Glos
Canterbury: Kent v Yorkshire
Lord's: Middlesex v Essex
Weston-super-Mare: Somerset v Northamptonshire
Edgbaston: Warwickshire v Lancs
Worcester: Worcestershire v Leics

Thursday, August 5th

OLD TRAFFORD—ENGLAND v INDIA
(Second Test, five days)

Saturday, August 7th

Leyton: Essex v Leicestershire
Swansea: Glamorgan v Yorkshire
Cheltenham: Glos v Worcs
Wellingborough: Northants v Kent
Weston-super-Mare: Somerset v Nottinghamshire
The Oval: Surrey v Hampshire
Hove: Sussex v Derbyshire
Coventry: Warwicks v Middlesex

Wednesday, August 11th

Headingley: Yorkshire v India
Leyton: Essex v Somerset
Cheltenham: Glos v Northants
Blackpool: Lancashire v Middlesex
Eastbourne: Sussex v Kent
Worcester: Worcestershire v Glam
Edgbaston: Warwickshire v Scotland

Saturday, August 14th

Trent Bridge: Notts v India
Cheltenham: Glos v Hampshire
Folkestone: Kent v Glamorgan
Leicester: Leicestershire v Lancs
Lord's: Middlesex v Surrey
Northampton: Northants v Derby
Eastbourne: Sussex v Somerset
Edgbaston: Warwickshire v Worcs
Hull: Yorkshire v Essex

Wednesday, August 18th

Folkestone: Kent v Worcestershire
Leicester: Leicestershire v Glam
Northampton: Northamptonshire v Nottinghamshire
Taunton: Somerset v Middlesex
Edgbaston: Warwickshire v Essex

Thursday, August 19th

THE OVAL—ENGLAND v INDIA (Third Test, five days)

Saturday, August 21st

Chesterfield: Derbyshire v Glos
Chelmsford: Essex v Kent
Cardiff: Glamorgan v Somerset
Bournemouth: Hants v Lancashire
Kettering: Northants v Surrey
Trent Bridge: Notts v Warwicks
Worcester: Worcestershire v Sussex
Bradford: Yorkshire v Leicestershire

Wednesday, August 25th

Hove: Sussex v India
Chelmsford: Essex v Worcestershire
Bristol: Gloucestershire v Surrey
Bournemouth: Hants v Yorkshire
Old Trafford: Lancashire v Derbys
Lord's: Middlesex v Somerset

Saturday, August 28th

*Taunton: Somerset v India
Derby: Derbyshire v Glamorgan
Chelmsford: Essex v Notts
Canterbury: Kent v Hampshire
Old Trafford: Lancashire v Worcs
Leicester: Leicestershire v Northants
The Oval: Surrey v Yorkshire
Hove: Sussex v Middlesex
Edgbaston: Warwickshire v Glos

Wednesday, September 1st

Worcester: Worcestershire v India
Southampton: Hants v Somerset
Trent Bridge: Notts v Kent
The Oval: Surrey v Derbyshire
Hove: Sussex v Northamptonshire
Edgbaston: Warwicks v Yorkshire
Scarborough: England XI v England Under-25 XI

Saturday, September 4th

Lord's—Gillette Cup—Final

Scarborough: T. N. Pearce's XI v India

Wednesday, September 8th

Bristol: Gloucestershire v Sussex
The Oval: Surrey v Glamorgan
Scarborough: County Knock-out competition

Saturday, September 11th

Southampton: Hampshire v Surrey
Harrogate: Yorkshire v Northants

SUNDAY LEAGUE FIXTURES, 1971

Sunday, April 25th

Chelmsford: Essex v Glamorgan
Bournemouth: Hampshire v Notts
Leicester: Leicestershire v Glos
Edgbaston: Warwicks v Lancashire
Worcester: Worcestershire v Kent

Sunday, May 2nd

Bristol: Gloucestershire v Lancashire
Leicester: Leicestershire v Somerset
Trent Bridge: Notts v Glamorgan
The Oval: Surrey v Essex
Hove: Sussex v Northamptonshire
Worcester: Worcs v Middlesex
Harrogate: Yorkshire v Derbyshire

Sunday, May 9th

Chelmsford: Essex v Notts
Bristol: Glos v Derbyshire
Gillingham: Kent v Glamorgan
Old Trafford: Lancashire v Hants
Bath: Somerset v Sussex
Dudley: Worcestershire v Northants
Middlesbrough: Yorks v Warwicks

Sunday, May 16th

Ilkeston: Derbyshire v Somerset
Bristol: Gloucestershire v Surrey
Portsmouth: Hampshire v Northants
Lord's: Middlesex v Yorkshire
Horsham: Sussex v Leicestershire
Edgbaston: Warwickshire v Kent

Sunday, May 23rd

Buxton: Derbyshire v Essex
Ebbw Vale: Glamorgan v Middlesex
Northampton: Northants v Kent
Trent Bridge: Notts v Leicestershire
Yeovil: Somerset v Lancashire
The Oval: Surrey v Worcestershire
Edgbaston: Warwickshire v Sussex
Sheffield: Yorkshire v Glos

Sunday, May 30th

Chesterfield: Derbyshire v Notts
Swansea: Glamorgan v Warwicks
Gloucester: Gloucestershire v Worcs
Portsmouth: Hampshire v Leics
Old Trafford: Lancashire v Essex
Lord's: Middlesex v Somerset
Northampton: Northants v Surrey

Sunday, June 6th

Ilford: Essex v Northamptonshire
Tunbridge Wells: Kent v Sussex
Leicester: Leicestershire v Derby
Lord's: Middlesex v Lancashire
Nottingham: Notts v Surrey
Brislington: Somerset v Glos
Worcester: Worcestershire v Hants

Sunday, June 20th

Neath: Glamorgan v Leicestershire
Gillingham: Kent v Gloucestershire
Old Trafford: Lancashire v Derby
Peterborough: Northants v Notts
Weston-super-Mare: Somerset v Yorkshire
Guildford: Surrey v Hampshire
Hove: Sussex v Worcestershire
Edgbaston: Warwicks v Middlesex

Sunday, June 27th

Derby: Derbyshire v Kent
Lydney: Gloucestershire v Glam
Southampton: Hants v Warwicks
Old Trafford: Lancashire v Surrey
Lord's: Middlesex v Essex
Worksop: Nottinghamshire v Sussex
Taunton: Somerset v Northants
Hull: Yorkshire v Leicestershire

Sunday, July 4th

Harlow: Essex v Sussex
Maidstone: Kent v Yorkshire
Leicester: Leicestershire v Warwicks
Lord's: Middlesex v Hampshire
Northampton: Northants v Glam
Trent Bridge: Notts v Lancashire
Torquay: Somerset v Surrey
Worcester: Worcs v Derbyshire

Sunday, July 11th

Chesterfield: Derbyshire v Northants
Westcliff: Essex v Somerset
Cardiff: Glamorgan v Sussex
Portsmouth: Hampshire v Glos
Old Trafford: Lancashire v Kent
Leicester: Leicestershire v Worcs
The Oval: Surrey v Yorkshire
Edgbaston: Warwickshire v Notts

Sunday, July 18th

Folkestone: Kent v Leicestershire
Brackley: Northamptonshire v Glos
Glastonbury: Somerset v Hampshire
Byfleet: Surrey v Glamorgan
Hove: Sussex v Middlesex
Stourbridge: Worcestershire v Essex
Headingley: Yorkshire v Lancashire

Sunday, July 25th

Cardiff: Glamorgan v Worcs
Bristol: Gloucestershire v Essex
Southampton: Hampshire v Derbys
Old Trafford: Lancashire v Sussex
Trent Bridge: Notts v Kent
The Oval: Surrey v Middlesex
Edgbaston: Warwicks v Somerset

Sunday, August 1st

Derby: Derbyshire v Warwickshire
Cardiff: Glamorgan v Somerset
Lord's: Middlesex v Leicestershire
Bedford: Northamptonshire v Lancs
Newark: Nottinghamshire v Worcs
Bradford: Yorkshire v Essex

Sunday, August 8th

Leyton: Essex v Hampshire
Swansea: Glamorgan v Yorkshire
Cheltenham: Glos v Warwickshire
Leicester: Leicestershire v Lancs
Wellingborough: Northampton v Middlesex
Frome: Somerset v Nottinghamshire
The Oval: Surrey v Kent
Hove: Sussex v Derbyshire

Sunday, August 15th

Derby: Derbyshire v Middlesex
Bristol: Gloucestershire v Notts
Canterbury: Kent v Somerset
Leicester: Leicestershire v Essex
Eastbourne: Sussex v Surrey
Edgbaston: Warwicks v Northants
Scarborough: Yorkshire v Worcs

Sunday, August 22nd

Aveley: Essex v Kent
Cardiff: Glamorgan v Hampshire
Lord's: Middlesex v Gloucestershire
Kettering: Northants v Leics
Trent Bridge: Notts v Yorkshire
Edgbaston: Warwickshire v Surrey
Worcester: Worcs v Somerset

Sunday, August 29th

Chesterfield: Derbyshire v Glam
Chelmsford: Essex v Warwickshire
Maidstone: Kent v Hampshire
Old Trafford: Lancashire v Worcs
Leicester: Leicestershire v Surrey
Lord's: Middlesex v Notts
Hove: Sussex v Yorkshire

Sunday, September 5th

Bournemouth: Hampshire v Yorks
Canterbury: Kent v Middlesex
Old Trafford: Lancashire v Glam
The Oval: Surrey v Derbyshire
Hove: Sussex v Gloucestershire
Dudley: Worcestershire v Warwicks

Sunday, September 12th

Bournemouth: Hampshire v Sussex
Bradford: Yorkshire v Northants

MINOR COUNTIES FIXTURES

MAY

19—Bramhall: Cheshire v Yorks II
24—Old Trafford: Lancs II v Ches
29—Reading School: Berkshire v Buckinghamshire
30—Spalding: Lincolnshire v Suffolk
Jesmond: Northumberland v Durham
York: Yorkshire II v Lancs II

JUNE

2—Wroxeter: Shropshire v Cambs
6—Macclesfield: Cheshire v Staffs
9—Shrewsbury: Shropshire v Somerset II
Chatteris: Cambridgeshire v Bedfordshire
Millom: Cumberland v Yorks II
14—Chester: Cheshire v Lancashire II
16—Tadcaster: Yorks II v Lincs
20—Kendal: Cumberland v Lancs II
21—Jesmond: Northumberland v Staffordshire
23—Hartlepool: Durham v Staffs
March: Cambridgeshire v Lincs
Jesmond: Northumberland v Yorkshire II
27—Bishops Stortford: Hertfordshire v Bedfordshire
28—Wolverhampton: Staffordshire v Norfolk
30—Wisbech—Cambs v Norfolk
Taunton: Somerset II v Shrops
Elland: Yorks II v N'berland

JULY

3—*Buckingham—Bucks v Suffolk
4—South Shields: Durham v Cheshire
Jesmond: Northumberland v Cumberland
Cleethorpes: Lincs v Norfolk
7—Hitchin: Herts v Cambs
Old Trafford: Lancashire II v Northumberland
9—Wadebridge: Cornwall v Somerset II
11—Wallasey: Cheshire v Shropshire
Penrith: Cumberland v Durham
14—Stoke: Staffordshire v Lincs
Hertford: Herts v Norfolk
17—Bedford School: Bedfordshire
Hertfordshire
18—Northwich: Cheshire v Durha
Workington: Cumberland
Northumberland
19—Bedford School: Beds v Shrop
Helston: Cornwall v Berkshire
Old Trafford: Lancashire II
Yorkshire II
21—Bedford School: Beds v Suffol
Sidmouth: Devon v Berkshire
Scunthorpe: Lincs v Cambs
22—Norwich: Norfolk v Bucks
23—Sherborne School: Dorset
Berkshire
24—*Luton: Beds v Bucks
*Norwich: Norfolk v Cambs
25—Oswestry: Shropshire v Cheshir
Torquay: Devon v Somerset I
26—Maidenhead: Berks v Dorset
Stevenage: Herts v Bucks
Norwich: Norfolk v Staffs
Swindon: Wilts v Oxfordshire
28—Norwich: Minor Counties
India (3 days)
Luton: Beds v Cambs
Lincoln: Lincs v Yorkshire II
Jesmond: Northumberland
Lancashire II
Oxford: Oxfordshire v Dorset
Bath: Somerset II v Wiltshire
Ipswich School: Suffolk v Buck

AUGUST

1—Blackhill: Durham v C'berlan
Cheadle: Staffordshire v Ches
2—Reading: Berkshire v Cornwa
Blandford Forum: Dorset
Wiltshire
Norwich: Norfolk v Herts
4—Reading: Berks v Oxfordshire
Norwich: Norfolk v Lincs
Taunton: Somerset II v Devo
Felixstowe: Suffolk v Herts
Salisbury: Wiltshire v C'wall
6—High Wycombe: Bucks
Oxfordshire
Taunton: Somerset II v C'wa
Cambridge: Cambridgeshire
Hertfordshire

7—*Norwich: Norfolk v Suffolk
9—Windsor: Berkshire v Wiltshire
Oxton: Cheshire v N'berland
Dorchester: Dorset v Cornwall
Newcastle-under-Lyme: Staffs v Durham
Tring: Hertfordshire v Suffolk
Oxford: Oxfordshire v Devon
Harrogate: Yorkshire II v Cumberland
11—Bray: Berkshire v Devon
Stone: Staffs v N'berland
Cambridge: Cambs v Shrops
Devizes: Wiltshire v Dorset
13—Shaftesbury: Dorset v Devon
Oxford: Oxfordshire v Berks
14—*Chesham: Bucks v Herts
15—Wellington: Shropshire v Beds
16—Camborne: Cornwall v Dorset
Banbury: Oxfordshire v Bucks
Trowbridge: Wilts v Somerset II
18—Paignton: Devon v Dorset
Sleaford: Lincs v Staffs
Lowestoft: Suffolk v Norfolk
Chippenham: Wiltshire v Berks
20—Exeter: Devon v Oxfordshire
21—*Wing: Bucks v Berkshire
22—Felixstowe: Suffolk v Beds
23—Poole Park: Dorset v Oxfordshire
Old Trafford: Lancashire II v Cumberland
Jesmond: N'berland v Cheshire
25—Truro: Cornwall v Devon
Witney: Oxfordshire v Wilts
Castleford: Yorks II v Cheshire
28—*Amersham: Bucks v Beds
29—Chester-le-Street: Durham v Northumberland
Bury St. Edmunds: Suffolk v Lincolnshire
30—Beaconsfield: Bucks v Norfolk
Penzance: Cornwall v Wiltshire

*Matches played on Saturday and Sunday.

SECOND XI FIXTURES, 1971

APRIL

28—Edgbaston: Warwicks v Glos

MAY

5—Hove: Sussex v Hampshire
Leicester: Leics v Northants
Trent Bridge: Notts v Worcs
Aylesford: Kent v Surrey (3 days).
6—Bristol: Glos v Glamorgan
10—Worcester: Worcs v Glamorgan
Edgbaston: Warwicks v Lancs
12—Derby: Derbyshire v Northants
Gloucester (Dowty Rotol): Glos v Worcs
Leamington Spa: Warwicks v Nottinghamshire
Dover: Kent v Middlesex (3 days).
Byfleet: Surrey v Sussex (3 days)
17—Old Trafford: Lancs v Derby
Abergavenny: Glamorgan v Northamptonshire
Birmingham (Mitchell & Butlers): Warwicks v Sussex
19—Stinchcombe: Glos v Northants
Old Trafford: Lancs v Leics
Southampton: Hampshire v Middlesex (3 days)
24—Northampton: Northants v Worcestershire
Hove: Sussex v Warwickshire
26—Retford: Notts v Derbyshire
Old Trafford: Lancashire v Northamptonshire
Edgbaston: Warwicks v Surrey (3 days)
27—Andover: Hampshire v Kent
31—Hove: Sussex v Middlesex

JUNE

2—Derby: Derbyshire v Leics
Worcester: Worcs v Glos
Corby: Northants v Notts
Ealing: Middlesex v Hants (3 days)
7—Old Trafford: Lancs v Notts
9—Blossomfield: Warwickshire v Northamptonshire
Basingstoke: Hants v Surrey (3 days)
Hastings: Surrey v Kent (3 days)

14—Loughborough: Leics v Glam
Knowle & Dorridge: Warwick v Worcestershire
16—Worcester: Worcs v Derbyshire
Coalville: Leics v Notts
21—Nottingham (Boots): Notts v Warwickshire
23—Winchmore Hill: Middlesex v Kent (3 days)
Oval: Surrey v Warwickshire (3 days)
24—Bristol: Gloucestershire v Hants
Newark: Notts v Glamorgan
28—Derby: Derbyshire v Warwicks
Wellingborough: Northants v Lancashire

JULY

1—Bootle: Lancashire v Worcs
5—Hadleigh: Essex v Kent
Nottingham: Notts v Lancs
7—Bournemouth: Hants v Glam (3 days)
Norbury (N.W. Bank Limited): Surrey v Middlesex (3 days)
8—Northampton: Northants v Gloucestershire
12—Portsmouth: Hants v Sussex
14—Northampton: Northants v Derbyshire
Dudley: Worcestershire v Lancs
Coalville: Leics v Warwicks
15—Tunbridge Wells: Kent v Sussex
Edmonton: Middlesex v Essex
19—Collingham: Notts v Northants
Bournville (Cadburys): Warwickshire v Leicestershire
21—Derby: Derbyshire v Notts
Old Trafford: Lancs v Warwicks
Worcester: Worcs v Northants
Norbury (N.W. Bank Limited): Surrey v Kent (3 days)
22—Southgate: Middlesex v Sussex
26—Cardiff: Glamorgan v Notts
Ashton: Northants v Warwicks
28—Brockworth: Glos v Warwicks
Roehampton (Bk of England) Surrey v Northamptonshire
29—Loughborough: Leics v Derbys
Newport: Glamorgan v Worcs

AUGUST

4—Bedworth: Warwicks v Derby
Northampton: Northants v Leicestershire
Horsham: Sussex v Surrey (3 days)
5—Dagenham: Essex v Middlesex
9—Derby: Derbyshire v Worcs
Stratford-on-Avon: Warwicks v Glamorgan
Leicester: Leics v Lancashire
11—Horton: Northants v Glam
Nottingham (John Player Ground): Notts v Leics
Hornsey: Middlesex v Surrey (3 days)
12—Sittingbourne (Bowaters): Ker v Hampshire
16—Southampton: Hants v Glos
Worcester: Worcs v Warwicks
18—Usk: Glamorgan v Glos
Dudley: Worcestershire v Not
Byfleet: Surrey v Hants (3 days
23—Dartford: Kent v Essex
25—Derby: Derbyshire v Lancashi
Pontypridd: Glamorgan Warwickshire
30—Worthing: Sussex v Glamorga

SEPTEMBER

1—Mitcham: Surrey v Glamorga (3 days)

Printed by John Gardner (*Printers*) Limited, Liverpool and published by
© THE DICKENS PRESS, 161 Queen Victoria Street, London, E.C.4.
SBN 85090 297 5